D1084051

brainstorm

AN INVESTIGATION

OF THE MYSTERIOUS

DEATH OF FILM STAR

NATALIE WOOD

by criminal law authority

SAM PERRONI

A POST HILL PRESS BOOK
ISBN: 978-1-63758-373-9
ISBN (eBook): 978-1-63758-374-6

Brainstorm:
An Investigation of the Mysterious Death of Film Star Natalie Wood
© 2021 by Samuel A. Perroni
All Rights Reserved

www.nataliewoodbrainstorm.com

EDITORS: Julie Kastello, Milwaukee, Wis., and Paul Dinas, New York, N.Y.
COPY EDITOR: Kristine Krueger, Minocqua, Wis.
PAGE DESIGN: Cheryl A. Michalek, Milwaukee, Wis.
BOOK JACKET ARTWORK AND WEBSITE DESIGN: Thoma Thoma, Little Rock, Ark.
AUTHOR PHOTOGRAPH: Stephen Thetford Photography, Fayetteville, Ark.

No part of this publication may be reproduced, stored in a retrieval system or trans-mitted in any form or by any means—electronic, mechanical, photocopy, recording or any other—except for brief quotations in printed reviews, without the prior permission of the author.

Post Hill Press
New York • Nashville
posthillpress.com

Published in the United States of America
1 2 3 4 5 6 7 8 9 10

I dedicate this book to my dear wife, Pat,
who spent many lonely hours without me
during a challenging time in her life.
She understood my passion for this work
and the measure of truth craved by me
and so many of Natalie's fans.

"Tempt not a desperate man."
—Shakespeare

table of contents

acknowledgments

THIS BOOK OWES ITS DETAIL AND ACCURACY TO THE BLUE-RIBBON experts, former homicide investigators, private detectives and research assistants scattered from coast-to-coast, who dug as deeply as they could after so many years to find material witnesses, articles, and archived records and documents relevant to Natalie Wood's death. They are Kevin Brechner, a relentless researcher and kind soul; Jan Morris, who volunteered countless hours and impressed me regularly with her communication techniques, detail and accuracy; Sherry Joyce, my former ace legal assistant, and her husband, John; Jade Vinson, my bright, young personal assistant who learned she has a knack for being a private investigator; Summer Pruett, my former secretary/personal assistant who skillfully churned out brief after brief in my CPRA lawsuits while navigating the mind-numbing morass of procedural rules in Los Angeles County; Diane Richards, a skilled research technician in North Carolina; Linda Hudson and Detective Tommy Hudson; Robert Pozos, Ph.D; Christina Stanley, M.D.; Jonathan Unwer, PharmD; Barry Jewel; and Bob Hardin.

I would also be remiss if I didn't extend my heartfelt appreciation to: Pamela Eaker, Paul Wintler, Curt Craig, William Peterson, John Claude Stonier, Ron Nelson, Doug Urata, Barbara Sherman, Karl Lack, Ron Hunter, Doug Bombard, Ginger Blymyer and Kitty Kelley; Marilyn Wayne, who persisted in the face of unjust law enforcement degradation to do the right thing; and Lana Wood, for helping me the best she knew how during a most painful time in her life.

Thanks to Dave Nath and Peter Beard of Story Films Ltd., two fine British movie producers who inspired me with their creativity and desire to achieve excellence and who focused my attention on several aspects of my investigation that would have been merely touched upon without their thoughtful insight; and Kiera Godfrey, Peter Beard's better half, who was so supportive of this endeavor.

A special thanks to Brenda Longstreth-Cabral for her perfect transcriptions of taped conversations and videos, and to my dear friends Mary Ann Liscio and Hope Sunshine, who gave me so much encouragement and advice along the way.

I would like to acknowledge my personal editor, Julie Kastello, for her creativity and superb attention to detail; Paul Dinas for his invaluable suggestions and keen insight into how material should be presented to the reader; Kristine Krueger for her consummate copy editing; Cheryl Michalek, the best book designer around; and the Thoma Thoma marketing team led by the talented Shawn Solloway for a brilliant cover design and website.

Finally, my sincere gratitude to Katharine Sands, my wise and persistent agent who refused to give up; Beth Karas, a gracious and skilled analyst who always believed in me; and all of the dedicated people at Post Hill Press who tackled the difficult job of publishing this book on a decidedly abbreviated schedule, including my perceptive editor Debra Englander, who recognized the value of my work, and senior publicist Devon Brown, a proud Arkansas native with an eye for promotion.

My solitary mission writing this book was to help the public understand why events occurred the way they did in Natalie's case so they could form their own judgments about them. If I make any money, I intend to give it to charity in Natalie's memory.

foreword

NEARLY 40 YEARS HAVE PASSED SINCE BELOVED SCREEN STAR NATALIE Wood drowned off the coast of Catalina Island. And there have been very few days since then that I haven't thought about what might have been. You see, my fiancé, John Payne, my 8-year-old son, Anthony, and I were aboard John's sailboat, *Capricorn*, which was moored—unbeknownst to us—across the fairway from Natalie's yacht, *Splendour*, on the night she died. We did not know it at the time, but we were "ear witnesses" to some of the last terrifying minutes of her life.

Shortly before midnight on Saturday, November 28, 1981, John and I were awakened by a woman's desperate cries for help. We could tell from her cries that she was in the water near *Splendour*, but it was too dark to see her. I wanted to jump in to find her, but John talked me out of it. In this skillfully written book, Sam Perroni explains in perfect detail our efforts to help the woman and how we thought she was being rescued by a man who said, "Hold on. We're coming to get you." Her cries stopped a short while later.

But the end of the woman's cries for help was not the end of the tragic incident for me. It was just the beginning. I was not prepared for what I would face—simply for trying to do the right thing. When John and I learned Natalie had drowned, we called the lead detective on her case to report what we had heard that night. He never bothered to call us back. I was insulted and angered that a detective would make no effort to contact me for more information. I felt dismissed as a witness.

So, I called the *Los Angeles Times*, because I believed someone needed to know what we had heard. It was only after the *Times* published my account that I was telephoned by a crime scene investigator from the Los Angeles County Sheriff's Department. And the same day, an anonymous threatening note was left for me at my place of business.

During the LASD's 1981 investigation into Natalie's death, no one ever took the time to talk to John or me *in person* or to determine if we were credible witnesses. In doing what good citizens ought to do, we were not only snubbed by the investigators, we were attacked by the lead detective as publicity hounds.

Those events fueled other challenges to our credibility over the years, including during the LASD's so-called "reopening" of Natalie's case in 2011, which caused me to question ever getting involved.

Since 1981, every time the subject of Natalie Wood's death comes up in public, I become uncomfortable and nervous. It was—and still is—so surreal, confusing and frightening for me. However, my willingness to write this Foreword stems not from my desire for you to believe my personal account. Instead, I seek to encourage others similarly situated to press for the truth no matter how difficult it may become.

Due to Sam's unselfish efforts, my faith in truth-seeking was restored when I read the remarkable, fact-based revelations contained in this book. Little did the occupants of *Capricorn* know that instead of being vehicles for truth, we were obstacles to overcome in an LASD cover-up. Now, as I look back through the prism of Sam's meticulous timeline, it becomes crystal clear why no one seemed interested in *what* we heard and *when* we heard it. Yet, unlike the "eyewitnesses" on *Splendour* that night, our story has never changed.

Sam's piece-by-piece, person-by-person investigation unveils lies, deceit, violence, greed, brazen arrogance, dirty cops and Hollywood scare tactics, and it finally identifies the true cause of Natalie's death and the culprit behind it. Now, Natalie can rest in peace.

— Marilyn Wayne, September 2021

introduction

I first took notice of celebrated screen star Natalie Wood in 1961. I was 12. She was 22. As I remember it, Natalie was being interviewed on television about *Splendor in the Grass*, a film she was making with newcomer Warren Beatty. I don't recall anything she said that day. To be honest, I was too hypnotized by her perfect beauty—even in black and white. It was love at first sight. To me, there wasn't a lovelier woman on the planet.

The exact moment I learned of Natalie's death is also firmly etched in my mind. It was November 29, 1981, a little before noon on a Sunday morning in Little Rock, Arkansas, when a special report was broadcast over my car radio. Natalie Wood was dead. Her body had been found early that morning floating facedown in the waters off Santa Catalina Island.

The news hit me like a sucker punch. My mind couldn't process the fact that this beautiful, brilliant actress had died that way at the peak of her career.

As I remember, very few details were given about the tragedy other than Natalie had apparently taken a dinghy out for a ride and drowned. Later, I would hear that a fingernail was lodged in the side of the dinghy where she had desperately tried to claw her way to safety. I eventually found out that wasn't true, but the image itself was horrible. The loss I felt was vivid and real. But Natalie was gone, and that was it.

However, I thought about her death on and off for the next 30 years. Every time a new book or tabloid article about her was published, the "facts" described about her death never seemed to add up. As a seasoned criminal law attorney, I felt there was more—much more—to the story. Even after her case was "reopened" in 2011, the investigation seemed phony.

When I retired from the practice of law in 2008, I was 60 years old and had spent 37 years working in some facet of the criminal law business. I was teaching a course on white-collar crime at the William H. Bowen School of Law in Little Rock and consulting for a couple of criminal defense lawyers on the side.

In 2014, I read a biography about Natalie Wood that inspired my pursuit of one of the most scandalous, heartbreaking and frustrating cases of my career—to find the truth behind her mysterious death.

What drove me to engage in a complex and costly investigation of the death of someone I had only known through movies, television and books? I didn't need the attention and publicity. I had garnered more than my fair share while actively trying criminal cases. I didn't need something to keep me busy. I had plenty to do.

My answer is simple. I believed admirers like me needed closure. We needed more than vague accusations or sensational sound bites about Natalie's "accidental" demise. We needed the truth, and if possible, we needed justice.

Many of the official files surrounding the original and subsequent investigations had not been made public. They were buried in the archives of the Los Angeles County Sheriff's Department, Los Angeles County Department of Medical Examiner-Coroner and Los Angeles County. When these agencies stonewalled my repeated public information requests, I brought three lawsuits against them. In doing so, I gained access to investigative files, autopsy records and photographs, which helped me uncover countless details about Natalie's death that have never been viewed by the public.

Following my instincts and training as a prosecutor, I set out to corral as much of the truth as I could and present it to readers in a logical fashion. To date, information has come in bits and pieces of untested theories. I wanted to see if there was any credible evidence out there that would suggest Natalie's death was a homicide, and if so, the identity of the most likely suspect or suspects. Of course, the primordial trail led in the direction of Natalie's husband, Robert Wagner. But, I wanted to know, *Why? Why would Robert Wagner want Natalie dead?* Shouldn't that be the foremost question on anyone's mind before accusing him of such a heinous crime?

My intent was to present the facts I found in a format that would enable readers to judge for themselves who was ultimately responsible for the tragic circumstances that ended Natalie's brilliant life and the integrity of the agencies responsible for gathering the evidence in her death investigations. If you're reading these pages, I've happily succeeded.

prologue

AT 7:44 A.M. ON A BRILLIANT SUNDAY, NOVEMBER 29, 1981, NATALIE WOOD'S body was spotted floating off the shore of Santa Catalina Island. The celebrated actress had spent Thanksgiving weekend boating with her movie and TV star husband, Robert J. Wagner Jr. For the pleasure cruise, Dennis Davern captained the couple's stately, 60-foot Bristol yacht, *Splendour*. Their sole guest was Academy Award-winning actor Christopher Walken, Natalie's costar in the soon-to-be-completed film *Brainstorm*.

Since around 1 a.m. when Wagner alerted locals his wife was missing, island residents—along with Baywatch lifeguards, the Coast Guard and the Catalina Island sheriff's office—had been searching for Natalie and the yacht's 13-foot inflatable Zodiac dinghy.

Doug Bombard, owner of Doug's Harbor Reef & Saloon, was one of the searchers. Bombard managed several operations at the secluded Isthmus, including its Harbor Patrol service. As he steered his Harbor Patrol boat toward a red bubble floating about 100 yards off Blue Cavern Point, his "heart sunk." Motoring over, he discovered the bubble was a red down jacket, the same type and color his friend Natalie Wood had worn Saturday night at his restaurant. The jacket had ballooned up with air, so it looked "kind of like a life preserver" for the petite film star.

According to Bombard:

> Her feet and legs were hanging underneath her…almost in a standing position…like she was just suspended there. Her arms were out, and her face was in the water…with her hair floating on the water around her. I turned her over. Her eyes were open. I knew she was gone.

At 43, the celebrated film star appeared to have drowned.

The yacht's dinghy had been found earlier, around 5:30 a.m., by two of Bombard's employees against the rocks at Blue Cavern Point, near the location of Natalie's body. They described the condition of the dinghy to a sheriff's deputy, who wrote in his report, "The key was in the ignition, which was in the off position. The gear was in neutral and the oars tied down, and it appeared as if the boat had not even been used." Natalie's body and the Zodiac had drifted over a mile from *Splendour's* mooring site before they were recovered.

With the aid of two searchers, Bombard carefully lifted Natalie over the side of the patrol boat and gently placed her faceup on the open deck. Her body was clad in only the red, long-sleeved down jacket, a flannel cotton nightshirt, wool socks and some jewelry.

The news of Natalie's death stunned the world. Her many fans were heartbroken. Media representatives around the globe clamored for answers as to how and why the international star ended up in the ocean and drowned in the middle of the night. Special news reports consumed the airwaves in the U.S. and Europe. And rumors and speculation quickly took shape as fact.

Natalie's fear of deep, dark sea water was well known, and it didn't make sense that she had left the yacht by herself in the middle of a cold, dreary, starless night in a dinghy. The press and public wanted to know what really happened. And for 40 years, conflicting and unfounded stories were all they were told.

Until now.

CHAPTER 1

star-studded cruise

THE PROSPECT OF BAD WEATHER THANKSGIVING WEEKEND 1981 was likely unknown when the Catalina Island cruise was planned. Natalie Wood finished location filming on the science fiction movie *Brainstorm* on October 27 and had returned to MGM studios in Los Angeles with other cast members and staff to finish up the remaining scenes. Her husband, Robert Wagner, had been on Maui, Hawaii, from November 2 until November 12, shooting scenes for his hit TV series *Hart to Hart*. The couple frequently relaxed on their yacht in the lovely Southern California port, a favorite destination of Hollywood celebrities. On this weekend, their only guest was Natalie's costar in *Brainstorm*, Christopher Walken.

The cruise escort, Dennis Davern, was hired by the Wagners when they acquired the yacht *Challenger* in 1975. They renamed it *Splendour* in honor of Natalie's hit film *Splendor in the Grass*. Included in the deal was a 13-foot Zodiac dinghy they named *Valiant*, a humorous tribute to Wagner's film *Prince Valiant*.

To fully understand and appreciate the complex woman who became an internationally known and beloved star, it is important to understand her upbringing. Natalie was born into a troubled Russian émigré family, and her mother, Maria, greatly influenced her from an early age.

As a young woman, Marusia (Maria) and her family escaped repression at the hands of the Russian Revolution Bolsheviks and settled in China. Part of an expat Russian community, Maria immersed herself in "Romany magic" practiced by local gypsies. As the story goes, on one occasion, she had her fortune told by a gypsy who warned Maria to "beware of dark water." That same gypsy told Maria her second child "would be a great beauty, known throughout the world."

Maria's superstitions and phobias shaped her three daughters in many ways for the rest of their lives. For example, because her mother had shared the gypsy's prophecy, Natalie became terrified of deep, dark water and never learned to swim.

Maria married a Russian-Armenian regimental captain, Alexei Tatulov, and they had a daughter, Ovsanna (Olga). He arranged for the family to immigrate to the United States, and they settled in San Francisco. Unfortunately, within a few years, Tatulov left Maria and Olga for another woman. After the couple's divorce, Maria married her ex-husband's friend Nikolai (Nick) Stephanovich Zakharenko and had two more daughters: Natalia (Natalie) Nikolaevna Zakharenko on July 20, 1938, and Svetlana (Lana) Zakharenko on March 1, 1946. Nick changed his family's last name to Gurdin.

Nick didn't make a great deal of money and drank to excess. Finances were always a problem. There was often turmoil in the house, compelling Maria to take the girls to a local hotel to avoid her husband's alcoholic rages. That may have been a reason for Maria's obsession with movies and show business. Perhaps she saw it as a ticket out of her dismal life. That, and the gypsy prophecy about her cute and talented second daughter's future fame.

But make no mistake about it, Maria was a survivor. Cunning, strong-willed, dramatic and colorful, she used those traits to do what she felt necessary to fulfill the fortune teller's prophecy that her second-born child would become famous.

Renowned Hollywood director Irving Pichel was shooting his film *Happy Land* in nearby Santa Rosa in 1943. Maria found out about the filming and took Natalie to the set. The true circumstances as to how Pichel came to notice Natalie are debatable, but what is clear is that Maria got the attention of the famous director by, among other things, having Natalie sing "a little song." Pichel was impressed and gave her a part.

For the role, Natalie had to drop an ice cream cone in front of a drugstore and then cry. No doubt coached by Maria, she did just that—right on cue. Natalie's impressive cameo in *Happy Land* endeared her to Pichel for the rest of the filming.

Energized by her small but effective victory, Maria moved the family to Los Angeles. Maria had secured the second floor of a house that belonged to a ballet teacher she had met in San Francisco. When the family was settled, Maria tracked down Pichel at Universal-International Pictures.

Pichel was conducting a search for a child to appear in his film *Tomorrow Is Forever*. The role was a young Austrian orphan with a German accent who would perform alongside two prominent stars, Orson Welles and Claudette Colbert. Natalie was 6 years old, and her mother persuaded Pichel to let her test for the part. At the audition, she ended up playing her character perfectly, astonishing Pichel, his producer and the president of the company and getting the part.

Her first scene in the movie was with Welles. He was instantly smitten with Natalie and said in a *Life* magazine interview that he found her talent "terrifying." He later noted she was already a perfect professional. Having played her role with critical acclaim, she received the *BOXOFFICE* Blue Ribbon citation.

After that, Maria negotiated a personal contract with Universal-International as the proprietor of Natalie's services. Maria would also sign a three-year contract with Famous Artists Agency to represent Natalie, insisting on veto rights for every offer Natalie received through their efforts.

Natalie's success pulled her family out of poverty and gave her father a job as a studio carpenter, but Nick continued terrorizing the family with his drunken rages for years to come.

When Natalie secured her first movie contract, she also got a new last name. Studio executives wanted something more marketable and chose "Wood." She didn't like it at first, but the dutiful child did as she was told. Focused on her film career, Natalie had been shuffled from school to school, had missed the latter half of grade school because of filming schedules and hadn't learned to read. So, she practiced her lines by having her mother, half-sister Olga and a dialogue coach read them to her. She had a good memory and learned her lines flawlessly. It wasn't long before people in the business started calling her "One-Take Natalie."

Following *Tomorrow*, Natalie was cast opposite Maureen O'Hara as Susan Walker, the little girl who didn't believe in Santa, in the low-budget Twentieth Century-Fox film *Miracle on 34th Street* in 1947. The role earned her "The Most Talented Juvenile Motion Picture Star of 1947" award from *Parents' Magazine*. No one knew it at the time, but it would become Natalie's first classic film and thrust her headlong into the spotlight.

After *Miracle*, Natalie's stock went through the roof. By the time she was 8, her mother shrewdly rescinded her contract with Universal-International and instructed Famous Artists to commence negotiations with Twentieth Century-Fox. When the dust settled, Natalie had a rich seven-year deal with Fox, including an agreement to pay Maria for answering Natalie's fan mail. Natalie appeared in 21 films, working with such Hollywood icons as James Stewart, Fred MacMurray, Bette Davis and Joan Blondell.

One of those films was the 1949 movie *The Green Promise*. Natalie played Susan Matthews, a young farmer's daughter who yearns to raise lambs. But because of land erosion caused by her father, a great storm threatens their farm, including the lambs. So, Susan braves dangerous flooding conditions to save the animals. In one scene, Natalie is required to run over a bridge designed to dramatically collapse behind her into a torrent of water below. Instead, as Natalie crossed the bridge, it prematurely gave way.

Figure 1: 1965 photo of Natalie Wood showing a bracelet on her left wrist covering her abnormality, visible upon close examination
(Getty Images/Silver Screen Collection)

Natalie reached the other side with only a distended left wrist. However, because her neurotic mother didn't believe in going to doctors, the bone in Natalie's wrist was not set properly. When it healed, it protruded noticeably. She was very self-conscious of the deformity, and as a result, Natalie rarely went out or made a film without something—a bracelet or watch—covering that wrist.

In 1955, Natalie got the opportunity to star in *Rebel Without a Cause*, a drama about juvenile delinquency and teenage alienation. Natalie, who was 16, costarred with James Dean, Sal Mineo and Dennis Hopper. Her family, agent and others weren't happy about the controversial role as Judy, a rebellious teenager who falls in love with James Dean's bad-boy character. Natalie fought to play the part and eventually won out. The film was a sensation and received three Academy Award nominations, including one for Natalie for Best Actress.

Her dramatic role in *Rebel* also brought the teen star a great deal of sexual attention, not only from some castmates and the film's 43-year-old director, Nicholas Ray, but from older married stars like Frank Sinatra and others in Hollywood. According to her sister Lana, Natalie was raped by a well-known older star who enticed her to his room by offering her a role in one of his films. Natalie, her mother and her other confidants kept it quiet for fear of ruining her career.

On the outside, Natalie appeared to have achieved every young actress' dream. Rich and

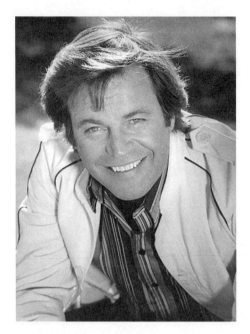

Figure 2: Robert J. Wagner Jr., costar of the TV series *Hart to Hart*, in a 1981 publicity photo (Getty Images/ABC Photo Archives)

beautiful, she was mobbed by good-looking young men and attended glittering parties with legendary celebrities. Her public image was fixed as a glamorous starlet who was always in control. But on the inside, Natalie was emotionally immature and needy.

When Natalie received her first Academy Award nomination, she was noticed by handsome, playboy actor Robert Wagner. She had been smitten with the Twentieth Century-Fox contract player since she was 11 and met him in a chance encounter on the studio lot. At the time, Natalie told her mother, "When I grow up, I wish that I could marry him."

Wagner, known by friends as "R.J.," was born in 1930 in Michigan, the only son of wealthy socialite parents. In 1937, his father moved the family to California and settled in Bel Air. Wagner claimed he witnessed, at age 12, a life-forming experience at the Bel-Air Country Club. In his 2008 memoir with Scott Eyman called *Pieces of My Heart: A Life*, Wagner reported while watching the suave male idols of the day who were country club members—Cary Grant, Fred Astaire, Clark Gable and Randolph Scott—he decided he wanted to be "in that club."

Blessed with astounding charm, good looks, a beaming smile and exceptional golf skills, he eventually entered the business of his dreams. Using his father's connections, Wagner secured a small part in the 1950 William Wellman production of *The Happy Years*. Following that, he signed with Henry Willson, an important film and TV agent with a reputation for representing handsome young men with whom he became infatuated. Among his most famous clients were Rock Hudson and Tab Hunter. He got Wagner a contract with Twentieth Century-Fox.

Between 1951 and 1957, Wagner appeared in 19 films with most of his critical reviews being less than stellar. Try as he might, Wagner wasn't able to make the leap from supporting roles to the upper echelons of stardom as he had hoped. But he was a master networker, relying on his charm to cultivate relationships that could further his career. As a teen, he dated Susan Zanuck, daughter of the head of Twentieth Century-Fox studio's Darryl F. Zanuck, which no doubt helped him become a contract player there. Despite his lackluster career, by age 26, Wagner was one of Hollywood's most eligible bachelors. He had affairs with a host of famous starlets, including 18-year-old Natalie Wood.

On July 20, 1956, at his invitation, Wagner escorted Natalie to the premiere of his most recent film, *The Mountain*, in which he was cast as the brother of Spencer Tracy's character. He and Natalie had been dating for a while by then. Less than five months later, in Beverly

Hills' chic Romanoff's restaurant, Natalie finally got her girlhood wish. Wagner proposed, handing her a champagne glass with a diamond-and-pearl engagement ring at the bottom that "glittered among the bubbles." It was inscribed with "Marry me." Swept off her feet, Natalie accepted, and the couple was married in Arizona on December 28, 1957. Wagner was 27. Natalie was 19.

The tabloids and movie magazines were all over the fairy-tale story of young Natalie catching the man of her dreams. Photographed with dazzling smiles in lovers' poses, the two movie stars beamed young love from magazine covers all over the world. They were America's dream couple, and there was no doubt in Natalie's mind at least, that her marriage would endure the stresses of Hollywood life and provide the union she yearned for to bring her personal happiness.

The pair used Natalie's money to purchase a mansion in Beverly Hills, a boat and new cars, and they hit the nightlife circuit with a vengeance as "members in good standing of Frank Sinatra's Rat Pack," according to *Movie Life* magazine. All the while, they gushed and cooed over each other in what appeared to be "one continuous honeymoon," as Natalie's mother described the marriage in 1958.

Publicly, everything seemed perfect until 1961. During filming of *Splendor in the Grass* with Warren Beatty, Natalie returned home to find Wagner having an affair with another man. The couple separated, shocking fans who had no suspicions anything was amiss. Natalie never spoke about the facts behind their breakup, allowing speculation that an affair with Beatty split up her marriage.

With a divorce imminent, Wagner left for Europe where he appeared in only five films between 1961 and 1966, achieving positive critical recognition in just one—a supporting role in *The Pink Panther*. During this period, Wagner married actress Marion Marshall, the ex-wife of Stanley Donen, a prominent American film director. In time, Wagner's marriage to Marion produced a daughter, Katharine, known as Katie.

In the nine years following her divorce, Natalie made a string of classic films in addition to *Splendor in the Grass*, including *West Side Story* and *Love with the Proper Stranger*. She received two more Academy Award nominations, a Golden Globe Award and the Foreign Press Association's award for world's favorite actress. She also spent eight years in psychotherapy learning to deal with her failed marriage to Wagner, two broken engagements and a host of emotional problems that had dogged her since childhood. It made her a stronger person and gave her the personal self-confidence that had eluded her most of her life.

Natalie married a second time, in 1969, to Richard Gregson, a sophisticated British entertainment agent, film producer and screenwriter. They had a daughter, Natasha. But the marriage ended in divorce a little over two years later when Natalie discovered Gregson having an affair with her secretary.

Meanwhile, Wagner and his new family returned to Hollywood in 1966 where he signed with Universal Studios. After appearing in three more films, Wagner got what would turn out to be his big break. In 1967, powerful television mogul Lew Wasserman suggested to Wagner that his medium was television. At the time, television wasn't considered on the same level as full-length feature films. So, Wagner balked. But Wasserman persuaded him to accept the lead in *It Takes a Thief*. The TV series about a sophisticated thief who works for the U.S. government ran for three seasons, and Wagner's performance earned him an Emmy Nomination for Best TV Actor. In spite of this success, Wagner continued taking minor film roles, hoping to achieve recognition as the big-name movie star he always wanted to be. Soon after the TV series ended, Wagner and Marion separated. He filed for divorce on October 14, 1970.

However, only in Tinseltown could two celebrities marry each other, divorce, marry others, have a child with their new respective spouses, divorce again, then remarry over a decade later. But that's exactly what happened in the lives of Natalie Wood and Robert Wagner.

Wagner spent most of 1971 "haggling" over divorce settlement terms with Marion. By the time the divorce decree was filed on December 10, 1971, he was dating Tina Sinatra, his longtime friend's daughter, and he was broke. Friend John Foreman, producer of *Butch Cassidy and the Sundance Kid* among other notable movies, and his wife, Linda, invited Wagner and Natalie to a party they were hosting at their home. The two attended "unescorted," according to Wagner.

He claimed they didn't talk, but said in his memoir that when they looked at each other, "a light went on in both of us." The following day, Wagner phoned Natalie. When the conversation ended, Wagner said that Natalie volunteered, "if the situation with Tina changes, maybe we could get together."

According to Suzanne Finstad, author of the 2001 book *Natasha: The Biography of Natalie Wood*, Wagner became engaged to Tina. Wagner denied the relationship got to that level. Natalie's half-sister, Olga, however, told Finstad that when she was with Natalie during a cruise around Sardinia, Italy, although worried about Wagner's engagement to Tina, Natalie spent the trip "fantasizing" about a reunion with him, "hoping to make her life right again." Later, Natalie said she had been thinking of Wagner ever since her divorce from Gregson.

In January 1972, *The Hollywood Reporter* scooped that Wagner and Natalie were "dating again." That ended his relationship with Tina. Wagner had taken Christmas presents to Natalie and Natasha, and later in the month of January, he invited Natalie to his Palm Springs home. He said when she got off the plane, "It was instant reaction" and "before anybody knew it, we fell in love all over again."

Even so, Natalie's mother and sisters were immediately concerned. But Natalie believed it was meant to be and that Wagner would be different this time.

Their renewed storybook romance created an amazing media and public frenzy and so captivated fans that bodyguards were needed to walk them through the crowd at the 1972 Academy Awards. Old Hollywood was back, and one of the most glamorous stars of the time believed there were "happy endings after all."

The couple remarried on July 16, 1972, aboard the borrowed yacht *Ramblin' Rose*, and the two honeymooned in Paradise Cove and the Isthmus at Catalina Island. They settled in Palm Springs, where they redecorated Wagner's comfortable home. Natalie began focusing on motherhood, placing her career to the side. But the public and media were ecstatic. This time, observed *Movie Life*, the couple found "what they were looking for all along" and now "love is forever and ever." Behind the scenes, however, Wagner was in a great deal of debt, including back taxes, alimony, child support and potential liability for a breach of contract case filed by Universal Studios. And Natalie bailed him out.

But Natalie's career ambitions were never far from the surface. Shortly after the birth of their daughter, Courtney, in 1974, the couple bought a home in Beverly Hills, and Natalie began inching back into show business. Her comeback began with a string of television and silver-screen movies, some memorable, some not. Among them was the 1979 made-

Figure 3: In 1972, Robert Wagner remarries Natalie Wood aboard *Ramblin' Rose* as his daughter, Katie, looks on. (Mart Crowley)

for-TV version of *From Here to Eternity*, which earned her a Golden Globe and an Emmy nomination.

Wagner's own career picked up considerably after his second marriage to Natalie with regular appearances in the television prisoner-of-war series *Colditz*; a part in the highly successful film *The Towering Inferno* with the iconic Steve McQueen, legendary Paul Newman and celebrated Faye Dunaway; and a lucrative contract with television producers Aaron Spelling and Leonard Goldberg.

By the mid-1970s, Wagner's career in television took flight. It began with the modestly successful CBS detective series *Switch*, which lasted three seasons, ending in August 1978. *Switch* was followed by Wagner's signature Spelling-Goldberg production *Hart to Hart*, which premiered August 25, 1979. The award-winning series ran for five seasons with Wagner playing Jonathan Hart, a suave, smart and extremely wealthy businessman married to a beautiful freelance journalist played by Stefanie Powers. Together, they outsmarted thieves, spies and most often murderers, solving cases law enforcement couldn't. Years later, the director of *Hart to Hart*, Tom Mankiewicz, described Wagner during this period as the "small-screen Cary Grant."

By 1980, Natalie was well on her way to reigniting her movie career. After appearing in a chilling TV drama *The Memory of Eva Ryker* that spring, she and Wagner decided to take a quiet vacation in the south of France. But before the trip was over, Natalie was given an opportunity to star opposite three Academy Award-winning actors in *Brainstorm*.

She was also asked to play the lead in the stage play *Anastasia* at the Music Center in Los Angeles, with rehearsals to begin in January 1982, as soon as she finished *Brainstorm*. The

Figure 4: Christopher Walken and Natalie Wood in a scene from *Brainstorm*
(AMPAS/Michael Childers)

play was going to be her stage debut, and she was looking forward to it "like crazy," according to Mankiewicz, her close friend. After the LA performances, the producers planned to take it to Broadway in New York.

Natalie was ecstatic about *Brainstorm*. Wagner not so much, because after preliminaries in Northern California, the role required that Natalie be away from home for six weeks filming in North Carolina. Within a few weeks of the start of location shooting and less than two months before the fateful *Splendour* cruise to Catalina, rumors were rampant in Hollywood that Natalie and Walken were having an affair. That prompted Wagner, who had admittedly been jealous of some of his wife's previous leading men, to take a mid-October trip to Raleigh-Durham to check up on her. In his memoir, Wagner claimed when he returned to LA, he felt Natalie was only being "emotionally unfaithful." And from all appearances, he agreed to Natalie's invitation of Walken on their cruise to prove it.

But the incidents that transpired on that deadly Thanksgiving weekend in 1981 tell another story of darker motives amid jealous rage.

CHAPTER 2

the "official" account

DOUG OUDIN, ACTING HARBORMASTER FOR TWO HARBORS, MADE his call to the U.S. Coast Guard at 3:26 a.m. Sunday, November 29, 1981, to report a missing woman in a Zodiac dinghy. First Petty Officer Gallagher took this troublesome report after overhearing radio transmissions from *Splendour* that the missing woman was Natalie Wood. Gallagher reportedly dispatched the Coast Guard cutter *Point Camden* to the scene, saying it should arrive around 5:30 a.m.

According to Oudin, he had been awakened by Don Whiting, the night manager of Doug's Harbor Reef & Saloon, and Bill Coleman, the restaurant's cook, "about 1:15 a.m." Whiting later told authorities that he and Coleman woke Oudin between "2:30 and 2:45 a.m." Based on solid information I now possessed, Whiting's timing was more accurate. My attempt to confirm these facts with Whiting and Coleman failed. Both were deceased. The significance of the time discrepancy, however, will become clear later with the narrative from Paul Wintler, an Isthmus maintenance troubleshooter who encountered Wagner at Isthmus Pier around 1 a.m. Sunday.

In any event, Oudin and Whiting went to *Splendour* to talk with an "intoxicated" and "dazed" Wagner, who discouraged them from contacting authorities, wanting to keep the search "low-key to avoid unnecessary or sensational attention from the news media." Whiting apparently asked if Wagner had any idea where Natalie would take the yacht's dinghy, and Davern spoke up: "Boss, do you think she could have gone to the mainland?" Wagner replied, "Yes, that's a possibility." The mainland was over 32 miles from Isthmus Cove, where *Splendour* was moored.

By all accounts, efforts to locate Natalie by locals and members of the Harbor Patrol at the Isthmus had been in progress for at least two to three hours before Oudin's Coast Guard call. But their search had been largely confined to the Isthmus mooring sites, beach, tiny community and dock shoreline because Wagner initially said he believed Natalie went back to the restaurant's bar. And their intense hunt had to that point been fruitless.

After conversing with Wagner, Davern and Walken, Whiting and Coleman continued the search by expanding to the shoreline outside the cove near Blue Cavern Point. Oudin, who was not interviewed by investigators in 1981, recounted his involvement in *Between Two Harbors*, his 2013 memoir. Oudin claimed after his initial contact with "all three men," he returned to the Harbor Patrol office to initiate further action.

"At precisely 5:15 a.m.," Whiting, in Harbor Patrol Boat 6, reported that he and Coleman had found the Zodiac floating in a "kelp bed" at "the rock face" near Blue Cavern Point. The area was approximately 1-1/4 miles northeast of Isthmus Pier. The keys were in the ignition in the off position, the gear was in neutral, the oars were in place and the bell props were in the water. In other words, the dinghy appeared as though it had not been used and had floated to its current position. While clearly inadvisable from an investigatory standpoint, the two searchers started the dinghy and used it to continue their probe for the

Figure 5: *Splendour's* dinghy, *Valiant*, is secured to a rescue boat after Natalie Wood's body is found in 1981. (Los Angeles Times)

missing movie star.

After the dinghy was discovered, Oudin claimed he contacted the sheriff's department and Baywatch lifeguards, reporting what he believed was now a "life or death matter." He also returned to *Splendour* to tell Wagner the dinghy had been found. Wagner, Davern and Oudin then returned to the pier. According to Oudin, that's when Wagner, now "painfully sober," stood "forlornly at the rail of the pier, head between his hands staring at the black water below" and mumbled, "She's terrified of the water. She doesn't even like to swim in the water. It scares her." Of course, at that point in time, there was no evidence Natalie was in the water.

LASD Deputy R. W. "Bill" Kroll, assigned to Avalon Station Unit 137, Catalina Island, was contacted by Avalon Sergeant J. Dyer at 5:55 a.m. regarding a "missing woman in a Zodiac." When the dinghy was found 40 minutes earlier, no one knew a drowning death was involved. Wagner led everyone to believe Natalie took out the dinghy late Saturday night to return to the bar. Nevertheless, at 6:15 a.m., an hour after the empty Zodiac discovery, Kroll updated Sgt. Dyer and requested LASD search and rescue Sikorsky helicopter AIR-53 be dispatched to assist by combing the area where the dinghy was retrieved. Kroll also requested Avalon's search and rescue team "for a ground search of 'Blue Cavern Point'."

According to Gavin Lambert, Wagner confidant and author of the 2004 biography *Natalie Wood: A Life*, Wagner telephoned longtime screenwriter friend and employee Mart Crowley "shortly before seven a.m." and exclaimed, "She's gone! She's gone!" In a 2020 HBO documentary about Natalie's life jointly produced by Natasha Gregson Wagner, Crowley confirmed the call.

Approximately 45 minutes later, Kroll reported the rescue helicopter observed what was believed to be Natalie's body "floating approx 250 yds North of Blue Cavern Point." From all indications, the helicopter and Doug Bombard saw the somber scene around the same time, because Oudin said Bombard radioed to call off the search seven minutes later.

∽∽∽∽∽∽∽∽

As a result of lawsuits against Los Angeles County agencies, I received copies of files on Natalie's death from the coroner's office and sheriff's department. Among the documents were those establishing the timeline of Deputy Kroll's investigation that morning.

Avalon's LASD satellite office triggered the request for the Homicide Bureau's involvement somewhere between 7:45 a.m. and 8:30 a.m. When Deputy Kroll's assignment ended around "0937 hours" Sunday, he had been to *Splendour* to conduct a "complete search;" conducted interviews with Davern and Wagner, who had remarkably similar stories; examined Natalie's scantily clad, partially jeweled body, observing injuries to her nose and bruises on her arms and legs; and interviewed eight local witnesses. His 10-page handwritten report was approved for distribution to "Homicide" by Lt. S. L. Collins. Yet, inconsistent with what he saw and his actions summoning homicide detectives, Kroll classified his "confidential" complaint report as a "490"—"PERSON DEAD/APPARENT ACCIDENTAL DROWNING."

I had the distinct feeling after scrutinizing Kroll's official report that the file classification was brought about by Lt. Collins attempting to protect Wagner's and Walken's celebrity. That was high on the list of questions I had for Kroll, a deputy with 12 years of experience, who was No. 1 on my "Most Wanted" list. But my anticipation of interviewing him was short-lived. Kroll drowned on April 22, 1996, free-diving off Little Gibraltar on Catalina Island.

Kroll had recently retired from the sheriff's department at the time of his untimely demise. For me, his death was another frustrating irony in the many uncanny and troubling events tied to Natalie's death.

∽∽∽∽∽∽∽∽

Dr. Thomas T. Noguchi was chief pathologist for the Los Angeles County Department of Medical Examiner-Coroner when its call center received word of Natalie's death at 8:30 a.m. Pamela K. Eaker, described as an experienced and "skilled" investigator by Dr. Noguchi, got the nod to head to the scene. As a coroner's office first responder, Eaker was assigned to travel to Catalina Island via the LASD Aero Bureau in Long Beach, examine the body, determine time of death parameters, locate, collect and document evidence and facts to be used by the forensic pathologists to determine the cause and manner of death, and report back.

When I had the opportunity to interview Eaker in 2018, she told me Natalie's case came in as "an apparent accidental

Figure 6: Dr. Thomas Noguchi, LA County coroner, speaks at a 1981 press conference on Natalie Wood's death. (Getty Images/Bettmann)

drowning," and she knew it was the famous actress before she got to Catalina Island. Initiating the case as an accident was completely inconsistent with Dr. Noguchi's protocol in unexplained death cases. But, that's how Eaker got her instructions after the cause of Natalie's death was reported to the coroner's office by LASD Homicide "Detective Morck" as a "probable drowning in [the] ocean."

Eaker authored a five-page report for Dr. Noguchi concluding, in the face of unexplained injuries to Natalie's body, that her death was an accident and "foul play is not suspected at this time."

When the chief pathologist held an afternoon news conference November 30, a few hours after Natalie's autopsy, he declared her death was "not a homicide, not a suicide. It was an accident." Dr. Noguchi explained he and his team had "completed the investigation and the preliminary autopsy" and announced:

> Miss Wood—it appears, based on our investigation, around noon—pardon me; around midnight—shortly after midnight of Sunday morning, she apparently attempted to get onto the dinghy, slipped and fell in the water, unable to return to the dinghy or the boat. And later her body was found about a mile away. The boat—the dinghy was also found close to the shore.

It took roughly *32 hours* from the time Natalie's body was pulled from the cold Pacific Ocean for the coroner to proclaim to the world that her death was a tragic accident.

Dr. Noguchi also told those in attendance Natalie "slipped, hitting her head and drowned and that there was no evidence of foul play" and related that an abrasion to Natalie's face may have caused her to be "rendered unconscious." Finally, he reported that with a blood alcohol level of 0.14 percent, Natalie was "legally intoxicated" and referred to her condition as "slightly inebriated."

Then, Dr. Noguchi dropped a bombshell. He told the large crowd of reporters that before Natalie disappeared, "a heated but nonviolent argument" had ensued between Wagner and actor Christopher Walken, a guest on the yacht. The room erupted. Dr. Noguchi then added:

> Argument apparently took place, not involving Miss Wagner, but Mr. Wagner and the other actor. And, Miss Wagner apparently did not get involved, and apparently that may be the cause of herself separating from this group.

There was nothing in Dr. Noguchi's forensic autopsy report that stated, or even suggested, that Natalie was rendered unconscious. The report was quite the contrary. At autopsy, Natalie's head and skull were examined by pathologists and her brain was examined microscopically by a neuropathologist with negative results. Moreover, there was nothing in the autopsy report about a "nonviolent argument" between Wagner and Walken. So, where did Dr. Noguchi get his information and how did he come up with those conclusions?

The next day, December 1, Dr. Noguchi's administrative chief of staff, Richard Wilson, got into the act. He granted a personal TV interview immediately after Natalie's funeral in which he elaborated, then contradicted his boss:

> Now we said from the beginning that we don't think she was knocked unconscious when she went in the water. We think what happened is she stepped down to the swim step, which is at the rear of the yacht, she attempted to board this rubber dinghy, which is somewhat unstable. We feel that the dinghy slipped away from the back of the yacht and then she fell into the water. At that time she scraped the left side of her face on this swim step. *It was not severe enough to cause unconsciousness* [emphasis added], at least that is what we believe. So therefore, her going into the water, becoming disoriented, probably panicking, screaming for help, it all ties right in with our belief that it was an accidental drowning.

At the news conference the day prior, Wilson had added this about an argument:

> There was an argument between Mr. Wagner and the other gentleman, the actor, I can't remember his name right now. It was a nonviolent argument. In other words, they were arguing about general purposes, we don't know specifically why. There was no physical altercation. *Each of the two gentlemen were examined, looked at by our investigators, as well as sheriff's investigators, there were no physical marks or whatever* [emphasis added]."

The preceding paragraph appeared to suggest that after the coroner's office staff learned of the argument, they were suspicious that a physical altercation may have occurred. Of course, that was completely reasonable under the circumstances. The trouble is, there was nothing in the coroner's file that substantiated the assertion that Wagner and Walken were examined for "marks or whatever" by anyone at the coroner's office, or the LASD, for that matter.

The argument issue was followed up by this exchange:

> **News reporter:** Was the argument serious enough to make her feel that her safety was in danger and therefore she had to leave that yacht?

> **Wilson:** No, according to the information we have, no, there was no danger, she felt no danger at all. *The argument was not over her* [emphasis added].

I tried to locate Richard Wilson to get answers about something I knew for a certainty he and Dr. Noguchi had discussed. I hoped to find his current address, but the common last name and the inability to obtain personnel records of Los Angeles County employees frustrated my efforts and those of my investigators. But I know one thing for a fact: If Wilson is alive, he's intentionally staying under the radar and has done so for 40 years.

One day later—Wednesday, December 2, 1981—sheriff's investigators set up a major conflict between the two agencies by disavowing Dr. Noguchi's argument announcement. The front page of the *Los Angeles Times* read: "Dispute Before Wood's Death Now in Doubt." The reporter wrote:

A sheriff's homicide detective Tuesday disputed coroner's statements suggesting that actors Robert Wagner and Christopher Walken were arguing heatedly aboard an anchored yacht early Sunday when Wagner's wife, actress Natalie Wood, drowned.

"I don't know where the coroner got that information," said investigator Roy Hamilton. "We talked to Wagner and Walken and there was no indication that there was any argument."

Hamilton added, "I think he (Dr. Noguchi) was juicing it up a little bit."

Figure 7: Detective Duane Rasure leads the 1981 LA County Sheriff's Department probe into Natalie Wood's death. (CBS' *48 Hours*)

At the same time Eaker got her assignment, veteran LASD Detective Duane Rasure and Crime Scene Investigator Roy Hamilton "were detailed to investigate the circumstances surrounding the death of Victim Natalie Wood Wagner." They were to depart from Long Beach in the LASD Aero Bureau's Sikorsky helicopter with Eaker, a photographer by the last name of Garrison and personnel from the sheriff's department information bureau to handle contacts with the media.

After leaving Davern the gut-wrenching responsibility of officially identifying Natalie's body, Wagner and Walken, "at their request," were whisked off the island—in the same helicopter that had assisted in locating Natalie—a little over an hour after her body was discovered.

When they arrived in Long Beach, the two celebrities were ushered into the captain's office, where Rasure and Hamilton were waiting. Wagner's interview, initiated at 9:54 a.m., lasted six minutes. After Rasure gave Wagner a pass allegedly because of Wagner's "emotional" condition, Wagner departed with his friend Mart Crowley and went directly to his psychiatrist, who "told him how to break the news to the children." Of course, assuming that's true, he was too late, since Natasha, who had spent the night with a friend, had already heard from a radio report that her mother's lifeless body had been found in the ocean.

Walken's interview at the Aero Bureau began at 10 a.m. There's no indication how long it lasted. By the brevity of investigators' notes and the fact they were on the island being "briefed" by Deputy Kroll by 10:50 a.m., Walken's interview must have been no more than 15 to 20 minutes tops. Beginning with CSI Hamilton's notes, this is what Walken told investigators about Saturday:

Saturday night went out. Had drinks. I had a lot. She can't drink. Had

2—RJ and I had a small beef. I ran out door. Came back and she went down to her room. RJ and I made up. Hugging each other. Didn't hear boat start. I thought she went to bed. I thought she thought we were a bunch of assholes. I think Davern noticed dinghy gone. *We looked for dinghy then looked for her* [emphasis added].

Detective Rasure's notes added a few more details:

Saturday went to Isthmus at night— The Bar had drinks— Back to boat. Nat not too much—not a drinker— Wagner and Chris into small beef—off the boat. Chris ran out the door. Nat—sitting there. Seemed to disturb Nat. She went to her room. Did not hear the motor—or small boat. Possibly after midnight. Thought she went to bed. Dennis (boat captain) observed dinghy gone—? Shore boat came and Wagner went to look for her. Came back and could not find her or dinghy.

Four days later, when the investigators interviewed Walken a second time, in the presence of his criminal defense lawyer, Walken said after they discovered Natalie and the dinghy were missing, "they all felt that she had gone ashore in the Zodiac, probably back to the restaurant." Walken then told them, according to Rasure's notes, "it didn't mean too much to him because he knew she had gone ashore the night before and stayed at Avalon. So, he just went to his stateroom and went to sleep." Hamilton wrote in his notes that Walken said he "slept all night."

The statement was markedly inconsistent with Walken's narrative Sunday morning before he lawyered up. In his first statement, Walken told investigators when they discovered both Natalie and the dinghy were missing, they "looked for her and the dinghy." Moreover, according to Whiting and Oudin, they both talked to Walken before the Coast Guard was called.

Walken was 38 years old when he made his first, and probably last, trip to Catalina Island. When the coroner allegations of an argument surfaced during Dr. Noguchi's press conference, the press understandably asked Walken about its validity. On December 2, he told a *Los Angeles Times* reporter, "I don't remember the coroner being there."

∽∽∽∽∿∽∽∽

Approximately 30 minutes after arriving on the island, the investigators interviewed Davern, who told them all four of them slept on the yacht Friday night. When confronted with the truth that he and Natalie stayed in a hotel in Avalon, Davern said he wanted "to talk to RJ and his attorney before talking about that." And when questioned about broken glass observed by Kroll on the yacht's salon floor, both investigators' notes reported Davern said it was due to "rough seas." And Hamilton's notes stated Davern said, "maybe six wine bottles were broken."

Moreover, when asked about an "argument" between Wagner and Walken on Saturday evening, Davern said he would "rather not say." To any reasonable person, an answer like that would raise grave suspicions about what really happened during Wagner and Walken's "small beef." Yet, *less than 48 hours* after Natalie's body was recovered, Detective Rasure was publicly expressing his view to London's *Daily Mirror* that Natalie's death was an accident. And, the following day, Rasure gave the *Los Angeles Times* his take on the argument issue:

> Sheriff's homicide Sgt. Duane Rasure said Tuesday [December 1] he plans to reinterview Wagner, in seclusion at the couple's Beverly Hills home, and Walken, staying at the Beverly Wilshire with his wife, who arrived on Monday from the East Coast.
>
> Rasure said he intends to find out exactly what the two men discussed— and whether there actually was an argument in the true meaning of the word.
>
> "I'm hearing all kinds of rumors," he said. "But we don't know. ... In four or five days we will have all the answers."

As for the answer to why a famed film star with a publicly expressed fear of dark water would choose to clamber into a small boat at 1 a.m. on a cold night, sheriff's investigator Hamilton said:

> "According to the people we talked to, it was not uncommon for her to take the dinghy out on a nice night. She was very familiar with it."

By the time Hamilton made his statement to the press about Natalie taking out the dinghy on a "nice night," the two investigators had been told by several locals involved in the case that the night was anything but. Witnesses described it as "very cold," "light drizzles" and "breezy" with "white-capped" waters.

Notwithstanding inconsistent statements, unexplained injuries to Natalie's body, reports of witnesses who provided evidence that Natalie may have been in the water next to *Splendour* calling for help and questionable conduct by the only real suspect, on December 11, Detective Rasure took action to officially render case number 081-00898-1873-496, Wagner, Natalie Wood, inactive and classify the file as a "496"—"PERSON DEAD, ACCIDENTAL DROWNING." As far as the two law enforcement agencies were concerned, their investigation was complete, and it was "case closed" on the death of Natalie Wood Wagner.

～～～～～～

Now that you know the "official" account, let's focus on Wagner's actions from the time Natalie's body was discovered until the day of Natalie's funeral.

First, while still on Catalina Island, Wagner refused to make the official identification of his wife's body, instead leaving the painful job to Davern.

Wagner then requested that he and Walken be flown by the LASD's rescue helicopter to Long Beach, leaving Davern to fend for himself and seek public transportation to the mainland.

When Wagner arrived at the Long Beach Aero Bureau, he was interviewed by LASD investigators for a mere six minutes and then released. When Wagner eventually returned home, his lawyer, Paul Ziffren, had already arrived and assumed the role of personal spokesman. Together, they came up with a statement for the press summarizing the events surrounding Natalie's death. It read:

> While Mr. Wagner was in the cabin, Mrs. Wagner apparently went to their stateroom. When Mr. Wagner went to join her, he found that she was not there and that the dinghy was also gone. Since Mrs. Wagner often took the dinghy out alone, Mr. Wagner was not immediately concerned.
>
> However, when she did not return in 10 to 15 minutes, Mr. Wagner took his small cruiser and went to look for her. Unable to find his wife, Mr. Wagner contacted Doug Bombard, whose company leases Isthmus Cove, and who operates a harbor patrol service there.

That same afternoon, Wagner called Dr. Joseph Choi, one of Dr. Noguchi's trusted deputy coroners, who had been assigned the task of performing Natalie's autopsy. He requested an early "post-op"—another word for autopsy—for the following day (see *Figure A*, Page 258) because Natalie's burial was scheduled for Tuesday, December 1.

When Davern finally made it to the house Sunday after identifying Natalie's body, he was taken upstairs to Wagner's spacious bedroom, where he was greeted by Wagner and Ziffren. According to Davern, he was told by the duo to say nothing and to meet with a criminal defense lawyer they had hired for him. Davern, who had been living on *Splendour*, said Wagner also instructed him to start living at the Wagners' house instead.

Still that day, Wagner was composed enough to walk from room to room acknowledging the crush of famous guests who came to pay their respects. Among those Wagner spoke to was Army Archerd, a well-respected columnist for *Variety* magazine who wrote about the gathering.

The following day, Monday, November 30, was Natalie's autopsy. Wagner remained secluded in his home, but his lawyers, clearly at his direction, were hard at work. Wagner met with Davern to tell him to call his lawyer and to use a driver he had hired to transport Davern to the appointment.

On the day of Natalie's funeral, Tuesday, December 1, Wagner found time to revise his earlier press release. According to Catherine Mann of *Entertainment Tonight*, this version read [emphasis added]:

> What happened is she went downstairs in the boat to the master bedroom, and R.J. thought she was going to sleep. And then he went down there *ten or fifteen minutes* later. When he found out she was gone, he noticed the dinghy was gone. *And then he went out with his boat to try to find her. And then he immediately called the Coast Guard* and they made a search and did not discover her or the dinghy until this morning about 8:00.

Wagner also managed to sign the sworn declaration and petition required to probate Natalie's estate. (See *Figures 8* and *9*, next two pages.) The document, prepared by Ziffren's law firm, included a complete copy of Natalie's will. And, as is the case with so many pieces of this mysterious puzzle, the entire probate file was sequestered from public view by the probate clerk until I brought it to light in 2018. And sometime during the week after Natalie's death, Wagner had a 45-minute visit with Jill St. John, the actress who later would become his wife.

Most of what you have just learned took place behind the scenes or under the radar.

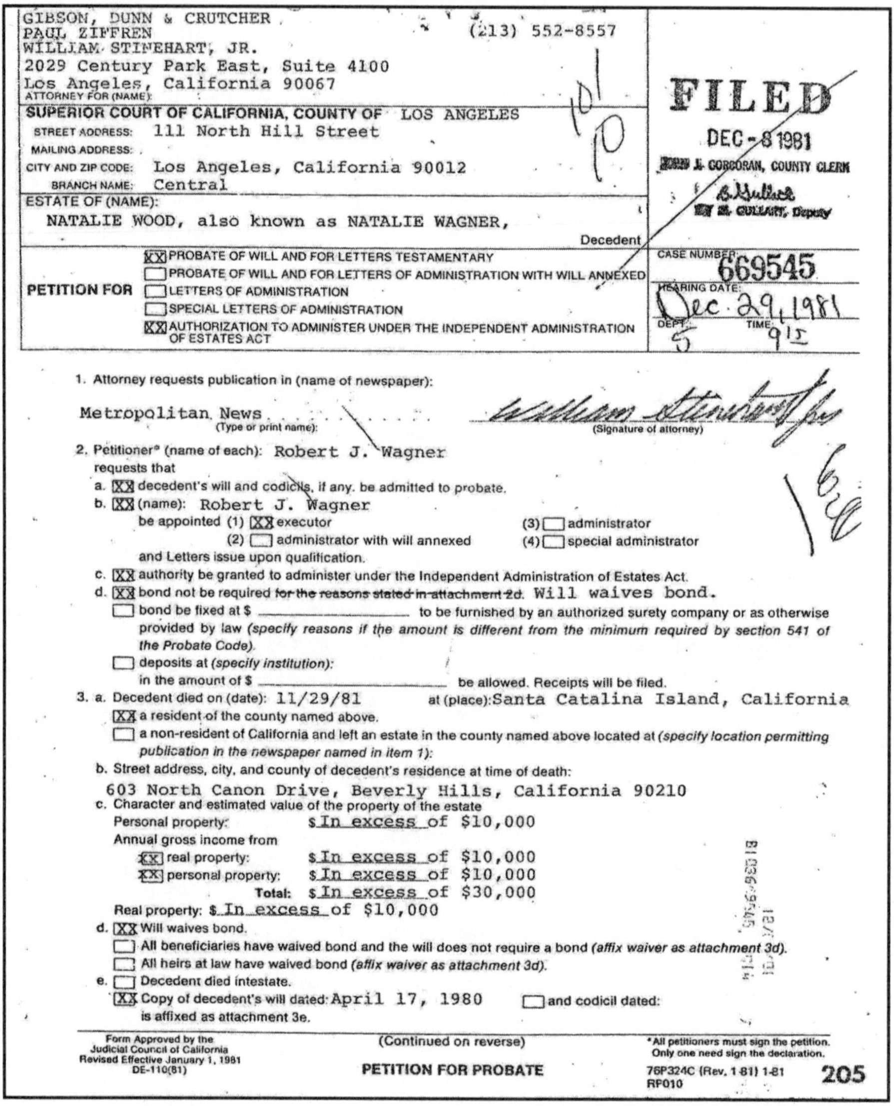

GIBSON, DUNN & CRUTCHER
PAUL ZIFFREN (213) 552-8557
WILLIAM STINEHART, JR.
2029 Century Park East, Suite 4100
Los Angeles, California 90067
ATTORNEY FOR (NAME):

SUPERIOR COURT OF CALIFORNIA, COUNTY OF LOS ANGELES
STREET ADDRESS: 111 North Hill Street
MAILING ADDRESS:
CITY AND ZIP CODE: Los Angeles, California 90012
BRANCH NAME: Central

ESTATE OF (NAME):
NATALIE WOOD, also known as NATALIE WAGNER, Decedent

FILED
DEC - 8 1981
JOHN J. CORCORAN, COUNTY CLERK
BY B. GULLART, Deputy

PETITION FOR
[XX] PROBATE OF WILL AND FOR LETTERS TESTAMENTARY
[ ] PROBATE OF WILL AND FOR LETTERS OF ADMINISTRATION WITH WILL ANNEXED
[ ] LETTERS OF ADMINISTRATION
[ ] SPECIAL LETTERS OF ADMINISTRATION
[XX] AUTHORIZATION TO ADMINISTER UNDER THE INDEPENDENT ADMINISTRATION OF ESTATES ACT

CASE NUMBER: 669545
HEARING DATE: Dec. 29, 1981
DEPT: 5 TIME: 9:15

1. Attorney requests publication in (name of newspaper): Metropolitan News (Type or print name): (Signature of attorney)

2. Petitioner* (name of each): Robert J. Wagner requests that
a. [XX] decedent's will and codicils, if any, be admitted to probate.
b. [XX] (name): Robert J. Wagner be appointed (1) [XX] executor (2) [ ] administrator with will annexed (3) [ ] administrator (4) [ ] special administrator and Letters issue upon qualification.
c. [XX] authority be granted to administer under the Independent Administration of Estates Act.
d. [XX] bond not be required ~~for the reasons stated in attachment 2d.~~ Will waives bond.
[ ] bond be fixed at $ ______ to be furnished by an authorized surety company or as otherwise provided by law *(specify reasons if the amount is different from the minimum required by section 541 of the Probate Code).*
[ ] deposits at *(specify institution):* in the amount of $ ______ be allowed. Receipts will be filed.

3. a. Decedent died on (date): 11/29/81 at (place): Santa Catalina Island, California
[XX] a resident of the county named above.
[ ] a non-resident of California and left an estate in the county named above located at *(specify location permitting publication in the newspaper named in item 1):*
b. Street address, city, and county of decedent's residence at time of death:
603 North Canon Drive, Beverly Hills, California 90210
c. Character and estimated value of the property of the estate
Personal property: $ In excess of $10,000
Annual gross income from
[XX] real property: $ In excess of $10,000
[XX] personal property: $ In excess of $10,000
Total: $ In excess of $30,000
Real property: $ In excess of $10,000
d. [XX] Will waives bond.
[ ] All beneficiaries have waived bond and the will does not require a bond *(affix waiver as attachment 3d).*
[ ] All heirs at law have waived bond *(affix waiver as attachment 3d).*
e. [ ] Decedent died intestate.
[XX] Copy of decedent's will dated: April 17, 1980 [ ] and codicil dated: is affixed as attachment 3e.

Form Approved by the Judicial Council of California Revised Effective January 1, 1981 DE-110(81)
(Continued on reverse)
PETITION FOR PROBATE
*All petitioners must sign the petition. Only one need sign the declaration.
76P324C (Rev. 1-81) 1-81 RP010
205

Figure 8: Page 1 of the petition for probate signed by Robert J. Wagner on December 1, 1981
(Natalie Wood Wagner probate file)

While the public and press had many questions about how Natalie could end up in the ocean in the middle of the night, they weren't getting any answers. The three surviving members of the pleasure yacht *Splendour* weren't talking, and credible, independent information was hard to find. Moreover, it looked as though Wagner's explanation was going to

ESTATE OF (NAME):
NATALIE WOOD, also Known as NATALIE WAGNER, Decedent   CASE NUMBER:

PETITION FOR PROBATE

f. Appointment of personal representative
  (1) Appointment of executor or administrator with will annexed
    ☒ Proposed executor is named as executor in the will.
    ☐ No executor is named in the will.
    ☐ Proposed personal representative is a nominee *(affix nomination as attachment 3f(1))*.
    ☐ Other named executors will not act because of ☐ death ☐ declination ☐ other reasons *(specify in attachment 3f(1))*.
  (2) Appointment of administrator
    ☐ Petitioner is a nominee *(affix nomination as attachment 3f(2))*.
    ☐ Petitioner is related to the decedent as:
  (3) ☐ Appointment of special administrator requested *(specify grounds and requested powers in attachment 3f(3))*.
g. Proposed personal representative is a ☒ resident of California ☐ non-resident of California ☒ resident of the United States ☐ non-resident of the United States.
4. a. *(Complete in all cases.)* The decedent is survived by
    (1) ☒ spouse   ☐ no spouse.
    (2) ☒ parent   ☐ no parent.
    (3) ☒ child   ☐ no child.
    (4) ☐ issue of predeceased child ☒ no issue of predeceased child.
  b. No surviving child or issue of a predeceased child has been omitted from the list of heirs (item 6).
  c. *(Complete only if no spouse or issue survived the decedent.)* The decedent
    (1) ☐ had no predeceased spouse.
    (2) ☐ had a predeceased spouse whose heirs are named in the list of heirs (item 6).
    (3) ☐ had a predeceased spouse who had no heirs.
  d. *(Complete only if no parent or issue survived the decedent.)* The decedent is survived by
    (1) ☐ a brother or sister or issue of a predeceased brother or sister. None has been omitted from the list of heirs (item 6).
    (2) ☐ no brother or sister or issue of a predeceased brother or sister.
5. ☒ Decedent's will does not preclude independent administration of this estate under sections 591—591.7 of the Probate Code.
6. The names, residence or mailing addresses, relationships, and ages of heirs, devisees, predeceased devisees, legatees, and predeceased legatees so far as known to petitioner are ☐ listed below ☒ listed in attachment 6.
    NAME AND RELATIONSHIP   AGE   RESIDENCE OR MAILING ADDRESS

7. ☒ Number of pages attached: 20 pages
Dated:. December 1, 1981 . . . .   X _____
                                  (Signature of petitioner)

I declare under penalty of p___ under the laws of the State of California that the foregoing is true and correct and that this declaration is exec___ (date):. 12/01/81. . at (place) LOS Angeles, California . .

Robert J. Wagner . . . .   X _____
  (Type or print name)   *(Signature of petitioner)*

Figure 9: Page 2 of the petition for probate signed by Robert J. Wagner on December 1, 1981
(Natalie Wood Wagner probate file)

be largely unchallenged until the public heard from one tenacious tabloid.

Within days of Natalie's death, the *National Enquirer* carried a story headlined: "Medical Expert's Shocker: Natalie Didn't Drown," which suggested Dr. Noguchi may have been wrong in concluding Natalie's death was an accidental drowning. The article highlighted one key fact—several "mysterious" bruises, some fresh, were found on Natalie's body and Dr. Noguchi had offered no explanation for their existence. Not only that, the article said:

> The actress' strange demise followed an emotionally charged evening— during which she drank heavily and fought publicly with hubby Robert Wagner on California's Catalina Island. Later that night, the couple got into a squabble aboard their yacht anchored nearby—and a weekend guest, actor Christopher Walken—also argued with Wagner, insiders said.

Insiders said? What insiders? Only three people were with Natalie on *Splendour*. They were the only possible "insiders," unless one of them had said something to a friend. *Was one of them the source for the revelation that Wagner and Natalie got into a "squabble" and that Wagner and Walken also argued? Or was it some official who secretly wanted the public to know the truth?* All the same, with this information and the bruises, LASD investigators had ample evidence of a suspected homicide within hours of Natalie's death. Yet, the case was quickly closed as an accident.

The same *Enquirer* article also contained comments by C. R. McQuiston, a top expert in voice stress evaluation. McQuiston said Dr. Noguchi and his administrative chief of staff, Richard Wilson, weren't being fully truthful during their explosive news conference the day after Natalie's death. The story said, "After examining stress patterns of the duo's key statements using a Psychological Stress Evaluator (PSE), a machine that was widely used by police at the time for truth detection, McQuiston came up with these observations and findings:

> **Noguchi**: "The cause of death will be certified as accidental drowning."

> **McQuiston**: "His stress pattern shows he is not comfortable with this statement and implies there's more to it than he's saying."

> **Noguchi**: "It is most unfortunate that wine and champagne caused this accident."

> **McQuiston**: "Dr. Noguchi stresses heavily on 'wine' as being the cause…this suggests he is trying to drive home a point while not totally believing it himself."
>
> ****

> **Wilson**: "The argument [between Wagner and Walken] was not over her [Natalie]."

> **McQuiston**: "Wilson is throwing a wild stress pattern in stating 'not over her.' This suggests that she actually WAS involved somehow and that something happened that he isn't going to reveal."

Summing up, McQuiston declared: "Voice stress tests on both men's statements indicate that the full story of Natalie's death was not being told. There's something hanging—suggesting they know more than they are willing to disclose."

Forty years ago, a tabloid smelled a rat. Now, I needed to talk to Dr. Noguchi and Wilson to get to the bottom of things. I was confident both knew more than they had revealed.

CHAPTER 3

unresolved and unsettling

IT WAS EARLY JANUARY 2014 AND I WAS RETIRED FROM MY CAREER AS A criminal defense attorney. As I read the concluding sections of Finstad's biography of Natalie, I became curious where the author had obtained the official information provided by witnesses. In checking the book's "Notes," I found references to "Detectives Duane Rasure and Roy Hamilton's official notes and/or the 1981 Natalie Wood file in the L.A. Sheriff's Department Archives."

Someone gave Finstad the official sheriff's department file, I concluded. That was unusual. Based on my experience, investigative files like Natalie's are generally not subject to public disclosure—even after a case is closed.

Furthermore, I knew the sheriff's department had "reopened" Natalie's case in 2011 with great fanfare, so I wondered, *What had it done with the case since then?*

There was plenty of published material from witnesses and others involved for the LASD to analyze.

In a 1985 *Star* magazine article, Davern, *Splendour's* captain, had described a jealous Wagner angrily smashing a wine bottle in front of Natalie and Walken in the yacht's salon, resulting in a humiliated Natalie storming off to the master stateroom.

Vanity Fair reporter Sam Kashner included damning quotes from Davern in his 2000 article "Natalie Wood's Fatal Voyage." Moreover, Davern's longtime friend Marti Rulli helped him describe his version of events in their 2009 book, *Goodbye Natalie, Goodbye Splendour*. It included a sensational claim that Natalie and Wagner had a titanic quarrel shortly before Natalie disappeared.

Plus, several years before publishing their book, Davern and Rulli had talked with Finstad. In her book, she reported stunning claims of a series of late-night phone calls between Davern and Lana Wood.

The last chapter of Finstad's book is titled *Act Five: Dark Water (1980-1981)*. In it, Finstad spends 52 pages laying out her version of the weekend events leading up to Natalie's death. The final climax quotes Lana as telling Finstad that 10 years after Natalie perished, Davern called her with a drunken confession. Finstad's precise words are:

> Natalie was in the ocean alongside the boat, yelling, while R.J., who was still furious, and desperately drunk, continued the argument from on board the boat. "Dennis was very panicky. He was sitting, and would say, 'Come on, let's get her.' And he said R.J. was in such a foul mood, at that point that Dennis then shut up." Time slipped away, Davern told Lana, "until all the sound stopped."
>
> When he and R.J., "beyond drunk," went back to look for Natalie, she was missing, the skipper told Lana, "and that's when everybody panicked."

"That's all Dennis would ever say to me," relates Lana. "I never got anything else out of him about that. There was (sic) a lot more times when he would call me and say how miserable he was, and he didn't know if he could live with this, and on and on and on and on and on."

Anyone reading this account would come away with the reasonable conclusion that both men knew when Natalie was in the water. *Could that possibly be true? Did they both just let her drift off into the blackness to drown?* I asked myself. *And where was Christopher Walken during all of this?*

But there was something suspicious about the Lana Wood passage. While Finstad used quotation marks to indicate Lana's verbatim remarks, she didn't put the dramatic first sentence in quotes—indicating she was paraphrasing what she claimed Lana told her. If Lana's account had been a taped interview or in writing, Finstad would have certainly placed that first damning sentence in quotes.

I would later meet Lana in person, and she eventually told me the Finstad version was "incorrect," "really poorly written" and "sloppy and so mixed-up." Lana insisted she never told Finstad that Davern knew when Natalie was in the water. And, Lana wouldn't be the only person to tell me Finstad seriously misquoted them.

So, why the sudden interest by the sheriff's department in Natalie's case in 2011? Davern's claims of a violent argument between Walken and Wagner and a screaming fight between Natalie and Wagner that fateful Saturday night in November 1981 had been out there for years.

∽∾∽∾∽∾∽

After reading Davern's alleged drunken "confessional," I promptly closed Finstad's book in disgust and searched out my wife to announce I was going to investigate Natalie's death.

It was obvious to me the authorities in Los Angeles were sitting around waiting for Wagner to come in and confess. Of course, that would never happen. Wagner and Walken have had good criminal defense lawyers backing them up since 1981. And Wagner, predictably so, has refused any official interviews since his conversations with the investigators in 1981.

If what Finstad says has any truth to it, Wagner and Davern let her drown. If that's true, the only question that remains is *Why? And, why didn't the authorities make a beeline for Davern after Finstad's book came out in 2001?*

∽∾∽∾∽∾∽

In my experience, it's quite unusual for detectives to spend three years reinvestigating a circumstantial evidence homicide case with the potential suspects known to them. There were three—Wagner, Walken and Davern. After potential suspects are developed, the norm is to establish access or opportunity to commit the homicide. That happens by assuming there was, in fact, a homicide—which should always be assumed by detectives in every unexplained death case.

As Barry A. J. Fisher, former director of the LASD's Scientific Services Bureau, and his son, David, said in their thorough text *Techniques of Crime Scene Investigation*, "All investigators should develop a healthy skepticism. Things often are not as they seem." Armed with that skepticism and the assumption of homicide, an experienced investigator should compose a crime theory. Expressly, what happened? How did it happen? When did it happen? And, finally, why did it happen?

With the "why" or "motive" question, criminal investigators should ask why a potential suspect would want the victim dead. Every investigator worth his or her salt knows this. Jealousy, envy, financial gain, marital discord and passion are classic motives that have been a part of the human experience since the beginning of humanity. But, to discover them, a detective must dig and follow his leads. He can't belittle, ignore or shrug off any clue presented to him, and he must use his instincts. Nine times out of 10, if the "why" question is answered, a prime suspect will be identified.

Who were these new sheriff's detectives, and who did they regard as suspects? I questioned.

In Natalie's case, there were four healthy adults: three men and one beautiful woman aboard a 60-foot yacht moored in Isthmus Cove. Catalina's Isthmus, a narrow strip of land connecting the two parts of the island, is home to the town of Two Harbors, so named because Isthmus Cove harbor is on the northeast side of the Isthmus and Catalina Harbor is on the southwest side.

The four adults returned to their yacht after having drinks and dinner at the only restaurant on that part of the island, and sometime later that dreary night, the beautiful woman ended up dead in the cold Pacific Ocean. The LASD had jurisdiction of the case because Catalina Island was part of Los Angeles County. The three men on the yacht should have been considered suspects from the moment Natalie's body was found.

Yet, the LASD has never stated publicly or in writing that any of the men were suspects. In fact, on November 11, 2011, at a press conference orchestrated by the sheriff's department (see Page A-1), a reporter asked point-blank if Robert Wagner was a suspect in Natalie's death. Lt. John Corina, the department's homicide spokesman, answered flatly, "No."

I knew if the sheriff's officials were being honest, Lt. Corina would have said, "All three gentleman are suspects until we determine otherwise."

Something's not right, I reasoned. *Things are not adding up.*

Once an investigator has exhausted every lead in a homicide investigation of a bona fide suspect, he should take his findings to the district attorney for a decision to either prosecute or close the file. The prosecutor—not the police—must prove a defendant's guilt beyond a reasonable doubt. So, where does the Los Angeles County District Attorney stand on Natalie's case? Has the sheriff's department ever forwarded the Natalie Wood file to the DA's office for review?

The public has never heard from the Los Angeles County DA. In 1981, the office, headed by Los Angeles County Board of Supervisors appointee John Van de Kamp, was conspicuously silent when Natalie's body was found. It was silent in 2011 under the leadership of career prosecutor Steve Cooley—who worked under Van de Kamp when Natalie drowned—when the LASD reopened the case. And it has been silent through hundreds of articles and books about the mystery of Natalie's death to date.

The DA could have put an end to the continuing uncertainties about this case. Perhaps the DA couldn't solve the mystery, but the office could have demanded the files, and after investigation and review, charged a prime suspect or announced once and for all that there would be no prosecution of anyone for Natalie's death unless someone confessed. The DA has always known that, yet the office remained on the sidelines while key witnesses died off and critical evidence was lost due to the passage of time. *Why?*

And there was another investigative tool for finding the truth available to the California authorities in 1981 and 2011—a coroner's inquest.

Given the unexplained circumstances surrounding Natalie's death, why didn't the district attorney or the sheriff call for an inquest at the time? If Dr. Noguchi was interested in the truth, why didn't *he* call for a jury inquest into Natalie's death? Or, why haven't his successors done so?

At an inquest, Walken, Wagner and Davern could be subpoenaed and examined under oath in public. Natalie's longtime hairdresser could be called to testify about Natalie's real thoughts on her marriage leading up to that fateful Thanksgiving weekend in 1981. Bank, credit card and phone records and probate documents could be subpoenaed and experts used to review the evidence. Even Willie Mae Worthen, the Wagners' longtime, live-in housekeeper, could have been summoned to testify. The law enforcement agencies knew about the use of an inquest as a means for reaching the truth. So, why the lack of effort?

Thirty years later, if Los Angeles County Sheriff Lee Baca and his detectives were truly motivated in 2011 to uncover the truth when they reopened Natalie's case, why didn't they demand an inquest? Even Dr. Lakshmanan Sathyavagiswaran, the chief medical examiner-coroner/interim director for Los Angeles County who dramatically changed Natalie's autopsy report from accidental "drowning" to "drowning and other undetermined factors" in a May 2012 Supplemental Report, recognized the lingering questions concerning her death. Why didn't he conduct his own inquest? There is only one reasonable conclusion: In 2011, they were not genuinely interested in the truth.

Embarking on my investigation, I knew there were a lot of questions that needed to be answered. And I didn't know if I could answer them. But deep down, I wanted to know what happened to Natalie Wood. And, in my opinion, the authorities appeared to be doing nothing to resolve the suspicions of murder that had been lingering over her case for nearly four decades.

⌁⌁⌁⌁⌁⌁

You might be asking, why murder? Why not manslaughter or some other homicide crime? Under California law, both voluntary and involuntary manslaughter were long ago lost to the statute of limitations. The California statute of limitations in 1981 gave prosecutors six years from the date of the offense to prosecute someone for voluntary manslaughter and three years for involuntary manslaughter. Murder has no statute of limitations.

From what I knew about Natalie's case, it would boil down to two simple questions: *Was someone responsible for Natalie, who couldn't swim, ending up in the ocean in the middle of a cold, dark November night? And, did that person knowingly let her drown?* If those questions were answered in the affirmative, then under the California Penal Code in 1981, that person could have been prosecuted for second-degree murder with implied malice aforethought.

California recognizes that malice can be either "express or implied." Malice is "implied" when a "killing results from an intentional act;" the "natural consequences of the act are dangerous to human life;" and that act "was deliberately performed with knowledge of the danger to, and conscious disregard for, human life."

To constitute the crime of second-degree murder, there must also be, in addition to the death, an "unlawful act or omission which was the cause of the death." Under the established law, "a cause of death is an act or omission that sets in motion a chain of events that produces as a direct, natural and probable consequence of the act or omission a death and without which the death would not occur."

Going in, I recognized that without a full confession, Natalie's case would need to be investigated as a circumstantial evidence case. Under California law, circumstantial evidence is "evidence that, if found to be true, proves a fact from which an inference of the existence of another fact may be drawn."

I knew this wouldn't be easy. The biggest problem, though, was not logistics or my personal issues, it was my lack of legal process. In an actual criminal investigation, a law enforcement officer can get a grand jury or prosecutor's subpoena to compel the production of records or the attendance of witnesses if they refused to cooperate. Or, an investigator could obtain a search warrant. I wouldn't have those powerful tools. The LASD certainly had access to one or the other by going to the district attorney or judge. But whether the investigators requested and used those tools in 2011 remained to be seen.

CHAPTER 4

corpus delicti

ARMED WITH A CELL NUMBER I GOT FROM TWO BRITISH PRODUCERS, I sent Lana Wood a text at the end of 2016 introducing myself and explaining that I was going to be in Los Angeles in January. I wanted to meet with her to discuss some things about her sister and something I read in her book *Natalie: A Memoir by Her Sister*. She responded within minutes and said she would be happy to talk with me.

In late January 2017, we met at the Westin Bonaventure Hotel in Los Angeles. I will disclose more details about our interactions in another chapter. However, because it sheds light on the use of circumstantial evidence in criminal cases, I want to share part of our conversation from that first face-to-face meeting.

I decided to start with something Lana was familiar with.

> **S.P.:** I've been around this business a long, long time. I've seen every kind of investigator you can imagine, from the dishonest ones to the terrific ones to the lazy ones and in between. And I can tell you that the folks investigating this case have been sitting around waiting for Robert Wagner to come in and confess.

Lana laughed, but I was serious.

> **S.P.:** They haven't been investigating the case. If they were, they would have realized a long time ago that Wagner wasn't talking.
>
> **Lana:** No.
>
> **S.P.:** But if the detectives were any kind of investigators, they would know they had something better than Robert Wagner coming in and telling them more lies. The contradictory statements he's made over the years in books, magazines and newspapers.
>
> **Lana:** Yes.

I had filed a lawsuit against the sheriff in late 2015, and the LASD had recently told Rulli I was "interfering with their investigation" of Natalie's death by trying to get their records. Rulli told Lana. I was in a lather and needed to say my piece.

> **S.P.:** Without a confession, this is a circumstantial evidence case. The LASD could have tried to get a prosecutor on board. Somebody who had been around for a while. Somebody who understood how you prove a circumstantial evidence case. Yet, according to the sheriff's lawyers, they never contacted the prosecuting attorney's office.

Lana: That's not good.

S.P.: While the years were passing by, critical witnesses were dying. A prosecutor can't prosecute a case with dead witnesses. So, I resent the fact that they accused me of interfering with the progress of their investigation. There's nothing that could be further from the truth.

Lana: I don't understand the subterfuge. I really don't.

S.P.: I think I understand their motive now that I've spent so much time digging into this. They don't want the public to appreciate the kind of evidence they had when people were alive.

Lana: Why?

S.P.: Because, at the least, it would be embarrassing for the department. At worst, it would show the public there has been an ugly cover-up.

Lana: Without question.

S.P.: Now, it's too late. They had suspicious circumstantial evidence in 1981.

Lana: Yes.

S.P.: People can draw inferences. That's what circumstantial evidence is all about. When I was a prosecutor, I used to tell the jurors in my criminal cases, "The defense says there's doubt because this is a circumstantial evidence case. Well, let me tell you something about circumstantial evidence. It's January in Wisconsin. You're getting ready to go to bed. You look outside. It's cold—very cold. Stars are shining. The moon is out. It's a beautiful night, only it's very cold. You get up the next morning, you open the drapes and there's snow on the ground. Now, you didn't see it snow. So, if somebody asks you, 'Did it snow? You can't honestly say, 'I saw it snow last night.' But what you can do is reasonably infer that because it was in Wisconsin and so cold and there's snow on the ground, it snowed."

Lana: I love that.

S.P.: For example, in your sister's case, Davern has things to say about what happened on that boat. There is other evidence to substantiate what he says. In a real case, jurors can put two and two together, and guess what? They can come up with four. Legally, that happens every day in courtrooms across America. For Natalie, the only real way to approach the complete truth is to have a jury trial. Have it prosecuted by a skilled DA and defended by a sharp criminal defense attorney in front of an honorable judge. Then, you will get as close to the complete truth as you will ever get.

Lana: I would take it.

S.P.: I know you would. I wish I could give it to you. But maybe I can get close.

I wasn't sure if I was preaching to the choir or if Lana was just being agreeable to be agreeable. Notwithstanding, I sensed her hurt and frustration. She seemed confused, yet comfortable with what I was trying to accomplish.

During our discussions, I realized Lana was no different than most ordinary citizens. Until they serve on jury duty, they don't really understand what's needed to prove the commission of a criminal homicide. It's not only a matter of evidence, it's an appreciation of the law. Unfortunately for Natalie's case, it's likely *you* will receive more instruction on the law of murder than the detectives in Natalie's 2011 investigation. To demonstrate that, I want to share something from an actual California murder case, *The People of California v. Eric Christopher Bechler.*

The trial in that case resulted in a life sentence for a young man who was convicted of murdering his wife on her birthday, which also happened to be the couple's marriage anniversary. Sadly, the couple had young children.

On a calm, sunny afternoon, Gary Greene was sailing with some family members and friends in the open ocean off the coast of Newport Beach. There was a 1- to 3-foot ocean swell with a light chop, but no big waves. About 4 miles off Abalone Cove, Greene saw a man in the water holding onto a boogie board. Nearby, a motorboat was circling at a fast rate of speed. As Greene approached the scene, he could hear the stranded man yell, "My wife, my wife, my wife."

According to Greene, the man in the water seemed distraught or in shock. As Greene got closer, he heard the man yell that his wife had fallen out of the boat. Greene immediately called the Coast Guard, threw the man a life jacket and tried to calm him as he pulled him near his vessel. During the tense 45-minute wait for the Coast Guard, the man held onto the boogie board, stared straight ahead and said nothing. Orange County sheriff's deputies responded to the distress call and pulled the man into their boat.

In an emotional condition, the man—Eric Bechler—explained to deputies that he and his wife, Pegye, had rented a boat to celebrate their fifth wedding anniversary and Pegye's birthday. They drank margaritas, ate snacks and sunbathed, and he rode the boogie board while Pegye drove the boat towing him. Bechler said he suddenly hit a wave or a wake and went under the water. When he came up, he couldn't see Pegye. The unmanned boat was traveling in circles and he couldn't catch up to it. The last time he saw Pegye, Bechler said she was seated on the top of the back part of the driver's seat.

After managing to stop and secure the rental boat, the sheriff's deputies inspected it. The boat was neat with no wrappers, chips or crumbs on the deck. For about two hours, searchers combed the area looking for Pegye. Bechler asked deputies to search the coastline because "maybe she swam to shore." They testified during the search, Bechler appeared to be sobbing, but "seemed" to shed no tears.

While others continued the search, deputies took Bechler to shore with the rental boat in tow. Within Bechler's earshot, they mentioned the possibility media might be present on the dock when they returned. Bechler was quiet on the trip to shore, but upon disembarking, he became very upset. He sobbed, his shoulders heaved, and deputies had to help him walk up the gangway. Once inside the sheriff's office, Bechler calmed down and could walk on his own. No media representatives were present.

The next morning, Coast Guard investigators went to Bechler's house, and he related basically the same story he had told sheriff's deputies. He appeared to be crying as he spoke, but the investigators reported they saw no tears.

When Coast Guard investigators examined the boat that day, they found one towel laid out in front of the motor, two duffel bags, a cooler containing a canteen half filled with margarita mix, a pair of sunglasses on a seat and a backpack. A large duffel bag contained only a magazine. A second duffel contained various items, including chips, other snacks, toiletries and clothing. Bechler's backpack contained black plastic bags, lubricant and a vibrator. Investigators also found a rope measuring 40 feet, 8 inches long. They found no blood on the boat or on any clothing retrieved from the boat.

Later the same day, investigators returned to Bechler's home and found him curled in a fetal position on a couch. He again appeared to cry, but shed no tears.

The next day, Bechler was interviewed by Coast Guard investigators at the police station. Bechler gave additional details about what happened the day Pegye disappeared, but his story stayed the same as he had stated the previous day.

Five days later, Orange County sheriff's investigators talked to Bechler. His story remained the same. Apparently, during the many interviews, Bechler told the investigators he and Pegye "rarely fought," were "so happy" and had a "very strong, wonderful marriage."

But friends and neighbors would tell investigators the couple argued "frequently and heatedly." Two or three years before Pegye disappeared, Bechler had confided in his best friend that he didn't want to be around her anymore, but he didn't want a divorce because he "would lose the money and the kids."

During their diligent search, investigators determined employment and financial issues were straining the couple's marriage. Pegye had built up a lucrative business and sold it. After the sale, the Bechlers were allowed to stay on as employees, but were let go about four months before Pegye's disappearance. They had, however, planned for their security in the event of a tragedy. Each was the beneficiary of $2.6 million in life insurance on the other's life.

A massive search of the area over the course of three days turned up nothing. Investigators later determined Pegye was a triathlete and a "terrific" swimmer. But sadly, Pegye's body was never found and, according to the appellate court record, "she has not been seen or heard from since" the day she disappeared.

Nearly three years later, after a relentless investigation aided by a scorned girlfriend, Bechler was charged with murder.

During the trial, one of Pegye's friends testified that she noticed Bechler appeared solemn and upset around Pegye's family, but outside their presence, he appeared more jovial and happier "than she had ever seen him."

And, three months after Pegye's disappearance, Bechler started seeing a woman. That stormy relationship ended two years later, following the girlfriend's claims that Bechler made incriminating statements and then tried to get her to lie about their conversations. At trial, Bechler denied his girlfriend's allegations, claiming they were a "drug-induced fantasy."

The prosecution had no direct evidence proving how Pegye ended up in the water. No witnesses who saw Bechler shove Pegye out of the speedboat or harm her in any way. And there was no body, so no evidence proving how Pegye died. Yet Bechler was charged with murder and convicted, and the case was affirmed on appeal notwithstanding claims of insufficient evidence. *So, how did the court reconcile the evidence against Bechler with the law of murder in California?*

⤙⤙⤙⤙⤙⤙⤙

The appellate court in Bechler's appeal began with an analysis of *corpus delicti*, or "the body of the crime" of murder. That principle of law is, "the fact of injury, loss, or harm, and the existence of a criminal agency." Under California law in 1981, *corpus delicti* needed to be established for a jury independently of a defendant's "extrajudicial statements, confessions, or admissions." That is, what a defendant said outside the courtroom to others. However, the degree of a crime, for instance, the difference between first-degree and second-degree murder, could be established by a defendant's extrajudicial admissions.

In 2002, the California Supreme Court held that a constitutional provision passed by the voters in 1982 abrogated the extrajudicial statements rule. From that point, convictions were only required to be supported by some proof of *corpus delicti* "aside from or in addition to" a defendant's extrajudicial statements.

Whether someone charged with Natalie's 1981 death could be convicted using the post-1982 rule is certainly subject to reasonable debate. But—and this directly relates to Natalie's case—it has always been the rule that proof of *corpus delicti* "may be circumstantial and need not be beyond a reasonable doubt." Specifically, the amount of evidence needed is "not great" and only " 'a slight or *prima facie* showing' permitting a [jury] inference of injury, loss, or harm from a criminal agency" is needed to sustain the prosecution's burden of proof.

Corpus delicti has two elements in the context of a murder trial. First is the death of the alleged victim, and second is the existence of some criminal agency as the cause. Production of the missing person's body or of evidence of the means used to produce a death is *not* essential to the establishment of *corpus delicti* or to sustain a murder conviction.

If murder is charged, the burden of proving *corpus delicti* can be met by the prosecutor with "evidence which creates a reasonable inference that the death could have been caused by a criminal agency, even in the presence of an equally plausible noncriminal explanation of the event." For example, being pushed in the ocean versus falling in accidentally.

The prosecution is also not obliged to "eliminate all inferences tending to show a noncriminal cause of death but need only introduce evidence from which a reasonable inference can be drawn that a criminal agency could have caused the death." For example, if two causes could reasonably be inferred from the evidence, one supporting an accident and one supporting a criminal homicide, the inference of homicide is legally sufficient to prove the criminal agency element of *corpus delicti*.

Finally, evidence of jealousy, envy, financial gain and marital discord can be used to prove one spouse had a motive and the intent to murder the other.

⤙⤙⤙⤙⤙⤙⤙

I found many of the factual similarities between Bechler's and Natalie's case remarkable. However, I found the contrast between how the U.S. Coast Guard and Orange County law enforcement officers treated Bechler and how the Los Angeles County Sheriff's Department treated Wagner in 1981 and 2011 to be most damning.

The Coast Guard investigators were immediately on the scene interviewing Bechler. The Coast Guard, which also had jurisdiction over Natalie's death because it occurred on the high seas, never got a crack at interviewing Walken, Davern or Wagner. But I believe they tried in 1981 and were rejected outright by the LASD.

The day after Natalie was found, Coast Guard investigator Lt. McCoy called Detective Rasure about "his [McCoy's] responsibility" in the "Wood drowning." I discovered the telephone message in the records I ultimately obtained from the sheriff's 1981 archived file on Natalie's death. There was no documentary evidence that Rasure responded. Although Rasure must have told McCoy something McCoy didn't like, because the following day (inferred by the telephone message order in the 1981 file), there was a notation of a telephone number for a Captain Simon Zerbos, another Coast Guard investigator, who was most likely McCoy's superior.

I searched in earnest for Lt. McCoy and Captain Zerbos without success. But I have no doubt they called Rasure about wanting to conduct an investigation in Natalie's case and he, and perhaps the sheriff himself, brushed them off.

In Natalie's case, Wagner was released by Detective Rasure after a six-minute interview because, as you will learn, he was "quite shook." Bechler, on the other hand, was kept at the Orange County Sheriff's Department until he composed himself. Then, he was interviewed by the deputies. Furthermore, the following day, Bechler was interviewed by Coast Guard investigators twice—even though on one occasion he was on the couch "in a fetal position." Several days later, Bechler was interviewed by Orange County detectives.

You will also learn that Detective Rasure and CSI Hamilton spent less than 30 minutes examining *Splendour* and the Zodiac dinghy in Natalie's case. And, other than taking photographs, no evidence collection occurred on the Wagners' yacht or dinghy. In comparison, in Bechler's case, a full and complete forensic examination of the speedboat was conducted.

Moreover, the investigators immediately asked Bechler questions about his relationship with his wife to uncover any marital discord and began immediately investigating the truth of Bechler's responses. Investigators also began looking into the Bechlers' finances to determine if there was a second motive to kill Pegye.

By contrast, in Natalie's case, I determined that investigators made no effort to discover evidence of marital discord or financial gain as possible motives for her death. In fact, during a sworn deposition on May 3, 2016, I questioned Detective Ralph Hernandez, the lead detective in the 2011 LASD investigation. After a contentious exchange with him and his lawyer, I learned the LASD file on Natalie's death showed no indication her probate file was examined in 1981, and since the case was reopened in November 2011, no one in the Homicide Bureau had either obtained or seen her probate file.

After all was said and done in Bechler's case, Orange County detectives stayed focused on his suspicious activities for *more than two years.* You will learn that in Natalie's case, the LASD's 1981 investigation was effectively over *in a few hours.* And the 2011 investigation was effectively over in *less than eight weeks.*

CHAPTER 5

a second opinion

BEFORE PAT AND I LEFT TO SPEND THE SUMMER OF 2016 IN RHODE ISLAND, I wrote to several expert pathologists. I hit the jackpot when Dr. Christina Stanley, Chief Medical Examiner for the State of Rhode Island, agreed to consult with me.

When we met, Dr. Stanley could not have been more pleasant. With light brown hair tied in a ponytail and wearing a weathered baseball cap with nautical shorts and a T-shirt, her thin frame gave her an athletic look. I guessed her age at about 45. Pat thought she was younger. But, her most endearing characteristic was her genuine interest in me and what I was doing. And, she liked to talk.

At her request, I had already emailed her Natalie's autopsy report and some typed witness statements. I also told her that Natalie couldn't swim and was terrified of deep, dark sea water. Thankfully, Dr. Stanley came prepared.

The narrative portion of Natalie's 1981 autopsy report is a mere six pages long. However, what's in that narrative is not nearly as telling as what's not.

For example, while reading Dr. Noguchi's 1983 memoir *Coroner*, I noticed he mentioned that his office's chief consultant on ocean accidents, Paul Miller, said he found "fingernail scratches on the starboard side of the dinghy, which shows she was trying to climb into it." There's nothing in the official autopsy report about Miller or fingernail scratches. What's more, I found nothing in the narrative report indicating the coroner's office took fingernail clippings or scraped under Natalie's nails for evidence of rubber or, more importantly, skin or blood.

If Dr. Noguchi had wanted to confirm what Miller told him, the best way was to inspect Natalie's fingernails and collect nail clippings. And, if Dr. Noguchi had wanted to determine if Natalie had been in an altercation, the classic forensic method was to check under her nails for skin or blood belonging to someone else.

This was when my suspicions of Dr. Noguchi's true motives first surfaced. *Was Dr. Noguchi intentionally avoiding the identification of potential evidence that might implicate a celebrity?*

Natalie's death was detailed in the first chapter of *Coroner*, Dr. Noguchi's bestselling book about celebrity deaths. By 1983, the public was starving for information about her death. Up to the point of the book's publication, Dr. Noguchi had shared no specifics publicly about Natalie's bruises, scrapes and scratches, Miller's involvement in the investigation or the method used to determine the time of death. I'm convinced the $14.95 book wouldn't have been nearly as bestselling without the chapter on Natalie Wood's death. No other chapter contains as much sensational, never-before-published autopsy material.

Natalie's official autopsy report was signed by three forensic pathologists: Dr. Noguchi as the chief medical examiner-coroner, and Dr. Choi and Dr. Ronald N. Kornblum as deputy medical examiners. The report is dated December 4, 1981, but the autopsy was performed November 30, 1981, between 9:30 a.m. and 1:30 p.m. A five-day lag in preparing a narrative report in this type of case in 1981 was a fast turnaround. It's obvious the pathologists felt some pressure to get it out.

Dr. Choi signed and dated the report December 5, 1981, indicating to me he was assigned the case. Dr. Noguchi supervised and Dr. Kornblum assisted. In *Coroner,* Dr. Noguchi described Dr. Kornblum as his "deputy chief of the forensic medicine division" and said Dr. Choi was "one of my most skilled deputy medical examiners." *I realize it was Natalie Wood, but if this were just a simple accidental drowning case, why three pathologists?*

∽∾∽∾∽∾∽∾∽

Before my meeting with Dr. Stanley, I decided to research both deputy medical examiners. As I had feared, Dr. Choi died on January 3, 2012, and Dr. Kornblum in September 2008. Fortunately, their obituaries provided valuable clues about why they were called in to help with Natalie's case.

Dr. Kornblum, former chief medical examiner of Ventura County, California, was considered an expert on choke-hold deaths. Dr. Choi, it turns out, was an authority on strangulation cases. *Did Dr. Noguchi believe Natalie was choked or strangled?* The narrative portion of the autopsy report contained no suspicions of that sort, and Dr. Noguchi conveniently omitted any reference to the specialties of Choi and Kornblum in his book. *Was there some injury to Natalie's body that I had missed while scrutinizing the autopsy report? Something I had overlooked?* I had a lot of questions for my new consultant.

During our first session, Dr. Stanley and I started with bruises—the first topic of conversation for anyone reviewing the autopsy results in Natalie's case. I learned later there were more telling injuries to Natalie's body. But I was initially focused on Natalie's leg and right forearm bruises.

At least 30 bruises were specifically identified on body diagrams during Natalie's external examination. (See *Figures 10* and *11,* next two pages.) However, nine were identified on the back of both legs, all the way up to about the midpoint of her hamstrings. In *Coroner,* Dr. Noguchi said the posterior leg bruises measured "a half inch to two inches."

Dr. Stanley remarked, "Having spent a good bit of time on fishing yachts, I could understand bruises on the front of her shins. But, the back of her legs?"

Seeing the baffled look on her face, I pressed her to explain.

She continued, "This is what I found strange…the amount of bruising on the back of her legs. I was looking at me. I get a lot of bruises [on my legs]. I'm not too bad now. There's just one right now on the front. But I don't have any back side. It's strange to me—these bruises on the back of her legs. It's very weird. You get bruises two major ways. One, you get hit really hard. Two, you can get a bruise if you're pushing against a bone."

Obviously puzzled, Dr. Stanley worked through the possibilities. "It's strange. Is she trying to get back on the dinghy? It was really helpful to know that she couldn't swim, because I was having real trouble putting this together. Because why didn't she just swim to shore? So, did she stay with the dinghy? Try to board it? But you shouldn't bruise against an inflatable rubber Zodiac. And, if she got up that high, she would be in the dinghy."

Then another thought occurred to her. "Maybe you're getting your legs squished? You know with [yacht] staterooms, your mattress may be low, and you've got that surround edge…that wooden edge. It could be that she was pushed onto the bed. Do you know if their yacht had the wood surround below the mattress?" Dr. Stanley asked.

With that keen observation, I wondered whether it was possible to discover the length of Natalie's legs. *If the stateroom bed had a wooden surround, would the height match up with location of the bruises on the back of Natalie's legs?* Lana would tell me later she was almost exactly the same height as Natalie—5-foot-2—and her inseam was 26 inches, meaning it was likely it would

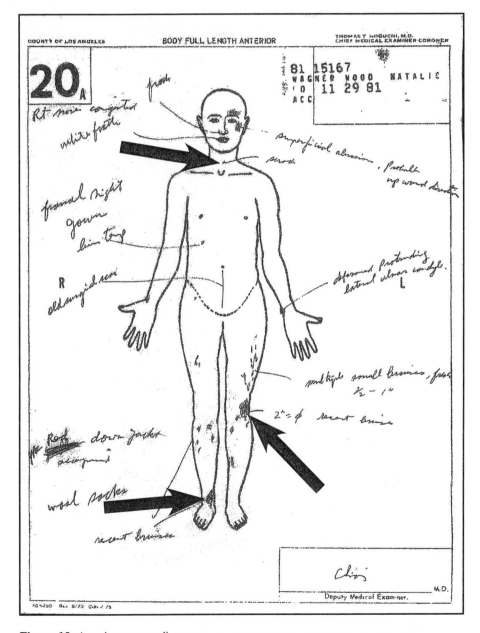

Figure 10: Anterior autopsy diagram (Los Angeles County Department of Medical Examiner-Coroner)

have been no more than 13 inches from the floor to the back of Natalie's knee.

"At this point, the only thing official I have is the autopsy report," I answered. But her comments raised a distinct possibility as to how back leg bruising injuries could occur during a physical struggle in the small confines of a yacht stateroom.

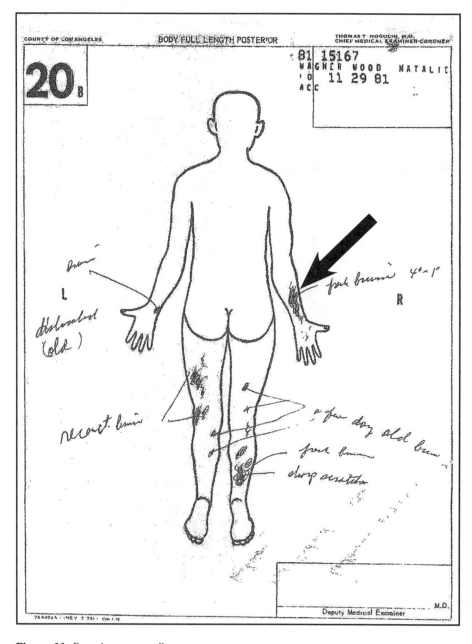

Figure 11: Posterior autopsy diagram (Los Angeles County Department of Medical Examiner-Coroner)

∽∽∽∽∽∽

My next topic with Dr. Stanley was whether, forensically, a pathologist could really tell if a bruise was old or new. The autopsy report labeled several bruises as "fresh." Natalie was found floating facedown in the ocean. The surface water temperature at that time was recorded by Eaker as 62 to 63 degrees. The air temperature was 63 degrees. Of course, it would have been colder at midnight. *Would cold water have affected her bruises?* I inquired.

Dr. Stanley gave my question some thought. "Bruises are really hard to judge," she began. "We've all had bruises. Sometimes you hit yourself and you see the bruise pretty quickly, and sometimes you don't. The deeper bruises take longer to be visible on the surface. A bruise is just blood that's no longer in a blood vessel. It's no longer circulating. You get bigger bruises in areas where you have superficial veins—like the tops of your hands. So, it depends on where the bruise is…which makes it really hard to say how old bruises are by looking at them."

Then Dr. Stanley added, "But, the really interesting thing about this case is they actually took microscopic sections and looked at some of the bruises microscopically. That's the best

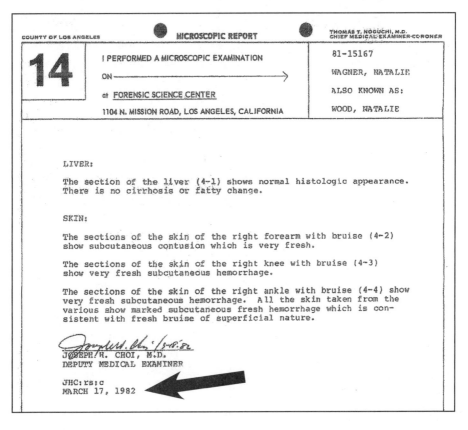

Figure 12: Dr. Choi's microscopic examination report on Natalie's liver and bruise sections
(Los Angeles County Department of Medical Examiner-Coroner)

way to date a bruise. They looked at the skin tissue under a microscope and they're calling them 'very fresh' in the report…specifically the big one on her right forearm, the big one on her left knee and a good-sized one on her right ankle, and a few others.

"If you look at bruise tissue microscopically, you're looking for cellular reaction…inflammatory cells," she explained. "You usually see those 12, 18 to 24 hours after onset. So, when they're calling them 'very fresh,' that means probably less than one day.

"Remember, to have a bruise, you have to have blood pressure," she continued. "And, you have to be alive to have blood pressure. Also, I don't think the temperature of the water—at 62 to 63 degrees—is going to have any significant relevance to the size of a small bruise. It's cold, but not cold enough to decrease the size. But, the contusion on the right forearm may be another story."

Now, I was beginning to understand the significance of the outside surroundings during the time Natalie was in the water.

"The right forearm bruise… Is there any significance to its location?" I asked.

"This forearm bruise, this is kind of a weird bruise, too," she began. "It could very well be defensive. Dr. Choi is calling it lateral. Lateral is going to be under—more than maybe on top of the forearm. So, that makes you think it's more under the forearm. Dr. Choi refers to it being a 4-inch by 1-inch diffuse bruise. I never use 'lateral' personally. I use 'radial' and 'ulnar' to avoid confusion. A layperson wouldn't know that. Dr. Choi's drawing shows it a little more on the side. But, to me, the drawing looks like it's what I would call dorsal, ventral and then radial. It's not a place where you would bump yourself."

"And the size of it?" I promptly probed.

"The size is significant. She's a little lady. And for a 43-year-old, that's a big bruise in not a real vascular area. There are two reasons why bruises are big. One is there is a lot of force, and, two, they bleed for a long time," Dr. Stanley explained.

From my personal experience with violent crime cases, I knew about assaults and defensive wounds. When people are attacked, they instinctively try to defend themselves. They put up their forearms, scratch, cover their heads, kick with their feet—all in an effort to protect themselves. At autopsy, assault victims invariably show bruises on the tops of the hands, under the leading forearms, and so forth. Natalie also had bruises on the back of her right hand.

I would later learn from Lana that Natalie was right-handed. Lana's forearm measured 9-3/4 inches (almost exactly the mean forearm length for an adult female, according to a 1989 Polish medical study). Knowing Natalie was similar in size to Lana, the bruise on the underside of her right forearm most likely covered nearly half its length.

The same was true about the bruises on Natalie's left knee and right ankle—both measured 2 inches in diameter. Natalie weighed 115 pounds, according to Lana. Based on her small physique, 2-inch bruises probably covered most of Natalie's knee and ankle.

Yet, the autopsy report signed by three experienced pathologists wrapped up by saying, "Most of the bruises on the body are superficial and probably sustained at the time of drowning." "Superficial" means that the bruise wasn't deep. So, in their conclusion, they ignored the big, unexplained deep bruises and had no basis to say that most of Natalie's bruises were sustained "at the time of drowning."

That Dr. Choi described the classic defensive bruise on Natalie's right forearm in such a confusing way was the second time I felt the forensic evidence may have been manipulated to support a conclusion of accident. But I would defer judgment until I dug deeper into the facts with Dr. Stanley.

"They say that right forearm bruise was recent," I continued.

"Yes. It's recent, and the cold may have even decreased the clotting," Dr. Stanley responded.

"So, perhaps the bruise would have been even bigger if she hadn't been in the cold water?" I theorized.

"It's possible, but all in all, I find these bruises to be quite excessive for someone her age. There are also a lot of bruises in strange places. She wasn't an alcoholic, was she?" Dr. Stanley asked.

I handled her question by saying, "I noticed they checked her liver."

"Right," Dr. Stanley responded, after consulting the report. "No cirrhosis or fatty change. This was excellent. Dr. Choi did take a section of the liver. He specifically said there was no fatty change. So, she's not an alcoholic."

"Are there any patterns to the bruises that you could see?" I asked.

"No patterns. No characteristic patterns. As a matter of fact, Dr. Choi says here in the external description narrative about the bruises, 'There is no particular pattern,' " Dr. Stanley answered.

"Can you match a bruise to something that caused it—like, for example, if Natalie hit her arm on something trying to board a dinghy?" I continued.

"You can," Dr. Stanley quickly answered. "Items can very often leave distinctive bruises."

Following up, I asked, "Did they state they compared the big bruise on Natalie's forearm with anything on *Splendour's* dinghy?"

Dr. Stanley's response was an unequivocal, "No."

Dr. Choi must have been asking himself the same questions in 1981 that Dr. Stanley was asking me. But the answers he got at autopsy were not declared in his narrative. The large bruises were recent, the leg bruises may have occurred in the stateroom, some bruises were consistent with defensive wounds, Natalie wasn't an alcoholic and there were no discernible patterns to any of the bruises.

Then Dr. Stanley said something that jolted me. When Natalie's body was found, she was clothed in a red down jacket, a cotton nightshirt, wool socks and some jewelry. "She's wearing a down jacket…it's really hard to get out of the water in a down jacket. The sleeve would have been covering her forearm, protecting it. So, that big forearm bruise had to have happened before she went into the water—quite likely in the stateroom."

That's when the clouds started clearing for me on Natalie's injuries.

"How about the abrasions on the left side of Natalie's face?" I asked. "If she fell or was pushed off the boat towards the dinghy and she hit the dinghy with her face, could that explain the abrasion on her face?"

Dr. Stanley looked at the anterior body diagram and said, "I think that's more likely than her being struck by something, like a hand, a fist or getting pushed into something. This is an area that if you get an impact, you're going to get bruised. But, because the dinghy is rubber, it wouldn't tear her face up. Falling facedown on the dinghy safety line could also account for the abrasion as it slid across her face."

The face abrasion was a perfect entry point for my troubling question about the expertise of the pathologists involved in Natalie's case.

"Something's really bothering me," I blurted out. Dr. Stanley looked at me with concern. "There were three pathologists on Natalie's case and two were experts in choke holds and strangulation. And I can't figure out what prompted that," I continued.

"Let me look at the diagrams," Dr. Stanley said reaching for her file. After a few seconds, she pointed to the anterior body diagram and said, "What's this?"

It was such a tiny notation that I needed my magnifying glass to examine it. Together, we zeroed in on the diminutive entry at the midline of Natalie's throat.

"Dr. Choi's handwriting is difficult to read in places, but that says 'scratch'," Dr. Stanley exclaimed.

That was it. The narrative portion of the autopsy report states the neck organs "were dissected" and showed "no traumatic injuries," concluding there was no "evidence of strangulation." It was a carefully worded entry that avoided commenting on evidence of a *choke hold*. Dr. Stanley agreed with my conclusion that the scratch was choke-hold evidence that likely prompted the entry of Drs. Kornblum and Choi and the dissection of Natalie's neck organs.

I had overlooked Dr. Choi's "scratch" notation because it isn't mentioned in the narrative. Nonetheless, Dr. Stanley agreed it could have been caused by a fingernail. In spite of that, no skin sections of the scratch were examined microscopically by the forensic pathologists.

As we carried on our conversation, I learned Dr. Stanley and her husband were familiar with Catalina Island and Blue Cavern Point. The Wagners' dinghy was found against the rocks at Blue Cavern Point, and Natalie's body was found approximately 250 yards to the north.

"So, if she's 250 yards from Blue Cavern Point…the point is a mile and a half from where she went into the water," Dr. Stanley stated. "I think that's a long way to stay together without her holding on to the dinghy, because she and the dinghy have very different floating characteristics. The dinghy is going to be up high and rolling somewhat, and she is in the water and is going to be subject to the current. So, to me, the proximity of where she was found in relation to the dinghy suggests she held on to the dinghy for a while."

"Perhaps she was holding on to or tangled in the ropes or safety lines or…maybe the motor or one of the oar handles, if the dinghy had them," I suggested.

"Right. The motor may be big, so that's something else that could have caused some of her front leg bruises," Dr. Stanley said.

"How about the tides affecting the movement of the body and the dinghy?" I asked.

"According to the National Oceanic and Atmospheric Administration website, at 11:07 p.m. that Saturday, it was high tide. At 3:14 a.m. on Sunday, it was low tide. That's going to pull her out. The prevailing winds and currents are in that direction. It all makes perfectly good sense. But, it's perfectly clear she doesn't swim, so that explains why she doesn't let go of the boat for so long," Dr. Stanley answered.

"Unless she was tangled in the dinghy's painter line," I added. A painter line, sometimes called a bowline or towrope, is used to tie a dinghy to a dock or vessel, or to tow it behind another boat. Most dinghies have two painter lines, one at the front and one at the rear.

"That's very possible," Dr. Stanley said, with a look of revelation.

"Bodies that go into the water for that short period of time are usually found pretty close to where they go in," Dr. Stanley remarked, as an afterthought.

"How about Natalie's intoxication level?" I asked. "According to the lab report, she registered 0.14."

"Yes. She was pretty intoxicated. Point 14, for someone her size, that's drinking seven drinks fast. It's probably drinking more drinks slowly," she said.

"A little while ago, you said you thought Natalie was with the dinghy in the water for a while," I summarized.

"Yes, that's my opinion," Dr. Stanley said.

"So, if you have wool socks on your feet and you're in the ocean kicking, what's going to happen to the socks?" I asked, anticipating she would say they would slide off.

"They may or may not come off. Shoes are probably going to come off, but we must not assume Natalie was kicking. If she didn't swim, maybe she didn't know to kick. I did two drownings recently. One guy was in the water for two or three weeks, and he still had his socks and shoes on. I was kind of surprised. But you never know," Dr. Stanley said.

"Now, let's talk about time of death," I said. "On Page 4 [of the autopsy report] it says that Natalie's stomach contents contained 500 CCs of semi-solid, partially digested chicken or fish. The waitress and Davern said she had fish for dinner. While she's in the water, I suppose her body is still digesting food?"

"Somewhat. But her body is also trying to survive," Dr. Stanley replied. "In cold water, the body is not going to waste its energy on digesting food. It will some, but I think it helps a little bit with determining that she was in the water pretty soon after she ate. She did go in the water within a few hours of eating. I feel confident of that."

"So, it helps more with when she entered the water and started experiencing hypothermia and distress than on when she died?" I confirmed.

"Yes," Dr. Stanley said.

"Would the digestion factors hold true for the two pills Dr. Choi described as 'a vitamin-like substance'?" I continued.

"The pills—it depends on where in the intestines they are. I think she took those pills before she ate, because they were found further down in her system," Dr. Stanley noted.

"What about the toxicology reports showing Natalie had Darvon or propoxyphene, and cyclizine in her system? Any significance to the levels that were found in her blood?" I asked.

"The level of propoxyphene—Darvon—is consistent with her being prescribed that pain medication. Cyclizine, which is sold under the brand name Antivert, is a seasick medication. The levels aren't very significant. And, just having those two things at those levels, combined with alcohol, is totally insignificant in terms of her ability to think and function. The other thing with the propoxyphene is this could be falsely elevated because it's a heart blood specimen. It would be concentrated in the heart. But you might want to check that out pharmacologically," Dr. Stanley advised.

"You also might want to check with a hypothermia expert on hypothermia's effect on the ability to think and function," Dr. Stanley recommended. "That might be more significant than the alcohol and prescription drugs."

∽∽∽∽∽∽∽

In my final in-person session with Dr. Stanley, she began, "We touched on this, but Dr.

Choi's report doesn't describe her hands very much. He doesn't describe her fingernails. We don't have that information. That would be helpful. Did he examine her nails? Maybe he did and he just forgot to dictate it. I always describe the nails. But, remember, this is not a regular autopsy. His boss is circling around, grabbing nasal swabs, talking to everyone.

FORENSIC SCIENCE CENTER
COUNTY OF LOS ANGELES

SEXUAL ASSAULT EVIDENCE DATA SHEET

THOMAS T. NOGUCHI, M.D.
CHIEF MEDICAL EXAMINER-CORONER

81

☐ Complete Procedure – Kit # ______
☒ Modified Procedure

Initiated as a Special Processing Case by:
Coroner's Investigator J.G.N.
Date: 11/30/81 Time: 1000
Location: ☒ FSC ☐ At Scene ☐ Other

CC# 81-15167

Decedent's Name Wagner, Wood, Natalie

☐ Male ☒ Female

	At Scene	At FSC	Collected by:	Not Collected
A. GENERAL EVIDENCE COLLECTION:				
1. NAIL SCRAPINGS collected?	☐	☐		☒
2. NAIL CLIPPING(S) collected?	☐	☐		☒
3. Decedent's HAIR collected (other than pubic hair)? ✓ Head __ Facial __ Chest ✓ Arm	☐	☒	J.G.N.	☐
4. BITE MARK evidence processed?	☐	☐		☒
5. TOOLMARK evidence processed?	☐	☐		☒
B. SEXUAL ASSAULT EVIDENCE COLLECTION: Collection Started: Date: 11/30/81 Time: 1000				
1. EXTERNAL STAINS detected and swabbed? #	☐	☐		☒
2. NIPPLES swabbed?	☐	☐		☒
3. MISCELLANEOUS EVIDENCE collected from body surface? # envelopes ______ *	☐	☐		☒
4. PUBIC REGION:				
a. "Foreign material" collected?	☐	☐		☒
b. Pubic hair combed?	☐	☐		☒
c. Pubic hair collected? (Decedent's Pubic Hair Kit)*	☐	☒	J.G.N.	☐
d. External genital area and pubic hair swabbed/one smear made?	☐	☐		☒
5. ORAL area swabbed/two smears made?	☐	☒	J.G.N.	☐
6. ANAL area swabbed/two smears made?	☐	☒		☐
7. Female victim only:				
a. VAGINA SWABBED/two smears made?	☐	☒	J.G.N.	☐
b. VAGINAL ASPIRATE collected?	☐	☐		☒
c. If yes, ☐ with injection of saline. ☐ without injection of saline.				
8. Completed Sexual Assault Kit sealed with evidence tape?	☐	☒	By: J.G. Njavro	

Collection Completed: Date: 11/30/81 Time: 1015
* not enclosed in kit

C. REMARKS (Explain any deviation from routine procedure):

Evidence Tag and this form reviewed by DME prior to autopsy.

Deputy Medical Examiner [signature] M.D. Date: 11-30-81 Time: 1210

White: To Sr. Investigator to be placed with medical papers prior to autopsy.
Pink: To be enclosed in kit.
Yellow: To accompany Kit to laboratory (Do not Enclose in Kit).

76S422S—PS 9-80

Figure 13: Rape kit evidence collection form prepared by coroner's investigator Jim Njavro

(Los Angeles County Department of Medical Examiner-Coroner)

There are probably a fair number of people at this exam. His boss is sticking his hands in the body. It can be unnerving in itself. I can imagine Dr. Noguchi wanting to do that, having met him. He's a very egotistical guy. Not a bad person, he just had the ego, I guess, it took to be the chief."

I was gripped by Dr. Stanley's observations. We talked about rigor mortis and the significance of blood in Natalie's heart chamber. And the clues I could possibly gather from the

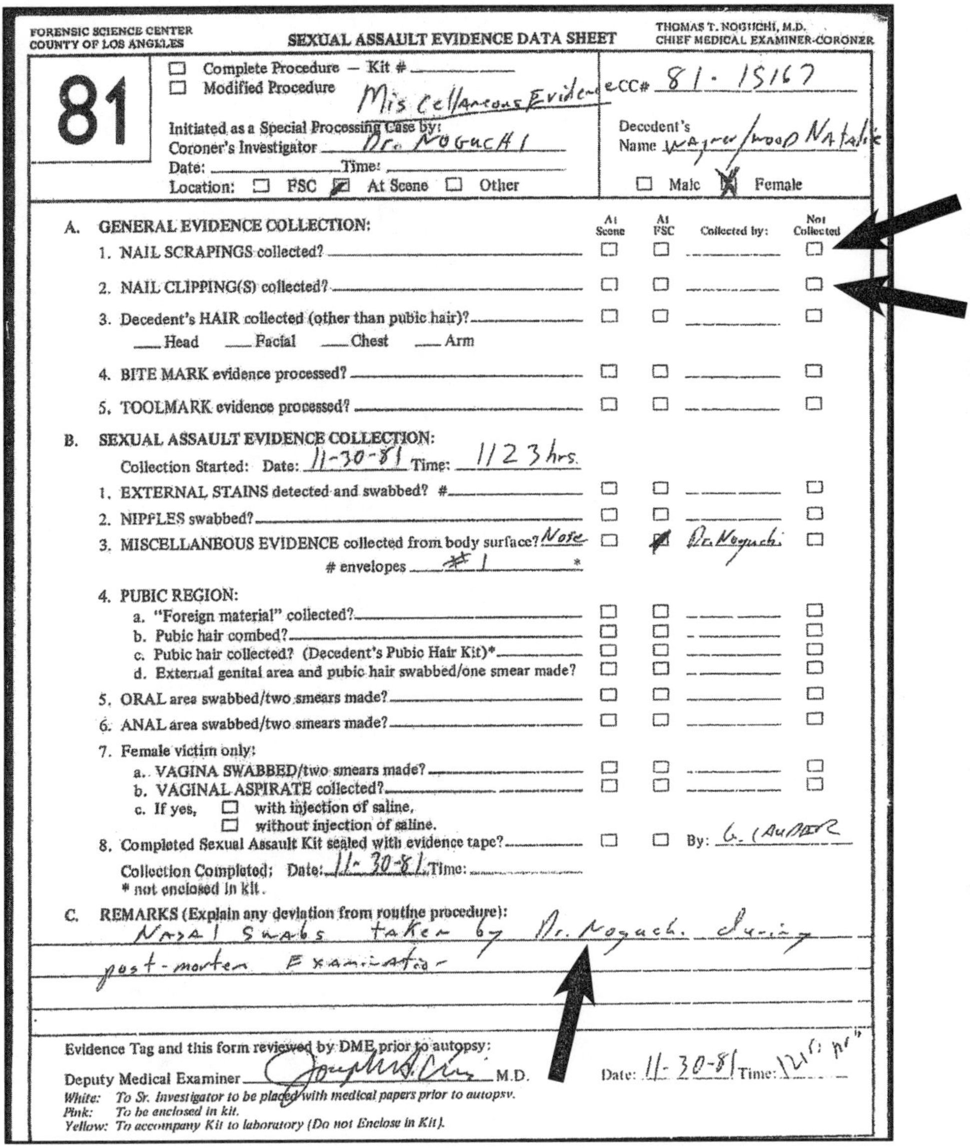
FORENSIC SCIENCE CENTER
COUNTY OF LOS ANGELES

SEXUAL ASSAULT EVIDENCE DATA SHEET

THOMAS T. NOGUCHI, M.D.
CHIEF MEDICAL EXAMINER-CORONER

81

☐ Complete Procedure — Kit # ______
☐ Modified Procedure Miscellaneous Evidence

Initiated as a Special Processing Case by:
Coroner's Investigator Dr. NOGUCHI
Date: ______ Time: ______
Location: ☐ FSC ☒ At Scene ☐ Other

eCC# 81-15167
Decedent's Name Wagner/Wood Natalie
☐ Male ☒ Female

	At Scene	At FSC	Collected by:	Not Collected
A. GENERAL EVIDENCE COLLECTION:				
1. NAIL SCRAPINGS collected?	☐	☐		☐
2. NAIL CLIPPING(S) collected?	☐	☐		☐
3. Decedent's HAIR collected (other than pubic hair)? ___Head ___Facial ___Chest ___Arm	☐	☐		☐
4. BITE MARK evidence processed?	☐	☐		☐
5. TOOLMARK evidence processed?	☐	☐		☐
B. SEXUAL ASSAULT EVIDENCE COLLECTION: Collection Started: Date: 11-30-81 Time: 1123 hrs.				
1. EXTERNAL STAINS detected and swabbed? #	☐	☐		☐
2. NIPPLES swabbed?	☐	☐		☐
3. MISCELLANEOUS EVIDENCE collected from body surface? Note # envelopes #1 *	☐	☒	Dr. Noguchi	☐
4. PUBIC REGION:				
a. "Foreign material" collected?	☐	☐		☐
b. Pubic hair combed?	☐	☐		☐
c. Pubic hair collected? (Decedent's Pubic Hair Kit)*	☐	☐		☐
d. External genital area and pubic hair swabbed/one smear made?	☐	☐		☐
5. ORAL area swabbed/two smears made?	☐	☐		☐
6. ANAL area swabbed/two smears made?	☐	☐		☐
7. Female victim only:				
a. VAGINA SWABBED/two smears made?	☐	☐		☐
b. VAGINAL ASPIRATE collected?	☐	☐		☐
c. If yes, ☐ with injection of saline, ☐ without injection of saline.				
8. Completed Sexual Assault Kit sealed with evidence tape?	☐	☐	By: G. Lauber	

Collection Completed: Date: 11-30-81 Time: ______
* not enclosed in kit.

C. REMARKS (Explain any deviation from routine procedure):
Nasal Swabs taken by Dr. Noguchi during post-mortem Examination

Evidence Tag and this form reviewed by DME prior to autopsy:
Deputy Medical Examiner [signature] M.D. Date: 11-30-81 Time: 1215 hrs

White: To Sr. Investigator to be placed with medical papers prior to autopsy.
Pink: To be enclosed in kit.
Yellow: To accompany Kit to laboratory (Do not Enclose in Kit).

Figure 14: Rape kit evidence collection taken by Dr. Noguchi (Los Angeles County Department of Medical Examiner-Coroner)

fact that Natalie's bladder contained 300 CCs of amber-colored urine at death. I learned that all three of those points should be analyzed in greater depth with experts in pharmacology and hypothermia. My mind was swirling over where I could find consultants with that type of expertise.

But before that, I wanted to discuss something that had puzzled me since I first read Natalie's autopsy report. Two separate rape kit forms had been completed. One was filled out by Jim Njavro, a coroner's investigator, at 10:15 a.m. November 30, 1981. (See *Figure 13*, Page 42.) The second was completed by Dr. Noguchi about an hour later. (See *Figure 14*, previous page.) Both were signed by Dr. Choi at 12:10 p.m.

Both contained a "General Evidence Collection" section listing the routine collection of nail scrapings and clippings. This prime evidence is collected to, among other things, help investigators identify the perpetrator of an assault—sexual or otherwise.

The Noguchi form indicated "nasal swabs" were the sole evidence taken by the chief coroner. The Njavro form indicated some standard items of evidence were collected. But it conspicuously had the "Not Collected" boxes checked for both nail scrapings and clippings. That meant the decision to pass on these critical pieces of evidence was intentional.

This failure to collect crucial evidence—combined with the other troubling irregularities in the autopsy report—led me to suspect an intentional cover-up by the coroner's office.

So, I asked Dr. Stanley: "Why would the pathologists get a rape kit in Natalie's case?"

"Because she's a young woman who died under suspicious circumstances," Dr Stanley quickly responded.

"Why nasal swabs?" I followed up.

Dr. Stanley explained nasal swabs were used to check for cocaine in 1981. Then, Dr. Stanley said askance, "It's interesting that he did that. It's particularly specified that he did that."

Why were two rape kit forms completed? I believed then, as I believe now, that Dr. Noguchi was looking for something sensational for his news conference that would cause a distraction from Natalie's multiple unexplained bruises and scratches, and other items pointing to her possible involvement in a physical altercation. Something that suggested Natalie's death was her own doing. *What better, more salacious answer to her death than it was the product of an alcohol and cocaine cocktail?*

To me, it was beginning to look like Dr. Noguchi and his two deputy pathologists turned their heads from anything pointing to an altercation as a contributing factor in Natalie's death. There were too many suspicious items that were ignored or required follow-up for that not to be the case. *But, why?*

CHAPTER 6

half-life

TO ZERO IN ON NATALIE'S TIME OF DEATH WITH AS MUCH PRECISION as possible, I took Dr. Stanley's advice to heart and began looking for someone who understood forensic pharmacology. Pharmacists know considerably more about prescription drugs and their potential effects on people than doctors. Then again, when you think about it, that's very logical. The time they spend in school learning about drugs far outdistances that of physicians.

For example, my local pharmacist—Jonathan Unwer—spent four years at the University for Medical Sciences in Little Rock earning a doctorate in pharmacology. And he had four years of practical training as a pharmacist.

I was visiting with him about some puzzling issues in Natalie's autopsy when he agreed to help me. I explained I wanted to determine her time of death.

Over the years, tabloid "experts" and Lambert in his biography of Natalie have generated sensational headlines with unsupported theories suggesting she was abusing drugs. Some even went so far as to say Natalie died as a result of mixing drugs with alcohol. *Was that possible?* I wondered. *And would an examination of the drugs' half-lives—the time it takes for 50 percent of a biological substance to distribute outside the bloodstream under normal biological processes—help me determine the time of death?*

At our first meeting, Jonathan explained that pharmacology is the scientific study of drugs and how they are used in medicine. The definition includes the study of a drug's composition, its therapeutic qualities and its effects on humans.

Pharmacokinetics is the study of how a body absorbs, distributes, metabolizes and excretes drugs—meaning when you take medicine, how long it takes it to start working, how long it lasts before you have to take more, and how long before the medicine's effects wear off.

Forensic pharmacology is the study of laboratory-based drug toxicology focusing on the pharmacologist's area of expertise in forensic science. However, forensic pharmacologists were not readily available to medical examiners when Natalie died.

There were pharmacologists in 1981, and drug information was, for the most part, available for forensic pathologists or toxicologists. We have now had nearly 40 years for the scientists to conduct additional case studies, making the expertise more refined today. But the basic information on drug reactions, distributions and effects on the people who used them was generally available in 1981 for those taking the time to study the research.

Before our meeting, I had sent Natalie's complete autopsy report to Jonathan. It included Eaker's report and a document entitled "Medication & Evidence Record." (See *Figure B*, Page 259.) The record was prepared by Eaker on November 29, 1981, and contained a list of outstanding prescriptions Natalie had at the time of her death.

Jonathan and I got into Natalie's case by starting with the prescription list.

"Does this record mean she was taking everything on this list?" I asked.

"Well, looking at the list, I can tell you she wasn't taking everything at the time. I just think this was a list compiled by Miss Eaker—either by being provided prescription bottles or calling the pharmacy where Mrs. Wagner got her prescriptions filled," he answered confidently.

There were nine toxicology reports requested by Dr. Choi, asking for an analysis on cocaine, codeine, morphine, ethanol (alcohol), propoxyphene, phenothiazines, cyclizine, volatile gases such as methane and butane, ethchlorvynol, trichlorethanol, caffeine, other neutrals, barbiturates and phencyclidine. But we weren't able to determine if a toxicology analysis was requested for each medication on the "Medication & Evidence Record."

"How was the toxicology analysis done on the items requested by Dr. Choi?" I asked.

"From an analysis of Mrs. Wagner's cardiac blood. On Page 3 of the report, it states that the blood was taken from her heart," Jonathan answered.

Dr. Stanley had already alluded to the fact that Natalie's Darvon level may have been "falsely elevated" because it was based on a "heart blood specimen," so I asked Jonathan a question for which I thought I knew the answer. "If you want to do the most accurate toxicology analysis, is that the best place to take blood?"

"Based on my research, it's very clear that the optimum place to take blood for a post-mortem toxicological analysis is the femoral artery. My research shows that information was available in 1981," Jonathan responded, lifting his brow.

I learned from Jonathan's research that at death, some drugs, as well as alcohol, tend to concentrate more in the central blood—the heart, for example—which would cause the postmortem drug concentration to be higher than the actual concentration at the time of death. The technical name for this is "postmortem drug redistribution."

Postmortem drug redistribution is the process that sometimes takes place after death by which drugs and other chemicals move between tissues, organs and bodily fluids. It can result in the migration of drugs between blood and tissue. The rate and extent of this movement vary according to several factors, including the nature of the drug, and the time between death and the postmortem specimen collection.

That's extremely important in Natalie's case. According to Jonathan, Natalie's cardiac blood was taken approximately 33 hours after death, and cyclizine and alcohol, both detected in Natalie's blood, were susceptible to postmortem drug redistribution.

"The significance of that is the pharmacokinetics of cyclizine can be a strong indicator of time of death in Mrs. Wagner's case," Jonathan pointed out.

Here's why. The toxicological findings for cyclizine were detected at the level of 0.045 mg. In pharmacology, that measurement is 45 nanograms per milliliter, which is abbreviated "45 ng/ml." The medication record had cyclizine as the fifth item on Natalie's medication list—"Antivert 12.5 mg."

Based on Jonathan's professional experience concerning medication compliance, he believed Natalie took Antivert to help her with motion sickness and nausea. Moreover, in his opinion, based on his experiences with people taking Antivert, Natalie took an Antivert tablet shortly after she got back to the yacht.

Because the blood sample was taken from cardiac blood and because cyclizine would exhibit some drug redistribution after death, it was Jonathan's opinion that it would cause the postmortem drug concentration to be slightly higher than her actual concentration at time of death.

"So, what significance does that have in this case?" I asked.

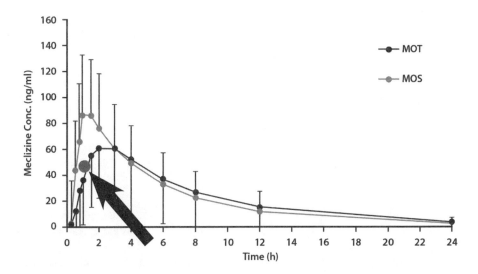

Figure 15: Arrow points to the time it takes for meclizine to reach its peak concentration in the blood stream after a human receives a single dose of meclizine oral tablet (MOT; 25 mg). Also shown is plasma concentration-time course of meclizine oral solution (MOS; 25 mg). Cyclizine and meclizine are first-generation antihistamines used to treat motion sickness.

(Data: *Journal of Clinical Pharmacology*; Graphic Design: Thoma Thoma)

"OK, let me see if I can explain it this way. Cyclizine—Antivert—has an onset of action of around one hour. Typically, this means people take it one hour or less before its needed effect. Cyclizine also has what we call a Tmax—time to peak drug concentration—of 3.11 hours, plus or minus 1.35 hours, with a Cmax—peak drug concentration—of 68 ng/ml. The time to peak drug concentration means the time it takes a drug, after it is ingested, to reach its peak with it steadily going downhill, like a bell-shaped graph," Jonathan explained.

As Jonathan explained peak drug concentration, he handed me a bell graph that was indeed worth a thousand words. Starting at the bottom from zero to 24 hours, cyclizine reaches its peak somewhere between two and three hours and then starts a gradual decline. The vertical bar shows the drug concentration in the blood stream. These are averages based on extensive studies of the medication's effect. When cyclizine reaches its peak concentration, it's approximately 68 nanograms per milliliter.

In Jonathan's opinion, even though the reported postmortem drug concentration was 45 ng/ml, he believed it was actually slightly less. Central blood, or cardiac blood, will potentially exhibit a higher postmortem drug redistribution due to diffusion of the drug from organ tissues, like the gastrointestinal tract. This can easily cause higher postmortem drug concentrations compared to the actual drug concentrations a person has before death.

Furthermore, cyclizine is metabolized predominately by an enzyme in the liver. That's how it gets into a person's system. Since most enzymatic processes exhibit temperature dependence, it can be expected that hypothermia would cause alterations in the Tmax and Cmax parameters of the prescription drug Antivert.

Jonathan looked very hard for specific case studies reporting the effects of hypothermia on cyclizine concentrations, but was unsuccessful in finding something material. However, it was his opinion based on the medical literature he read, that the normal time it takes cyclizine to reach its peak plasma concentration would be slowed down by hypothermia conditions.

Under normal metabolic conditions, Jonathan said Natalie would have a therapeutic maximum concentration of 68 ng/ml at 3.11 hours, plus or minus 1.35 hours. This computes to 1.76 to 4.46 hours, or an average of approximately three hours. Natalie's reported postmortem drug concentration for cyclizine was 45 ng/ml—marked on Jonathan's bell graph with a large dot. (See *Figure 15*, previous page.)

Under normal conditions, Jonathan believed it would take close to two hours to reach 45 ng/ml. If Natalie went to her stateroom at 10:45 p.m. and immediately took her Antivert—which Jonathan thought was "probable"—it would put her time of death at 12:45 a.m. max.

"Like I said, though, *with the redistribution and hypothermia factors*, if she took the Antivert when Wagner said he last saw her, around 10:45, her time of death would have been a little earlier, at max, around 12:15 a.m."

Placing Natalie's time of death between 11:45 Saturday evening, at a minimum, and 12:15 Sunday morning, at a maximum, is critical to understanding what I call the "Fatal Gap" and its relationship to Natalie's death. The Fatal Gap is the period of time between Natalie's confirmed disappearance—around 10:45 p.m. Saturday evening—and the time Wagner reached out for help—around 1 a.m. Sunday. If Natalie died during that period of time—as the toxicological evidence indicated—Wagner's inaction under circumstances he created, if intentional, was a direct cause of her death.

But there was more toxicological evidence to back up the time of death conclusion.

∾∾∾∾∾∾

Another prescription drug that showed up in Natalie's toxicology report was propoxyphene, commonly known as Darvon. Listed first on Natalie's medication list, it is generally prescribed for the relief of mild to moderate pain. According to Jonathan, there was nothing abnormal about the Darvon concentration in Natalie's blood, confirming Dr. Stanley's statement that the level of propoxyphene was consistent with her "being prescribed that pain medication."

That told me a lot about Natalie and her habits. Habits that were consistent with her personality as a disciplined mother and actress. The record reflected that Natalie's Darvon prescription—a combination of 65 mg hydrochloride, 389 mg aspirin and 32.4 mg caffeine—was written on November 15, 1981. The prescribing physician's instructions were to use the drug "as directed."

The record indicated that 65 Darvon capsules were dispensed November 15. Counting the day the prescription was filled through November 28 totaled 14 days that Natalie had been taking the medication. There were 37 capsules remaining in the bottle at the time Eaker began marshalling Natalie's medications for the evidence list. So, Natalie consumed 28 capsules, or an average of two capsules per day. The maximum daily dosage in 1981, according to my expert, was one capsule every four hours or six capsules per day.

"So Natalie wasn't abusing Darvon?" I asked.

"Not by a long shot," Jonathan said emphatically.

As for Darvon's peak concentration, Jonathan said, "Looking at her plasma concentration, detected at a level of 0.07 ng/ml, the Tmax of a 100-mg tablet of Darvon should roughly be 0.15 IUG/ml. I think she was on the uphill slope of the bell graph that we talked about and, in my opinion, it's more than likely that she also took the Darvon less than two hours before her death."

"Could hypothermia slow down peak plasma concentration for Darvon?" I asked.

"Yes, but it would depend upon how long Mrs. Wagner was in a hypothermic state before she died," Jonathan said. "If she wasn't in a hypothermic state for a long time, then it wouldn't be that big of an issue. That would go for cyclizine as well."

I questioned Jonathan about the significance of Natalie's stomach contents in relation to our pharmacological issues. He pointed out that the pathologists described a few patchy areas of "red discoloration" in her stomach contents. They offered no explanation for it. The pathologists said that the small intestine contained two pills which were not dissolved and appeared to be a large size. They described them as a "vitamin-like substance by the appearance and by the smell."

Jonathan was skeptical. "I believe the two pills were the Darvon capsules," he stated. "A Darvon capsule in the stomach will release the medication and leave behind what we call a ghost capsule. I'm of the opinion—because Darvon comes in red colors and is made with D & C Red No. 33—that the red discoloration was due to the red dye used in Darvon. Antivert comes in a tablet and would not show up in the stomach."

Looking at both Darvon and Antivert, the blood concentrations and Jonathan's research gave him the foundation for another opinion. "It tells me more than likely Mrs. Wagner ingested Antivert and Darvon at the same time," he said.

Other than a miniscule amount of caffeine, the only other substance detected in Natalie's blood was ethanol at a level of 0.14 percent, 0.04 percent above the 1981 legal limit in California for driving while under the influence.

"Based on the central blood factor of postmortem drug redistribution, which also applies to alcohol, it's my opinion that her blood alcohol level was lower than 0.14 percent before she died. How much, it's hard to say. But, definitely lower," Jonathan opined.

Of course, it also meant Natalie was drinking alcohol and at some point, she took her Darvon. That combination would cause respiratory depression according to Jonathan. That is, the rate she was breathing would slow down. That's not helpful if you are in the water. And, being under the influence of alcohol "affects your judgment, reaction time, balance and mobility," according to Jonathan.

∽∾∽∾∽∾∽

It has been reported by many people close to her that Natalie took a sleeping pill nightly before bed. So, I turned my questioning toward sleep medications. Jonathan told me Placidyl, Dalmane and Valium listed in Eaker's medication record can be taken as sleep aids. But based on the dates of the prescriptions and the instructions, his opinion was Natalie was probably using only the Dalmane or Valium as a sleep aid.

Considering the half-lives of those drugs, if Natalie had been taking them regularly at bedtime, Jonathan said they would have shown up on the toxicology report if she took them within the last few days of her death. He was genuinely puzzled over the pathologist asking for a report on cocaine and other illegal drugs, but skipping over some of Natalie's prescription medications.

Natalie could have taken something, but we don't know what or when, because her blood apparently wasn't tested for her sleep aids.

⌒⌒⌒⌒⌒⌒⌒

Because I had heard an expert claim that one of Natalie's medications made her particularly susceptible to bruising, I asked Jonathan to research that question for me. He examined all her medications, and only Bactrim DS carried the possibility of making her prone to spontaneous bruising.

Natalie was taking Bactrim DS, one tablet every 12 hours, and prescribed 20 tablets on November 3, 1981. Bactrim DS is a combination of two antibiotics and is generally prescribed to treat a wide variety of bacterial infections, like ear infections or urinary tract infections. Bactrim DS, like alcohol, also has certain blood anticoagulation properties. That could mean Natalie was susceptible to spontaneous bruising, except the probability of that happening "would be miniscule," Jonathan concluded.

"I researched that and based on the literature I was able to find from the drug manufacturer's FDA filing, they did not define a frequency at which anticoagulation was reported as a side effect, which typically indicates a frequency of less than 1 percent," he added.

As with many similar unconfirmed theories in Natalie's case, while "possible," it was "highly unlikely" that Natalie experienced some spontaneous bruising using Bactrim DS.

But, Jonathan was emphatic—"You could never have a spontaneous contusion" since it requires "an impact of some sort."

CHAPTER 7

cold water

I HAD NEVER USED A HYPOTHERMIA EXPERT IN MY PRACTICE OF LAW. IT was a subject that had escaped my grasp over the years. I'd heard about it, of course. But I knew nothing about its cause and effects and how it killed people. And, surprisingly to me, the condition had never been fully investigated in Natalie's case. It seemed everyone was treating her death like a typical drowning. But it was nothing of the sort. Natalie drowned in cold saltwater. I'm confident she experienced some degree of hypothermia before her death. Likewise, I had a feeling that from a forensic standpoint, hypothermia made a difference not only in the manner, but also the timing of her death.

Determined to find someone to answer my questions, I went to the library and began reading books on the subject. Three items looked to me to be a perfect way to learn about cause and effect. One book in particular, *Human Performance in the Cold*, by Laursen, Pozos and Hempel, was most helpful in appreciating the hypothermia factors present in Natalie's case.

When I finished reading the text, I attempted to make contact with one of the authors. I started with Robert S. Pozos, Ph.D., because he appeared to be one of the foremost authorities on the subject of hypothermia.

I sent him a detailed email, figuring the chances of a response from a busy professional to an unknown writer were not good. But, four hours later, Dr. Pozos replied, "Be happy to help you. Send the questions."

Dr. Pozos is a professor of biology at San Diego State University. His education includes a bachelor's degree in biology and organic chemistry; a master's in physiology and biophysics; and a doctorate in physiology and biophysics. He has extensive experience studying human response to environments including conducting ethically approved human experimentation dealing with hypothermia, hyperthermia, cold-induced vasodilation as well as local cooling experiments.

Spending over a half-century studying the effects of hypothermia on humans, Dr. Pozos has written more than 50 articles, book chapters and papers on the subject of cold's effects on humans. But the writings of interest to me in Natalie's case included four chapters in books dealing with primary and secondary hypothermia, and his published books *Hypothermia, The Nature and Treatment of Hypothermia*, and the aforementioned *Human Performance in the Cold*.

To his unequaled credit, Dr. Pozos also established the hypothermia laboratory at the University of Minnesota Medical School, Duluth and was one of the chief civilian scientists at the Naval Health Research Center in San Diego.

∽∽∽∽∽∽∽

My first request for Dr. Pozos was to clarify the definition of hypothermia. "We've all heard the term, but what is it scientifically and medically?" I asked.

"Well, hypothermia is simply a physical condition that occurs when the body's core temperature falls below a normal body temperature of 98.6 degrees—that's Fahrenheit—to 95 degrees Fahrenheit, or cooler. Think of it as the opposite of heat stroke," he answered.

A body's core is the brain, the heart, lungs and other vital organs, like the kidneys and liver. I was surprised to learn that the body's core temperature gets cooler more quickly in water than air.

"It's much faster in water. It can, in some cases, cause body heat to be lost 25 times faster," Dr. Pozos emphasized.

But every human body doesn't lose core body temperature evenly inasmuch as there are many factors that determine when a person becomes hypothermic in cold water.

"It can depend, for example, on what kind of clothing the person is wearing to help trap body heat," Dr. Pozos explained. "It can depend on a person's personality...are they the type who would panic and give up, or a survivor like Rose in *Titanic*? Their physical condition is also important, that is, are they in good shape, like swimmers or hikers? It would depend on what the outside—what we call environmental—temperature is. Everyone will react differently to cold water, even under the same conditions."

"What are the symptoms of hypothermia?" I continued.

"To begin with, and we have all experienced this in our lives, if you jump in a cold lake or ocean, at first you gasp. It's called torso reflex. The gasping is an inhalation response, the sucking in of air, reflexively, for the body to get more oxygen for survival. Only problem is, you can also suck in water. And, some people hyperventilate, particularly those not accustomed to cold water. They can't stand the discomfort for any significant period of time. There's also pain that's associated with cold stress, just like when you put your arm in cold water," he responded.

I asked, "If you can't swim, would the torso reflex be different?"

"The initial immersion can initiate cold shock," he answered. "If you can't swim and you panic, it could very easily prolong the initial cold shock. Prolonged cold shock can incapacitate you and result in drowning, sometimes in minutes. People can also experience hallucinations, disorientation and loss of short-term memory during the early stages of cold stress."

"What happens after the torso reflex?" I continued.

"After the gasp, your skin begins to cool, and your body constricts surface blood vessels to conserve heat for your vital organs," he said.

Thinking about the food in Natalie's stomach, I asked, "Would that have any effect on your ability to digest food?"

"Absolutely," Dr. Pozos replied. "It's going to slow that process down. Our research has shown that."

That scientific fact may not have been considered by the pathologists in determining Natalie's time of death. Reading between the lines, it appeared to me the nature of her stomach contents was the primary factor used to determine the time of death. That and rigor mortis. But in cold water, the presence of stomach contents can't be the only factor used to determine time of death.

"The next thing would be that your blood pressure and heart rate increase, and muscles tense and shiver," Dr. Pozos continued. "There's a benefit to that, because it produces more body heat. However, it also results in a loss of dexterity and motor control. Just like plastics get stiff when they get cold, so do muscles and tendons." Tetany—the inability of muscles to contract or relax effectively—results in jerky, uncoordinated movements, staggering and loss of the ability to perform even simple tasks like zipping up a jacket.

"Actually, we have found that a decrease in muscle strength occurs earlier than does the shiver," Dr. Pozos noted. And mild hypothermia can result in slurred speech. To me, this would explain why any cries for help by Natalie would only continue for a brief period of time. Her fear of water, combined with cold shock, shivering and tetany, would result in her being physically unable to cry out for more than a few minutes.

This supported the initial account made by one of the occupants of the sailboat *Capricorn* moored near *Splendour* that night. On December 3, 1981, Marilyn Wayne told CSI Hamilton the cries for help she and John Payne, her fiancé and owner of the sailboat, heard lasted "five minutes." Years later, she would remember for Finstad and Rulli that the cries for help lasted 20 minutes. Since I have come to know Marilyn, I'm confident, that to her, the painful experience seemed like an eternity. But the accuracy of her first recollection of the event is borne out by the scientific evidence.

I learned from Dr. Pozos and my research that as hypothermia progresses, the shivering stops, but your coordination is severely impaired, and your confusion pairs up with incoherence. Extreme lethargy then combines with unconsciousness and you eventually drown, or have cardiac or respiratory arrest, and you die.

"Does the progression of hypothermia result in a greater loss of dexterity and motor control?" I questioned.

Dr. Pozos replied: "Right. Then as you get colder, your mental attitude and level of consciousness change. Your thinking processes and decision-making become slower. You begin to act confused or irrationally. Irrationality can even include resisting help, if it were presented, or even removing clothes. At lower core temperatures, speech is impeded due to the effect of cold on the brain. Then, as your core temperature drops to dangerous levels, you become semiconscious, then unconscious."

During the time we explored the particulars of Natalie's case, I expressed interest in factors that might hasten the rate in which she became hypothermic. By the time our discussions concluded, several factors were determined to exist in Natalie's case that would have accelerated her hypothermia.

The first was Natalie's blood alcohol level. According to Dr. Pozos, "Alcohol can actually accelerate the onset of hypothermia." It also impairs motor skills and magnifies the torso reflex.

I sent Dr. Pozos the toxicology report that indicated Natalie had a blood alcohol level of 0.14. I also explained that Jonathan Unwer was of the opinion that the level was actually lower because the sample used was taken from the heart instead of the femoral artery. With that information, Dr. Pozos advised me that although Natalie's blood alcohol level was above the legal limit, its effect on hypothermia would depend on the individual.

Then he noted: "The cold stress of the water would have sobered her up very fast. Actually, it might have kept her somewhat calm as she fought to get out. But I believe the cold water would have overpowered the ethanol's effect, at that level, to cause a vasodilation, that is, a rapid loss of heat. In short, it would not, in my opinion, have contributed much to her hypothermia."

And Natalie's flannel cotton nightgown would have helped increase the onset of hypothermia. "When it's wet, it's worthless as an insulator, and it's heavy," Dr Pozos said.

Natalie was wearing wool socks, but socks "wouldn't be a significant factor as an insulator, because her body would be redirecting blood flow away from her feet and hands to her core," Dr. Pozos explained. Moreover, Natalie wasn't wearing underwear to help insulate her from the cold. To fight off hypothermia, it's important to preserve body heat until you are rescued.

"You can't do that with nothing on and in this case, in the cold water, Miss Wood was practically naked except for a down jacket that I understand may not have been zipped up," he said.

There was only one way to confirm if Natalie's jacket was zipped up when she was found. I needed to ask the man who found her body that Sunday morning.

〜〜〜〜〜

As you may recall, Doug Bombard, owner of the Buffet-esque restaurant and bar, found Natalie's body. By the time we got to him, Bombard had just celebrated his 90th birthday but was still a spry, colorful fellow. My Illinois research assistant, Jan Morris, made a vacation trip to Catalina Island in 2016 to conduct the interview.

Jan's assignment was to get answers to certain questions I had about Natalie's down jacket and clothing, and to ask if there was a chance Bombard and the men helping him injured Natalie's body when they lifted her out of the ocean.

As they talked over lunch, Jan said Bombard's memory of the weekend in question seemed clear to her. He told her he and his family had managed the Isthmus area for nearly 25 years by 1981. In addition to the restaurant, his family managed nearly 400 moorings, a campground and a general store. He was friends with the Wagners and obviously liked them both.

During the early morning hours of November 29, Bombard said he was awakened and told Natalie Wood was missing in a rubber dinghy. He expressed regrets he hadn't been called sooner because, "Nobody knows that island like I do. As far as the winds and currents and things like that are concerned, I was the authority in the area. Maybe a little more knowledge about the area might have made a difference. I don't know…I've thought about that a lot."

Because Bombard's health has declined, I never got a chance to tell him that according to my experts, Natalie was gone well before the time he was called. Perhaps that might have eased his mind and erased his regrets.

Bombard said he got dressed and joined the search at Isthmus Pier. Driving Harbor Patrol Boat 4, with another boat following, he headed northeast out of the harbor—to the right—up the east coast. He hoped to find Natalie "clinging to the rocks or sitting up on a hill." He motored his boat near shore, thinking if Natalie had drowned, the way the current comes down the island and swings in, he would find her "inside the kelp line," the seaweed line that forms near the shore.

As he was trolling about a hundred or so yards off Blue Cavern Point, in front of steep cliffs above Perdition Cave, he spotted a "bright red bubble on the water" out by the reef. In 2011, CBS interviewed him about his efforts for an episode of *48 Hours*, and a video clip can be found at www.cbsnews.com/video/doug-bombard-on-finding-natalie-woods-body/.

Bombard had reported Natalie was found in an almost standing position and that suggested something to him. "Most people, if they don't have much fat on them, will sink to the bottom," he explained. Forensically, Bombard was correct about drowning victim bodies generally sinking, according to Drs. Vincent DiMaio and Suzanna Dana in their book *Handbook of Forensic Pathology*. Bombard continued, "Natalie didn't have an ounce of fat on her. That coat was the only thing that kept her up. Because of the bubble, though, it was actually pulling her face down into the water."

Bombard noted Natalie's jacket was open in front and she had "both arms inside the jacket." When her body was pulled into his boat, he said Natalie was wearing "some type of shirt or nightgown and what I call mukluks, those heavy socks with leather bottoms that the girls wore to keep their feet warm."

He and Jan discussed Natalie's long-sleeved down jacket in depth, and when Bombard found her, he said the jacket was "unzipped." So I took that information back to Dr. Pozos for his take.

∽∽∽∽∽∽

"First, the jacket would help decrease the rate of heat loss because it would act as a flotation device, allowing you to keep your head out of water, as well as an insulator," Dr. Pozos replied.

"Next, your critical heat loss regions are your head, your sides, your armpits and your groin. The jacket would have protected her sides and armpits, if it's on, but if it's unzipped, it would diminish the effectiveness of having it on. Ideally, you would want it zipped up.

"So, all in all, it would help decrease [the rate of hypothermia], but not to the optimum level you would desire," Dr. Pozos concluded.

Catalina Island didn't have a weather reporting station, so the weather there on November 28, 1981, was difficult to officially determine. The closest station was San Clemente Island, about 70 miles away. The conditions in both places wouldn't have been much different, according to my expert, who based his opinion on personal knowledge of the area and witness accounts from my files.

The high temperature Saturday on San Clemente Island was 59.9 degrees Fahrenheit. The low was 47.8 degrees, presenting an average temperature of 53.6 degrees. San Clemente also experienced 0.63 inches of rain that day. In Dr. Pozos' opinion, an environmental temperature in the high 40s to high 50s with light rain would increase the rate of hypothermia. "And if it was windy, or even a breeze, more of an increase," Dr. Pozos stressed. From the locals I talked to, there's always wind at the Isthmus.

Another factor for Dr. Pozos to consider was that Natalie couldn't swim. His response surprised me.

"Swimming or trying to—unless you know you can make it to shore—speeds up core body heat loss through convection," he said. "The more energy you use in cold water, the more your body cools off. You really should remain still, treading water if you don't have a flotation device, or hanging suspended if you do have one. But not being able to swim would affect you mentally. You must keep a positive outlook. Not panic. So, in this case, in my opinion, if Miss Wood couldn't swim, it would probably have increased her rate of hypothermia."

Can there be any doubt, based on her history, that Natalie panicked when she hit the water? I thought.

She was afraid of deep, dark sea water and would have been without question hysterical.

Furthermore, according to Davern, Natalie had a low tolerance to cold. Dr. Pozos said that would also "increase onset of hypothermia."

Finally, but not insignificantly, was Natalie's body size and build. Being 5-foot-2 and 115 pounds was no help to her in keeping warm. "Thin people lose body heat faster than overweight people. So, a person of that size, it would increase the rate of hypothermia," Dr. Pozos said.

By my count, that was seven factors that would have increased Natalie's rate of hypothermia and one—the down jacket—that would have only minimally decreased her rate because it was unzipped. By anyone knowledgeable in assessing her chances in the cold water, there's little doubt that Natalie was in serious trouble when the black ocean first wrapped itself around her petite body.

∿∿∿∿∿∿∿

In his work with the hypothermia laboratory in Minnesota, Dr. Pozos had the opportunity to determine general parameters for the length of time a person can survive in cold water. Taking into account the average person and ranges of water temperature, Dr. Pozos and his colleagues established a general gauge for the expected time the average person has before exhaustion or unconsciousness, and their expected time of survival.

Dr. Pozos spent a great deal of time in the waters up and down the coast of Southern California, including Catalina Island. In his opinion, if the surface water temperature at 7:44 a.m. November 29, 1981, at the Catalina Isthmus was 62 to 63 degrees Fahrenheit as reported by Eaker, the surface water temperature at 11 p.m. the night before "would have been, more than likely, in the range of the high 50s."

Armed with that opinion, he detailed the early hypothermia symptoms for a person like Natalie.

"With mild hypothermia—a core temp of between 95 to 90 Fahrenheit—a person would be shivering more intensely and perhaps be dizzy and nauseated," Dr. Pozos said. In addition to having trouble speaking, Natalie also might have experienced slight confusion and fatigue, having problems climbing into a raft, climbing a ladder or performing other manual tasks. When the core drops to 93, uncontrollable shivering develops.

So, according to Dr. Pozos, a mild level of hypothermia would affect a person's ability to hold onto a dinghy rope or motor. But, he added, "When hypothermia becomes moderate to severe, the shivering response stops. That's so, even though the hypothermia is getting worse." But, speech would be slurred or mumbling, there would be confusion and poor decision-making, the person would become drowsy with very low energy, and there would be a progressive loss of consciousness.

After being instructed on everything material to Natalie's death, I asked the ultimate question. "Assuming everything we have discussed is present in this case and further assuming she went into the water around 11 p.m. Saturday, do you have an opinion as to how long it would have been before mild, moderate and severe hypothermia would set in for Natalie Wood?"

Dr. Pozos thoughtfully answered, "Well, the only weapon she really had was the down jacket. It could have kept her warm in the sense that any captured water would act as an insulator. And, the jacket could have kept her buoyant as well as warm. But, specifically, in response to your question, in my opinion, it would more than likely have taken her one to two hours to become mildly hypothermic and another one to two hours to become moderately hypothermic and then, perhaps, it would have taken her another hour or so to become severe enough for her to actually die of hypothermia."

We know Natalie did not die of hypothermia, but within one hour, she could have experienced mild hypothermia. In that condition, the likely chain of events would have been that after the initial shock of entering the cold water, she called out until the symptoms of hypothermia began to set in and the shivering prevented her from speaking. She became weaker and more hopeless, and her low energy would have prevented her from holding on to one of the dinghy's painter lines or its pontoons for long. However, if she was tangled in the line, after being caught by the currents, she may have floated uncontrollably with the Zodiac out of the cove to the northeast toward Blue Cavern Point. But at some point, her face fell forward in the water. She didn't have the strength to keep her head up, and she drowned.

∾∾∾∾∾∾∾

For three months in the summer of 2018, American Media Inc. and Treefort Media produced the podcast *Fatal Voyage: The Mysterious Death of Natalie Wood*, which included witnesses, experts and writers with some direct or indirect knowledge of the events surrounding Natalie's death. I was asked to participate along with Nancy Grace, a former state court prosecutor and celebrity television journalist; Detective Hernandez, the reported lead detective in the 2011 LASD investigation; Davern; Rulli and others.

Aside from the obvious sensationalism injected by Davern and Rulli, who have now learned to express the right moneymaking buzzwords, the podcast addressed few important issues in Natalie's case. A new one, however, was generated from the forensically documented presence of "approximately 300 CCs of amber-colored fluid" in Natalie's bladder at the time of her death.

In the podcast, Grace proclaimed Natalie was "knocked out before she went in the water," according to "many medical personnel" or "she would have urinated upon drowning."

Grace didn't identify the "medical personnel," but added "when someone drowns, they void." Because Natalie's "bladder was full. That's a big indicator that she was knocked out before she went in the water," she opined.

Then, Detective Hernandez added his two cents' worth: "Approximately 300 CCs is a rather large amount of urine. … Having that amount of urine in her bladder can certainly lend to the possibility that she went in [to the water] unconscious."

For my part in the podcast, I was asked to support those particular theories and conclusions. With all due respect to Grace, I told the producers she was wrong to assume that in light of the cold water, air temperature, Wayne's and Payne's statements and the most likely time of death. Here's the basis for my conclusion.

When I asked Dr. Pozos about the urine in Natalie's bladder, I learned that drawing the conclusion that Natalie was "knocked out" before she entered the water due to the presence of urine was inconsistent with all existing circumstantial and scientific evidence.

A healthy adult bladder holds 600 to 800 CCs of urine. Natalie's contained 300 CCs. So, at most, given her petite stature, Natalie's bladder was half full at death. The micturition point—the point at which a person has the urge to urinate—is anywhere from 150 CCs to 300 CCs of urine. When a person comes into contact with cold water, his or her body increases direct blood volume to its core organs and away from its extremities to keep warm. The proper scientific name for that is "peripheral vasoconstriction."

Acute or sudden exposure to cold water induces a diuretic response due to "increase mean arterial pressure." In other words, scientifically, sudden exposure to cold water causes arterial kidney cells to sense an increase in blood pressure, which signals the kidneys to excrete superfluous fluid in an effort to stabilize [hold steady] the pressure. This means the kidneys increase urine production, which in turn fills the bladder. As the bladder fills, a person feels the urge to urinate. That's called "cold-induced diuresis." It's believed to occur after mental function decreases to a level significantly below normal.

With chronic exposure, that is exposure to cold water over a period of time, as the person progresses through the stages of hypothermia, there is a decreased amount of bodily activity. Everything is affected by cold water. So, the scientific probability is that Natalie did urinate when she first entered the water, but as time progressed, her body produced more urine while her overall metabolism slowed down. In other words, she produced urine but did not urinate again before she died, explaining the presence of 300 CCs of urine in her bladder.

Moreover, new forensic studies show that on autopsy, it's more common than not to find urine retention in the bladder with hypothermic deaths. According to Dr. Pozos and affirmed by Dr. Stanley, the presence of 300 CCs of urine in Natalie's bladder is indicative of her probably reaching the level of "mild hypothermia" before she drowned—not being "knocked out" before she entered the water.

"Her bladder was beginning to retain urine even though she was at or past micturition," Dr. Pozos said.

Of course, Grace's "knocked out" statement would also give rise to the reasonable question, *Was there evidence, beside the 300 CCs of amber-colored fluid in Natalie's bladder, to suggest Natalie was knocked out before she entered the water and drowned?*

As I've already pointed out, on December 1, 1981, Dr. Noguchi's administrative chief of staff said, "*Now we said from the beginning that we don't think she was knocked unconscious when she went in the water* [emphasis added]. Moreover, Wilson said the abrasion on Natalie's face "*was not severe enough to cause unconsciousness* [emphasis added]."

All three pathologists signed off on Natalie's autopsy report, which relied upon their personal observations coupled with an examination of Natalie's scalp tissue and brain. They found no evidence of head trauma serious enough to result in Natalie being "knocked out."

And remember, two years after the autopsy, Dr. Noguchi said in *Coroner*, "Because she had sustained no deep traumatic head wounds, we knew she had been conscious while in the water."

Yet, that didn't stop Finstad. Nineteen years after *Natasha* was published, she "updated" the book under a new title: *Natalie Wood: The Complete Biography*. The 2020 rewind boldly claimed that a May 2012 Supplemental Report for Natalie's autopsy signed by Dr. Lakshmanan Sathyavagiswaran, called "Dr. L" by the LASD detectives due to the difficulty pronouncing his name, "raises the possibility that Natalie may have been struck unconscious on the boat and tossed overboard." And the book dramatically added that the interim coroner "stated he believed that Natalie Wood was unconscious when she entered the water…"

Aside from the fact that the interim coroner stated no such thing in his report, a careful reading revealed Dr. L made no mention of any evidence to support Finstad's new theory. Perhaps recognizing that, Finstad quoted Vidal Herrera, "a photographer for the Coroner's Office," as saying he observed "significant wounds to Natalie's head." When I mentioned this to Eaker, she said she knew Herrera and had worked with him. But she responded with indignation to his claims. She said she had attended the autopsy, she didn't remember Herrera being present, and "there was no such trauma, I can tell you that for sure."

Sadly, Natalie drowned in cold saltwater. And while it was sensational to say she was "knocked out" and "tossed overboard," there was simply no credible evidence to substantiate such claims.

CHAPTER 8

first contact

THE VIEW FROM MY SMALL, SECOND-FLOOR TERRACE AT THE PORTOFINO Hotel was one of those Avalon spring scenes you see in travel magazines. Aided by the warm afternoon sun, sparkles from the ocean reflected off the sides of the moored sailboats as they slowly moved with the gentle breeze.

I can understand why people like Catalina Island, I mused. It had a good feel to it. But instead of soaking up the moment, I caught myself examining each vessel for the way its dinghy was tethered to the craft. *Most are trailing behind the boat, tied to the craft's stern with one painter line.*

A short time later, Paul Wintler, who worked many years for Doug Bombard in "troubleshooting maintenance," knocked lightly on the door of my room. I barely heard him, but he was right on time.

Paul was born in California and had moved from Santa Monica to Catalina Island. In 1981, he was 26 years old and lived in a "villa hut" on the beach in Isthmus Cove—on the "west side, right by the launch ramp." His home was a small building made of two-by-twos. Paul thought the huts were built during and after World War II. At one time, there were thousands of them all over the Isthmus, and a few of them had been preserved.

Mustached and heavyset, the troubleshooter wore khaki pants and a camouflage hat to our meeting. I had mailed him some notes from the 1981 investigation, a section of Detective Rasure's official report addressing his November 29, 1981, interview and excerpts from Finstad's book *Natasha*. His uneasy reaction when I pulled them from my file told me something was wrong.

"The records I got from my lawsuit included what I sent you. I'm going to show them to you again," I began.

"I was looking at them going, 'I don't know where some of this came from,'" Paul said, folding his arms and leaning back in his chair. "I don't quite understand some of it or where it popped up from."

"Did the sheriff's office come to see you again in 2011 when they reopened the case?" I began.

"Yes, they did," Paul answered sharply.

"When they came to see you, they should have let you see those notes," I explained.

"Well, they didn't. They had a report and they asked me a bunch of questions. I basically explained what went on. One guy was taking notes, I think. He would just say, 'You basically said what you said the last time.' And I'm looking at this now going, 'Where did this come from?' There are things there that are not right," Paul replied.

He seemed agitated at the discrepancies contained in the documents, so I changed the subject and showed him a boat mooring map of Isthmus Cove that I'd found on the Internet. He told me the place, including the moorings, hadn't changed much in over 30 years.

In 1981, Paul worked from 8 a.m. to 4:30 p.m. most days. Theoretically, he was off duty after that. If there were no emergencies, he was usually in his hut by 10 p.m. Generally, on

Saturdays, he would go to Doug's to listen to live music.

The reasonable likelihood is that Paul was at the restaurant that Saturday night, but he doesn't specifically recall seeing the Wagners there, since seeing movie stars in the Isthmus was routine for him.

"Tell me how, in 1981, people on the Isthmus boats would generally make phone calls to the mainland," I inquired.

"They didn't," Paul quickly replied. "People didn't have cell phones. If you had a marine radio, you could do it. But they were very expensive," he added.

∿∿∿∿∿∿

My earlier research revealed that by the mid-1960s, AT&T "Ma Bell" had switchboard operators in Los Angeles who, on weekends, placed radio calls from boats in the harbors, including Catalina Island, to land lines on the mainland. *Splendour* had a marine radio, according to records I would uncover later. A November bill to Robert Wagner from Redondo Marine reflected a charge of $34.20 for "marine radio" and $7 for "message handling."

The Wagners had phone service with Pacific Telephone and Telegraph, which managed the Bell System's telephone operations in California, including Intrastate Radiotelephone, Inc. and General Telephone of California. The Wagners' Pacific Telephone and Telegraph bill with an ending service date of December 13, 1981, reflects "long distance" charges of $339.87 and "zone charges" of $16.62, along with a monthly service charge of $158.40. With taxes, the bill was $545.12, or approximately $1,362 in today's dollars.

The idea that there was no way to make telephone calls from *Splendour* also conflicted with a crime scene photograph showing a white phone, attached to a long cord, in the yacht's salon. (See Page A-1.)

Unfortunately, I didn't have the full phone bills, or marine radio charges, to determine what radio calls or messages were made from *Splendour* between 10:30 p.m. Saturday, November 28, and approximately 9 a.m. Sunday, November 29, and—more importantly—to whom.

Like credit card statements, a lot can be gleaned from telephone records. In 1981 and 2011, the sheriff's department could have obtained a subpoena for all of the Wagners' phone records covering the pertinent period of time. It was one of the first moves I made in the white-collar crime prosecutions I handled. And phone companies are good about keeping old records. But I was doubtful, based on what I knew and had seen on the part of the investigators assigned to Natalie's case, that any effort was made to obtain phone records.

∿∿∿∿∿∿

As I continued with my interview of Paul, I said, "The first thing the detectives' notes say is that at approximately 1 a.m., you were awakened by music and you turned on your monitor."

"No. I was awakened by somebody yelling, 'Help!'" Paul said, quickly correcting me. "Of course, I rolled over and looked at the clock. That's why I said approximately 1 a.m."

Needless to say, I was astonished. This was contrary to what people have believed for the past 40 years. They claimed Paul was awakened by loud music and thereafter overheard a radio transmission from *Splendour* requesting help. Paul's words to me added a completely different dimension to the case. He had to know by my reaction that I was surprised by his statement. Yet, he was unflinching in his resolve, even when I confronted him with quotes from Finstad's book containing her conversation with him.

"She called me on the phone, but I told her the same thing I told you…and the cops," Paul stated calmly.

In my experience, when a witness makes that kind of correction, you had better take notice. He was unable to be more exact on the time he was awakened, but he remembered it was "around 1 a.m. and late."

When I asked if what he heard startled him, Paul explained, "What you have to understand was…back then, this was a once-a-week up to two- or three-times a-week thing for me. I would be woken up in the middle of the night by someone yelling, 'Help!' What I would do is throw on my clothes, walk outside, listen for it and figure out… Is it in the moorings? Or where is it? To figure out what I'm going to do. So, I threw on some clothes, came outside my house."

Paul told me he could tell the yelling was "coming from the pier." As he exited his tiny home, Paul could see a silhouette of someone standing on the partially illuminated pier. Walking down to where he heard the distress call, he recognized the person as Robert Wagner, whom Paul had met before.

He said Wagner was alone. Paul, clearly puzzled, added, "How he got there, I don't know. It's always bothered me. But he was on the pier."

When I asked why it had bothered him, Paul said, "Well, we ended up looking for Mrs. Wagner, who was supposed to be in their dinghy, and there were only three ways to get to the dock—swim, a dinghy or a shore boat. He wasn't wet, so swimming was out. And the shore boats weren't operating at that time of night. The dinghy was missing, so how did he get there?"

When he reached Wagner, Paul politely said, "Hello, Mr. Wagner. What's up? What's the problem?"

Paul said Wagner looked at him and said, "My wife's gone."

Paul said he replied, "OK. No problem. We'll just run the rows and see if she tied up to another boat." Paul apparently had experienced this kind of scenario before. He explained that many times he found a dinghy mistakenly tied up to the wrong boat and the person who had been operating the craft was sound asleep.

When I pressed Paul about whether that was all Wagner said, Paul said, "Truthfully, I don't remember the total words. But I remember him saying she was gone. She took the dinghy."

Paul described Wagner as being anxious about Natalie. "He was definitely worried about her."

Again, I pressed him, this time on Wagner's appearance. Were his clothes disheveled? Was his speech slurred?

"Not that I can remember," Paul replied. "If you're asking me was he drunk, I would say he wasn't stammering. He hopped right in the boat with me. He may have been a little drunk. It's like anything. By looking at somebody like that, you might say he's drunk because he fell in the boat. You know how someone is when they are drunk—kind of altered. They can't walk right. But he was walking very well. Wasn't weaving. He walked right into the harbor boat."

After Paul and Wagner got into the boat, Paul said they began going slowly back and forth between the boats in the mooring rows. According to the Isthmus mooring map, there were 13 mooring rows and Paul started in between the two rows closest to the pier. He emphasized to me they were "looking for the dinghy."

Paul knew where he could safely turn around and where he couldn't. As they covered the territory, Paul studied the area around each craft, working his way to where *Splendour* was moored.

When questioned, Paul said Wagner didn't mention anything about Natalie being in her nightgown or drunk. "He really just sat there as I made the rows."

He recalled that as they searched, he was "trying to reassure" Wagner they would find her "because I found I don't know how many people out there tied up to boats." They looked for Natalie between the boat rows for about an hour to an hour and a half. "There were a lot of rows to look at, and I was going slow," Paul said.

When he ran out of paths, Paul told me, "We didn't find her, so I turned to him [Wagner] and said, 'I think it's time we need to call in the cavalry.'" At that point, Paul was becoming more concerned. "We needed more people, so they could start looking in different directions and have a better search," he explained.

In response to Paul's comment about the cavalry, Wagner replied, "Fine. I need to find my wife." So Paul headed to *Splendour* to drop off Wagner. He specifically remembered approaching the yacht so he could "see if there was a dinghy sitting around the boat somewhere." No dinghy was present.

There is a witness out there who has never come forward with a piece of the puzzle—Wagner's explanation for needing to be dropped off at a lonely pier at 1 a.m. on a cold November morning. Is that witness now deceased? Or is he or she afraid to come forward and get involved? Whatever the reason, I'm still searching for the mystery witness.

As we continued our conversation, which Paul took very seriously, he said "two guys came out on deck" when he pulled up to *Splendour*. He didn't talk to them other than to say he was going to bring in more people. If they said anything to Paul, he didn't remember what it was. He confirmed for me that he dropped off Wagner "around 2 to 2:30" in the morning.

That Paul distinctly remembered that "two guys came out on deck" as he approached *Splendour* is crucial. The only people known to be aboard the yacht at that time of the night were Davern and Walken. If both men came out on deck around 2 a.m. to 2:30 a.m. as Paul recalled, that directly contradicts Walken's age-old claims of ignorance and being asleep all night.

༄ౚ౿ౚ౿ౚ౿ౚ౿

Paul motored back to the pier, docked his boat and went to the Harbor Patrol office. Given that the office wasn't kept locked, he was able to call Oudin, who had a phone on his boat in Catalina Harbor. Paul told me that before Oudin could get there, Whiting came to help. That's when Paul decided to return to *Splendour* to get a little more information from Wagner "about the dinghy and so forth."

While debriefing Wagner during his second visit to *Splendour*, Paul said, "I believe I remember him saying something about having a fight with Natalie and her going back to the bar." This defining information was shared with investigators on November 29, 1981, and it is confirmed in CSI Hamilton's official notes. Paul continued, "Wagner also said the dinghy was a Zodiac and described it for me."

Paul told me the captain said something to him, but he didn't remember what. But after speaking with Wagner and Davern, Paul transported Wagner back to the pier to talk to everyone at the Harbor Patrol office. He wanted Wagner to tell them what was going on, so that they all got the story right.

It was "around 3 a.m." when Paul and Wagner arrived at the pier. Paul recalled that contacting the Coast Guard "came up" during the discussion. "We didn't really like calling the Coast Guard right away…unless there was something really bad, you know. Like a boat sinking or such," Paul said. "The problem was that the Coast Guard would take forever to get there. It was easier for us to go find them and to deal with it. Baywatch had just gone onto basically a 40-hour week. They could only go on the overtime clock if there was a boat sinking or you knew obviously something was going on."

Wagner stayed at the Harbor Patrol office while Paul went back out searching. He volunteered to me that the wind was "on shore to the Isthmus," meaning the wind was blowing from the shore out to sea. He jokingly said it was called "our Isthmus breeze." The wind generally "comes down off the mountain at you" when you come around the point into the harbor.

"Dinghies don't do very well in the wind," Paul acknowledged. "It's like putting a motor on a balloon. So, I went around Blue Cavern Point looking."

There were certainly currents in the Isthmus as well. "If the water is pushing you away, which there is current around that point, it will move you along. Not fast, but it will move you…or the wind [will]…or both," Paul said.

During the early morning hours of the search, Paul remembered the weather was clear by 2:30 a.m. "The stars were out. Cold, but it was clear. I remember that we had a little bit of a moon." But earlier Saturday evening, Paul recalled some rain.

There were only five shore boats operating in the Isthmus in 1981, according to Paul. If an occupant of a boat moored in the harbor wanted a shore boat, the procedure was to blow the horn on his boat or to call on the CB radio. Paul recalled that shore boats "charged a buck, I think."

In concluding the interview, I once again mentioned the incorrect music scenario that the investigators and Finstad had reported.

"I don't know where that came from. I really don't. I told them what I'm telling you," Paul responded before I could finish my question. "There was no loud music. I knew how to take care of loud music. I knew where the breaker boxes were. All I had to do was flip a switch."

∽∾∽∾∽∾∽∾

On November 29, 1981, Deputy Kroll was scheduled to work the day shift starting at 7 a.m. But his plans changed after receiving a telephone call from his sergeant at the Avalon sheriff's station explaining that two Baywatch Isthmus lifeguards and a Coast Guard cutter were conducting a search for Natalie Wood Wagner. His sergeant explained Natalie "had been last seen aboard the 60 ft. vessel '*Splendour*' which was tied up to mooring #N-1 in Isthmus Harbor."

Kroll's assignment ended at "0937 hours" Sunday morning. His immediate supervisor eventually approved the 10-page confidential report classifying the matter as an apparent accidental drowning. But Kroll's report indicated "homicide" was requested, a routine procedure in unexplained deaths.

Even though Kroll classified the death as an apparent accidental drowning, Kroll seemed to be following the basic rule—the death was a homicide until proven otherwise.

Kroll's untimely death frustrated me beyond words. I had many questions for Kroll, who was the sheriff's department first responder in Natalie's case. In addition to being saddened by his death, I was looking forward to telling him how impressed I was with his report. Neatly printed by hand, the report was not only detailed, it was easy to read. Kroll included enough personal information so that anyone could have easily found the witnesses he interviewed. He carefully noted event times and set out clearly what the witnesses told him. And, most importantly, Kroll not only noted what he saw—he noted what he didn't see.

I read Kroll's report many times, and each time I found little details that were important for piecing together who said what to whom between the time Kroll arrived and the time he concluded his assignment. So, I feel very confident in relying on Kroll's report for the details I am about to relate to you.

After receiving his orders, Kroll headed to the Harbor Patrol office at the Isthmus where he made contact with Robert Wagner. Wagner was predictably brief. In his report, Kroll wrote:

> All of us, (vict., wit's Wagner, Davern, & Walken) were drinking in the main cabin of the boat when we realized Natalie wasn't around. We searched the boat and found that the Zodiac dinghy was missing. We then thought that Natalie had gone ashore to the bar. *This all took place around 12:00 midnight* [emphasis added]. When she didn't return by 1:30 AM I got on the radio & called the Isthmus to see if she was there. I got a hold of some guys who worked at the Isthmus and asked if they could check the Isthmus for Natalie. When the guys at the Isthmus checked and couldn't find the boat at the dock they started searching the bay, and contacting the Coast Guard.

Kroll's interview with Wagner took place between 5:55 a.m. and 6:15 a.m. Sunday. But, consistent with other troubling matters noted by me after reading Detective Rasure's official report, Kroll's interview with Wagner was omitted from it. I suspect this was done to avoid the glaring inconsistency between the statements Wagner made to Kroll and the statements Wagner made to Rasure at 9:54 a.m., 3-1/2 hours later. In that six-minute interview, according to the investigators' notes, Wagner told them he "started calling Harbor Patrol about 11:30" p.m. Wagner preceded that by saying, it was a "beautiful night" and Natalie "wanted to take dingy (sic) out." Those three statements were omitted from Rasure's official report as well.

After talking to Wagner, Kroll contacted John Claude Stonier and Roger Smith, the Baywatch Isthmus lifeguards who were searching the coastline by boat. Fifteen minutes later, Deputy Kroll accompanied Wagner to *Splendour* "in order to conduct a complete search of the vessel" *for Natalie*. That struck me as very odd. It was a 60-foot yacht, not a mansion.

Did Kroll sense something was amiss?

Kroll knew the locals had been out there and that the search for Natalie had been going on for five hours. *So why did the deputy feel the need to "conduct a complete search" of Splendour for Natalie at 6:30 a.m.?* My experience told me Kroll wanted to get a look at a potential crime scene before it was compromised. It looked to me that the search "for Natalie" was a pretext to search the yacht without a warrant, since any observations he made during the search for Natalie would have been considered evidence discovered "in plain view" and admissible in court.

Sure enough, Kroll didn't find Natalie. But he did observe something noteworthy that he included in his report. "While conducting the search I obs'd pieces of a broken wine bottle laying on the deck carpeting of the main salon. I also obs'd partially eaten food, empty wine bottles, and clothing scattered about the cabin," Kroll wrote.

Under normal circumstances, where celebrity didn't reign supreme, the matter would have looked suspicious to an experienced law enforcement officer. Wagner's claim to Kroll that he thought his famous wife went back to the isolated Isthmus bar alone in a dinghy "around midnight" was dubious, at the very least.

Moreover, Wagner's statements to Kroll, coupled with an admitted delay of an hour and a half between the time Wagner said he noticed Natalie was missing and the time he instigated a search, caused Kroll, in my opinion, to suspect there was much more to the story. Kroll was trained to look for evidence of a struggle or fight when someone is missing. That's why he noted what he saw aboard *Splendour*. He even took time to discern the glass on the floor was a wine bottle.

And, then there was Walken. *Where was he?* Wagner and Davern were interviewed by Kroll, but Walken was conspicuously absent.

∽∽∽∽∽∽

Kroll was the first law enforcement officer to step inside *Splendour* that Sunday morning. The homicide investigators and coroner's investigator took their turn hours later. Kroll's search took 15 minutes, and curiously, there was no indication in Kroll's detailed report that he talked to Walken. Kroll had to have entered Walken's stateroom during his search, and he listed Walken as witness "3 of 11." But unlike the other 10 witnesses, Kroll had no entries of anything Walken said except his age, city of residence, telephone number and that his business address was the "Beverly Hills Wilshire Hotel."

To me, the fact that Kroll obtained personal identification information indicated he did in fact talk to Walken. *So, why didn't he write down what he said?* Even if Walken told Kroll he was asleep and didn't know anything, it should have been noted, because at that point, Walken was a potential suspect in Natalie's disappearance. Based on Kroll's attention to detail in every facet of his work that morning, I suspected something was up when it came to Walken. Kroll would never forget to interview the third man on the yacht. So, it made me wonder if someone told Kroll *not* to interview Walken or *not* to include what he said, particularly when I knew Kroll interviewed Davern.

At "approximately 0645," Kroll reported he boarded the Baywatch Isthmus boat and met with Smith and Stonier. Together, they made a search patrol to Blue Cavern Point "with negative results." When they returned to *Splendour*, Smith and Stonier conducted an underwater search around and under the yacht, again "with negative results." In his report, Kroll made notes of his conversations with both lifeguards.

Shortly after the lifeguards performed the underwater search, Bombard spotted Natalie's body floating near Blue Cavern Point. Hearing that sad report, Kroll and the lifeguards raced to Bombard and assisted him with removing Natalie's body from the water. I'm confident that Kroll, experienced as he was, would have told me they were very careful with Natalie's body. That's what Bombard said, and there's no evidence to dispute it. This type of evidence negates any suggestion that the injuries found on Natalie's body were caused when she was lifted from the water. You can't bruise a dead body, but you can scratch one.

But this, in my opinion, is where the investigation, in Kroll's mind, turned from a "search and rescue" to a homicide investigation. Kroll didn't note it, but homicide was called not only because of an unexplained death, but because of the suspicious circumstances surrounding Natalie's disappearance and what he saw during his search of *Splendour.*

Kroll accompanied Natalie's body to the USC marine laboratory's hyperbaric chamber in Big Fisherman's Cove to wait for sheriff's homicide investigators and the coroner's first responder. While Kroll and the Baywatch Isthmus lifeguards were en route, Kroll noted "a visual examination was made of the vict. *A small laceration was obs'd on the bridge of the vict's. nose* [emphasis added]." He also saw "small bruises" on her arms and legs. I believe in his cursory examination of the body, he missed the big forearm bruise since, as Dr. Stanley pointed out, it was on the underside of her forearm. But the technical definition of a laceration is "a tear in tissue produced by blunt force injury," according to forensic specialists. That was vitally important, and only the autopsy photographs of Natalie's face could refute or verify Kroll's observations.

There was no mention by the pathologists of an injury to Natalie's nose. Of course, there would be no reason for Kroll to fabricate such an assertion. *One more mystery in a legion of mysteries concerning the handling of Natalie's death investigation,* I reflected. But that notation told me Kroll was thinking about a possible assault.

Kroll also stated that Natalie was wearing a "one piece dress, blue socks, and a red down jacket." He listed Natalie's jewelry in typical precise detail:

> Y/M ring (scarab beetle design) & Y/M chain bracelet on R/hand. L/ Hand, Y/M ring (square knot design) Y/M ring (numerous entwined circles) W/M ring with w/stones, Y/M jewelry chain around victs. waist.

It was fascinating to me that Kroll would recognize a "scarab beetle" ring. The scarab beetle is an Egyptian symbol for eternal life, and gold rings of that nature are rare unless custom-made. In any event, there was nothing to indicate Natalie had a bracelet on her left wrist when she was examined by Kroll. Moreover, I found it remarkable that Kroll's report ends with this emphasis: "It should be noted that none of vict. Wagner's jewelry or other personal affects (sic) were removed from the body."

It's almost as if this were an afterthought or added to the report at a later date. I couldn't tell without looking at the original report, but I felt it was added later because of a question Wagner would raise with Rasure about Natalie's jewelry a few days later. There was a diamond necklace Wagner bought Natalie in Avalon on Friday afternoon, worth about $12,000 today, that wasn't noted by Kroll, wasn't included on the personal effects inventory compiled by Eaker, and wasn't described by Davern as being found during the boat cleanup a week later.

According to Kroll's report, at "0830" hours, Davern appeared at the marine lab and "positively identified the body as that of vict. Natalie Wagner (Wood)." Kroll also seized that opportunity to take this statement from Davern about the foursome's movements:

> We ... had gone ashore in the afternoon to have dinner. We sat in the bar drinking until 7:00 PM or 8:00 PM and then had dinner. We left for the boat around 10:00 PM or 11:00 PM and continued drinking on board. At about 12:00 midnight we discovered Natalie was missing and the "Zodiac" was missing. We thought that she had just gone ashore and back to the bar. We couldn't go and check because we had no way of getting ashore. At about 1:30 AM when Natalie still hadn't returned, "J.R." (sic) (wit. Wagner) contacted some Isthmus employees (wit's 4 & 5) [Bill Coleman and Don Whiting] and asked them to look for Natalie on shore. When they couldn't find her ashore, a search of the harbor was started.

There was nothing in Kroll's report to indicate he asked Wagner or Davern about the broken glass and clothes on the floor. It was another mystery that seemed uncharacteristic for the seasoned deputy. But perhaps Kroll decided to leave those questions to the homicide investigators. Moreover, Davern's and Wagner's stories to Kroll were suspiciously similar in detail. That smacked of collusion.

Furthermore, as I carefully read Davern's statement, something immediately caught my attention. He told Kroll, "We couldn't go and check because we had no way of getting ashore." I knew that was untrue, because Wagner obviously got to shore, specifically the pier, around 1 a.m.—and he got there some way other than swimming.

Upon concluding the interview, Kroll told Davern "to return to the '*Splendour*' and remain there until contacted by sheriff's homicide detectives." Davern complied. But he wasn't interviewed by investigators until 11:20 a.m. and it wasn't on *Splendour*. Kroll, obviously at a superior officer's direction, "picked up" Davern at 10 a.m. and escorted him to the pier after Kroll "secured" *Splendour* and the Zodiac for "homicide's disposition."

～～～～～～～

According to the records I obtained from LASD investigators, their first interview of Davern took place "in the Sheriff's Station in Isthmus Harbor." After Davern was interviewed, Kroll helped take statements from witnesses on the island, including Ted Bauer, 26, the bartender at Doug's Harbor Reef & Saloon.

On my fourth trip to Avalon, I made an effort to find Bauer. Not surprisingly, Bauer had left his employment at Doug's establishment. After hitting every bar in Avalon, I found a local who knew Bauer, but lost track of him in the '90s after Bauer "got in a little trouble with the law."

So, once again, I was compelled to rely upon what Bauer told Deputy Kroll and Lt. Collins:

> At about 3:30 PM Bob & Natalie Wagner along with 2 other men (movie people) came into the bar & started drinking; Natalie drank rum. They continued to drink until 7:30 PM or 8:00 PM; they were quiet & didn't cause any problems. Neither Natalie or Bob Wagner acted drunk, but both the other males appeared intoxicated by the time they went in to dinner at about 7:45 PM. At about 10:00 PM I saw them again and all four parties appeared intoxicated. At 10:15 PM all 4 made a toast & broke their wine glasses. All 4 left right after the toast & Natalie was pretty "shaky." Don Whiting, restaurant mgr., called Kurt Craig at the Harbor Patrol office to tell him they were on their way down and to make sure they got back to their boat.

Bauer also told the officers Natalie "had been dressed in designer jeans (blue), a yellow sweater, and a red down jacket." As for jewelry, Bauer said she had on a "*necklace* [emphasis added] & 2 or more rings." The necklace probably wasn't the mysterious diamond necklace since Bauer would most likely have remembered that stunning piece of jewelry.

So, what happened to the necklace Natalie was wearing and the expensive diamond necklace?

The jewelry Natalie was wearing Saturday night would eventually play an important role in my effort to determine the sequence of events, including who dropped Wagner off at the pier and the time Natalie entered the water.

CHAPTER 9

the bond girl

HISTORY SHOWS THAT HOLLYWOOD WAS PRIMARILY THE INVENTION of Eastern European Jewish immigrants and their offspring. Furthermore, 20th-century organized crime in America was primarily a Jewish-Italian joint venture. And for at least three decades between the '50s and '80s, the trio of Sidney Korshak, impeccably dressed fixer and low-profile mob-connected entertainment attorney; Lew Wasserman, the refined head of Chicago-based, mobbed-up Music Corporation of America (MCA); and Paul Ziffren, the respectable, politically connected Los Angeles lawyer; combined to be called the "triumvirate of absolute power in Hollywood." All three were Jewish.

Korshak and Wasserman were the best of friends, and Ziffren entertained Korshak at his home. When the three men worked together, there wasn't a politician that couldn't be elected or destroyed, not an issue that couldn't be made or closed, and not a deal that couldn't be created or killed. And all three power brokers had solid connections to Natalie and Wagner.

Concededly, for many years there was "a well-established tradition of symbiotic codependence and mutual regard between Hollywood and organized crime." Korshak was described by former Chicago FBI agent Bill Romer as the "most important contact the Mob had to legitimate business, labor, Hollywood, and Las Vegas." Author Kitty Kelley in *His Way: The Unauthorized Biography of Frank Sinatra* traced Korshak's roots to Al Capone. His power ranged inextricably into the lives of Wasserman, Sinatra, Teamsters president Jimmy Hoffa, and Ronald Reagan, our 40th president. Sinatra's ties to Korshak began in earnest in 1954 when he hired Korshak to represent him in the ill-fated "wrong door raid" involving baseball legend Joe DiMaggio. And Korshak's wife, Bernice "Bee" Stewart, a former model, was maid of honor at Sinatra's 1976 marriage to Barbara Marx.

In 1962, Korshak, whose open and notorious infidelities were legend, began a long-standing affair with red-headed playgirl Jill St. John. The FBI described the relationship as "Korshak's only known weakness." Gus Russo, in his acclaimed book *Supermob*, reported it was common knowledge that Korshak was "keeping" St. John, including setting her up in a Beverly Hills apartment, buying her a home in Aspen, Colorado, and sustaining her "special passion"—luxurious jewelry. It has also been established that Korshak—who was "like brothers" with Cubby Broccoli, the producer of many James Bond films—was responsible for arranging St. John's part as Bond Girl Tiffany Case in the 1971 film *Diamonds Are Forever*, a role that the film's screenwriter, Tom Mankiewicz, said was intended for Lana Wood. But, inexplicably to Mankiewicz, the roles were reversed, and Lana ended up playing the part intended for St. John—Plenty O'Toole, the Bond Girl who was assassinated after a brief appearance in the film. Korshak also had legendary, must-be-invited-to parties at his fabulous beach house that Natalie first attended when she was 19, before her first marriage to Wagner.

Jill Arlyn Oppenheim was born in 1940 to a Jewish couple in Los Angeles. When she was young, her stage mother changed her last name to the more Hollywood sounding "St. John." Her career in entertainment started in radio and television in 1946 at age 6 and, along the way, she crossed paths with Natalie Wood and Stefanie Powers as they were all members of the Children's Ballet Company.

When she was 16, the quick-witted St. John married Neil Dubin, an heir to a linen fortune. After a year, they divorced, and two years later, she married Barbara Hutton's son, Lance Reventlow, race car playboy and heir to the F. W. Woolworth retail fortune. Their marriage lasted three years, ending in 1963. St. John's third husband was Grammy Award-winning singer Jack Jones. The couple divorced in 1969 after roughly two years of marriage.

Early in life, St. John wanted for nothing, and after her divorce from Reventlow, she became a glamorous and confirmed jet-setting sexpot. Her liaisons for the next 12 years are part of Hollywood lore. From Italian jewelry czar Gianni Bulgari to President Nixon's National Security Advisor, Henry Kissinger—who she described as "a friend for life"— each relationship appeared calculated to advance her career, enhance her connections or improve her net worth.

She had talent, no doubt, and she was as smart as a whip with an alleged IQ of 162. That's probably why men were attracted to her—that and her striking beauty. And she was nobody's fool. She knew where she wanted to go and had a good idea of how to get there. Her carefree journey included dating married men, like Korshak, and ladies' man Frank Sinatra. Within two years of her divorce from Reventlow, St. John's sex life was explored amid questions of promiscuity in a *This Week* magazine article titled, "Two Many Jacks for Jill," where it was rumored she had recently turned down a marriage proposal from Sinatra.

St. John's film career began to take shape as a contract player for Universal Pictures in 1956 and, a few years later, with Twentieth Century-Fox, where she met Robert Wagner. According to George Jacobs, Sinatra's valet from 1953 to 1968, Wagner was "crazy" about St. John. The St. John/Sinatra/Wagner timeline becomes important to Natalie's case by 1963. That year, St. John appeared with Sinatra in *Come Blow Your Horn*, a comedy for which she was nominated for a Golden Globe Award. St. John was having an affair with Sinatra by at least late 1963. And once you were one of Sinatra's girls, to him, you were always a Sinatra girl.

In 1967, she did two movies with Wagner: *How I Spent My Summer Vacation* and *Banning*. The same year she made another film with Sinatra, *Tony Rome*. Wagner's marriage to Marion Marshall was getting shaky by 1969 amid allegations by Marion that Wagner was having extramarital affairs. By June 1970, Wagner and Marion were separated.

According to reports citing St. John, she entered voluntary exile in Aspen beginning in 1972, the year Wagner remarried Natalie. But conveniently in early 1981, St. John decided to return to Hollywood and rent an apartment in Beverly Hills, just about the time Natalie started preparation work on *Brainstorm* at the Esalen Institute in Northern California.

∽∽∽∽∽∽∽∽

A romantic relationship between Sinatra and Natalie was formed well before she met Wagner. In *Natasha*, Finstad presents a strong case of a 1953 affair between the two, quoting Olga Viripaeff, Natalie's half-sister, and three other credible sources.

In 1953, Natalie was 15. Sinatra was 38 and married. And, it's not clear whether her affair with Sinatra was before, during or after her well-known affair with director Nicholas Ray. But Sinatra's romantic liaison with Natalie was "conducted in top secret" because Natalie was a minor and Sinatra didn't want to end up like Errol Flynn, Charlie Chaplin "or, later, Roman Polanski," according to Sinatra's valet.

In *His Way*, author Kitty Kelley shared this quote from makeup man Beans Ponedel: "He [Sinatra] was real good to his girls. He gave them all parts in his movies." For her part, 19-year-old Natalie costarred with Sinatra and Tony Curtis in the film *Kings Go Forth*—released on June 28, 1958. Natalie had married Wagner the previous December with Sinatra's blessing. In fact, according to George Jacobs, Sinatra encouraged Natalie to marry Wagner.

But, the strong connection between Sinatra and Natalie continued notwithstanding her marriage to Wagner. For instance, on July 20, 1959, Natalie turned 21. For that occasion, Sinatra orchestrated an exclusive birthday party for her at Romanoff's in Hollywood, at the time the undisputed restaurant of the stars. The place was packed with A-listers, including Spencer Tracy and a beaming-on-the-outside Robert Wagner.

For Natalie's 22nd birthday, Sinatra sent her 22 bouquets—one each hour for 22 hours. If that wasn't enough, he hired 22 musicians to serenade her.

The romantic relationship between Natalie and Sinatra was rekindled when Natalie separated from Wagner in June 1961. It was short-lived, like the vast majority of Sinatra's liaisons, but their closeness continued. He "adored this tiny beauty" and was "very protective of her," claimed Jacobs. In 1972, after Natalie remarried Wagner, the couple continued spending time with Sinatra at restaurants and parties.

Figure 16: Frank Sinatra throws Natalie Wood a surprise 21st birthday party at Romanoff's in Hollywood in 1959.

(Getty Images/Murray Garrett)

So, there really is no question about Sinatra's affinity for Natalie. And when Natalie died, Sinatra was one of her pallbearers.

Because of Natalie, Wagner also became close to Sinatra. After Natalie and Wagner divorced the first time, Wagner—who by his own admission was broke—became engaged to Sinatra's daughter Tina, again with Sinatra's blessing. Wagner was 41. Tina was 24.

Wagner broke off the engagement to Tina, for which Sinatra forgave him, right before he got back together with Natalie in 1972. The timing of their second marriage would turn out to be crucial in understanding Wagner's true motives at the time of Natalie's death. But that will be sorted out in more depth later.

Significantly, however, Sinatra and Wagner had one other thing in common. As you have learned, Sinatra started his relationship with Jill St. John in 1963 and starred in two films with the mischievous beauty between 1963 and 1967. Wagner also appeared in two movies with the stunning actress, and she was featured in the 1979 pilot for Wagner's series *Hart to Hart*. As you know, Wagner eventually married St. John after Natalie's death, once again with Sinatra's blessing. But the details of how and when the two became romantically involved are shrouded in mystery and deception.

On August 28, 1982, almost exactly nine months after Natalie's death, a feature article written by David Wallace appeared in *People* weekly magazine entitled, "Friends Say It's Love." St. John told Wallace that while she had lived in Aspen for 10 years, she returned to Los Angeles in *the summer of 1981* because, as she put it, "I never wanted to let my name die." And, notably, photographs of a scantily clad St. John appeared in the July 1981 issue of Canadian-based *Rustler* pornographic magazine, marking her second entrée into the world of men's entertainment magazines. Her first was in the March 1960 issue of *Playboy* where she appeared in provocative poses semi-nude.

In 1986, Diana Maychick and L. Avon Borgo wrote their unofficial account of Wagner's life called *Heart to Heart with Robert Wagner*. The first paragraph of the "Acknowledgments" reads: "Although this book is by no means an authorized account, Robert Wagner did speak with us before the project began."

Other than Wagner's statements to the first responders and his two interviews with Detective Rasure and CSI Hamilton, he had not spoken publicly or officially about the details of that fatal Thanksgiving weekend for nearly five years. So, what triggered his meetings with Maychick and Borgo? The answer will be forthcoming, but first let's get back to Jill St. John.

In *Heart to Heart*, the following passage about Jill St. John appears:

> Although she denies making the first move, Jill freely admits that she wanted to see R.J. She sent flowers to him the day after Natalie died. He never received them, however, because he'd asked that all gifts and flowers be sent to nearby Children's Hospital. That didn't matter, though, as Jill had also asked Tom Mankiewicz, her boyfriend at the time and creative consultant on "Hart to Hart," to bring them together somehow. "When Natalie passed away," said Jill, "I told Tom that I would like to see R.J. sometime, to tell him how badly I felt for him and to ask if I could help in anyway. About a week later Tom took me over to R.J.'s house to see him, and we talked for about forty-five minutes. Then I didn't see R.J. again. I didn't call him and he didn't call me."
>
> For reasons that are not clear, *about two months* [emphasis added] after the initial encounter, Mankiewicz decided to get Jill together with R.J. again. Inviting Jill to dinner, Mankiewicz asked R.J. and Kate [Wagner's daughter with ex-wife Marion Marshall] to join them. "We had a good time at dinner," recalled Jill, "and the next day R.J. called and asked me out."

A bit further along, Maychick and Borgo say, "Their relationship was never kept a secret, but, due to R.J.'s lingering need for seclusion, the press was slow to pick up on it."

Not surprisingly, the "new love" prompted questions. Hollywood wanted to know how Wagner could start a relationship so soon after Natalie's death. "I don't like solitude," Wagner told the authors. "I get anxious when I'm alone." To others, the authors said Wagner responded, "I don't give a damn what anyone thinks."

It would be nice to get Wagner and St. John under oath for some cross-examination about their relationship and when it started. Because, if I understood everything Maychick and Borgo along with Wagner said correctly, St. John asked her current boyfriend to bring her and Wagner together "somehow" shortly after Natalie's death. And later, "for reasons that are not clear," that same boyfriend asked St. John and Wagner, with his oldest daughter in tow, to a dinner party. And all of this supposedly happened "about two months" after Natalie died. And, after putting on the full-court press with her boyfriend as matchmaker, St. John told Maychick and Borgo she had to "think about it for a while" before accepting a date with Wagner. Yet, their relationship was "never kept a secret"? You be the judge.

Not one word was included in *Heart to Heart* or *Pieces of My Heart*, or for that matter in Lambert's book, *Natalie Wood: A Life*, about how the girls, particularly 7-year-old Courtney and Natalie's 11-year-old daughter, Natasha, felt when a new woman showed up within weeks of their mother's death, eventually moving in that same year.

Twenty-two years after *Heart to Heart* was published, Wagner changed the couple's dating timeline when he said this in *Pieces*: "Jill and I first went out for dinner with Tom Mankiewicz and my daughter Kate *about six months* [emphasis added] after Natalie died. A few days later, I called Jill and asked her out."

With the stretched "about six months" assertion, as with other materially inconsistent statements Wagner made over the years, I was confident Wagner was hiding more than the beginning of a relationship with St. John.

꙰꙰꙰꙰꙰꙰

At this point, I want to frame the timeline for Wagner's movements between October 28, 1981, and November 14, 1981, to create a reasonable picture of his activities and likely motives.

Hart to Hart producers planned to shoot an episode of the series in Hawaii starting in early November. It's typical for actors shooting on location to arrive a few days before filming begins. So Wagner likely arrived in late October and came without Natalie because she was working on the mainland.

According to Don Chapman in his November 4, 1981, gossip column for *The Honolulu Advertiser*, Wagner attended a birthday party for Stefanie Powers at the Hyatt Regency Maui in Lahaina on Monday evening, November 2. Chapman reported the *Hart to Hart* episode was being filmed at the hotel that week.

Beginning Wednesday, October 28, 1981, and ending November 5, 1981, purchases from Maui appeared on a First Interstate Bank Mastercard credit card in the name of Natalie Wood. The first purchase was on October 28 at "The Logo Shop" in Kapalua where the highly rated Plantation [golf] Course is located. Wagner played the sport. "I love to golf," he said in his memoir. But, Natalie didn't.

The second and third purchases were on October 30 at "Monteleone Designs" and the "Whaler's Pub" in Lahaina. The fourth was October 31 at "The Ambrosia Restaurant" in

Kihei, about 25 miles from the Hyatt Regency Maui. On November 3, there was another transaction at Monteleone Designs in Lahaina.

The Mastercard statement reflected three more purchases on November 4: "Whalers Chest" and "Lahaina Scrimshaw Factory" in Kaanapali and "Superwhale" in Lahaina. There was another purchase at Lahaina Scrimshaw Factory in Kaanapali the next day, November 5, as well as a purchase at "Coral Garden Gifts" in Lahaina.

Kaanapali Beach offered a variety of activities, including whale watching, surfing, scuba diving and sightseeing tours as well as shopping and dining at the Whalers shopping center. The Lahaina Scrimshaw Factory, in particular, sold hand-carved ivory, bone and turtle shell, ranging from budget-priced souvenir items to museum-quality pieces.

The October 29, 1981, issue of Raleigh, North Carolina's *The News and Observer* reported that filming on Natalie's movie *Brainstorm* "wrapped up" late "in the evening" on Tuesday, October 27. For Natalie to be in the Logo Shop of the Plantation Course during business hours on October 28, she would have had to fly on a red-eye 5,000 miles from North Carolina directly to Maui in secret.

Who was using Natalie's credit card in Hawaii if she wasn't there? And, why? The credit card document in Natalie's probate file was "page 1 of 3," meaning two pages were missing. In addition, the new transactions on the card totaled $1,143 for November. That told me there were most likely other Hawaii purchases through November 12, but the pages were unavailable for my inspection.

Someone went on a sightseeing and shopping trip in Maui with Natalie's card between October 28 and November 5. Based on all I've read, Wagner didn't seem like the type to go off shopping, drinking and whale watching alone.

Brainstorm wasn't finished shooting its interior scenes, and Natalie hadn't seen her girls in weeks. In 2001, Finstad quoted Louise Fletcher, Natalie's costar, as describing Natalie's reaction to being away from her children this way: "She was always talking about her kids. Missing them, what they were like. She mentioned them all the time, and called them, having conversations at night."

It isn't reasonable to believe that after nearly a month in North Carolina she would leave *Brainstorm* filming and immediately fly incognito to Maui for 10 days, considering how much she missed her girls and the amount of wrap-up filming work that awaited her in Los Angeles.

Wagner's personal Visa credit card showed no Hawaii purchases between October 28 and November 12. However, Wagner and Natalie had a joint First Interstate Bank Mastercard credit card, which reflected Los Angeles, Hollywood and Beverly Hills purchases during the *Hart to Hart* Hawaii filming time period, including purchases at "Nickelodeon" on Wednesday, November 4 (bearing handwritten notes of "Xmas gifts—Kids" and "Tapes"); "Licorice Pizza" on Friday, November 6; "St Laurent Rive Gauche" on November 7 and 11; "The Bikini Shop" on Monday, November 9; and "Ahmanson Theater" on Tuesday, November 10.

The handwritten notations on the statement, probably by someone assisting accountants or lawyers, stated "Gifts—Gregson Girl" and "Skirt" on the Saint Laurent Rive Gauche transaction descriptions and "Mrs. W" on The Bikini Shop transaction. Having spent many hours of my life in women's clothing stores, I know of nothing more personal to a woman or a girl than the purchase of a bikini. Consequently, the records strongly indicated Natalie was entertaining her girls from at least November 4 through November 11 using the jointly held Mastercard. Furthermore, the evidence strongly suggested Natalie purchased a bikini in Beverly Hills on Monday, November 9.

Interestingly, Wagner's Visa card reflected a $79.50 purchase (about $225 today) at "Ina's 14 Karat Shop" in Beverly Hills recorded on Tuesday, November 24. That was three days before his trip with Natalie and Walken to Catalina Island.

On Friday, November 27, Wagner, Walken and Natalie were on Catalina Island in the town of Avalon visiting, shopping and drinking. Walken said he bought a painting. Wagner negotiated with David Stein, owner and goldsmith of Off White Gallery, for the purchase of a 20-karat gold pendant with 0.74 carat diamond and a "special" handmade chain for $4,250 (about $12,000 today); a 14-karat Spanish "4 reale replica" coin pendant for $325 (about $915 today) and a strand of ivory beads and horsehead for $375 (about $1,050 today).

However, the jewelry wasn't paid for until after Natalie's death. The bill was submitted by Wagner to probate and paid from Natalie's estate. (See *Figure C*, Page 260.)

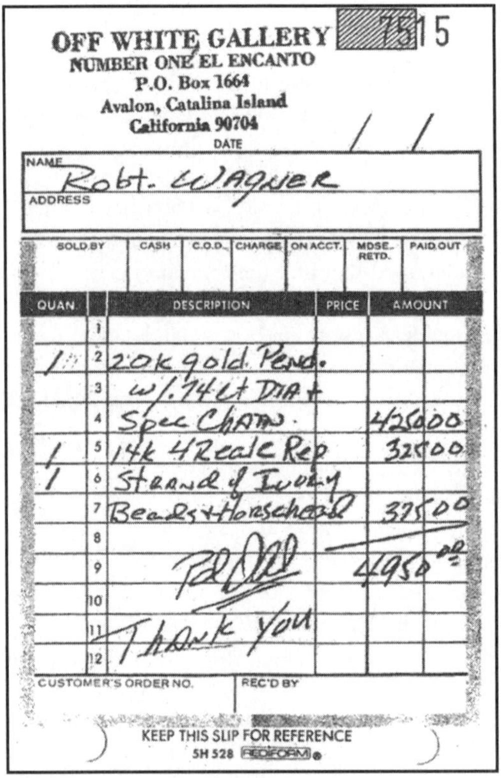

OFF WHITE GALLERY 7515
NUMBER ONE EL ENCANTO
P.O. Box 1664
Avalon, Catalina Island
California 90704

DATE / /

NAME Robt. Wagner
ADDRESS

SOLD BY	CASH	C.O.D.	CHARGE	ON ACCT.	MDSE. RETD.	PAID OUT

QUAN.		DESCRIPTION	PRICE	AMOUNT
	1			
1	2	20k gold Pend.		
	3	w/.74 ct DIA +		
	4	Spec Chain.		4250 00
1	5	14k 4 Reale Rep		325 00
1	6	Strand of Ivory		
	7	Beads + Horsehead		375 00
	8			
	9	[signature]		4950 00
	10			
	11	Thank You		
	12			

CUSTOMER'S ORDER NO. REC'D BY

KEEP THIS SLIP FOR REFERENCE
5H 528 REDIFORM

Figure 17: Robert Wagner's receipt for jewelry purchases at Off White Gallery (Natalie Wood Wagner probate file)

During my third trip to Catalina Island, I found a former longtime employee of Off White Gallery. Barbara Sherman, owner/manager of High Tide Traders in Avalon, graciously identified receipt number 7515 found in Natalie's probate file as handwritten by David Stein. Stein had passed away, but Barbara was familiar with his creations.

The jewelry Stein made included handmade Spanish coin replica necklaces, pendants and earrings, and during his travels, he collected unusual jewelry. Unfamiliar with the ivory beads and horsehead, Barbara thought it was probably a bracelet similar to a picture she pulled up online. (See *Figure 18*, next page.)

On December 3, 1981, Walken told investigators after he, Natalie and Wagner got to "Solomon's" in Avalon on Friday, Wagner *left* and went back to Stein's to "beat the price" for the diamond necklace. I have a high degree of skepticism that Wagner's excuse for returning to Stein's was only about prices. Here's why.

Davern claimed Natalie gave him an early Christmas present Friday night—a very nice "pieces of eight" necklace. Along with Natalie's diamond necklace, they might account for two of the items Wagner bought from Stein. *But who ended up with the unique and expensive strand of ivory beads and horsehead?*

Moreover, the receipt omitted any reference to "pieces of eight earrings," which you will learn were identified by Davern as being purchased by Natalie. Stein sold Spanish coin replica earrings in his shop. So, this led me to believe Natalie made her own purchase with either cash or credit card. Considering the amount involved, she probably used a credit card.

The first page of Natalie's Mastercard statement reflected no entries past November 5. And while Natalie's estate paid $7,757.86 (about $21,850 today) to "American Express" for items "Charged Prior to 11/29/81," there was no American Express credit card statement in the probate file to support the payment. So, I was unable to verify whether Natalie paid for her purchases with her Mastercard, American Express card or cash. We know

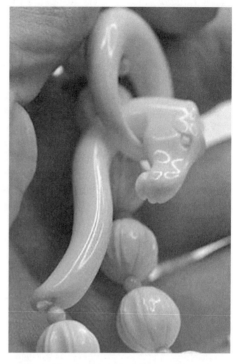

Figure 18: An Internet search turned up this photo of ivory beads with an ivory horsehead clasp that may be similar to the one Robert Wagner purchased in Avalon. (Jewelry Kingdom Hawaii)

Natalie had an American Express card with her Friday night because she used it to pay for her stay at the Pavilion Lodge in Avalon, according to desk clerk Linda Winkler.

Wagner was interviewed by investigators a second time, on December 4, 1981, in the bedroom of the couple's home on Cañon Drive in Beverly Hills. In *Pieces*, Wagner said he was "catatonic" after Natalie's death. "It was at this point that I went to bed and stayed there. It may have been for seven days, it may have been for eight. I was catatonic and I don't really remember. I didn't shower and I didn't shave."

"Catatonic" means a state of "immobility" or "unresponsive stupor." Yet, at the end of his second interview about his wife's death, Detective Rasure's notes reflected Wagner's only questions were, Did you "open a package with a wallet and boat papers?" and What "about jewelry" on the yacht?

Remember, on November 29, coroner records indicated "Mr. Wagner called" Dr. Choi and requested an early autopsy for Natalie "tomorrow" (Monday) because he planned her "burial" Tuesday. The following day, Jill St. John "sent flowers" to Wagner. A week later, she came for a visit. In addition, on November 30, while in his unresponsive stupor, Wagner's Visa card posted a purchase from "Merrin Jewelry Co in New York, NY" for $196 (about $550 today).

On December 1, 1981, two days after Natalie's death, the "catatonic" actor managed to sign a 20-page "Petition for Probate of Will" asking to, among other things, be appointed executor of Natalie's estate for the purpose of distributing that estate to Natalie's heirs. The petition was prepared by the Gibson, Dunn & Crutcher law firm on behalf of partners Paul Ziffren and William Stinehart Jr. Portions of the information for that petition would no doubt have been provided by Wagner, and no self-respecting attorney would have allowed a genuinely "catatonic" client to sign a document of that importance.

Later, it was reported Wagner and St. John "became an item" on Valentine's Day 1982, approximately 11 weeks after Natalie's death. And, the paparazzi caught them out on the town roughly three weeks after that. (See Page A-2.) But most telling was the passage in Wagner's memoir that ran immediately before the new "six months" claim. "We [Wagner and Jill St. John] had worked together in *How I Spent My Summer Vacation*, and *Banning* not to mention the pilot for *Hart to Hart*, and the association had been pleasant but purely professional, *despite the imaginings of my wife, Marion* [emphasis added]."

Wagner's second wife, Marion Marshall, apparently believed Wagner had more than a "purely professional" relationship with St. John. When suspicions of infidelity surfaced, Wagner claimed in his book that Marion actually accused him of having an affair with St. John.

"It was while I was doing *It Takes a Thief* [January 1968 to March 1970] that I began to stray off the marital reservation," he confessed to Eyman in *Pieces*. Then Wagner penned another falsehood:

> *I had always been able to resist extramarital gopher holes before* [emphasis added], but not this time. My relationship with Marion had been initially passionate, but that passed, and in our case friendship wasn't enough to sustain the marriage. If I had to ascribe my infidelity to one thing, I would say that it was the times. Everybody was going crazy, and I felt I had to make up for lost time.

Natalie divorced Wagner after their first marriage, according to Lana and others, because Natalie caught him scampering down an "extramarital gopher hole" with a male staff member in the couple's home. And now we know his divorce from his second wife was also due to infidelity since he needed "to make up for lost time."

I had seen it many times during my time in the law business. One spouse believes the other is having an affair, so he or she has an affair to even the score. There's more to come on the issue of infidelity, which will allow you to decide if Wagner's trail leads to the reasonable conclusion that filled with suspicious jealousy, he was off the "marital reservation" once again in the months before Natalie's death, and whether the evidence suggests the most likely paramour was Jill St. John—the horse lover who admittedly amassed such a valuable and huge collection of jewelry that she kept it in "vaults."

CHAPTER 10

red flags

IN MAY 2012, DR. L, WHO HAD HELD HIS POSITION AS CHIEF CORONER for only two months, created an international stir when he signed a "Supplemental Report" for Natalie's autopsy offering new conclusions about her death.

The media, and rightly so, reported extensively on Dr. L's decision to change the cause of Natalie's death from accidental "drowning" to "drowning and other undetermined factors." The manner of death was changed to "undetermined." Then, Dr. L added this: "How injury occurred will be listed as found floating in ocean. Circumstances not clearly established." This was big news, but as you will learn, the reopening of Natalie's case proved more of a frustrating disappointment for those interested in the truth and actually constituted a step backward in the search for answers as to how the superstar drowned in deep, dark waters.

The official 1981 autopsy file, which I had obtained through my CPRA lawsuit, included a crucial narrative by the coroner's office investigator. Eaker's report contained some significant facts and conclusions, the most important of which was an account of what Wagner told her after Natalie's body was found early Sunday morning, November 29, 1981.

The report said, "Spoke with Mr. Wagner who related that the last time he remembers seeing his wife was at 2245 hours [10:45 p.m.] Mr. Wagner, when he realized his wife was missing, placed a radio call for help." And, later in the report, Eaker said, "Mr. Wagner was also questioned regarding the possibility of suicide. However, he states that his wife was not suicidal."

What struck me immediately about Eaker's report was the fact that the time had been changed by hand from 2345 hours to 2245 hours. There were a few other handwritten changes as well as the initials "PE" at the end of the report. This told me a couple things about Eaker.

First, in an effort to be as accurate as possible, Eaker likely made the changes after her report was typed. If those changes were in her handwriting, it meant she carefully reviewed the report before it was sent to her supervisor—Senior Investigator Juan Jimenez—who also signed the report after stating "Approved." This procedure was not unusual for conscientious investigators who followed standard protocol.

Second, it gave me insight into Eaker and her personality type. She was meticulous. An investigator who paid attention to detail and her job. In Dr. Noguchi's book *Coroner,* he called Eaker "a skilled investigator." Since the case involved high-profile Natalie Wood, this skilled investigator was going to be sure she got it right.

In Eaker's report, she wrote that Don Whiting told her he heard *Splendour's* call for help at 1:30 a.m. Sunday. If Wagner last saw Natalie at 10:45 p.m. Saturday, that meant nearly three hours lapsed before help was sought. This is a critical set of facts.

In *Coroner,* Dr. Noguchi reported Eaker told him Wagner said this:

1. After the Wagner group returned to the yacht from dinner Saturday night, Wagner and Walken went to the "wardroom of the yacht for a nightcap while Natalie retired to her quarters."

2. The last time Wagner remembered seeing Natalie was *"at about quarter of eleven* [emphasis added]."

3. *"Sometime after midnight* [emphasis added], Wagner went to their cabin and noticed that his wife was not in bed."

4. When Wagner searched for Natalie "elsewhere on the yacht, he discovered that the dinghy was also missing."

5. Wagner wasn't concerned at first, because Natalie "often took the boat out alone. But as time passed and she didn't reappear, he became more and more upset, and finally radioed for help."

Most of this information was not contained in Eaker's report. (See *Figures D* and *E*, Pages 261-262.) Eaker told me she only told Dr. Noguchi what was contained in her report. *So, why did Dr. Noguchi claim Eaker told him those five things?*

In my opinion, Dr. Noguchi was intentionally trying to reduce the Fatal Gap—the time between when Wagner last saw his wife and when he called for help. Dr. Noguchi knew when he wrote *Coroner* the timeline was more than suspicious. Fabricating what Eaker reported was an obvious attempt to cover it up.

Yet, more than anything, I was troubled by the stark inconsistences between Dr. Noguchi's book and Eaker's report as well as Eaker's final reported conclusion.

Eaker saw "numerous bruises" on Natalie's "legs and arms." She also heard what Wagner told her about when he last saw Natalie and that when realizing she was missing, he "placed a radio call for help." Coupled with Natalie's injuries and what Whiting said about the timing of Wagner's call, why would Eaker conclude her report with, "No other trauma noted and foul play is not suspected at this time"?

In my experience, drawing a conclusion like that so early in an unexplained death investigation is unusual. This was a report about an investigator's findings at the scene. I found it strange Eaker would have had any reason to put a conclusion like that in her first responder's report. *Was she asked to do that because of the celebrities involved?* It was the coroner's job to determine cause and manner of death. *So was Dr. Noguchi looking for official support of accidental death from Eaker? Or did the sheriff's investigators influence her by telling her it was an accidental drowning case?*

Although a critical witness, Eaker hadn't been discussed much in tabloids or books. Finstad made only a passing reference to her in 2001, and Rulli and Davern did likewise in 2009.

∽∽∽∽∽∽

Detective Rasure's notes reflected that he and Hamilton "arrived at [Catalina Island] 10:45 a.m." Sunday. Eaker was with them. I knew she was essential to the truth, so I hired a driver take me to Lakewood, a suburb of Los Angeles bordered by Long Beach on the west and south.

As he slowly drove through the neighborhood, I noticed a tall, fair-skinned woman with Caesar-styled red hair working in the yard of a well-kept home we thought was Eaker's. Since I'd never seen a photo of her, I didn't know if we had the right person.

"Hi, I'm Sam Perroni. Are you Pamela Eaker?" I said cheerfully. I could tell she was startled by my presence.

"Yes," she said cautiously.

"I'm writing a book about Natalie Wood and I was wondering if you had a few minutes?" I asked, expecting a polite, "No."

"OK, sure," she said to my astonishment.

I admired the landscaping while walking up to the front door of her modest one-story home and made a mental note of how meticulous she was—right down to the clean and protected stray cat homes that graced a shady side of her house.

Eaker had retired from the LA County coroner's office. Her 11-year career as an investigator for the coroner began in 1979. At the time of her employment, she was working toward a degree in criminal justice at California State University, Los Angeles, which she completed in June 1982. She also worked a brief time for the Orange County coroner.

Eaker's duties as a coroner's investigator were straightforward and vitally important to the operation of the office. When the coroner was called to handle a death under Los Angeles County's jurisdiction, she was one of the staff who went to the scene to collect time of death evidence before the body was sent to the lab for autopsy. Her most important responsibility was to locate and document evidence and facts to be used by the pathologist to determine the cause and manner of death. That included developing time of death parameters, locating crime scene evidence, supervising the recovery of remains and gathering evidence to identify the body.

Time of death parameters, or postmortem interval (PMI), are facts that help establish the time of a person's death. If the length of time a person has been dead can be determined, with other circumstances, a pathologist can establish, or eliminate, a possible linkage between the victim and a suspect. So, Eaker's responsibilities were vital to any unexplained death investigation.

When I began asking Eaker questions with my notepad in my lap, she quickly went to a closet and retrieved a copy of her report in Natalie's case. It was almost as if she were expecting me. Her report was precise by any standard, giving her high marks, in my opinion, for being scrupulously careful. And her prompt recovery of the report told me the matter had been at the forefront for her recently, but she couldn't remem-

Figure 19: Pamela Eaker, coroner's office investigator, questions an official after a fatal fire. (Courtesy of Pamela Eaker)

ber much about what happened 35 years ago without referring to her report. It also told me she didn't want to make any mistakes—even with me, a writer.

In 1981, the coroner's office had a call center. When a call to the coroner would come in—perhaps from the police, a doctor or a hospital—the call center staff would tell the coroner's office supervisor on duty, "This is what we've got." The supervisor would then look it over and say, "We're going to need to go out." After that, the supervisor would assign the case to an investigator like Eaker.

Natalie's case came in as "an apparent accidental drowning," and Eaker was informed it was Natalie Wood before she arrived on the scene. In my opinion, Kroll made the call to the coroner's office call center. The phone call on Natalie's case, according to Eaker's file, came in at 8:30 a.m. Sunday. She guessed for me she would have been contacted around 9 or 9:30 a.m., and then assigned a coroner's case number.

Eaker estimated she got to the island around noon. Kroll's report indicated she and others arrived at "1045 hours." She first talked to some of the officers and locals about what had happened, and at some point, she said she briefly talked to Wagner. Eaker's memory was cloudy on the location of that interview. Based on Kroll's report, however, her contact with Wagner must have been at the Aero Bureau in Long Beach around 10 a.m. before she departed for Catalina. She told me she never saw Walken and never spoke to him.

Eaker had no doubt she talked to Wagner, because he told her he was "wanting to get home to the kids." She told me she specifically remembered that. Wagner also expressed concern that the children would hear about what had happened "on the news." Other than those statements, Eaker told me she had no memory of anything else other than what was in her report.

You would think because she was talking to a celebrity that she would remember every detail. But I got the impression from Eaker that she wasn't starstruck. She was just doing her job, and the details, outside of her report, were lost in the thousands of cases she worked during her time with the coroner's office.

"Did Wagner tell you about having a fight with Walken or his wife before she went 'missing'?" I asked.

"If he would have said anything like that, I would have put it in the report," Eaker replied. The reason for her emphatic answer is that a quarrel is potential evidence of the manner of death, given that a substantial number of the homicide deaths investigated by the coroner were the result of domestic violence.

"Did he tell you that Natalie didn't know how to swim and was afraid of dark water?" I continued.

"He didn't say anything like that to me," Eaker answered. "I would have remembered something like that and would have put it in my report."

"Did Wagner mention anything about angrily smashing a wine bottle on the coffee table in front of Natalie and Walken?" I asked, believing I knew the answer.

But, then Eaker surprised me by replying, "We knew about a fight."

I immediately perked up. "You knew about a fight? A fight between—" I started to ask before she cut me off.

"Wagner and Walken in the salon," she blurted out.

"But that's not in your report," I said to her.

"No. Wagner didn't tell me that. I learned that after I talked to Wagner," she explained.

But the implications were obvious.

෧෬෧෬෬෬෧

Eaker examined Natalie's body at the USC marine lab's hyperbaric chamber at about 1:30 p.m. Sunday. Natalie was lying in a "stokes litter," a plastic or metal stretcher-type bed used in search and rescue, and was "wrapped in a plastic sheet." Eaker carefully pulled back the plastic and saw that Natalie was dressed in a one-piece blue and red plaid flannel nightgown, and blue argyle wool-type socks. A red jacket, of "down-type" material, was at the foot of the litter.

Eaker assured me she didn't remove the down jacket. "Our people knew better," she insisted. Since Kroll stated emphatically that no personal effects were removed from Natalie's body, that left Baywatch Isthmus lifeguards Stonier and Smith or sheriff's reserve officer Michael Harvin—who was placed in charge of Natalie's body while Kroll assisted Lt. Collins in interviewing witnesses—as possible suspects in that major forensic gaffe.

Forensically, Eaker noticed numerous bruises on Natalie's arms and legs and said her eyes appeared a bit cloudy looking. Eaker explained that the more exposure the eyes have to air after death, the more cloudy they appear. Natalie was not wearing underwear, and although Eaker didn't check the tag, her recollection was the plaid nightgown Natalie was wearing was a "sleep shirt," like Eaker wore herself. As a consequence, she concluded the fabric was most likely cotton.

Eaker also checked Natalie's body for rigor mortis, noting there was no rigor mortis when she was pulled from the ocean—information she had to have obtained from Bombard or the lifeguards. Eaker also noted the environmental temperature—the air in the hyperbaric chamber—was 63 degrees Fahrenheit; Natalie's liver temperature was 65 degrees Fahrenheit at 1:30 p.m.; and the water temperature at 7:44 a.m. when Natalie was found was 62 to 63 degrees Fahrenheit. That information related to PMI.

Natalie was wearing some jewelry, and Eaker collected and listed it on the coroner's office standard property notepad. (See *Figure 20*, next page.)

According to Eaker, Natalie had one ring on her right hand and three rings on her left hand. She had a chain bracelet on her right wrist, but nothing on her left to cover her deformity. And she had a "yellow metal" chain with a charm around her waist under her nightgown. All consistent with Kroll's observations.

Eaker prepared a personal effects inventory for Natalie Wood Wagner and explained to me that the abbreviation "Y/M" and "W/M" on her inventory meant "yellow metal" and "white metal." She said investigators never used the words "gold" or "silver" because "that may not be what it [the metal] actually was." In addition, they never described items as "diamonds"; they used the phrase "clear chips." Her normal practice was to check the jacket pockets and note if she found anything. There was nothing noted.

Eaker didn't recall seeing any photographs that were taken of Natalie in the water at Blue Cavern Point and added that she didn't believe photographs were taken because "she was found by locals, not law enforcement."

Eaker's standard "Medication & Evidence Record" was prepared by calling Natalie's pharmacies and going onto the yacht and collecting all prescription bottles with Natalie's name on them.

I specifically asked her if she did anything in connection with the body that was different from her customary way of dealing with bodies because Natalie was a celebrity, and she responded, "No."

Then, I directed her attention to the first page of her report marked as "Continuation Sheet," where the time Wagner said he last saw Natalie looked like it had been changed from a typed number "2345 hours" to a handwritten "2245 hours," a change from 11:45 p.m. to 10:45 p.m.

That was the only time I saw her bristle before correcting me, saying, "It wasn't changed, I made an error and corrected it."

She informed me the correction was indeed in her handwriting and also that she was "pretty sure" it was supposed to be 10:45 p.m. because Wagner told her they got back to the boat between 10 and 10:30 p.m., and according to what he said, it wasn't long before he went downstairs and noticed Natalie was missing. Otherwise, according to Eaker, "it would have been as much as 1 hour and 45 minutes before he went downstairs, and I believe they weren't back at the yacht that long before Natalie disappeared."

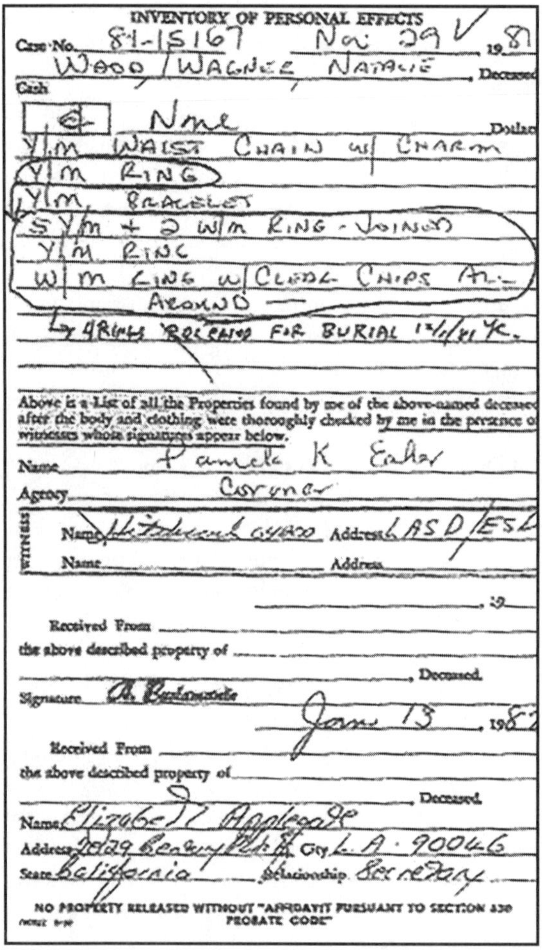

As time went on, and because I was terribly curious, I asked, "Did you report Natalie's case to the district attorney's office?"

"No, because I determined no foul play was suspected at that time," was her slightly defensive reply. I could tell then she still believed Natalie's death to be an accident. To feel otherwise would have required her to admit she might have been premature in her assessment of the objective findings. I understood. No one in forensic law enforcement wants to believe he or she missed a potential homicide. So, I left it at that. I didn't want to offend this nice lady.

Later, after we developed a friendly relationship, I sent her an email and asked, "Was it customary for you to insert your

Figure 20: Inventory of Natalie Wood's personal effects compiled by Pamela Eaker, coroner's office investigator
(Los Angeles County Department of Medical Examiner-Coroner)

subjective opinion in a report like Natalie's so early in an investigation and, if not, did anyone instruct you to add that language to your report?"

In her reply, she wrote, "It was a very typical ending to my reports." I had no reason to doubt her. She was sent to the scene of an "apparent accidental drowning," and she finished her report with no evidence from her boss or the LASD investigators to change her mind.

Of course, because so many years had transpired between the investigation and our discussion, Eaker's memory about what had happened that day was largely confined to what was in her report. But she was steadfast about what Wagner said and what she saw and heard.

I must say, however, I still find it odd she did not suspect foul play when she saw numerous unexplained bruises on Natalie's arms and legs. I never asked if she would have a different opinion today based on my newly found evidence, because it would have been an unfair question for me to ask and for her to answer.

<center>~~~~~~~~</center>

In Dr. Noguchi's memoir, he wrote after Natalie's autopsy was finished, he instructed Eaker, Dr. Choi, Dr. Kornblum and Wilson to meet in his office before his news conference. Dr. Noguchi outlined his preliminary finding of an accidental drowning, with alcohol playing a significant role. Then, according to *Coroner*, one of his staff said the reporters were really interested in "*why she left the yacht in the middle of the night* [original emphasis]." Dr. Noguchi then added, "Why hadn't she climbed back aboard the yacht when she was only one or two feet away?"

Both actions seemed to him to indicate Natalie was determined to get away from the yacht. At that point, Dr. Noguchi was told one of the sheriff's deputies had apparently reported that Wagner and Walken were quarrelling in the main cabin that night. Then Dr. Noguchi wrote that the "implications" of Natalie leaving because of a fight "fed right into the hands of those who had been speculating that some 'scandal' on the yacht had contributed to the famous star's death."

It's reasonable to conclude Dr. Noguchi and Wilson got the information about the quarrel from either Eaker relating what she had been told or by one of the LASD investigators during the autopsy. (Rasure attended the autopsy according to his report.) So I asked Eaker if she in fact attended a meeting November 30, 1981, in Dr. Noguchi's office before the news conference. She answered affirmatively.

I followed up with, "Do you remember if anyone else was there?"

Eaker told me she specifically remembered the meeting with Dr. Noguchi but could not recall everyone who was there. She said she believed Detective Rasure and "a major boat enthusiast who sailed often" being there along with Dr. Choi and Wilson. But that was the extent of her memory. The "major boat enthusiast who sailed often" had to have been Paul Miller.

Eaker told me she had never been called to a meeting like that while working for the Los Angeles County coroner's office. To the best of her recollection, the purpose was to review the autopsy findings and the results of the investigation itself. She said it was quite possible she may have learned the information about the fight between Wagner and Walken at that meeting.

The top-level meeting was a red flag for me. It signaled an unnatural approach to the official conclusions that ultimately came out of the coroner's office.

<center>~~~~~~~~~</center>

I knew I needed to concentrate on the statements from key witnesses made near the time of Natalie's death, and to avoid witnesses who were obviously trying to get their names in the paper. In general, the further out in time I went, the less reliable people were likely to be, particularly with the continued media interest and search for salacious sound bites.

Anyone interested in Natalie's death, including witnesses who might have relevant information on the guilt or innocence of potential suspects, was reading the newspaper and tabloid articles and watching the TV news shows. Depending on their opinions of the people involved or the subject matter, the articles or reports could influence the witnesses' memories or create opportunities for them to step into the spotlight.

I found a perfect example of this early on.

As you may recall, Roger Smith was a Baywatch lifeguard who helped in the search. He claimed in *A Cry for Help,* a "paper" he wrote years after Natalie's death, that he "had been running the Catalina Baywatch Isthmus lifeguard rescue boat operation for ten years" and was the "first lifeguard paramedic in the world."

Finstad briefly quoted Smith in *Natasha,* and Rulli and Davern relied heavily on Smith in their book *Goodbye.* Rulli described Smith as a "former Coast Guard Lieutenant" and "victim" of Natalie's death.

According to Smith, he responded to the search and rescue operations at 5:11 a.m. Sunday after the Coast Guard was notified Natalie was missing. He claimed he located the empty Zodiac dinghy and brought Natalie's body to shore after Doug Bombard pulled her from the water. Smith has also stated over the years that he examined Natalie's body for "foul play," removed her jewelry and flexed her fingers and, I learned later, that he removed Natalie's down jacket. Finally, he claimed while he possessed important evidence about her death, he was "never" interviewed in 1981 by the officials investigating it.

However, I would learn in my investigation that he was indeed interviewed at approximately 9:30 a.m. Sunday, November 29, by Deputy Kroll. Smith reported to Kroll that "he was first contacted regarding the missing person at 0515 HRS by the US Coast Guard." He and Stonier "responded to their patrol vessel to assist in the search, and upon learning that the Sheriff's Department had also not been notified, requested US Coast Guard contact Avalon sheriff's station."

Smith also told Kroll that at about 5:30 a.m. he and Stonier "were contacted by the Isthmus Harbor Patrol [and] advised the missing Zodiac dinghy had been found against the rocks at Blue Cavern Point." According to Kroll's report, the duo thereafter conducted a "coastal search" and an "underwater search" with "negative results." Finally, when Natalie's body was observed by the search and rescue helicopter, Kroll wrote that Smith and Stonier "assisted in recovering and transporting" it to the USC marine lab.

Moreover, although he said he "refused to talk to the media," Smith managed to be interviewed by a *Los Angeles Times* reporter a short time after Natalie's body was found for an article appearing the following day. Smith's reported statements, describing the area around Blue Cavern Point and the currents off the Isthmus, were insignificant to the overall investigation and largely benign.

Years later, Smith's tale was considerably inflated in *A Cry for Help*. Early in the paper, he wrote [grammar and punctuation errors have not been corrected]:

> I got down to the rescue boat and found out that Natalie had been missing since 1:30 A.M.
>
> I got a hold of the local Sheriff's deputy and told him to call his station and get a shore line search started and send their helicopter over from the mainland, Deputy Kroll came onboard with me. When Robert Wagner was questioned by the deputy on why he had not called us sooner? He exclaimed that because we were a public agency he did not want to get in the news, and he thought she might just be on another boat meeting someone.

By the time Finstad got *Natasha* published in 2001, Smith's tale became even more sensational and exaggerated. Finstad quoted him saying that *he and Stonier* had located the dinghy. "We swam it out of the cove…and when we swam it out, all the oars were in disarray. Everything was in disarray, as if somebody had been trying to climb back into it." Finstad also reported Smith noticed "scratch marks" on the *Valiant*.

A few paragraphs later, Finstad described Smith's involvement like this:

> Bombard used his boat radio to alert Baywatch he thought he had spotted Natalie. Lifeguard Roger Smith immediately radioed back to the Isthmus Harbor Patrol to alert Bombard to locate her but not touch her "because we might be talking about a homicide."

Several pages later, Finstad wrote that Smith said:

> "The Sheriff's Department just sort of wanted the whole investigation to go away. It was so disheartening, so confusing. Nobody wanted to know the real facts…it's kind of like an O.J. thing: it's a celebrity, so, 'Oh well,' they don't investigate it. They never asked me one question."

Eight years later, when *Goodbye* was published, Smith's version—with Rulli's spin on things—became even more shocking:

> When Deputy Kroll asked Robert Wagner why he hadn't called the Coast Guard immediately, Wagner's answer astounded Roger Smith. "You're a public agency, and I didn't want this to become public," Wagner responded. "I have my image to think about. We thought she took off to go boat-hopping and was out screwing around because that's the kind of woman she is."

After Smith said he examined Natalie's body, he also told Rulli, "I could have saved her.

She did not have to die. I believe that minutes could have made the difference."

Finally, my intuition about Smith was solidified in 2018, during the podcast *Fatal Voyage: The Mysterious Death of Natalie Wood*, when he persisted with his fabrications on finding the dinghy "in a crevasse" and allegedly "taking off Natalie's jewelry."

To me, it was very plain. Smith was a publicity seeker and sensationalist who was prone to exaggeration. A sensible investigator or veteran prosecutor would never use a witness like Smith. In court, he would be cut to ribbons with his blown-up version of events and his changing tale about Robert Wagner's statements at the scene.

Furthermore, his alleged removal of Natalie's jacket, examination of her body, removal of her rings and flexing of her fingers were—to put it mildly—a poor exercise of judgment. Not even a skilled crime scene investigator would dare handle an unexplained death corpse in this manner. And, frankly, the fact that Smith, a lifeguard, found it necessary to lift Natalie's nightshirt to "examine" her naked body for "foul play" was beyond troubling.

Contrary to his claims in Finstad's book and the podcast, Smith didn't find the dinghy. Don Whiting and Bill Coleman did, according to their statements to investigators. Furthermore, if Smith took jewelry off Natalie's body, no one has ever confirmed it. Davern never acknowledged he received any jewelry from Smith. Kroll inventoried Natalie's jewelry and stated emphatically that no "personal effects" were removed. And Eaker reported she removed Natalie's jewelry at the Forensic Science Center where the autopsy was performed and logged it in the records with official documentation.

But I got an idea from Smith's tales. His partner John Claude Stonier had retired and moved to Kailua, Hawaii. In my opinion, Stonier had been conspicuously quiet over the years. Another red flag for me. It takes a strong will to stay out of the limelight in a case involving the unfathomable death of an internationally acclaimed movie star.

It took me more than three years to talk to Stonier. But luckily, my new assistant, Jade Vinson, and her husband, Matt, were going to Hawaii and staying at a friend's house on the same island as Stonier's residence.

It was Jade's first time to surprise a witness. She reported back that Stonier said, "the weather was bad," and the "wind was blowing through the Isthmus clear out there." Stonier admitted he and Smith did in fact remove Natalie's jacket. But, contrary to what Bombard told us, Stonier told Jade, "It was zipped up and the zipper was crossed at the top. We had a time getting it off to observe what was going on."

Moreover, Stonier told Jade when he and Smith pulled up to *Splendour* (around 5:30 a.m. Sunday), he saw Wagner and Walken. And contradicting Smith, Stonier said they "didn't talk to any of them [Wagner, Walken and Davern], just the sheriff's deputy for his report." He also didn't mention removing Natalie's jewelry and deflected most questions by saying, "It's in our report."

I had never seen a report from the Baywatch Isthmus lifeguards, but Stonier indicated it would have been prepared by Smith. However, with Smith's tendency to embellish, he and his report would be unreliable as far as I was concerned.

CHAPTER 11

coroner to the stars

WHEN SOMEONE DIES FROM UNEXPLAINED CAUSES, IT'S MOST OFTEN the medical examiner-coroner who determines the official cause and manner of death. In high-profile cases, it's a safe bet the coroner will be the person everyone looks to for the truth.

Dr. Thomas T. Noguchi is no doubt Hollywood's most controversial and famous former chief medical examiner-coroner. High-profile work on notable deaths made him an international celebrity. He and his department were instrumental in the final assessment of the manner of Natalie Wood's death as accidental. But to understand whether he participated in a cover-up, we need to know more about how he became to be called "Coroner to the Stars."

Dr. Noguchi was born in Japan in 1927. After the war, following in the footsteps of his father, Dr. Noguchi enrolled in Tokyo's Nippon Medical School. Motivated by an incident with his father being charged criminally in the death of a young patient, Dr. Noguchi also enrolled in law school. But, since details of Dr. Noguchi's school life are scarce, the extent of his legal education is unknown.

However, from *Coroner*, we know he graduated from medical school in 1951 and interned at Tokyo University Hospital. Claiming he applied to "two hundred American hospitals for an internship," Dr. Noguchi said he received one reply—from Orange County General Hospital in Santa Ana, California. Thereafter, he served a series of residences at Loma Linda University School of Medicine and Barlow Sanatorium in Los Angeles, eventually becoming board certified in both clinical and anatomic pathology.

We get a glimpse of Dr. Noguchi's personality from his memoir, when he said he came to the United States because he considered it to be the world leader in technology and he wanted to "break new barriers and super-achieve." Studying "clinical and anatomic pathology," he wrote his "love for scientific detective work" inspired him to become an authority in the field of forensic pathology. In 1960, his efforts ultimately resulted in a position with the Los Angeles County Department of Medical Examiner-Coroner as a deputy medical examiner.

Almost from its inception, the Los Angeles County Department of Coroner was tainted with controversy. In 1957, a year after California passed its first laws establishing a medical examiner's system, Dr. Theodore Curphey, the former Nassau County, New York, medical examiner, became Los Angeles County's first coroner. Within a year, he became embroiled in a dispute with local morticians over delays in issuing death certificates. Shortly thereafter, his autopsy procedures were investigated by a grand jury, which accused him of misconduct. However, the Los Angeles County Civil Service Commission rejected the claims and Dr. Curphey continued his service until his retirement in 1967.

Dr. Noguchi apparently impressed his boss so much that two years after his appointment, when iconic actress/sex symbol Marilyn Monroe was found dead in her home, Dr.

Noguchi was assigned the case. In his book, he said he was routinely given the "more difficult scientific cases" because he was a university faculty member and board certified.

After conducting Monroe's autopsy, Dr. Noguchi prepared a report, and the coroner's office released it to the press. Controversy over Dr. Noguchi's findings of "probable suicide" began almost instantly when salacious claims of murder captured the imagination of conspiracy theorists. At the same time, the uproar put the young deputy coroner in the media spotlight for the first time.

When Dr. Curphey retired five years later, the Los Angeles County Board of Supervisors narrowly elected Dr. Noguchi to succeed him. However, Dr. Noguchi entered the position without the backing of the County Medical Association and the UCLA and USC medical schools. One Los Angeles Times report indicated his detractors viewed Dr. Noguchi as "too young and too inexperienced." In spite of this, breaking a tie vote, Supervisor Ernest E. Debs supported Dr. Noguchi's appointment.

Shortly after his selection, Dr. Noguchi felt he needed additional funding for his office. At the time, the person to see for county funds was Chief Administrative Officer Lindon S. "L.S." Hollinger, a longtime county employee whose brother was the former county auditor-controller. L.S. wanted ultimate control over county operations and didn't appreciate anyone challenging his authority. So, Dr. Noguchi approached L.S. on additional funding, and the bureaucrat promptly turned him down. Undeterred, Dr. Noguchi went over his head to the Board of Supervisors, which ultimately granted his request.

As a result, Dr. Noguchi became embroiled in a heated political battle. Eventually, it became so intense that he resigned. Later, convinced he was the victim of anti-Japanese prejudice, Dr. Noguchi rescinded his resignation and hired prominent local attorney Godfrey Isaac to sue for reinstatement.

At the outset, the board suspended Dr. Noguchi and appointed an acting coroner, denying there was any racial motivation. The formal firing took place on March 18, 1969. According to the official record, the charges against Dr. Noguchi were that he took drugs, had symptoms suggesting he needed psychiatric care, engaged in inappropriate behavior with female subordinates, was a poor manager and bullied his employees. After the board voted to take his job, Dr. Noguchi's lawyer appealed to the Civil Service Commission and pushed for the hearings to be broadcast by radio and TV. The board reluctantly agreed, and the show was on.

The commission's testimony quickly turned ugly with claims that Dr. Noguchi made morbid statements in the office, including wishing Bobby Kennedy would die because it would elevate his reputation as a coroner and that he hoped a 727 airliner would crash into a hotel to bring more attention to the office.

To blunt Dr. Noguchi's claims of racism, the County Counsel claimed Dr. Noguchi overworked a black employee who later died. In fact, a Japanese secretary, one of the women with whom he allegedly acted inappropriately, testified that Dr. Noguchi told her "he hated all niggers, he hated all Japs and he hated all Jews." To top it off, Dr. Noguchi was depicted as a power-hungry megalomaniac, and there was testimony from a UCLA psychologist that Dr. Noguchi was a "manic-depressive."

After seven weeks of testimony and hearings, during which Dr. Noguchi didn't testify, the commission adjourned. While it deliberated, Dr. Noguchi's supporters took out a full-page ad in the Los Angeles Times entitled, "A Plea for Justice." It listed a series of injustices to Dr.

Noguchi and noted "never has the Japanese-American community been more aroused."

A month later, the commission restored Dr. Noguchi to his position as chief medical examiner in a terse, two-line press release.

                     ∽∽∽∽∽∽∽

After the battle was over and his job secure, Dr. Noguchi became an ambitious patholo-gist who cherished his reputation and cultivated it by performing autopsies on high-profile public figures followed by sensational news conferences.

His career also displayed a pattern of filing autopsy reports concluding the manner of death as either accidental or suicide, a practice that put the onus on decedents' families to overturn the coroner's findings if they didn't agree. Between 1969 and 1974, a plethora of celebrity deaths plagued Los Angeles County, thrusting the already well-known coroner into the national spotlight despite his often controversial findings.

It began in August 1969 with the grisly murder of Sharon Tate. The pregnant actress was butchered in her Beverly Hills home by the Charles Manson gang. In April 1970, popular Swedish-American actress Inger Stevens died of "acute barbiturate poisoning." Dr. Noguchi ruled it was a suicide amid a cloud of controversy. In October of that year, singer Janis Joplin died of an accidental heroin overdose. Then, in April 1972, beautiful Sicilian-American actress Gia Scala was found on her bed, naked, bruised and lying on a blood-stained pillow. While the evidence suggested murder, Dr. Noguchi ruled her manner of death was a result of an accidental "acute ethanol and barbiturate intoxication." This is despite the fact that only three valium (which is a benzodiazepine, not a barbiturate) were discovered missing from a prescription bottle in her house and that very day she called police to evict some men from her home, one of whom returned that evening and claimed he found Gia's lifeless body.

While family and friends of some of the deceased were unhappy, in the general public's eyes, Dr. Noguchi's approval rating climbed as he became a prominent national figure. But in May 1974, that began to change when SWAT teams from the Los Angeles Police Department surrounded a one-story stucco house in south Los Angeles containing a radical group called the Symbionese Liberation Army (SLA).

The SLA was well-armed and violent, partially financing its activities with bank robber-ies and kidnappings. Donald DeFreeze, a fugitive from justice, was its leader. The group's highest-profile kidnapping was Patricia Campbell Hearst, the 22-year-old granddaughter of wealthy newspaper publisher William Randolph Hearst. Enormous pressure was placed on law enforcement to find her.

Then, in one of the more bizarre events in American criminal law enforcement history, Patty Hearst, the victim, joined the SLA and became a gun-toting criminal and bank rob-ber. Intrigued beyond description, America watched and listened as Hearst and the gang became some of the most hunted criminals in U.S. history.

After attempts to negotiate a surrender, police lobbed tear gas into the house, with the fierce gun battle that followed captured live on national TV. As bullets from police officers' automatic weapons riddled the little house, it suddenly burst into flames. Everyone inside was killed.

Dr. Noguchi was called in to identify the victims. When the examinations were finished,

Dr. Noguchi called the influential grandparents personally to tell them Patty had been spared.

However, when Dr. Noguchi called his standard, high-profile press conference, he declared that based largely upon past "psychological autopsies," he believed DeFreeze was suicidal and shot himself during the firefight. How he died was important to people in the African American community who claimed the police killed DeFreeze unnecessarily.

Dr. Noguchi had just formulated a new method of electron microscopy that analyzed trace metals left by bullets in bodies and had assigned his experienced staff to determine how the charred victims died. But the lab work was incomplete.

When the final analysis was ready, it was determined DeFreeze had been shot by the police department. Nevertheless, Dr. Noguchi refused to correct the death certificate, stating the cause of death was "suicide, homicide/undetermined." When asked why, Dr. Noguchi said it wasn't "absolutely wrong" and he was "very reluctant" to inform relatives about such a "minor" change.

While there were citizens in Los Angeles who were disgruntled over how their chief coroner spent his time outside his jurisdiction, national law enforcement, the pathology profession and Hollywood were fascinated by the high-profile coroner. In 1977, Dr. Noguchi traveled to Fargo, North Dakota, to testify for the federal government in the sensational Wounded Knee trial of Leonard Peltier. Peltier, a native American Indian, was charged with the shoot-out deaths of two FBI agents at the Pine Ridge Indian Reservation in South Dakota. Dr. Noguchi's appearance was rare for a full-time chief medical examiner who had his hands full in his own jurisdiction.

By this time, Dr. Noguchi had also made his entrée into the entertainment business. Reputed to be the inspiration for the hit TV series *Quincy, M.E.*, about an outspoken and brilliant crime-solving medical examiner, Dr. Noguchi lent his facilities and staff to the production company. In 1978, he played himself in the mondo horror film *Faces of Death* and later appeared in the documentary *The Killing of America*. Now, he really was the star pathologist for the city of stars. As far as Dr. Noguchi was concerned, things had never looked better for the LA County coroner's office and his career.

In 1977, Dr. Noguchi signed the incorporation papers for his personal consulting business: Los Angeles Institute of Forensic Sciences. His county secretary, on official stationary, wrote to the district attorney of Storey County, Nevada, to request $6,000 (about $25,000 today), a suite of first-class hotel rooms with color televisions, meals paid in advance, and limousine service for Dr. Noguchi's testimony in the murder case of Argentine heavyweight boxer Oscar Natalio "Ringo" Bonavena. The secretary said she was writing at the direction of a "publicist" hired by Dr. Noguchi's private institute. To use a county employee and official county stationary to conduct personal business is highly irregular by any professional standards. Yet apparently nothing was said.

∽∾∽∾∽∾∽∾

An example of Dr. Noguchi's creative conclusions is found in the case of Patricia Morris. She was the wife of an African American man who was killed in June 1980 during a struggle with officers of the Los Angeles Police Department. LAPD race relations were beginning to heat up by that time, and Mr. Morris' death stirred up his community. If the police were judged responsible for his death, it could ignite a political wildfire. After finally issuing his autopsy report on August 12, 1980—two months after the autopsy—Dr. Noguchi concluded the man's death was the result of a "cardiac arrest during a physical altercation due to or as a consequence of arteriosclerotic heart disease and blunt force injuries to the neck and soft tissues." Unsatisfied with that result, concerned citizens pressured Dr. Noguchi into conducting a coroner's inquest in the case.

A coroner's inquest in California is very similar to a grand jury investigation. It's presided over by the coroner, one of his deputies or a hearing officer selected by the coroner. The inquiry can take place in front of the coroner or an inquest jury, consisting of not less than nine nor more than 15 qualified county citizens. The jury's job is to pass judgment on the cause and manner of death.

Witnesses who had "any knowledge of the facts" could be subpoenaed to testify under oath in a public proceeding. Records, including phone records, could be subpoenaed and outside experts called to express their opinions. An inquest jury would also have been allowed to accompany the coroner to examine the body if necessary. And, under the law, the county sheriff or district attorney had the authority to request an inquest.

After hearing testimony and examining all relevant records, the inquest jury or coroner would have been required to render a verdict setting forth, among other things, the medical cause of death and whether the death was by "(1) natural causes, (2) suicide, (3) accident, or (4) the hands of another person other than by accident." If the findings were that the deceased met his or her death at the hands of another, the coroner was required to transmit the findings to the district attorney and police agency where the body was recovered.

In the Morris case, the inquest lasted two days, and the jury found that Mr. Morris was strangled to death. Despite the outcome, Dr. Noguchi signed Mr. Morris' death certificate two weeks later and certified his death was by cardiac arrest as he had originally reported. Patricia Morris appealed, seeking an order of the Superior Court compelling Dr. Noguchi to change the manner of death conclusion in her husband's death certificate from "accident" to death by "strangulation...at the hands of another person, other than by accident." The courts ultimately sided with Dr. Noguchi, citing his sole legal discretion to state the cause and manner of death.

The Morris case file leaves little doubt Dr. Noguchi succumbed to police pressure and authored a report and death certificate he knew contained half-truths. The forensic cause of Mr. Morris' death may have been cardiac arrest, but the cardiac arrest was caused by someone strangling him. "Strangling" became the manner of death. As a result of the courts' rulings, Dr. Noguchi now appeared beyond reproach.

By 1981, the ego-driven Dr. Noguchi had clearly established himself as a celebrity. Like Quincy, the TV character he inspired, Noguchi considered himself a brilliant forensic detective who used clues he uncovered in his investigations to solve mysterious deaths. The November 1981 death of William Holden, a respected movie star and on-again, off-again boyfriend of Stefanie Powers, was yet another opportunity for him to bask in the limelight.

In his memoir, Dr. Noguchi wrote, "It was my job, as mandated by law, to establish the 'manner, cause and circumstance' of death and to report it to the press and the public." There again, what Dr. Noguchi wrote was only partially true. Establishing the manner, cause and circumstance of death was indeed mandated by law. But, reporting his findings to "the press and the public" was certainly not legally mandated. It was merely part of Dr.

Noguchi's showboating persona.

Holden had been dead at least four days when he was found on the bedroom floor of his Malibu apartment with a 2-1/2-inch gash in his forehead. After visiting the scene and receiving a toxicology report showing Holden had a blood alcohol level of 0.22 percent, Dr. Noguchi concluded Holden was drunk when he fell, struck his head on a table and bled to death.

When Dr. Noguchi held his news conference and announced the gruesome ending to Holden's life, newspaper coverage of his statements began what Noguchi described in *Coroner* as "a professional crisis." Holden's friends—and Hollywood in general—were inflamed by the invasion of privacy, and the chief of the LAPD was openly critical of two *Los Angeles Times* articles that "characterized the deceased as a drunken recluse."

Then, 13 days after Holden was found dead, Natalie Wood's lifeless body was recovered off Catalina Island. Dr. Noguchi, who clearly relished the spotlight, held a press conference within hours of the autopsy. He described the November 30, 1981, event this way in *Coroner*:

> I've attended many dramatic news conferences after the deaths of world famous motion picture stars, but none so tense as the one following Natalie Wood's death. Rumors of foul play, as well as sexual scandal, were rocketing through the movie colony. And, it was my responsibility to produce the facts that would rebut or substantiate those rumors.

It's the professional responsibility of a coroner to ascertain the cause and manner of death, not to "rebut or substantiate" rumors. The facts should be enough, if reported accurately, to take care of any assumptions or theories made by interested parties. Moreover, what Dr. Noguchi said at the press conference and subsequent interviews deviated from his own book account.

These contradictions and misrepresentations support his past pattern of "creative forensic reporting"—manufacturing facts to fit his own agenda. Did his desire to be perceived as the authority in celebrity deaths prompt him to draw premature conclusions in Natalie's case? He loved the spotlight and sensationalized the circumstances of high-profile deaths in his jurisdiction. Was his claim that alcohol played a "significant role" in Natalie's death sensational enough to distract from unexplained injuries that were consistent with her being involved in a physical fight? Dr. Noguchi was still facing backlash for releasing "the last gory detail" of Holden's demise. Was his conclusion that "there was no evidence of foul play" in Natalie's case a maneuver to keep criticism from Hollywood at bay?

Despite his efforts to protect his job, the inflammatory details that Dr. Noguchi revealed about Natalie's death made him the target of Sinatra, the Screen Actors Guild and the Los Angeles County Board of Supervisors for, among other things, unduly sensationalizing celebrity deaths.

On the heels of Dr. Noguchi's conclusion that Natalie's death was accidental, a quote from the *Los Angeles Times* on December 28, 1981, was most telling:

> When Natalie Wood died…Noguchi was widely—though quietly—criticized by criminologists and some of his own staff who wondered how, given the evidence available to him, he had pieced together so graphi-

cally the details of the actress's last moments at Catalina Island.

To my knowledge, this was the first and only time there had been a public expression of doubt from within the coroner's office about Noguchi's conclusions in Natalie's case.

∿∿∿∿∿∿

After Natalie's death, Dr. Noguchi was interviewed by writer Douglas Stein over four successive evenings in Noguchi's comfortable Pasadena home. The ensuing article appeared in the November 1986 issue of *Omni* magazine. Stein's introduction called the 59-year-old pathologist a "renowned medical detective and forensic scientist." He went on to state that Dr. Noguchi was among the first big-city medical examiners to put together a staff of specially trained crime scene experts and that LA's Forensic Science Center employed state-of-the-art autopsy facilities and drug-testing, ballistics and "tissue-evaluation equipment."

Dr. Noguchi told Stein, "the medical examiner begins by visiting the crime or death scene to see for himself the circumstances surrounding the incident." However, there was nothing in the official autopsy report for Natalie Wood Wagner to indicate Dr. Noguchi, or the other pathologists on Natalie's case for that matter, visited the spot where Natalie's body was found or where the yacht *Splendour* was moored the night of her death.

Dr. Noguchi made it plain for Stein that "most crimes are still committed by a person known to have something to gain by the killing. From motive comes lead." This idea is as basic to homicide investigations as conducting a forensic autopsy. But in Natalie's case, there was nothing to suggest the LASD investigators or Dr. Noguchi's office attempted to determine motive evidence.

This was contrary to an elementary principle of forensic autopsy investigations as stated by Dr. Noguchi in *Coroner*: "In any case of unusual death, it is the first duty of medical examiners to suspect murder." In 2016, that principle was confirmed for me by Dr. Noguchi in a sworn deposition. Given this basic principle in unexplained death investigations, it is open to suspicion that "murder" had never been officially investigated in Natalie's case.

With Stein, Dr. Noguchi also claimed he had a fascination and expertise with wound "cause-and-effect relationships." What caused a bruise and how long it had been in existence "help identify the assailant," he said.

As for bruises themselves, Dr. Noguchi emphasized, "A bruise with scratches or abrasions not only yields an impression of the object, but also gives the direction and force of the application" and "bruises have a whole spectrum of color changes."

According to Dr. Noguchi, he and his staff could define the bruise color changes in terms of hours by using the Forensic Science Center's new sophisticated electron microscope to target certain chemicals and enzymes. The Scanning Electron Microscope, or SEM, was so powerful it could analyze wound debris invisible to the human eye. If this equipment were used in Natalie's case, the abraded skin tissue on the left side of Natalie's cheek and forehead could have easily been examined to determine the presence of any substances, like rubber, dirt or foreign skin tissue, and the precise "direction" and "application" of the wound.

Yet, there was nothing in Natalie's case to indicate this was done.

The official autopsy report in Natalie's case only said: "The abrasions over the left cheek area appear to be superficial and fresh. These abrasions are *brush type abrasions* [emphasis added] on the vertical dimension." While patently incomplete, this does tell us the abrasion was observed close enough to tell it was a scraping injury, as opposed to an "impact abrasion" or a "patterned abrasion." And the abrasion was "on the vertical dimension" (up and down) suggesting it was linear in nature.

Moreover, the Forensic Science Center owned another sophisticated microscope—Transmission Electron Microscopy, or TEM—that could project images of tissue cross sections to visualize cell damage up to powers of a half-million. With this microscope, tissue cross sections of any bruise, contusion or abrasion could be examined to determine the depth of the injury, indicative not only of its age, but the amount of force it took to make it. The 1981 autopsy report in Natalie's case stated that cross sections of some of the larger bruises—the bruises on her right forearm, right ankle and left knee—were, in fact, taken. But the results of any examination were not mentioned in the autopsy report. Instead, under the heading "Musculoskeletal System," the autopsy report said: "There are numerous small, superficial skin bruises over the legs but there are no deep contusions noted on the sections."

Another half-truth. The larger, fresh bruises were essentially ignored by Dr. Noguchi and his deputy pathologists in the official autopsy report.

Furthermore, none of the bruises had been examined for color changes that would help pinpoint whether they occurred within a matter of hours, a procedure within Dr. Noguchi's expertise and custom. The report used the word "superficial" eight times to describe the bruises. And the pathologists concluded their report with, "The autopsy findings are consistent with drowning in the ocean. The time of death is difficult to pinpoint, but it appears to be about midnight of November 28, 1981. *Most of the bruises on the body are superficial and probably sustained at the time of drowning* [emphasis added]."

The intentional use of the word "superficial" suggested to the outside world that the bruises were minor when, in fact, certain strategically placed bruises were clearly not and could have been caused by a physical struggle *before* Natalie went into the water.

〜〜〜〜〜〜

Dr. Joseph Choi was a Korean-educated pathologist who attended medical school at Chonnam in Gwangju, Korea. Between 1970 and 1982, he worked homicide cases for the LA County coroner's office and was also on the USC medical staff, teaching pathology as a medical school associate professor. As one of Dr. Noguchi's deputies and a forensic pathologist, he was responsible for determining cause and manner of death, natural or violent. That is, his job was to study and perform autopsies of decedents to compile the necessary anatomical and physical findings to arrive at the cause and manner of death.

Dr. Choi, not Dr. Noguchi, examined bruise tissue cross sections under a microscope. The injuries on Natalie's left knee and right ankle were assessed by Dr. Choi as fresh, deep or "subcutaneous" hemorrhages. Yet the official microscopic report signed by him noted, "All the skin taken from the various [sections] show marked subcutaneous fresh hemorrhage which is consistent with *fresh bruise of superficial nature* [emphasis added]." The conflict between the terms "subcutaneous" and "superficial" was obvious. Wounds can't be both. Yet they were described as "superficial bruises." Significantly, Dr. Choi's microscopic report wasn't issued until March 17, 1982—*nearly four months after Natalie's death was ruled as accidental.*

Why was this information withheld and not included as an addendum to the official report? I believe the omission was intentional since the nature of the wounds could be linked to some level of physical violence, rather than an accidental fall into the water.

✤✤✤✤✤✤✤

Dr. Noguchi didn't mention scratches on Natalie's body in the official autopsy report either. During autopsies in 1981, a technician would usually prepare contemporaneous notes on body diagrams while the pathologist examined the body and called out his observations. In Natalie's case, Dr. Choi prepared the forms himself. Those diagrams, which are vitally important in documenting evidence for future use in court, depositions or official inquires, made two references to scratches. One was on Natalie's right calf on the posterior diagram. It read "deep scratches." The other was in the middle of Natalie's throat. It said "scratch" in Dr. Choi's very small handwriting.

During Dr. Choi's 12 years with the LA County coroner's office, he developed a specialty in strangulation cases, authoring medical-legal articles on the subject. Another deputy coroner in the office who assisted with Natalie's autopsy, Dr. Kornblum, was a nationwide expert in choke-hold deaths, testifying in law enforcement excessive force cases. After handling 112 strangulation autopsy cases, Dr. Choi and another colleague, in cooperation with the USC Medical School, published a paper in the 1985 *Annals of Otology, Rhinology & Laryngology* under the title "Strangulation." The first page of the article stated, "Abrasions or fingernail scratches may be present in the throttling victim from the assailant's or the struggling victim's hands." Those abrasions or scratches can happen when an assailant grabs the victim by the throat with the assailant's thumb in the center of the trachea causing "fingertip marks" or "fingernail scratches."

After completely reading Dr. Choi's study, I came away convinced the scratch on Natalie's throat was caused by a fingernail or thumbnail. However, no effort was made forensically to determine the cause of that scratch. Although the Forensic Science Lab had the equipment to do so, Dr. Choi didn't analyze microscopically the skin tissue at the site of the scratch on Natalie's throat or the bruises on the back of her right hand to see if they were caused by a thumbnail or fingernail. If he had, the findings could have yielded evidence about the hand that caused the injuries, i.e., whether it was a right or left hand and the size of the thumb or finger.

One way to determine if Natalie scratched her own throat or if she scratched someone during a struggle was to take samples from under her fingernails. But we know from the autopsy report that Natalie's fingernails weren't clipped or scraped to determine the presence of someone else's blood or skin or other foreign material. Neither was there a mention of checking Natalie's nails for cracks or breaks.

These omissions are exacerbated by the fact that not one, *but two*, experts in the field of strangulation and choke-hold deaths participated in Natalie's autopsy. It simply couldn't have been an oversight. They failed to microscopically analyze the throat scratch or *were told not to perform the test*. The proof of that is in the "External Description" section of Natalie's autopsy report. The throat scratch isn't mentioned, even though it appears on the body diagram.

This revelation is even more damning when we consider that Miller told Dr. Noguchi he saw markings that could be fingernail scratches on the Zodiac dinghy's side. If the marks were deep enough to be noticeable as fingernail scratches, then the likelihood is rubber particles would have been found under Natalie's nails. If rubber particles were present, it would establish three things. First, it would prove Natalie was conscious and alive in the water next to the Zodiac. Second, it would show Natalie was trying to board the Zodiac but was so low in the water she was incapable of reaching over its pontoon. Finally, if she did not have the strength to haul herself into the Zodiac, it would indicate she was, for a period of time, capable of screaming for help, which supports the statements of Wayne and Payne that they heard someone in the water near *Splendour* the night Natalie died.

◠◟◠◟◠◜◠◜◠

One of the principal indications of strangulation is the presence of petechial hemorrhage in the victim. A petechia is the pinpoint bursting of blood capillaries after blocking off blood flow, leaving a small red spot in or near the eyes, face or heart. During her autopsy, Natalie's eyes, face and heart were checked for the presence of petechial hemorrhage. According to the official report, all were negative. At the same time, the pathologists did find evidence of petechial hemorrhage on the face of Natalie's lungs.

Petechial hemorrhage, including spots on the lungs, was first recognized by pathologists over 150 years ago in suffocation deaths. Since then, researchers have concluded that a violent struggle can increase cardiac output and raise blood pressure, thereby enhancing the occurrence of petechiae on the lungs, heart and other body parts. Based on my discussions with Dr. Stanley, it's uncommon to find petechial hemorrhage in ordinary drowning deaths. But Natalie had petechial hemorrhage on her lungs. And the pathologists in Natalie's case offered no explanation for their presence.

While we know Natalie wasn't strangled to death, there was now classic forensic evidence to corroborate Davern's claim that Natalie was involved in a screaming, cussing argument, which caused the petechial hemorrhage on her lungs.

◠◟◠◟◠◜◠◜◠

Dr. Noguchi's public deception about Natalie's death was not finished with his news conference and official autopsy report. On August 29, 1988, seven years after her death, he was invited to be a guest on *The Late Show* with Ross Shafer. On that program, Dr. Noguchi told millions of viewers, in response to an insightful question by Shafer, that Natalie "had bruises on the inside of the arms which the *pattern matches with protruding objects* [emphasis added] on the dinghy."

Undoubtably, Dr. Noguchi was of the opinion that petite Natalie, who couldn't swim, was able to reach over the side of the rubber dinghy from the water with such force that she caused a contusion—through her down jacket—that stretched nearly halfway down her right forearm.

In *Coroner*, Dr. Noguchi said the rubber sides of the dinghy "were large and cylindrical" and it would have been difficult "under the best of circumstances" for her "to reach over them from the water to hoist herself up."

In Natalie's autopsy report, the three pathologists, with Dr. Noguchi at the helm, signed an autopsy report saying they found "no pattern to the bruises" to connect them to the dinghy or anything else. There was also nothing in the autopsy report stating they compared the bruise on Natalie's right forearm with any objects protruding from the "large and cylindrical" sides of the dinghy to see if "the pattern matches."

This information, coupled with the prime location of the forearm contusion where defensive assault wounds often occur, opened my eyes to the truth. I knew from my visit with Dr. Stanley that, in her opinion, the bruise to Natalie's right forearm was sustained *before* she went into the water. Now, I knew why Dr. Choi's complete microscopic information was not mentioned in the official narrative. It was intentionally omitted. Covered up. Buried forever.

From all appearances, Dr. Noguchi omitted vital findings and intentionally manipulated facts in Natalie's case to make them consistent with his self-preserving conclusions. He failed to perform routine inspections and omitted important details during the autopsy when he found doing so to be expedient. And he officially reported what he knew was necessary to quickly close Natalie's case as an accident and intentionally ignored leads and evidence pointing to something much more politically risky for him—a potential murder.

CHAPTER 12

overboard

I WAS LOOKING FOR A FIT MAN AROUND 80 WITH A FULL HEAD OF WHITE hair and a thick white mustache to match. A man whose face showed the creases and lines of a senior sailor. I had what I knew to be a good address for the Marina del Rey-based California Sailing Academy, Paul James Miller's mainstay for at least 50 years. Miller, a retired Naval Academy officer who graduated at the top of his class, was the sailing academy's director.

It was around 2 p.m. on a Tuesday in February 2016 when my driver and I arrived at the marina. The parking lot was empty. But the warm sun caused me to forget it was winter and the Pacific Ocean a little cold for sailors heading out to sea. Despite the lack of cars, I was not about to leave without trying.

We had called the academy's phone number, but several messages left by my assistant, as a "prospective student," went unreturned.

I knew Miller had been in town on January 24, 2012, from my copy of the Supplemental Report the Los Angeles County coroner's office issued May 20, 2012. Miller had attended a meeting with Dr. L, Dr. Noguchi, Detective Hernandez and others.

Miller's report for Dr. Noguchi in Natalie's case seemed the topic of conversation during the January 2012 meeting, given that it had been retrieved from the coroner's microfilm archives and distributed to Miller and the investigators for discussion. In *Coroner*, Dr. Noguchi said while Eaker was on the island "interrogating" people, he was "telephoning Paul Miller" for a "special investigation" of the Wagners' yacht and its dinghy. Dr. Noguchi claimed he initially made contact with Miller because of the "numerous" drowning fatalities in Los Angeles County and Dr. Noguchi's desire to "learn more about the factors which contribute to underwater accidents."

Dr. Noguchi also said Miller was "a deputy on the staff of the Los Angeles County Medical Examiner's Office" in addition to being Noguchi's sailing instructor.

During my legal battle with the coroner's office over records, the coroner's lawyers—even though admitting it in official pleadings—later disputed Miller's position as a deputy "on staff" since he was "an unpaid volunteer," according to Dr. Noguchi's sworn testimony in my case. That was further confirmation in my mind that Dr. Noguchi's chapter on Natalie's death was a sham.

In 1983, Dr. Noguchi described Miller as "a man who knew intimately the dangerous waters around Catalina Island." As it turned out, Miller claimed he was in Isthmus Cove on Saturday, November 28, 1981, in his 40-foot cutter, *Easy Rider*, and even dined at Doug's on Saturday night. Dr. Noguchi claimed in *Coroner* that Miller was "moored to the same buoy in front of the Wagners' yacht the night of the tragedy" and it was Miller who "first responded to Wagner's call for assistance."

Because of Miller's experience and presence on the scene Saturday night, November 28, Dr. Noguchi called him a "perfectly positioned expert." But there was no record of this perfectly positioned expert having been interviewed by the LASD investigators in 1981.

Dr. Noguchi's memoir was apparently the first time anyone outside of the coroner's staff knew about Miller and his work. And, when the meeting with Dr. L took place in 2012, over two months after Natalie's case was reopened, the new detectives still had not read Dr. Noguchi's book. "During the interview with the former Chief Medical Examiner-Coroner Dr. Noguchi, they [the LASD detectives] were made aware of a consultation report by one Mr. Paul Miller," Dr. L wrote in his Supplemental Report.

Miller's report had remained buried in the coroner's archives for 35 years. Now, I wanted to look Miller in the eye to confirm or dispute Dr. Noguchi's secondhand claims, hoping to finally reveal the truth about what Miller saw and reported.

I approached a poorly maintained two-story building and could see evidence of the California Sailing Academy's second-floor office, including signs and various sailing paraphernalia hanging in the windows.

Looping around the building, I was stunned to find there were no steps to the second floor. The stairwell was there, but the staircase had been removed. I looked for an elevator but found nothing. There was simply no way to get from the ground-floor parking lot to the second floor.

From what I could see, Miller's office looked eerily abandoned except for the name on the door and yellowed signs in the windows. There was no one around. So I started looking for life on the first floor. Nothing.

Puzzled, I went back to the drawing board on Miller and turned up a Paul Miller of the correct age in Portland, Oregon. A *National Enquirer* reporter had told me he talked to Miller just a few months earlier.

When we called the Paul Miller in Oregon, the person who answered denied being the former sailing instructor. Because we could find no obituary for Miller, if the Portland Paul Miller was telling the truth, it looked like our Paul Miller had disappeared.

Could he have known I was on his trail? Things were heating up again with my lawsuit and the *National Enquirer* carried two articles about my first case, mentioning that Miller's report was one of the documents I was seeking. I had my suspicions about his absence since one of the articles said I was looking for him with a subpoena.

In June 2016, I took the sworn deposition of Dr. Noguchi in my public records act lawsuit. Here is our exchange about Miller:

S.P.: Now, do you know Paul Miller?

Noguchi: I know him, yes.

S.P.: How long have you known Paul Miller?

Noguchi: On and off for many years.

S.P.: Do you know where he is?

Noguchi: No.

S.P.: Is he still alive?

Noguchi: Don't know.

∽∽∽∽∽∽∽∽∽

Over the years, we've tried every way we know to track down the elusive Paul Miller without success.

Nevertheless, as a result of my lawsuit, I came to know what he reported to Dr. Noguchi about his examination of *Splendour* and the Zodiac dinghy during the time it was sequestered in Catalina Island by the LASD. I considered lifting those portions I thought were relevant for you. But, in the interest of full disclosure, I decided in favor of revealing, for the first time, the full Miller report. (See *Figures 21, 22* and *23* on next three pages.)

Four photographs Miller included in his report were taken by a Polaroid camera, which used self-developing film to create instant prints. A big drawback that didn't become known until later was that the chemicals used to create the prints allowed the pictures to eventually fade away.

So, Miller's pictures were gone. More evidence lost due to the passage of time. However, the faded pictures can be reconstructed somewhat from the references to them in the narrative portion of the report. The first print was of *Splendour's* swim step, the second was its aft (stern) deck and the master stateroom French doors, the third was also of the stern deck, and the final print was of the dinghy's painter line.

What can you take away from Miller's January 28, 1982, report that casts light on the circumstances surrounding Natalie's death and Dr. Noguchi's intentions in 1981?

To start with, the report was prepared *two months* after Natalie's death. *Why?* That was one of the questions I had for Miller.

Next, according to Miller's diagram of the mooring sites in Isthmus Cove (see *Figure 24*, Page 106) and the actual mooring site rows, his vessel, *Easy Rider*, was moored at site J-1, *five* rows up from *Splendour*. It was not moored at "the same buoy in front of the Wagners' yacht," as Dr. Noguchi claimed in *Coroner*. The location of Miller's boat is important in judging his ability to see and hear sounds. His actual location, according to my personal measurements, research and observation, put Miller's vessel about 300 to 400 feet away from the Wagners' yacht.

Thereafter, Miller reported that at "1:50 a.m." Sunday, November 29, he made a radio call to Baywatch "to get some relief" from very loud music blasting from a house on the beach. In *Coroner*, Dr. Noguchi suspiciously, in my opinion, placed the time at "1:15 a.m."

Miller was not able to reach anyone on Channel 16, the marine VHF radio international distress frequency, but he reported that "someone" from *Splendour* "came on to the net and asked for a radio check." A radio check is a simple way to verify that a boat's VHF radio is operating properly. The boater tunes his radio to the proper frequency and then speaks into the microphone to request a radio check. Any boater within broadcast range who hears the request can reply.

At that point, according to Miller, *Splendour* asked if he was "cruising in the local area." *Cruising the area at 1:50 a.m.?* Of course, Miller gave a negative reply. But there was someone cruising in the area—William Peterson, the only shore boat operator on duty. *Splendour's* response to Miller was they "might have someone missing in an 11 foot Avon inflatable boat." Miller reportedly advised them that if they did, they should "call the Coast Guard." Miller said there was no response and, even though Dr. Noguchi claimed Miller was "a friend of the Wagners," Miller did not mention in his report that he recognized the voice.

[handwritten notes at top: Now 1 deceased / Natalie Wood Wagner / Case No 81-15167 / Report made 1-28-82]

follow-up Investigation

January 28, 1982   Dictation from Paul Miller
2:00 p.m.

(undersigned)

I was in the harbor immediately in front of the Splendor the
evening of the incident.   About 1:50 a.m. I had made a radio call to the
beach to get some relief of a problem -- a party on the beach had loud (very)
speakers on their front porch -- I wanted those turned down. I was not able
to reach anyone on Bay Watch on VFH radio, Channel 16. Someone on the
Splendor came on to the net and asked for a radio check. I replied and said
they were loud and clear. They then asked if I was cruising in the local area.
I replied, "No." They then said they might have someone missing in an
11 foot Avon inflatable boat. I stated that if they did, they should call the
Coast Guard. There was no response.
        During the day I had seen Natalie Wood driving the same small,
inflatable boat (Valiant) earlier -- she was alone.
        The following is the investigation, *with conducted* I did on the Splendor:
        I examined the vessel in front of the Harbor Patrol office. First
I examined the inflatable boat (Valiant) she had been in. I noticed multiple
scratches along the starboard side along the water line of the boat(which could
be Miss Wood attempting to get back into the boat) The swim step on the back of
the big boat (Splendor) -- see photo A -- measures 32 inches wide, and runs along
the entire beam of the vessel; it is 11 inches out of the water. There was a
rubrail (rubber) which runs entirely around the swim step. Between the rubber
rub rail and the rubber boat tied up, there would not be any noise of the small
boat banging against the back of the large boat during the night. There were
metal arms supporting the swim step on the back of the vessel covered with
barnacles and moss. There would be no indication that she was hanging on to the metal
arm unless there are multiple scratches on her hands. With the cut out sections
of the surface of the swim step, most people (unintoxicated) should be able to
climb back aboard. There were lines hanging from the inflatable boat (Valiant)

Figure 21: Page 1 of Paul Miller's report prepared for Dr. Noguchi (Los Angeles County Department of Medical Examiner-Coroner)

Page 2

which were within 9 inches of the water. Again, most unintoxicated people could
have been able to pull themselves up. However, since I have an identical
inflatable boat, I have personally seen as many as 3 unintoxicated women who
were unable to climb aboard this same identical type of inflatable boat.
(must paddle like crazy!)

My speculation is that due to the layout of the vessel (Splendor) which
has a main salon sitting area in the forward middle of the boat, the small
cabin which Natalie probably occupied 18 feet aft with a door in between,
another door from that small cabin onto the fishing deck all the way aft
(shown in Photo C), she must have exited from the after cabin aft door onto the
fishing deck (Photo C) then through the transom door, also shown in Photo C,
which was probably open, and then stepped onto the swim step to take a midnight
ride.

Due to the position of the ring in Photo C, used for tying up the rubber
boat (Valiant), she undoubtedly did untie the Valiant before attempting to
step into the boat. Untied, the boat probably drifted away and in attempting to step
between the swim step on the large boat to the Valiant, she missed.

The distance from the ring to the edge of the swim step was 66 inches.
The length of the painter or tie up line on the Valiant was 12 feet. This is
the reason she had to untie the line before getting into the Valiant. From the
point where she was in the water behind the Splendor, she would then be
30 feet from the area where the men were sitting. It had been raining and was
windy; the cabin windows were probably closed, along with the door into her
cabin. It is very likely that the men could not hear her scream. At times when
a person falls into very cold water, they are unable to scream due to the
coldness (Note: Mr. Miller has experienced this personally).

I figure she probably hung onto the bow line or painter of the dinghy
(Valiant) as shown in phto D, as it drifted across the bay in an easterly direction.

Figure 22: Page 2 of Paul Miller's report (Los Angeles County Department of Medical Examiner-Coroner)

Page 3.

In that she was wearing a down jacket, which was still on at the time of recovery of the body), her body weight would be increased by the wet down jacket.considerably. The down jacket probably contributed to her failure to get out of the water. The natural tendency is not to remove a jacket because of the coldness of the water.

Due to wind in that area and a tendency of the Valiant to be blown out toward the sea, and the more southerly drift of her body due to the current, after six hours the Valiant and the body would generally be found widely separated. The Valiant is like a balloon and would be blown by the wind, whereas her body would be more like a watermelon and would be carried by the current, each of which go in different directions in that area.

I feel that very likely she hung to the painter and tried to claw her way aboard the Valiant and possibly paddled with the boat toward the beach(where it was found) until she succumbed from hypothermia.

(1) My suggestions would be to check with Catalina Island Bay Watch for the water temperature at that time. Also then check the hypothermia tables to obtain how long she could have survived. I would also suggest that your office ask for (2) a transcript of the radio communications between the Splendor and the U.S. Coast Guard that evening between 0200 and 0500 a.m. I would be glad to examine the dialogue from a mariner's point of view. I suggest this merely to round out the investigation, and know that they do have complete transcript and tapes of these at the Coast Guard office, obtainable through the Coast Guard Commander at Long Beach, California.

Figure 23: Page 3 of Paul Miller's report (Los Angeles County Department of Medical Examiner-Coroner)

Nevertheless, Dr. Noguchi wrote this in *Coroner*:

> Suddenly the radio sprang to life with a different voice. *It was Robert Wagner* [emphasis added], although Miller didn't recognize his voice at first. He didn't sound nervous or excited. Miller described Wagner's tone as "quizzical" as he said, "*Easy Rider*, are you cruising in the vicinity?"

Based on Miller's written report, it seems clear that Dr. Noguchi fabricated this part of his book. Furthermore, since Walken knew nothing about radio checks, the call had to have been made by Wagner or Davern. However, the evidence clearly points to Davern, *not* Wagner, who made this particular call. As you learned from Wintler, Wagner wasn't on *Splendour* at 1:50 a.m. He and Wintler were searching the mooring rows for Natalie and the dinghy at the time. And, I believe Davern had a motive for calling when he did. Wagner was off the yacht and Davern was scared. He reached out for assistance without Wagner's authorization. And when Miller mentioned calling the Coast Guard, Davern ended the conversation.

Where Miller got the "11 foot Avon" boat is anyone's guess. Perhaps he confused the Wagners' dinghy with one of the many Avon inflatable boats in the cove that weekend. Or, there's another reasonable explanation. The call from *Splendour* was made by the person who dropped off Wagner at the pier in an Avon dinghy. But it is certainly another mystery

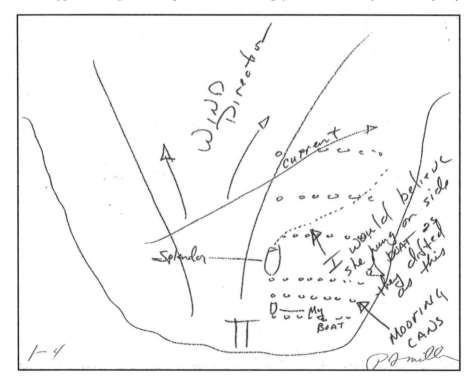

Figure 24: Paul Miller's sketch of mooring sites (cans) in Isthmus Cove (Los Angeles County Department of Medical Examiner-Coroner)

that needs to be cleared up with Miller.

Then, in his report, Miller added, "During the day I had seen Natalie Wood driving the same small, inflatable boat (Valiant) earlier—she was alone." Interestingly, someone printed the word "date" above the word "day" in that isolated sentence. Was there some question about what day Miller saw Natalie? At any rate, this sentence contradicts any notion that *during the day* Natalie couldn't operate the dinghy by herself.

According to his memoir, before the autopsy, Dr. Noguchi spoke to Miller over the phone and asked him to assist with the investigation by going to the Isthmus to examine the *Splendour* and the Zodiac dinghy. Dr. Noguchi claimed he requested that Miller specifically:

1. Examine the stern of the Wagners' yacht for any disturbance, or evidence of violence, that the police might have missed.

2. Check the dinghy for any sign of a struggle.

3. Examine the algae (marine plant growth) on the bottom of the swimming step for signs of disturbance. (Did she try to reboard the yacht?)

4. Check the sides of the dinghy for fingernail scratches. (Did she try to climb into the dinghy?)

∿∿∿∿∿∿∿

Studying Miller's report, I could tell he must have gotten in the water to take the measurements and examine both the dinghy and the yacht. Both vessels were in front of the Harbor Patrol office near Isthmus Pier. Miller started with the dinghy and "noticed multiple scratches on the starboard side of the boat along the waterline (which could be Miss Wood attempting to get back into the boat.)"

Miller never described the scratches as "fingernail scratches" and only speculated that Natalie could have made them in an attempt to board the dinghy. But here's what Dr. Noguchi quoted Miller as saying in his book: "There weren't any signs of a struggle in the yacht or the dinghy. There *were* fingernail scratches on the starboard side of the dinghy, which shows she was trying to climb into it."

I could now see why Miller was on the lam. Someone was lying and it was looking more and more likely it was Dr. Noguchi. It seems highly unlikely Miller would say such a significant thing to Dr. Noguchi and two months later fail to include it in his official written report. Additionally, Miller made no mention of looking for "signs of a struggle" aboard the yacht or viewing broken glass from a wine bottle on the salon floor. This could explain why the coroner's office fought me so hard in my lawsuit to get the Miller report.

And the "fingernail scratches" passage in Dr. Noguchi's book had even more significance than you might think at first blush. The starboard (right) side of the dinghy would be closest to the port (left) side of *Splendour* if the dinghy were tied port, parallel to the yacht, as Wagner would eventually claim in Lambert's book. That position would conveniently dovetail with Wagner's theory that Natalie couldn't sleep with the dinghy banging up against the yacht, so she went to retie the ropes and fell overboard at the swim step while facing the right side of the dinghy. Now it looked like someone else had been studying Dr. Noguchi's book.

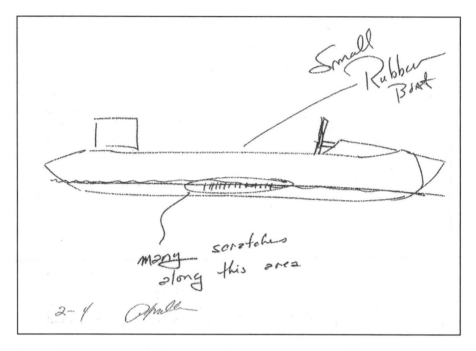

Figure 25: Paul Miller's sketch of the starboard side of *Splendour's* Zodiac dinghy (Los Angeles County Department of Medical Examiner-Coroner)

Miller's hand-drawn sketch of the dinghy showed the position of the scratches. Of course, scratches alone would not be conclusive evidence that they were made by fingernails since the Zodiac was found against the rocks. But Dr. Noguchi said he specifically asked Miller to check for scratches and thereafter, Dr. Noguchi intentionally failed to check Natalie's fingers and fingernails and obtain fingernail scrapings at autopsy.

I actually asked Dr. Noguchi in the 2016 deposition why a pathologist would get fingernail clippings at autopsy, and he told me under oath that "sometimes there is evidence found under the fingernails."

But imperative to investigating Natalie's death, Miller did something the LASD investigators didn't do. He made some important observations and took some weighty measurements. In order of notation by Miller, they are as follows:

1. *Splendour's* swim step measured "32 inches wide" and ran along the entire "beam" (width at the widest point of the yacht measured at the yacht's waterline) of the vessel.

2. The swim step was 11 inches above the water. (*Figure 26*, next page)

3. There was a rubber rub rail that ran entirely around the swim step.

4. "Between the rubber rub rail and the rubber boat tied up, there would not be any noise of the small boat banging against the back of the large boat during the night."

5. "There were metal arms supporting the swim step on the back of the vessel covered with barnacles and moss." (*Figure 26*, below)

6. There was no indication that Natalie was "hanging on to the metal arm unless there [were] multiple scratches on her hands."

7. "There were lines hanging from the inflatable boat (Valiant) which were within 9 inches of the water." (*Figure 26*, below)

8. The master stateroom was "18 feet" from the main salon of the yacht.

9. The distance was "30 feet" from the main salon of the yacht to the end of *Splendour's* swim step. (*Figure 27*, next page)

10. The distance from the stern eye-ring tie to the edge of the swim step was "66 inches." (*Figure 26*, below)

11. The length of the painter or tie-up line on the dinghy was "12 feet." (*Figure 26*, below)

12. In Miller's opinion, Natalie "probably hung on to the bowline or painter of the dinghy (Valiant)…as it drifted across the bay in an easterly direction."

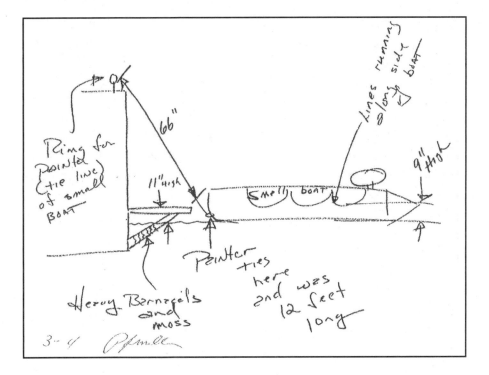

Figure 26: Paul Miller's sketch of side view of *Splendour's* swim step and dinghy (Los Angeles County Department of Medical Examiner-Coroner)

These were vital factual findings by Miller that can help determine the truth about how Natalie drowned and why her body ended up where it was found. The first finding is Miller's belief that because of the respective locations where the dinghy and Natalie's body were found—information obviously provided by Dr. Noguchi or the LASD—Natalie must have been holding on to the dinghy painter line in some fashion.

Natalie's body and the dinghy traveled over a mile from *Splendour* before they were recovered. Moreover, they were recovered in the same area. Those on the scene estimated Natalie's body was within 300 feet of the dinghy. In relation to the 5,280 feet in a mile, it's reasonable to infer that the dinghy and Natalie's body were close together when found.

I personally believe Miller's conclusion that Natalie traveled with the dinghy for a period of time before she drowned is not fallacious. His drawing (*Figure 24*, Page 106) demonstrated why and Miller explained it perfectly in his report:

> Due to wind in that area and a tendency of the Valiant to be blown out toward the sea, and the more southerly drift of [Natalie's] body due to the current, after six hours the Valiant and the body would generally be found widely separated. The Valiant is like a balloon and would be blown by the wind, her body would be more like a watermelon and would be carried by the current, each of which go in different directions in that area.

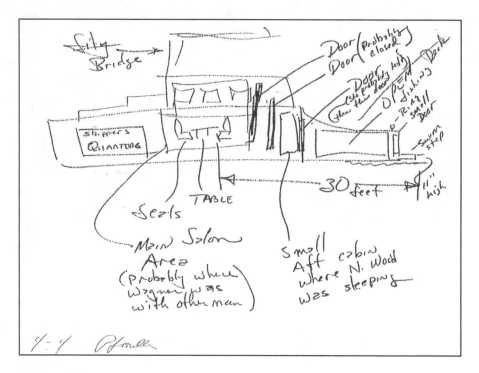

Figure 27: Paul Miller's sketch of port side view of *Splendour* (Los Angeles County Department of Medical Examiner-Coroner)

However, Miller made one unsupported assumption in his expert analysis. He assumed Natalie "hung onto" the painter line when she could have been entangled in the line. It can't be assumed Natalie was physically and mentally able to make any rational decisions, like intentionally grabbing a painter line or, for that matter, kicking her feet. People who are terrified of water they can't stand up in are, according to my research, so consumed by their terror that their only concern is getting air. And after a few minutes in the ocean, cold stress and hypothermia were taking their toll on Natalie's Spartanly clothed body causing her, initially, to lose muscle strength and shiver uncontrollably.

Splendour's swim step was only 11 inches above the water, but it can't be taken for granted that Natalie could make it to the step, even if she were only a few feet away.

✦✦✦✦✦✦✦✦

Dr. Noguchi, in *Coroner*, stated that he was "convinced" that Miller's "special" investigative report "would be conclusive." But Miller's report clearly showed that Dr. Noguchi didn't follow his ocean expert's suggestions on further investigating Natalie's case.

Miller recommended Dr. Noguchi check with Catalina Island Baywatch for the water temperature "at the time." While Eaker determined the surface water temperature at the time Natalie's body was found, no one checked with Baywatch for the surface water temperature between the time Natalie disappeared and the time of her death. Or, if they did, they didn't document it.

Next, Miller suggested Dr. Noguchi check the hypothermia tables to determine "how long she could have survived." As far as I could tell from the official autopsy report, no one gave much, if any, thought to how hypothermia could have affected Natalie's time of death.

Finally, Miller ended his recommendations with a suggestion "that your office ask for a transcript of the radio communications between the Splendor (sic) and the U.S. Coast Guard that evening between 0200 and 0500." He also offered "to examine the dialogue from a mariner's point of view." Miller even told Dr. Noguchi who to call—"the Coast Guard Commander at Long Beach, California."

The radio communication transcripts were a crucial piece of evidence on many fronts. But if Dr. Noguchi followed Miller's advice, the transcripts failed to make it into the coroner's official autopsy report or become part of Dr. Noguchi's book. The transcripts and the times of the communications, or whether there were communications from *Splendour* during that period of time, could have established the truthfulness of many claims regarding the Coast Guard and if help was called in by Wagner or Davern.

Over the years, Wagner has said he called the Coast Guard from *Splendour* after Natalie disappeared. The records could have confirmed or refuted Wagner's claims. In 2017, I submitted a federal FOIA request to the Coast Guard for the transcripts and was told they were only kept for 20 years. Now, the records are purportedly gone, like so many other pieces of evidence in Natalie's case.

Notwithstanding, Miller's report answered many questions and raised several issues. But a small detail nearly lost in the three-page report may dispel entirely Wagner's "banging dinghy" theory. Miller identified an eye-ring tie on the transom of the yacht (see *Figure 26*, Page 109) and took the time to measure the distance from that ring to the dinghy—"66 inches" or 5-1/2 feet. Miller didn't identify any other ties on the transom or stern of the yacht. Because the painter line was "12 feet" long, there was 6-1/2 feet of line that remained to tie the dinghy to the yacht eye-ring.

Miller measured the distance from the transom eye-ring tie because it was placed there for tying up the dinghy. It served no other yachting purpose. The eye-ring tie was on the starboard side of the transom (see Page A-2) while the swim step door was on the transom's port side. So, there would be no reason to step onto the swim step to retie the dinghy. Moreover, Miller verified the swim step edge was encased in a "rubber rub rail," making "banging" against a rubber dinghy extremely unlikely.

CHAPTER 13

down with the ship

IN 2009, 25 YEARS AFTER NATALIE'S DEATH, DAVERN AND RULLI AUTHORED *Goodbye Natalie, Goodbye Splendour*. While the bulk of their work appears to be a desperate attempt to shore up Davern's credibility with cheesy experiments, reenactments lacking foundation, hypnotists and lie detector tests, I still found Davern's core claims to have a ring of truthful content.

I started assessing Davern's credibility by testing the material statements he has made over the years—in his book and to authors, reporters and the LASD—against convincing evidence I discovered along the way. But first, an introduction to the yacht captain at the center of the mystery seems appropriate.

❧❧❧❧❧

Born in 1948 in Margate City, New Jersey, a suburb of Atlantic City, Davern joined the Navy after high school and was honorably discharged three years later. In 1974, Davern moved to Fort Lauderdale and landed a job refurbishing used East Coast yachts for resale on the West Coast.

A stately 1960 white, 60-foot Bristol, twin-screw diesel yacht named *Dizzy Izzy* was Davern's first project and the first yacht he personally operated. In 1975, Davern and his boss motored the refurbished vessel to lovely Marina del Rey, an upscale community near Los Angeles where the well-to-do and celebrated keep their floating toys. They planned to sell *Dizzy Izzy* in that teeming yacht dock, take the profits and return to Fort Lauderdale. But the lanky, bearded 27-year-old Davern liked what he saw and decided to make Marina del Rey home.

The yacht was eventually sold to Natalie Wood and Robert Wagner, who named it *Splendour*, along with an inflatable 13-foot Zodiac dinghy that the couple named *Valiant*, which provided transportation to shore.

❧❧❧❧❧

Ron Nelson, an unapologetic Natalie Wood fan, purchased *Splendour* in 1986 and painstakingly restored it to its former condition. But when I first contacted him in 2015, his "pride and joy for over 25 years" was moored in the Ala Wai, Hawaii, small boat harbor and up for sale. "Not because it's haunted as the tabloids have said, but because I'm in poor health," Nelson wrote.

In emailing me about his acquisition of a piece of Hollywood memorabilia to beat all others, Nelson reported that he and three of his friends brought *Splendour* across the Pacific from Catalina to Hawaii "on her own bottom," a trip that took 14 days. He agreed to send some renderings of *Splendour's* layout, but added "she is split level" with three staircases, standing about "20 FT above the water line…very tall and beamy, about 18 FT wide."

Nelson was asking $250,000. From the photos he provided, I could see the yacht had been altered since 1981. The back deck was fitted with a whirlpool and seating where a live well, ice maker, trash can and chairs used to be. (See Page A-3.) The galley and salon areas had also undergone modifications to provide more room for meal preparations. And some interior paint colors and fabric designs had been changed.

Meticulous, hand-drawn diagrams of the engine room, the yacht's two levels (the salon and wheelhouse) and its flybridge—the perch over the wheelhouse—were soon provided to me. (See *Figures F, G* and *H*, Pages 263-265.) In doing so, Nelson explained that the master stateroom, the twin bunk used by Walken and the queen berth all had locks on the doors—an essential fact in Natalie's case. There were French doors leading from the master stateroom to the back deck. But there was no way to the port or starboard side decks from the master stateroom. You had to walk up five steps to the main living quarters—the salon area—to access the side decks or hop up on the side of the yacht and carefully tread the ledge to the side deck.

Nelson's drawings provided important yacht details and measurements that would prove significant in understanding Davern's descriptions of the sights and sounds he heard Saturday night.

I stayed in contact with Nelson while he fought his illness in Hawaii and Mexico. Then, repeated emails to him went unanswered. I could find no information about him or *Splendour* until January 30, 2020, as I finished up this chapter. The *Honolulu Star-Advertiser* reported *Splendour* was demolished by the state of Hawaii because it had fallen into such disrepair that it was in danger of sinking. The newspaper said the 60-year-old yacht had been illegally moored and $12,000 in fees were owed because the owner had "not taken responsibility for the vessel."

My heart sank. That could only mean one thing—Nelson passed away. He loved *Splendour* too much to let her meet such an unceremonious end. I mourned the passing of Nelson and *Splendour*, the prized yacht that made such happy memories for Nelson, Natalie, her children and friends.

At the time of Natalie's death, Wagner, the personal representative of Natalie's estate, reported *Splendour* was "sold" during probate for $250,000. While nothing in the probate file explained how the yacht purchase was financed in 1975, it had no debt against it in 1981. So, it likely was purchased with Natalie's wealth inasmuch as three years earlier, Wagner was admittedly broke.

∽∿∽∿∽∿∽

Now, to get a feel for Davern's believability, the core narrative of the book it took Rulli and him decades to write and publish—meaning they had plenty of time to get Davern's story right—needs dissecting.

According to *Goodbye*, when Davern first met the Wagners in 1975, Wagner was 45 and Natalie was 37. He described them as a "stunning couple." At that time, the two were considered Hollywood royalty by many in the entertainment industry.

For several weeks after the purchase, the Wagners visited the yacht, always finding Davern "lovingly tending her." After a short while, the couple decided to let their captain go and ask Davern to be *Splendour's* skipper. (See Page A-3.)

In *Goodbye*, Davern related that Wagner enjoyed fishing and swimming with the girls while Natalie, who never swam, liked to relax, read scripts and needlepoint in her "perch" in the wheelhouse. "I got along great with Natalie. We spent a lot of time together on the boat," Davern said.

As far as Davern's relationship with Wagner, at first, Davern addressed his employer as "Mr. Wagner." But one day when the two were fishing, Wagner told Davern to call him R.J.—"like my other friends do." From then on, Davern used the nickname on the yacht and when he was invited to the couple's house for cookouts, pool parties and social parties, including their A-list New Year's Eve party.

(If true, the Wagners' housekeeper, Willie Mae Worthen, could have confirmed Davern's claims. Davern said he met her. Worthen was in her 80s when I started investigating, and she was still working for Wagner the last time I saw her mentioned in books or magazines. Maintaining a low profile until she died in 2017 at 90, she hadn't said a word publicly about Natalie's death, Davern or the children. But in 2011, a district attorney could have talked to her, under oath if necessary.)

By 1981, Davern, who was taking the Wagners out on the yacht almost weekly, was paid well to be at Natalie's beck and call—performing "any number of tasks, menial or large."

"I was their friend, not just an employee," Davern said. And Natalie trusted him with her children, asking him "to care for them, to take them on outings, to change Courtney's diapers, to feed them, to play with them." Most of all, if anything was bothering Natalie, Davern said he was around to take care of it.

This backdrop is essential for understanding how Davern responded to Natalie's needs on the yacht and would become important in my assessment of Wagner's "banging dinghy" theory. But before I address that, let's test some of Davern's other material book representations.

❧❧❧❧❧❧❧

On the trip to Catalina Island that Friday afternoon, November 27, 1981, Natalie was devoting her attention to Walken, and it was having an undesirable effect on Wagner. To ease the tension, Davern claimed in *Goodbye* that he offered everyone a Quaalude to help them *chill out*. In his *Star* magazine story published nearly 25 years before his book, Davern said all four of them "took a Quaalude."

In the late '70s and early '80s, Quaaludes (methaqualone) were the party pill of choice. A sedative-hypnotic drug, methaqualone was prescribed to treat insomnia and muscle tightness. Where or how Davern got his Quaaludes is unknown.

I asked my forensic pharmacology expert about methaqualone's elimination half-life. He informed me the half-life of a 300mg Quaalude is 20 to 60 hours. So, if Natalie ingested a Quaalude at noon that Friday, most likely remnants of the drug would be in her system at the time she died, around midnight Saturday. The coroner's toxicologists tested her blood for methaqualone as a "compound base," and there was no indication in the lab reports that methaqualone was detected.

That meant either Natalie didn't take her chill-out pill or Davern's statement about her taking one is untrue.

∽∽∽∽∽∽∽

According to Davern, after the Quaaludes, things slowed down Friday afternoon and Walken, who was seasick, went to his cabin to rest. As they approached Catalina Island, Wagner wanted to continue to the Isthmus for privacy, but Natalie wanted to shop. Since there was no shopping at the Isthmus, the party went to Avalon, the island's largest population center. The captain anchored *Splendour* near the Casino building, Avalon's remarkable signature structure. (See Page A-4.)

Generally, the closer to the Casino, the calmer the water. The boats are moored facing the sea, because the prevailing winds at that part of the island blow from the sea toward the city, and a boat is more steady and stable parked into the wind.

About the time *Splendour* pulled into the cove, Walken surfaced, apparently feeling much better. After dropping anchor, Davern removed the Zodiac from storage and agreed to stay behind and fix dinner while the trio went to shore in the dinghy.

According to Davern, while the famous threesome was in Avalon, they had drinks at El Galleon—a bar and restaurant—and went shopping, with Walken buying a painting and Wagner and Natalie purchasing some jewelry.

The three returned "about 8:00 or 9:00 p.m.—somewhere in there," according to Davern's 2011 petition statement, and he had dinner ready except for the steaks. Natalie mentioned she had purchased Davern "an early Christmas present." Things were pleasant for a while, but around 10 p.m., the skipper said the mood began to change.

Wagner mentioned to Davern that he wanted to move the yacht to the Isthmus. Davern ignored the comment. The Isthmus was 12 miles away along a rugged coast. With no moon, in the drizzly rain, it would be risky to say the least.

The four were enjoying cocktails when they finally sat down for dinner. As they ate, Davern said Wagner asked Natalie if she liked the diamond necklace he bought her. Natalie's response wasn't as enthusiastic as usual, and Davern thought her "near-indifference to the gift" annoyed Wagner.

At that point, Natalie gave Davern his present—a pieces of eight necklace. Davern described it as an imitation of an old-world coin sometimes called "pirate's gold." Noting Natalie had never bought Davern anything like that before, he claimed in *Goodbye* that "it was proof that he had grown to a new status in Natalie's world. He would treasure the gift of friendship forever."

(Davern wanted his readers to believe the international film star was thinking of him while she shopped on the island that Friday afternoon? Testing myself on the believability of that assertion, I asked, "How would you substantiate that if you were the prosecutor in a homicide case?" If it were true, Davern should have presented the necklace or at least a photograph of it if it was lost, stolen or sold. Not doing so just left more doubt about his credibility for professional skeptics like me.)

According to Davern, Natalie also showed him the pieces of eight earrings she bought for herself. The gift presentation set "a more positive mood" with "pleasant conversation and laughter," he claimed. Then Natalie said to Walken, "I wish *Brainstorm* could be released sooner than they expect."

Davern said "her comment totally changed the dynamics." Natalie and Walken began trading stories about the movie, filming problems and how Walken's recommendations had helped "save the show." The captain said he liked listening to Natalie, but while Natalie—"relaxed and animated"—continued the conversation about *Brainstorm*, "R.J. seethed."

According to Davern, it was late when Walken announced he was calling it a night. When Natalie said she was, too, Wagner stood up and said, "I'm moving the boat to the Isthmus. Now!"

Appalled, Davern recalled that Natalie replied, "What on earth for, R.J.? I don't understand." He said Wagner replied, "You don't have to understand. ... I feel like moving the boat, so I'm moving the fucking boat."

(Wagner's language, particularly using the word "fuck," is important in assessing Davern's account of the following day's events. Wagner's fondness of the four-letter word is obvious when it came to Natalie. In his memoir, Pieces of My Heart, there's a photograph on Page 131 of a young Natalie in dancing tights. Above the provocative picture is a quote that readers eventually discover has nothing to do with Natalie: "THAT FUCKING CUNT WILL NEVER WORK IN MY STUDIO AGAIN!" Under the photo, it says "Natalie."

In comparison, a couple chapters later, a lovely photo of his second wife, Marion Marshall, appears. Above it, the quote reads: "MY HEART STOPPED WHEN I SAW HER." Under it, it says, "My second wife, the beautiful Marion.")

According to Davern, Natalie was exasperated at Wagner's late-night plan and said, "R.J., don't be crazy. ... It's cold and dark. I'll leave the boat and go to the island before I'll go to the Isthmus tonight. Stop acting crazy! You're not going to move the boat tonight!" To which Wagner responded, "Watch me!" and headed for the wheelhouse.

Once again, a shaken Davern described Natalie's reaction. "She couldn't understand—neither could I, and I don't think I ever saw that kind of look on her face. She was completely flabbergasted." Davern continued, "R.J. was running around like a madman—up to the wheelhouse, gunning the engine, back down to the deck, messing with the rigging, you name it." Natalie pleaded with Davern to do something, saying she was going to the island if Wagner was moving the boat.

So Davern went to the wheelhouse to ask Wagner his intentions and tell him Natalie wanted to leave. According to Davern, Wagner was "drunk and mad" and his face was "beet red." Wagner yelled at him, "Then leave with her!"

Distraught and unsure what to do, Davern ran down to Walken's cabin and knocked. When Walken opened the door, Davern explained that Wagner intended to move the boat. "Want to help out here?" Davern asked. According to *Goodbye*, Walken advised him "to not get involved in any husband and wife dispute, ever."

(When Walken was asked about Friday night by sheriff's investigators on December 3, 1981, in his Beverly Wilshire Hotel suite with his attorney by his side, he described the scene as a "hubbub," defined as an "uproar" among other things. With this and other statements during his 1981 LASD interviews, he substantiated, in material part, Davern's version of Friday evening's argument.)

After Walken bowed out, Davern said he ran up to the wheelhouse a second time and confronted Wagner. After Wagner apologized, Davern suggested he talk to Natalie. Wagner responded, "No, go take her to the island. … Go stay with her, and keep an eye over her. Don't tell her I changed my mind. Just go."

As instructed, Davern went to Natalie, who already had her jacket on and bag ready. She was "hell bent" on leaving and wouldn't even let him pack a few things. According to *Goodbye*, Natalie looked "scared, bewildered, and plain sad" during the dinghy ride to Avalon. Davern told her Wagner was sorry, but Natalie wasn't interested.

The two went to El Galleon, where Natalie asked the manager about boats and private sea planes to the mainland. But it was close to midnight, and there was nothing available until morning. So, she asked him to find two rooms, which he reserved at the Pavilion Lodge.

(El Galleon manager Paul Reynolds confirmed this account with LASD investigators in 1981.)

Natalie's room, 126, was in the back of the hotel and Davern's room, 219, was in the middle. She paid for both with an American Express card. Because Natalie was worried someone might break into her room, Davern volunteered to stay with her. She replied, "I'd feel a lot safer if you would." So the beautiful star and her yacht captain opened a bottle of wine they had purchased on the way to the hotel, and Natalie took a sleeping pill.

According to Davern, Natalie was still very angry at Wagner and said, "He had no right to embarrass me that way in front of Christopher. … I was really enjoying myself and he ruined it." She explained, "I have a professional relationship with Christopher, and R.J. needs to respect that. I respect his relationship with Stefanie." Davern claimed Natalie added, "I don't go crazy over his co-star. It's his *job*." After talking more about the movie and Walken, Davern said Natalie told him, "I can't tolerate this kind of nonsense from R.J."

Reflecting on *Brainstorm's* location shooting, Natalie related that Wagner came to North Carolina in mid-October because, "He thought I was up to something." She told Davern she was not having an affair, then retorted, "Why on earth would I invite Christopher to share a weekend with us if I were?"

A bit later, Natalie announced, "Come Monday, R.J. will face the music on this. And he knows it!" When Davern asked what she meant, Natalie said:

> "I mean that I'll do something about this. I won't tolerate this kind of nonsense. It's getting old. R.J.'s jealousy gets the best of him. This isn't the first time he's gone crazy over my co-star. It's insane. He can't do this to me again! It's the drinking, Dennis. He's out of control, and I blame the booze. I'll see a lawyer if I have to. Maybe that will send the message loud and clear."

According to *Goodbye*, Davern was shaken by the lawyer comment, never suspecting things "had gone that far." Natalie then added, "What infuriates me the most is that he doesn't trust me. If he did, he wouldn't behave like this."

When it was time for bed, Davern, fully clothed, began getting himself situated on the floor. Natalie stopped him and said she would sleep under the lower covers and he could sleep under the bedspread. He said she thanked him for being with her and letting her talk. Then Davern claimed the troubled star said, "Dennis, I can't wait to fly my body out of here tomorrow."

That last statement, of course, was an omen of things to come. But the scene in room 126, more than anything else, told me why Davern's guilt eventually got the best of him. Natalie trusted Davern enough to confide in him and potentially cause a scandal for herself by spending the night with him in the Avalon hotel room. And when she needed him the most, he let her down.

(Over the years, Wagner tried to distance himself from Friday night by claiming the cove was so rough that Natalie wanted to spend the night on shore. That's contrary to Lambert's statement in his book that Crowley told him Natalie called Friday night from the dock at Avalon about "a terrible fight with RJ." Furthermore, Walken was the one prone to seasickness. If anyone wanted to leave the boat due to rough seas, wouldn't it have been Walken? And, I've seen no evidence that Avalon Harbor was rough Friday night.)

∽∽∽∽∾∾∾∾∾

According to *Goodbye*, when Davern awoke Saturday morning, Natalie readied herself, then left the hotel room. When she came back, she said they were returning to *Splendour* because she couldn't find a plane or boat, and she couldn't reach her friend Peggy or sister Lana to aid in her departure. Plus, she said she felt "bad about leaving Christopher alone with R.J." So, Davern begrudgingly took her back to the yacht.

When the pair arrived, Walken was still in his cabin. Natalie went to change clothes, and Davern joined Wagner, who was drinking coffee at the table in the galley. Out of Natalie's earshot, Davern told his boss he wanted to end the trip early. But Wagner sarcastically replied, "Nope. Natalie wants a pleasure cruise with her guest, and who am I to interfere with that?"

Without consultation, Wagner announced he planned to "bridle up and tow the dinghy" to the Isthmus, further upsetting the perturbed yacht captain. When Walken appeared, he was in cheerful mood, according to Davern, and "light and airy conversation started up as if nothing had transpired the night before." But Davern said when Natalie and Wagner spoke, "they didn't look at each other."

After the 12-mile trip to the Isthmus, *Splendour* was moored in the last mooring row in the cove. While tying the ropes, the puzzled skipper asked Wagner the reason for the move. Davern claimed Wagner said, "Because Natalie wants a weekend with Christopher Walken, and Natalie will get more than what she came for. *That's* why."

(Here, it's important to question Wagner's motive for moving the yacht from the active town of Avalon to the desolate area of the Isthmus. Was Wagner planning something? Some will say only Wagner can answer that, assuming he would speak honestly. I submit the circumstantial evidence of what happened next in the windswept inlet paints a clear picture of the truth.)

Once they were settled, Davern claimed in *Goodbye* that Natalie smiled sweetly at Wagner and said, "R.J., you wanted the peace and quiet of the boat this weekend, but Christopher is anxious to see the island. I'd like to take him ashore, if you don't mind. You're welcome to come along."

Davern said Wagner replied, "Sure. You two go and have fun. Dennis and I will join you later for dinner." Davern radioed for a shore boat. Natalie and Walken left through the swim step door, which was always left open when the girls weren't on the boat, while he and

Wagner waved goodbye from the back deck.

After Natalie and Walken went ashore, Davern said, "R.J., I think I need a nap. How about you?" The captain went to his quarters and tried to sleep. About 4 p.m., Davern said he and Wagner "were in the galley with a cocktail when R.J. decided he had given Natalie enough time alone with Christopher."

(The truthfulness of Davern's statements about how and when the four got to Doug's Harbor Reef on Saturday afternoon may seem insignificant, but the importance of this event cannot be overstated. If Davern is mistaken about this point, then his position on other points is subject to question. Furthermore, it's hard to swallow that after Friday night's events, Wagner would cheerfully let his wife go to a bar with Walken and patiently wait hours before joining them. Maybe it really happened that way, and the charade was also part of Wagner's plan.)

When Davern and Wagner arrived at Doug's Harbor Reef (see Page A-4), Natalie and Walken "were huddled together at the end of the bar, so totally engrossed in conversation that they had not even noticed R.J. and Dennis approach." Davern said Natalie, wearing her new pieces of eight earrings, greeted him pleasantly and offered a seat to Wagner, who was trying "hard to keep his anger in check." Davern and Wagner ordered scotch. Walken, according to Davern, "appeared a bit nervous."

When conversation slowed, Wagner gulped his drink and ordered another. After a few minutes, Davern said Wagner wanted to move to the dining room, but instead ended up making dinner reservations for 7 p.m. When their table was ready, the foursome created a predictable stir upon being seated. More drinks were ordered, but Wagner was unhappy with the wine list. So the dutiful captain offered to return to *Splendour* for "Soave Bolla," because he knew his employers both liked the wine.

As Davern stood to leave, Walken volunteered to accompany him. Aboard the Zodiac, Davern claimed he showed Walken how to maneuver in the dark with a flashlight, because the dinghy's headlight was out. He said they got three bottles of wine and smoked some marijuana. Davern estimated they were gone about 30 minutes. When the pair returned to the restaurant, they left one wine bottle in the dinghy "just in case."

(Walken's predilection for marijuana in 1981 appears all but certain with this incident and what you will learn about Lana's encounter with him after Natalie's funeral. If the LASD had checked the three men for alcohol and drugs after Natalie's death, Davern's claims could have been corroborated further.

The drug's popularity was on the upswing, but it was still illegal to possess, and the publicity of its abuse could ruin a career in those days. But this part of Davern's story also established one other thing for me. In addition to heavy drinking, Davern was into illegal drugs—Quaaludes and marijuana.)

The Wagner party ordered dinner and drank, among other things, a bottle of champagne sent to their table. Davern said the men had steaks, but "Natalie picked at her seafood. She was not pleased, so she ate only a few bites." They continued talking, and Natalie "chatted with fellow diners." Davern recalled a little girl asking for Natalie's autograph and an accordionist playing a song Natalie liked.

(All the events did happen, according to investigators' interviews of Whiting and waitresses Michelle Mileski and Christina Marie Quinn and the autopsy report that found "fish or chicken" in Natalie's stomach.)

When dinner was finished, Davern said Wagner was ready to leave, but Natalie wanted another drink. "Let's go now!" Wagner urged her. But Natalie said, "Oh, let's stay. I'm having fun." Davern claimed when Wagner went to the men's room, Natalie ordered more drinks while Walken watched and didn't say a thing.

(In Goodbye, Rulli took the opportunity to bolster Davern's credibility by relating Dr. Lyndon Taylor's encounter with Wagner on the way to the restroom. Dr. Taylor, owner of the sailboat Catacean moored at approximately site D-2, happened to be an expert on nonverbal communications, known as paralinguistics. Rulli wrote that Dr. Taylor "immediately recognized the bitter anger emitting from R.J.'s glazed-over eyes." Because every boat owner in Isthmus Cove that Saturday evening wasn't interviewed by investigators in 1981, Dr. Taylor wasn't contacted. But detectives in 2011 should've known about him and his probative evidence.)

∿∿∿∿∿∿

Davern recalled that when Wagner returned, he said, "Come on, Natalie, I want to get out of here" and threw "cold looks" around the table. Davern added that Wagner was getting angrier, like a "time bomb ticking louder and louder." Natalie finally succumbed to her husband's insistence.

As they left, Davern claimed Wagner staggered a bit, then put his coat over Natalie's shoulders. The foursome headed to the dock and climbed into the Zodiac. Once again, Davern slowly navigated with his flashlight in the dark, looking for the moorings. He noted it was "extraordinarily damp and cold, but there was hardly any wind." Davern said they were back on the yacht before 10:30 p.m.

(Restaurant employees corroborated Davern's account of Wagner's anger and the time the four left the restaurant.)

∿∿∿∿∿∿

In *Goodbye*, Davern said upon their return, everyone went to the salon and galley. Natalie "lit her beeswax candles" and asked for wine. While Davern opened the bottle, Natalie and Walken sat and talked on the couch, opposite the wooden coffee table inscribed with the word "*Splendour.*" Davern stood near Wagner, who "vigilantly watched Natalie as she entertained Christopher."

Wagner was silent for a bit, then interrupted to say he was unhappy about "how much *Brainstorm* had taken Natalie away from their home." According to the captain, Walken replied that it was "to be expected in the world of acting, especially for big stars" like Natalie.

Davern claimed Wagner's face turned bright red, and "he took one deep breath after another" as Natalie continued her conversation with Walken. Davern said, "Finally, R.J. burst and shouted at Christopher. 'So, what do you want to do to my wife?' ... 'Do you want to fuck my wife? Is that what you want?'"

Before the shocked trio could process Wagner's words, Davern said Wagner "grabbed the opened, half-filled wine bottle by the neck, pulled it up and back behind his shoulder for force, then brought it down fast and hard, crashing it against the coffee table." Natalie, Walken and Davern "threw their arms to their faces to shield against the shattering glass." Then, no one moved for "an eternity."

After that display of violence, Davern recalled that Wagner turned his back on everyone and he saw Walken's "hands start to shake" as he stood up cautiously, went to the door to the side deck (see Page A-5), stepped out and stood in the cold drizzle for a few moments. Then he reentered and went "directly to his cabin without a word." Once there, he closed his door behind him.

Davern said Natalie "looked mortified." She stood up and looked at Wagner, and Davern described her reaction like this: "'I won't stand for this, R.J.,' she hissed. 'This is outrageous, and I promise you, I will not tolerate it!' She stomped off to their stateroom and slammed the door behind her."

The captain said the incident happened right after they returned to the yacht, "maybe about ten forty."

(It took Davern 20 years to fully disclose the details of the scene in the salon. For 23 years, Wagner stood pat on his story of a friendly political "disagreement" with Walken and "rough seas" causing the broken glass. Walken has stayed hitched to his "small beef" and being "asleep when it happened" tale for 40 years. Today, there's no doubt Wagner hurled accusations at Walken before violently smashing a wine bottle over the coffee table. But it's the events that followed that have as their foundation Davern's eyewitness testimony.)

After Natalie left, Wagner said he was "embarrassed," according to the dismayed captain. "I could tell he wanted to go to Natalie to assess the damage. He told me to wait there, because he didn't really expect her to accept his apology. She'd probably throw him out of the stateroom." Davern said it was no later than 10:50 p.m. when Wagner went to apologize.

The master stateroom door was only about 15 feet away from the site of the assault in the salon. After Wagner went below, the yelling started. In *Goodbye*, Davern said, "I heard them screaming at each other so loudly that I couldn't even make out the words" and "all the curse words seemed magnified."

According to Davern, Walken didn't come out of his berth during all of this. The screaming and cussing continued, and Davern said it got louder and much worse. "I heard things being thrown around, hitting the walls, and it sounded like they were going at each other."

(I obtained three crime scene photographs of the master stateroom. All three show a disheveled bedroom. But the room had many wall hangings, including pictures, and none appear damaged or dislodged. There are no scuff marks on the master stateroom walls, but there is what appears to be a rather large crack or scratch on the inside of the hallway leading down to the master stateroom from the salon. See Page A-5.)

﹋﹋﹋

According to the frightened captain, he ran to the flybridge when the fight escalated. The flybridge is directly over the master stateroom, two decks up. "The fighting got louder, and then I heard R.J. yell, 'Get off my fucking boat!' or 'You can fucking leave the boat,' or something like that," Davern recalled.

(Since it wasn't Wagner's boat, the reasonable inference is a remark like that wouldn't set well with Natalie.)

In *Goodbye*, Davern said Natalie "screamed out again," so he went down to the master stateroom and knocked. He claimed it took "about thirty seconds" for Wagner to crack the door. He described Wagner's appearance as "horrible, just horrible, like he'd been in a fight." Davern said Wagner wedged himself in the opening and told the skipper to go wait for him; he'd be up in a bit. Davern said he didn't see or hear Natalie. "Everything was quiet."

When Wagner closed the door, Davern stood for "a few seconds" listening. He didn't hear anything, so he returned to the flybridge as instructed and turned on a light. Then he heard voices again, and the master stateroom door to the back deck opened and closed.

According to Davern, he could see most of the back deck from the flybridge. He ran to the plastic isinglass window overlooking the back deck, but it reflected the light and obstructed his view. Davern claims he wanted to intervene, but since he was told to leave, he "felt helpless to intrude." He "peeked out" and Wagner saw him, so he "ducked back real fast." When they started yelling again, he "put on loud music so they wouldn't think [he] was trying to listen to them" and thought the music would "help cover their voices so nearby boaters wouldn't hear."

(There have been inconsistent witness statements over the years concerning the existence of loud music Saturday night. Occupants of nearby boats—Paul Miller, Dennis Bowen and Laurel Page—reported hearing loud music while Janet May, owner of another boat, and Bombard employees Paul Wintler and William Peterson heard nothing. I believe there was loud music; it came from Splendour as Davern succeeded in drowning out the Wagners' screams from the back deck.)

The skipper said the couple was under the wheelhouse ledge, and while he couldn't see them, he saw shadows and could tell "Natalie was in her nightgown." Davern continued by saying, "Natalie was screaming—or yelling, then I heard *nothing*." He claimed he waited a few minutes, looked again and saw Wagner and Natalie together. He didn't hear yelling but kept the music on as a precaution. After "ten to fifteen minutes passed," Davern said he turned off the music and heard "boat sounds," the type you "get used to and don't really think about."

The concerned captain quickly went through the salon to the starboard side door. He took the side deck to the back deck and came up behind Wagner. When Wagner turned around, he hustled Davern off the deck and through the master stateroom. Then Davern quoted Wagner as frantically saying, "Natalie's missing. I've been looking all over for her, and she's not here. Help me find her, Dennis. You go forward and check the rooms."

Davern claimed he was "dumbfounded" by Wagner's words. "What do you mean, she's missing?" he asked. Davern said Wagner cut him off, and said, "She's missing, Dennis," and looked into his eyes. "He froze my insides with that look."

(This is where a prosecutor would use circumstantial evidence, including the timeline, to establish the most likely time Natalie went into the water in an effort to corroborate this part of Davern's story. The constructed timeline begins with the foursome returning to the yacht after dinner.

According to Whiting, Davern and Wagner, it was before 10:30 p.m., the time Whiting said Curt Craig, a Harbor Patrol officer, got off work, but after 10 p.m., according to Whiting. With that, you would note Wagner's early morning statement to Eaker on November 29, 1981, that the last time he saw Natalie was "10:45 p.m." and his statement to the LASD on December 4, 1981, that "15 minutes" after Natalie went below, he went down and she was "not there."

Next, you would establish Walken's narrative—from Hamilton's notes of Walken's December 3, 1981, LASD interview—that "ten minutes" after he walked back in from stepping outside following his "beef" with Wagner, Natalie "went to her room" and "ten minutes later," Davern noticed the dinghy was gone.

Finally, you would establish Wayne's and Payne's statements to investigators that they heard a woman's cries for help between "11:05" and "about midnight."

An inference of Natalie's obvious anger at Wagner's admitted display of jealously and violence would corroborate the master stateroom quarrel and forensic evidence would substantiate a physical altercation between Natalie and Wagner, supporting Davern's account of the screaming and banging sounds. The three forensic pathologists established the time of death as "about midnight," and the forensic pharmacology and hypothermia evidence supports that conclusion.

Taken as a whole, you could reasonably infer that there was a fight between Natalie and Wagner in the master stateroom that spilled out on the deck between 10:45 and 11 p.m.; Natalie was in the ocean between 11:05 p.m. and midnight—Payne and Wayne heard cries for help during that time—and Natalie perished about an hour after entering the water as established by her stomach contents, the peak drug concentration calculations for her prescription drugs and well-settled hypothermia phases.)

Davern said Wagner had him search the front of the yacht while he rechecked the back. Davern expected to find Natalie in his room, but she wasn't there. "Then I checked the empty cabin. I hoped it was all a crazy mistake. I checked every head. I even checked Chris's room. He was sound asleep," Davern said.

His search "took less than ten minutes." When he returned to the back deck, he noticed "the dinghy was gone." Davern said he met Wagner in the wheelhouse, where his boss told him Natalie must have taken the dinghy to shore. Davern claimed he suggested they put on their searchlight, but Wagner said, "No!" When Davern told Wagner to radio for help, Wagner refused.

At that point, Davern claimed Wagner opened a bottle of scotch and poured him a drink. The captain said his head was spinning. Natalie was either in the dinghy or in the water, and "one was as illogical as the other." So Davern said he "*had* to believe she was in the dinghy." He claimed he only drank some of the scotch to keep Wagner's trust.

(Crime scene photos of the galley trash cans help corroborate Davern's story. There appears to be a scotch bottle in one can. See Page A-6.)

〰〰〰〰〰

Davern said he "kept jumping up saying, 'Let's call a search' but R.J. kept rejecting the idea, saying he couldn't afford the bad publicity." Davern said he was scared and Wagner urged him not to "panic and cause a scene." So, the shell-shocked captain tried to sort out what had happened while he drank to appease his employer. After more than an hour, Davern claimed Wagner "suddenly started crying—really crying and saying 'Dennis, I know it. *She's gone, she's gone, she's gone.*" Davern said he held Wagner while he cried.

After comforting Wagner, Davern again urged him to call for help. Davern said Wagner finally made a call to the Coast Guard "around one-thirty."

(There is no independent evidence of Wagner calling the Coast Guard. But a radio transmission was made from Splendour around that time.)

To contradict statements in the three press releases Wagner issued after Natalie's death about taking out his "cruiser," "speedboat" or "small boat" to look for her, Davern stated the Wagners owned no other boats beside *Splendour* and the Zodiac dinghy: "Wagner didn't have a cruiser to take out. He lied from day one."

(The truthfulness of this event has been largely ignored over the years. Was Wagner's first attempt to find his wife a trip to the pier or a vague call picked up by night restaurant manager Don Whiting? The Whiting call scenario has been the storyline for almost four decades.

Because the Wagners didn't own a cruiser or speed boat, most people assumed Wagner didn't search for Natalie. Wagner's transportation may not have been a cruiser, but according to Wintler, he managed to reach the pier. So, what motivated Wagner to go to the pier? It's reasonable to believe it was a bona fide attempt to find Natalie. But, on the other hand, a reasonable person could conclude, based on the circumstantial evidence, that his trip was a masquerade designed to create a diversion.)

〜〜〜〜〜〜

According to Davern, while the two drank, they discussed what to say to those who responded to the call for help. Davern said Wagner instructed him to leave the broken wine bottle in case Walken said Wagner smashed it. He said he would explain "only if Chris mentioned how it got there."

(The collusion between Davern and Wagner to get their stories straight is corroborated by accounts each gave to the investigators, including the broken glass fabrication. And Davern's first statement to LASD investigators contained his measured falsehoods. He lied about where Natalie spent Friday night, and when confronted with the truth, he stated that he wanted "to talk to RJ and his attorney before talking about that.")

〜〜〜〜〜〜

After catching him in a lie about Friday night, Rasure let Davern go. Davern got the first passenger boat back to the mainland, where Wagner had a car and driver waiting to escort him to North Cañon Drive.

Davern was taken through the throng of reporters outside the gates of the Wagners' home to Paul Ziffren. From there, he went to Wagner's bedroom, where he found his boss sitting on the edge of the bed crying. Ziffren advised Davern he couldn't represent him and Wagner, but it was important he have an attorney. Then Ziffren told Davern, "We've hired Mark Beck, who will talk to you tomorrow."

Davern claimed Wagner said, "I won't be going to the funeral, but I want you to go, Dennis." Davern reported Ziffren replied, "We have to talk, R.J."

(Similar to refusing to identify Natalie's body, Wagner was going to skip Natalie's funeral until his lawyer explained how it would look. Was Wagner's desire to avoid the event because he didn't want to see his handiwork? Or, because he wanted to lay the haunting memories of Natalie's death on the young boat

captain? Or both? Either way, you could reasonably infer that it was a bizarre way for an "innocent" man to act after his wife's death.

At the time, Mark Beck was practicing criminal defense law, among other things, in Los Angeles. Based on the type of lawyers who represented Davern and Walken, you could conclude that Ziffren was orchestrating the representation because he sensed a criminal law problem.

Davern has stated he didn't pay for his representation. Beck's records would confirm this fact. No one knows whether Wagner also paid for Walken's lawyer. But one thing is certain. Beck had divided loyalties between Davern and Wagner if Wagner was paying his fees. And subsequent conduct with Davern would call into question whether Beck's principal loyalty was to Wagner.)

When Davern called Beck, the meeting was set for Tuesday morning, the day of Natalie's funeral. At Beck's office, Davern said his lawyer wanted him to sign a statement, so Davern did. He claims the statement was given to Rasure.

(I see no reason for Beck to obtain a signed statement from his own client. It would serve no purpose in his representation of the captain. When something like that happens, it's usually done to protect someone else. With knowledge of that fact, it would be reasonable to infer the statement was an insurance policy in case Davern turned on Wagner.

There was no mention of Davern's signed statement in Rasure's official report, but if it were in fact disclosed to Rasure, it guaranteed that if Wagner were charged with a crime, his lawyers would be entitled to the statement by operation of law—assuring them of a first-rate tool to attack Davern's credibility by claiming he lied to get a better deal.

Furthermore, knowing what someone thought was important to include in Davern's false exculpatory statement—a statement designed to express innocence that is later determined to be false—would help Davern's credibility when he repudiated it. But, according to Rulli, Davern was never given a copy and doesn't remember what it said.)

∽∾∽∾∽∾∽

After the LASD released *Splendour* and the Zodiac, Wagner told Davern to retrieve the yacht. Joined by three of Wagner's friends—Frank Westmore, Tommy Thompson and Eddie Butterworth, all makeup artists—the four made their way to the Isthmus on Sunday, December 6, 1981. The men boarded the vessel through the stern deck doors and entered the master stateroom, which Davern described as "tossed up." He said while Westmore was tidying the bedroom, he found one of Natalie's pieces of eight earrings "on the floor in the corner."

After cleaning the yacht, the foursome returned to the mainland, where Wagner instructed Davern to remove *Splendour's* contents and store it in the guesthouse. But Davern purloined Natalie's beeswax candles and the *Splendour*-inscribed coffee table. According to Rulli, "It was the table Dennis needed to keep, for unexplainable reasons."

(The crime scene photos substantiate that the master stateroom was "tossed up." The earring was a crucial piece of evidence, and Westmore could have corroborated Davern's claim, if the earring had, in fact, been found. But Westmore died in 1985. Checking with Thompson was not possible; he died in 2002. I tried to talk to Butterworth, but he didn't want to help. He died in 2018. I asked Rulli about the earring and she told me it "was boxed up with the other things.")

∽∿∽∿∽∿∽

From the day Natalie died, Davern lived on Cañon Drive, and Wagner called the shots on his whereabouts. On one occasion, Davern said he wanted to stay with his girlfriend past 10 p.m. but was muscled into a waiting car by "two of R.J.'s brutes." Davern claimed he was ordered to never talk to anyone about Natalie's death "or there'd be legal consequences."

Davern said he stayed in the upstairs guest bedroom and an alarm system prevented him from opening his bedroom door at night, going downstairs or making phone calls. A bodyguard was stationed near the front door, and a driver escorted him everywhere "for months."

(In the 1985 Star story, Davern said he lived with Wagner for "three weeks.")

According to Davern, when he suggested moving, Wagner went "nuts," saying he couldn't leave "until things died down." Wagner also requested the captain not contact anyone who sent him messages, even his own mother. And Davern said he didn't.

After Natalie's death, Davern claimed he and Wagner depended on each other for "comfort and support" and drank scotch almost nightly in Wagner's den. But they never talked about *"that night."* With the exception of Wagner's outings with St. John and work on *Hart to Hart*, Davern said Wagner "was a recluse for about a year." The arrangement also caused Davern's split with his girlfriend.

Between the house and the yacht, Davern claimed he was "watched *all* the time." He explained Wagner said, "it was for [his] own protection," and Davern believed him. Reporters swarmed Cañon Drive for weeks after Natalie's death, and Wagner didn't want him "to get cornered by them." But the stress took its toll.

(In my research, I didn't find one reference disputing Davern's narrative about living in the Wagners' home for a period of time, being chauffeured around and being sequestered from family and friends. Surely if it were false, a member of Natalie's family or Willie Mae Worthen would have challenged the assertions.)

∽∿∽∿∽∿∽

After the first meeting with his lawyer, Davern returned because the LASD wanted to talk to him again. The second meeting was Thursday, December 10, 1981. When Davern arrived, according to Detective Rasure's official report, Steven Miller, another criminal defense attorney, was with Beck.

Davern claimed in 2011 that Beck gave Rasure the statement Davern had signed on his first visit to the lawyer's office. Davern assumed Rasure read it.

Rasure wanted to know why Davern and Natalie stayed on the island Friday night. As planned, Davern said "rough seas." Davern also said the tone of the cruise was "fine," as he and Wagner had agreed. When Rasure asked if he had anything to add, Davern claimed he looked at Beck and Beck signaled him, so Davern said, "No." According to Davern's 2011 petition statement, Rasure left and he "never saw him again."

(But Davern did, in fact, see Rasure again on March 5, 1982, in Beck's office. Details of that interview will be discussed later in this chapter.)

∿∿∿∿∿∿

Wagner eventually lined up Davern with a job as an extra on *Hart to Hart* and paid his Screen Actors Guild fees. Davern said he also worked on other television shows as well as films and commercials. Even though he had no experience, he got parts "people wait years to get."

(I've seen nothing to contradict this setup. But, investigators in 2011 could have obtained documentation from the Screen Actors Guild and, perhaps, still photos of Davern's scenes from movies, TV shows and commercials.)

Before his work as an extra, Davern said Wagner gave him checks—"a thousand here, two thousand there"—for working on the yacht. Wagner told him "to call his accountant anytime" if he needed money. The checks Wagner gave him totaled "Maybe ten thousand, or a little more," according to the captain.

(If this were true, why haven't we seen copies of the canceled checks to corroborate it? The bank that had cashed or deposited the checks, if given the approximate dates and amounts, could have searched its records since many keep them for decades. Davern and Rulli started their book-writing and media campaign in the 1980s. The banks certainly had the records then. A photocopy of a canceled check or two would have gone a long way in establishing the truth of Davern's claims that he was paid to keep quiet.)

Davern described himself as a "wreck" during his time living with Wagner. He said he had terrible dreams about Natalie, drank constantly and finally went to therapy, paid for by Wagner. But things didn't get better. He was "petrified" and "scared" for his life because he was "ordered to say nothing" and frightened with suggestions the FBI might get involved. So, he "did what he was told."

(Who did Davern see for therapy? It would have been easy to document he was a patient and get records of his appointments and the name of the person who paid his bills. However, there is something that corroborates part of Davern's claims. In the summer of 1980, The New York Times reported the SEC was investigating ABC for paying Hollywood producers Spelling and Goldberg "tens of millions of dollars" from the Charlie's Angels production under suspicious circumstances.

The investigation came on the heels of a continuing probe by the LA County District Attorney to establish if officials of ABC and Spelling-Goldberg Productions took part in a "scheme to defraud profit participants in the television series Charlie's Angels." A few months later, the Los Angeles Times reported the FBI had launched an inquiry "into possible criminal involvement or racketeering in the entertainment industry," including "allegations of fraud concerning the Charlie's Angels television series." The Wagners were "victims" because they had a Charlie's Angels profit participation contract with Spelling-Goldberg.

The investigation continued for months, causing great angst in the industry before the DA and FBI closed their files. Wagner was interviewed by FBI agents in their "inquiry." This would explain Wagner's idea to use the FBI to intimidate Davern and Davern's belief that Wagner knew what he was talking about.)

∽∾∽∾∽∾∽∾

On the first anniversary of Natalie's death, Davern said Wagner wanted to take Katie, Natasha and Courtney to Switzerland to get away from the media. Davern wanted to join them, but Wagner wanted Davern to "go his own way." This, Davern related, is when Wagner started pushing him away.

Davern said Wagner insisted he visit his family in New Jersey, so Davern went home. Wagner paid for the trip and gave him a thousand dollars. When Wagner and his family came home from Switzerland, the captain returned to California. Davern later said after about 18 months, he was allowed to move out. Then, Wagner pushed him even further away.

Davern returned to live on *Splendour*. Without notice, Davern said Wagner "gave the yacht away" to a nonprofit called the Sea Scouts in September 1983. Shortly thereafter, Davern's studio work slowed, even though there was plenty of work. He said other extras were called in daily, while Davern only landed "about one part a week." He suspected Wagner was behind the decline. By 1985, Davern claimed he had "no studio work" at all.

In January 1984, his ex-girlfriend Yolanda Alanis gave an interview to *Star* magazine. Davern phoned Wagner to say he had no involvement in the story, but Wagner didn't return his calls. So Davern went to Wagner's mobile home on the *Hart to Hart* set. In *Goodbye*, Davern recalled the conversation that followed:

> R.J. threw his hands in the air with exasperation. "Stop it! Just stop it, Dennis," he scowled. "I don't give a fuck anymore who says what! So, give it the fuck up, Dennis, okay? It's over!"
>
> "Well, I just want to let you know that I had nothing to do with it," Dennis meekly explained.
>
> "With what, Dennis? So fucking what, what that bitch had to say! I don't give a fuck if you sell out, too. But, mark my words, *no one* will *ever* make a movie or publish a book about Natalie in *my* lifetime. Yeah, I *can* control that!"

(Sinatra made a similar declaration. In Kelley's tell-all biography of the entertainer, she wrote, "During an unguarded moment Frank once said that he would never allow the story of his life to be told. 'Never. That will never happen as long as I have any control over the project.'" Wagner loved to imitate his idols.)

Davern's last meeting with his boss occurred when the skipper visited Wagner at his new home to inform him he had decided to tell his story in *Star*. When Wagner answered the door, Davern started to explain the reason for his visit, but said Wagner left for a few moments. When he returned, Wagner had a $2,000 check and said, "Take this as final payment for odd jobs and make it from here on your own." Davern hadn't seen Wagner more than a couple of times in months, much less done any odd jobs for him.

∽∾∽∾∽∾∽∾

In *Goodbye*, Davern emphasized what was common knowledge in the industry when his book was published: Natalie was afraid of ocean water. In all the years Davern was captain, he said he never saw her go into the ocean, or swim, wade or even touch the water.

(Natalie's fear of deep, dark water was confirmed by Walter Grauman, her director for the 1980 television movie The Memory of Eva Ryker. *Natalie plays dual roles—mother and daughter—in the story about the survivors of a sunken luxury liner. After her death, Grauman was interviewed and shared this conversation he had with Natalie about one of several water scenes in the film:*

"There's a scene on the beach in which Brad Dillman, who is playing the heavy, is chasing Natalie down the sandy water's edge, and she's supposed to run into the water and swim to try to get away from him. And so I was describing what I wanted Natalie to do, and she says, 'Walter, I have to ask you a favor.' And I said, 'What?' And she said, 'I am deathly afraid of deep water.' And particularly dark...in the dark. But deep water...black water. And she said, 'Please don't make me do that.' So I said 'OK, I'll figure another way to do it. We'll use a stunt double to get you into the water.' And I did.")

∽∽∽∽∽∽∽

To further assess Davern's credibility, I conducted an additional examination of some statements he made over the years.

Davern's first official statement to homicide investigators occurred at the sheriff's station in Isthmus Harbor at 11:20 a.m. Sunday, November 29, 1981. Overall, the captain continued his original narrative, which he now says was false. However, he did say two significant things: the Zodiac was "usually tied to stern" and the trip "to the island" was "very rough," causing six wine bottles to break.

(Of course, we know rough seas had nothing to do with the broken wine bottle. But the statement about where the Zodiac was tied when the foursome returned to Splendour on Saturday night—and who tied it— has become a bone of contention in the storyline of Natalie's death. In his book, Davern flatly stated after participating in his second interview with Detective Rasure, he never saw him again. But Rasure's official notes proved that statement is false.

On March 5, 1982, Davern met with Rasure a third time at his lawyer's office. Davern was asked whether Wagner knew he spent the night with Natalie in her hotel room Friday. Davern said he told Wagner "later." He was also asked about the "movements" of everyone after they returned to the yacht Saturday night. Davern said he couldn't recall. But he did say Wagner "tied the Zodiac to the center tie." In his book, however, Davern was insistent he himself tied the dinghy parallel with the yacht's stern using both painter lines secured at the transom tie cleats, so it was tight against the swim step. He emphasized this to rebut Wagner's "banging dinghy" theory, which required Natalie to step on the swim step to retie the dinghy. In the March 5 interview, Davern had no reason to lie about who tied the dinghy. But for his book, he steered in another direction to try to make an emphatic point to refute Wagner.)

A boat's transom is the part of the stern where the two sides of the hull meet. According to Davern in *Goodbye*, chrome tie cleats were located 12 feet apart—the width of the back deck—on *Splendour's* stern. (See Page A-6.) When the Zodiac was tied to these stern cleats, Davern explained "the dinghy can be and usually is retied *from the deck.*" In other words, "no one has to leave the boat and step out to the swim step to secure the dinghy."

(In his book, Davern didn't mention another place the dinghy could be tied—an "eye-ring tie" on the starboard side of the transom away from the swim step door on the port side. Yet, the same thing holds true for a dinghy tied to the eye-ring—you don't have to get on the swim step to tighten a loose dinghy painter line. All of this runs counter to Wagner's claim that Natalie must have slipped on the swim step attempting to retie the Zodiac.

On the other hand, photos show the stern of Splendour underwent at least one modification while the Wagners owned it. The stern is white in a photo taken October 8, 1976. See Page A-7. In a photo taken later, but before Natalie died, the stern has a teakwood-type finish. Also on Page A-7. In both, it appears there is a chrome handle, cleat or similar accessory on both the port and starboard sides of the upper portion of the stern's exterior. It's possible the Zodiac could have been fastened to one or both of those pieces of hardware if the painter lines were tied to the stern. Moreover, the 1976 photo shows two items that appear to be ladder rungs on the starboard side of the stern's exterior which are not present in the later photo.

Unfortunately, every dated photograph I have seen of Splendour after Natalie's death had a covering over the stern that blocked the name of the yacht and any hardware, making it impossible to tell whether further modifications eliminated the hardware shown in the photo with the teakwood finish.

Finally, in the March 5 interview, Davern also admitted he recalled the "RJ and Walken argument and Walken walking out on deck" and that he thought "Nat and the Zodiac [were] missing about the same time" the argument occurred. That's inconsistent with a timeline statement he made to Kroll that they discovered Natalie missing "about midnight.")

Davern's third interview was aligned with Wagner's December 4 interview in most material respects. But this time, Davern said Natalie was "knowledgeable of the boat," she and Walken "went ashore in [the] Zodiac" when they left the yacht Saturday afternoon, and he and Wagner followed later in a shore boat.

(As you may recall, in his book, Davern said Natalie and Walken left Splendour in a shore boat as he and Wagner waved goodbye. The captain also firmly asserted he and Wagner left Splendour for Doug's in the Zodiac. Of course, this position was necessary to buttress his claim that Natalie didn't know how to operate the dinghy and never drove without him. Yet, there is now no doubt Natalie knew how to drive the Zodiac and took it out during the day alone, if Miller, who had no reason to lie, is to be believed.

In his second interview with LASD investigators, Davern also said Wagner tied the dinghy to the yacht's stern Saturday night and Walken "interfered" with Wagner and Natalie's "conversation about her being away," which upset Wagner. Davern said after Walken went outside, Natalie went below. He claimed "normally" she would return to say goodnight, but "he did not see her again." And when Wagner went to check on her, she was gone and they thought she "went ashore." After that, Wagner "called [a] shore boat and went ashore." This was Davern's first and only representation that Wagner managed to get a shore boat to take him to the pier to apparently look for Natalie. From Wintler's statements, we know Wagner got to the pier alone. But who escorted him is still a mystery.)

From everything I've read, Davern didn't speak with *anyone* about the events of Thanksgiving weekend until his paid interview—$26,000 (about $63,000 today)—with *Star* magazine in July 1985.

The *Star* article was a multipage, running narrative with dramatic color illustrations. But later Davern claimed he didn't tell the *Star* "everything." Davern failed to mention his claim of Natalie and Wagner's screaming fight in the master stateroom and back deck shortly before she disappeared. He said he omitted it because he was afraid of Wagner and worried he might be sent to jail.

Davern said he only gave the *Star* interview because Walken gave one to *Star* in June 1985 and "lied." I suspect that was partially true. There's nothing to show he was gainfully employed from the time Wagner cut ties with him. He was also an admitted drunk. So, his payday from *Star* was a welcome sum of money until the next payment for his "story." My conclusion is supported by Finstad in her book *Natasha*. She wrote that Rulli said Davern vacillated on going public about the events. Then, "when his funds were totally depleted," he decided to talk to the tabloids.

The *Star* exposé featured Davern as the author along with Brian Haugh, a *Star* reporter. It recounted a story so inconsistent with what Davern would later say in his 2009 book that it's hard to know where to start. Of course, Davern's mention of Quaaludes ensured that "drugs" made the article's headlines along with "bitter jealousy." Davern also toned down Wagner's vulgar language by stating Wagner said, after smashing the wine bottle, "What are you trying to do? Seduce my wife?"

Davern wrote for *Star* that he and Wagner drank until "after midnight" before Wagner went "below," and Wagner stayed in the stateroom "about a half-hour" before returning to tell him Natalie was missing. But the captain did say, "He [Wagner] signaled to the shore boat and he went in by the shore at the Isthmus, but found nothing."

As for identifying Natalie's body, Davern said her down jacket was folded over her and he was shown her jewelry, including "gold earrings" and a "diamond ring" (which, in 1985, he claimed Wagner gave her Friday night after the trio shopped in Avalon). Then, Davern wrote, "Her face was puffy and she looked so white. They showed me some bruises on the body, but I didn't want to look."

After the *Star* splash, for the next 15 years, Davern was alone in a world still hungry for the truth in Natalie's case. That's when Finstad and Kashner hit the scene.

∿∿∿∿∿∿

Davern claimed in *Goodbye* he got his drinking under control by 1986. But subsequent events cast considerable doubt on that assertion. Around 1991, he made a series of drunken calls to Lana Wood. In those calls, you will learn Davern told Lana there were things he "couldn't bring himself" to tell and "uglier things" she didn't want to know.

(In his 2009 book, Davern denied he knew when Natalie was in the water and implied, with half-baked polygraph examinations, that the book contained the whole truth. But he doesn't deny making drunken phone calls to Lana in 1991.)

Between 1991 and 2000, Davern and Rulli were hustling to get their book out, including an ill-fated appearance in 1992 on Geraldo Rivera's *Now It Can Be Told* television show. Then came a likely paid appearance in the 2000 British documentary *The Final Day*. In its fourth episode titled *Natalie Wood*, Davern recited his latest version of what happened. Among other things, he said after the Saturday evening fight between Natalie and Wagner in the master stateroom, *Wagner returned to the bridge* about 11:30 p.m., "tousled, sweating profusely, as if he had been in a terrible fight, an ordeal of some kind." A short while later, they determined Natalie and the dinghy were gone.

(The British documentary is the third version of what Davern said happened after hearing the master stateroom fight between the two stars Saturday night. In Goodbye, Davern said after the altercation, he left the flybridge for the back deck and "came up behind R.J. and there was no Natalie. R.J. **turned around and looked at me like he saw a ghost** *[emphasis added]."*

In 2011, Davern appeared on the television show Nancy Grace. The energetic host began with the question, "Was there an argument on the yacht?" In an uninterrupted narrative, with this rendition Davern said when it became quiet after Natalie and Wagner's screaming quarrel, he went to the back deck. When he got there, "Robert Wagner was standing there **leaning his back against the back of the boat** *[emphasis added] facing the boat and he said that Natalie was missing.")*

In 2000 and 2001, Davern, or Rulli on Davern's behalf, provided details on the events in November 1981 to Kashner for *Vanity Fair*. He told Kashner that he and Wagner drank until 1:30 a.m. before Wagner said he needed to check on Natalie, "returning a few minutes later to say she was gone." Of course, this is inconsistent with statements made to Deputy Kroll and LASD investigators, in his interviews with *Star* and Grace, in the British documentary and in his book.

Another inconsistency concerns the injuries Davern claimed he saw when he identified Natalie's body. In his 1985 *Star* interview, he said the authorities tried to show him "bruises on the body" but he "didn't want to look." However, in his 2009 book, Davern said he "noticed bruises on her body" and her "face appeared swollen."

Davern's next official statement occurred in 2011 when he and Rulli were shepherding a petition to reopen Natalie's case. A typed statement, purporting to be Davern's all-inclusive narrative of what happened Friday and Saturday along with events following Natalie's disappearance, merely said this about her injuries: "I noticed bruises on her body."

Then, by 2018, Davern and Rulli, resolved to the fact Wagner wasn't going to be charged with murder, proved they were willing to milk Natalie's death for all it was worth. The late-summer 2018 podcast was sold to me as a genuine attempt to lay out some of the truth in Natalie's case. Lana, Rulli, Davern, Detective Hernandez, Lt. Corina, Nancy Grace and Roger Smith were featured along with a list of "experts." I was also asked to appear as an unpaid expert on a few subjects.

Among the disheartening things about the podcast were producers using Baywatch Isthmus lifeguard Roger Smith, who said things Davern and Rulli had to know were false; allowing Rulli to run amok with the facts; and showcasing Davern, who lowered himself to exaggerate the evidence further. Asked about viewing bruises when he officially identified Natalie's body, his response for the podcast was:

> It was horrible. She had more bruises on her body than you can imagine. I said to myself, "This poor woman was beat." She had bruises on her face, she had bruises on her wrist. There were a number of bruises. I can't remember exactly where they all were located, because after I looked at her face, I just didn't want to look anymore.

In three previous detailed official accounts and in his book, Davern didn't mention bruises on Natalie's face or wrist, or that Natalie "was beat." Although Natalie did have an abrasion on the left side of her face and, according to Kroll, a small laceration on her nose, three pathologists as well as Pamela Eaker, Deputy Kroll and two investigators made no mention of "bruises" on her face. Natalie had plenty of bruises, but they were in large part on the inside of her right arm and on the front and back of her legs. Moreover, Natalie only had one old, small bruise on the tip of her left wrist deformity. (See *Figures 10* and *11*, Pages 35-36.)

<center>~~~~~~~~~</center>

Efforts to rehabilitate Davern's credibility at this point may be difficult to impossible on several levels. There seems to be little doubt he's prone to exaggeration and capable of being manipulated into uniting his position with the narrative du jour. However, the core elements of Davern's narrative can be summarized in the form of seven questions.

Did Davern have a conversation with Natalie on Friday night in the hotel room about her anger, frustration and intentions over Wagner's jealousy of her leading men? Did Wagner, in a profanity-laced manner Saturday night after dinner, scream accusations of intended infidelity toward Walken before violently smashing a wine bottle over the coffee table in the yacht's salon? Was Natalie present when the bottle was smashed? Did Natalie angrily leave the salon for the master stateroom with Wagner following her minutes later? Was there a screaming, cussing, banging fight between Natalie and Wagner in the master stateroom that spilled out on the back deck? Did Natalie disappear somewhere around 11 p.m. Saturday? And, did Wagner try to cover up what happened Saturday night by delaying a search, fabricating a false narrative, keeping Davern hostage in his home and attempting to buy Davern's silence with money and employment?

I've already presented evidence answering some of these questions. The remainder will be addressed later in this journey of truth. Then, in Chapter 22: *Summation*, I will piece together the evidence that corroborates Davern's core narrative.

CHAPTER 14

out of the shadows

CURT LEE CRAIG WORKED FOR DOUG BOMBARD AS A HARBOR PATROL officer in 1981. CSI Hamilton's handwritten notes identified Craig as a "Harbor Patrol Master" and the descriptive information obtained by Deputy Kroll said that Craig was 26 years old, a white male and lived in the Isthmus. Kroll listed Craig as witness "7 of 11," but apparently left Craig's interview for the experienced detectives.

We searched high and low for Craig. Through the years of my investigation, four research assistants, three retired detectives and I searched diligently for several material witnesses. We determined witnesses were deceased. We had witnesses who were "hiding out" or didn't want to be bothered. We discovered witnesses who had become mentally incompetent. Some witnesses didn't want to talk. But we never had a material witness vanish without a trace—until Craig.

Then, in July 2019, my persistent assistant found a Curt Lee Craig in Broken Arrow, Oklahoma. For three years, we had been searching for "Kurt Craig" because that's how Deputy Kroll spelled Craig's first name in his report.

Expecting no response, I sent a handwritten letter to Broken Arrow to see if he was the person we were looking for. Five days later, I received a text of confirmation. As far as I knew, this was going to be the first time in 38 years anyone had discussed the events of Saturday evening, November 28, 1981, with the former Harbor Patrol officer outside of a brief conversation with Rasure and Hamilton at 2:50 p.m. on November 29, 1981.

My money was on Craig or Peterson, the Saturday evening shore boat operator, as the person who escorted Wagner to the pier before Wagner accompanied Wintler on his "boat row" search for Natalie and the dinghy. What Wagner may have given as his excuse for needing a ride to the pier at 1 a.m. is something that needs to be exposed.

When we got the chance to visit via Skype, what Curt Craig told me was certainly illuminating. It just wasn't the revelation I was expecting.

In 1981, Curt lived in a small cottage in the Isthmus. "It was the highest-up residence in the Isthmus," he said. During the winter, he was the "only Harbor Patrolman." His employment with Bombard began in March 1980, giving him 20 months on the job by November 1981. (See Page A-8.) The Saturday night Natalie disappeared, Curt was working with Peterson.

In a videoconference, I asked him to share his memories of that night. I wanted to watch his mannerisms. After confirming that in 38 years he had only been interviewed by officials in 1981, he confidently told me he had gotten a call around 10 p.m. Saturday from Don Whiting, a good friend and night manager at Doug's Harbor Reef. Whiting wanted him "to keep an eye on" Wagner and his party as they went out to their boat.

"So, I knew I had to be discreet in doing this. I didn't want to be standing outside staring at them. And so I opened the door to the Harbor [Patrol] office, which had a glass window in it, and I could see their reflections," Curt said. Then he revealed this:

> I turned around briefly just to make sure what I was seeing was correct. And Natalie was out in front of them [Wagner, Walken and Davern] by about 10 feet. And they appeared to be—this is what I told the detective or whoever it was—that they appeared to have been drinking. I didn't say they were drunk. This was a point of contention with Doug Bombard and myself after this happened. He called me to his office and I got my ass chewed out by him, saying that I made a "stupid and irresponsible remark"—his exact words. I'll never forget it.
>
> What am I to do? Lie to a deputy? No. I didn't know at the time that I was supposed to be lying.

Agitated, Curt pressed on by saying the foursome crossed over and went down to the dinghy dock. That's when he lost sight of them. He told me he was "almost positive" he left the office at that point and went to the opposite side of the pier to look down at their dinghy. That's when Wagner screamed out, "I broke my fucking arm!"

His memory was cloudy over whether he looked over the side of the pier "pre- or post-" Wagner screaming, but thought Wagner was the first one into the dinghy inasmuch as "he fell in because he was so intoxicated." After that, Curt said Wagner "started laughing and cussing and stuff like that." According to Curt, the Wagner party left the dinghy dock and went "all the way out there" since "they were more out in the outer area [of the mooring rows.]" As a precaution, Curt said he asked Peterson to go there and check to make sure they "got on the boat OK." Then Curt added, "If I remember right, he did that."

Because the official report and investigators' notes from Curt's Sunday afternoon interview said he described Natalie as "screaming" and being "drunk and pissed off," I specifically asked him about that. Curt looked at me seriously and said, "I don't remember that, and I'm pretty sure I would if it happened." He emphasized that the only "scream" he heard came from Wagner.

Curt continued his narrative by telling me that after the Wagner party was safely on their boat, he went home and "went to sleep." (He was off duty at 10:30 p.m.) Much later, Whiting responded to *Splendour's* call for help on Channel 16 VHF. He came to Curt's cottage but couldn't wake Curt or his roommate.

In the morning, before Natalie's body was found, Curt eventually became involved in the search for Natalie by going "boat to boat" and "house to house" because "there was some type of feeling" that Natalie was "upset and she left"—to "most likely get away from Robert Wagner." He didn't remember where he got that information, but he was instructed by Oudin not to mention Natalie's name during the search.

Furthermore, according to Rasure's handwritten notes, after Natalie's body was recovered, Curt apparently talked to Warren Archer, owner of the vessel *Vantage.* Curt gave the investigators his information on Archer. Rasure's notes for Curt said, "[Vantage] People asked *Splendour* people over for a drink. *Observed dinghy tied up to Splendour* [emphasis added]." No time of day was noted.

Hamilton's notes said Archer "saw *Avon* [emphasis added] tied to *Splendour*." As a matter of fact, Hamilton crossed out the word "Zodiac" in his notes and wrote "Avon" above. In 1981, Avon Inflatables manufactured dinghies that were certainly distinguishable from Zodiac dinghies. Most telling, however, Rasure wrote in his official report that Curt stated the "*Zodiac* [emphasis added] ... was tied up to the *Splendour*" at the time of Archer's call. The conflict supports the presence of another person on *Splendour* after Natalie and the Zodiac disappeared.

At that point, I turned the conversation to Payne, Wayne and the sailboat *Capricorn*. I wanted to know if Curt talked with them Sunday morning while he was searching, and if he did, did they talk about hearing screams the night before. He said he did acquire that information, but thought it came from another searcher.

However, on December 4, 1981, the *San Bernardino Sun* carried a Los Angeles Associated Press report of Marilyn Wayne hearing screams Saturday near midnight. With the headline, "Witness says she heard screams from direction of Wood's yacht," the article reported Curt as saying he happened onto *Capricorn while looking for Natalie on Sunday* and "was told of the screams." Apparently, the *Sun* contacted LASD investigators about that report, and they "refused comment." This establishes that the screams were reported to Craig, who was looking for an unidentified missing person, by Payne and Wayne before Natalie's body was found, negating any suggestion that Payne and Wayne were seeking notoriety.

Curt didn't help me solve the Wagner pier transportation mystery, but some extremely important information was derived from our conversation. First, the effort to protect the Wagners began with connected locals in the Isthmus. Second, if what Curt said is truthful—and it certainly appears so—Rasure intentionally manipulated his official report to cast drunkenness away from Wagner and onto Natalie. Finally, Wintler's report to me, and earlier to Rasure, that Wagner said he had a fight with Natalie before she disappeared had made its way through the Isthmus grapevine very early in the search.

And most significantly, every boat was contacted by locals during the search for Natalie and *no one* reported seeing or hearing anything unusual except Payne and Wayne. Furthermore, other than Payne and Wayne, no one reported anyone in the water crying for help, either as a drunken prank or a serious incident. You will learn the significance of that cannot be understated when it comes to a *bona fide* assessment of the current LASD detectives' theory of the evidence in Natalie's case.

❧❧❧❧❧❧

From the official report and investigators' notes, it was clear Peterson was awake and working at *1:05 a.m.* According to Hamilton's notes, Peterson provided information about a "harbor check" he made at 12:45 a.m. during which he "didn't notice a dinghy." Unfortunately, Hamilton didn't clarify if that meant he didn't see *Splendour's* dinghy or if he didn't notice any dinghies in the harbor.

But in Rasure's official report, he wrote that Peterson stated "at approximately 12:45 a.m. he had been requested by members of the Long Beach Coast Guard to make a harbor check looking for a boat which was overdue." During this check, according to Rasure's report, Peterson "had observed nothing unusual." Strangely, the information Rasure included in his official report about Peterson never appeared in the notes of either investigator.

Initially, the obvious questions for me were, *What boat was overdue? Why did the Coast Guard request a "harbor check" of the Isthmus at 12:45 a.m.?* And, finally, *Why did Rasure change what Peterson said about not noticing a dinghy to "he had observed nothing unusual"?*

If the Peterson references related to Natalie and the Zodiac dinghy, it established that Natalie and the dinghy were gone from the yacht *before 12:45 a.m.*, at least, and that someone called the Coast Guard about something that required a harbor check shortly before 12:45 a.m.

We searched a long time for Peterson with no success until my assistant found a prospect in Hawaii. I wrote another letter asking if he had worked in the Isthmus in 1981. In a stroke of improbable and ironic luck, the same day I heard from Craig, I received an email from Peterson. In his thoughtful reply to my letter, Peterson said something that struck a familiar chord in my investigation:

> Having been there and having seen how this unfortunate incident has been portrayed over the years, I feel somewhat obligated. My little segment of "truth" may not reveal any undiscovered secrets, but such as they are, I am willing to share my memories.

We began a dialogue by email and our communications were professional and serious. Peterson wanted the truth out there in Natalie's case. I wanted to oblige.

Peterson informed me that shortly after graduating from college in 1970, he joined the U.S. Coast Guard and served until 1975, ending his active service as a lieutenant. In November 1981, he was employed by Doug Bombard as a shore boat driver and lived with his wife and children in a small home on the south side of the Isthmus, close to the road to Avalon.

He worked the weekend evening shifts from "perhaps 5 or 6 p.m." until the restaurant bar closed—"often as late as 2 a.m." He told me the bar tended to stay open until the crowd left. "But during the shoulder months [off-peak season including November] it might easily close at 10 p.m.," he added.

Peterson explained that by November, "the harbor is mostly empty during the week and only a bit fuller on the weekend." In fact, he said business in the Isthmus "fell off substantially at the end of November." However, Thanksgiving weekend in 1981 was "rather fuller than usual for that time of year," he recalled.

Since Natalie's death, he had been interviewed by officials twice about his knowledge of the events the weekend Natalie died. The first time was Sunday, November 29, 1981, at the "outside deck of the Isthmus snack bar." The second was in Hawaii after the investigation was reopened in 2011. He informed me in both instances he remembered telling them about seeing the Wagner party come down the ramp to the dinghy dock late Saturday night and seeing "one or more of the party sliding on the damp ramp."

Peterson also said an occupant of the yacht *Vantage* called on the VHF radio requesting Peterson come to his yacht. "This was well after midnight and he appeared to me to be inebriated," Peterson said. The owner, Warren Archer, wanted him to "invite the Wagner party from the *Splendour* over…for a drink." Because he was "going off duty," Peterson said, "I declined to pass on his invitation." Undaunted, Archer then asked Peterson to "deliver a bottle of champagne to the Wagner boat." Peterson "declined to do this as well."

According to Craig, *Vantage* was moored "one row shoreward" from *Splendour* and "the second boat in from the fairway" (mooring N-2). The fairway is the entry passageway within the mooring field.

I had initially provided Peterson with a list of questions, but in a follow-up email, I asked him if he remembered loud music Saturday night. He responded, "I do not recall any loud music that night. Normally there is music (with a DJ) and dancing on the outside deck by the bar—but that evening was late in the season and the weather was not the best. The only activity I recall was taking place inside the bar and restaurant—and even that was earlier in the evening."

Then we discussed the official report and investigator notes regarding the Coast Guard "harbor check" entry. Unfortunately, time had taken its toll on Peterson's memory regarding that event, most probably because it was routine at the time it happened. But after a follow-up question, Peterson provided me with some highly enlightening information on Coast Guard harbor checks in November 1981. His explanation is as follows:

> In 1981, the LA County Baywatch had only been stationed at Two Harbors for a couple of seasons. Our Harbor Department was still the primary contact for the USCG to call for missing or overdue boaters. When a call came into the USCG SAR (Search and Rescue) Operation Center in Long Beach, the duty crew would usually contact the Harbor Departments of the surrounding bays—such as Two Harbors and Avalon—and ask them to do a "harbor check" looking for such-and-such a vessel, sailboat or powerboat, of so many feet with a certain hull color, etc., with so-and-so passengers aboard. During normal operation hours, the harbor check would be performed by the Harbor Patrol on their patrol boat (assuming they did not already have the [missing] boat listed as having been assigned a mooring during the day). After hours, they usually called the shore boat operators on Channel 16 VHF.

> I doubt if this [the harbor check] was ever an official procedure—more of a neighborly request for assistance. An honest-to-goodness "mayday" call would involve scrambling more assets—Coast Guard cutters, patrol boats, and helicopters—to do a coordinated search. Most often, however, calls from family or friends reporting overdue boats could be resolved by having the locals look over the harbor and see the missing vessel tied up to a mooring with the crew ashore in the bar.

> Before Baywatch, our local Harbor Patrol, shore boats, and mooring boats were the primary first responders—not only locating, but also rescuing boats in trouble.

Our next subject was the cries for help reported by Payne and Wayne. Peterson was skeptical of them because of what he believed was their failure to respond to the situation. He told me he "never heard any screams or loud arguments that entire evening." But he voluntarily conceded that "the engine of my shore boat was running most of the evening, and it is possible that I would not have heard any such sounds." And, a harbor check "could have included the nearby coves of Cherry and Fourth of July. If so, I could have been out of Isthmus Cove when whatever happened at *Splendour* took place."

Finally, I asked Peterson this question: Before you closed up Saturday night, did you carry anyone from *Splendour* to the pier? He replied, "I do not recall picking anyone up from *Splendour* at any time that evening. That I believe I would have remembered clearly considering the events."

Once again, I failed to solve the mystery of how Wagner got to the pier before his late-night harbor boat row search with Wintler, but the combination of investigator notes, Rasure's report, my interviews with Craig and Peterson and reasonable inferences establish a defining series of events.

At *12:45 a.m.* Sunday, Peterson performed a harbor check. The only reported or mentioned event that would have given rise to that action was Natalie's disappearance. Peterson didn't notice "a dinghy." The only dinghy we know of that was the subject of any inquiry that night was *Splendour's* Zodiac. At that point, only three people knew about those two matters: Wagner, Davern and Walken, even though Walken claimed in 1983 he was "asleep when it happened."

At 1:05 a.m., Peterson reported *Vantage* owner Warren Archer called asking Peterson to invite the Wagners over for a drink. At the same time, an "inebriated" Archer reported he saw an "Avon dinghy" tied up to *Splendour*. Someone else, who hasn't come forward, was on *Splendour* at 1:05 a.m. in an Avon dinghy after Natalie and the Zodiac disappeared. I'm certain that person, or persons, dropped Wagner off at the pier.

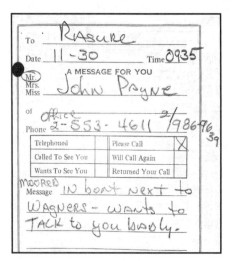

Figure 28: Message of the first phone call from John Payne to Detective Duane Rasure
(Los Angeles County Sheriff's Department)

But, most discouragingly, Peterson told me "at least a quarter to 50 percent of the dinghies at the [Isthmus] dock that day were Avon or Avon knock-offs." The mystery of Wagner's transportation to the pier early Sunday morning remains. But I'm convinced that whoever gave Wagner a lift to the pier owned or operated an Avon dinghy.

∽∽∽∽∽∽∽∽

On November 29, 1981, LASD investigators were on the island until at least 6:15 p.m. interviewing witnesses. Yet no attempt was made to contact *Capricorn's* occupants until 11:15 a.m. the following day. And that contact was precipitated by two frantic telephone messages left by Payne with the Homicide Bureau at 9:35 a.m. and 10:13 a.m.

Rasure must have instructed Hamilton to return Payne's call. After providing Hamilton with his complete contact information, Payne described what he, his fiancée and her 8-year-old boy witnessed Saturday night, according to CSI Hamilton's notes of his *telephone conversation* with Payne:

He was moored near the Wagners. At midnight he heard women (sic) yelling. "Help—Help, Someone please help me." This was coming from

direction of near stern of *Splendour* in the water. He thought it was someone in a dinghy that was from another boat moored on the opposite
side. His girlfriend woke up and heard it too. He also heard a man's
voice coming from opposite boat yell in a mocking voice "OK, Honey,
we'll get you." This voice sounded drunk and there was a loud drunken
party on this boat. He did not hear any noises coming from the *Splendour*.

I can state without reservation that if I had been given this information as a district attorney in this high-profile case, along with Wagner's dubious statements on November 29,
Walken's admission of an argument with Wagner shortly before Natalie disappeared, the

way Natalie was dressed when her body was
found, Natalie's unexplained injuries, and
Wintler's statement about Wagner saying he
and Natalie quarreled, I would have made a
beeline to Payne.

The investigators had no idea of the cal-
iber of people on *Capricorn* and that's not
something you can determine with a phone
call. The autopsy hadn't been completed
and the microscopic and toxicological tests
weren't finished. For all Rasure knew, Natalie could have been choked and thrown
overboard to drown. But, instead of aggres-
sively following those serious leads, Rasure
dismissed Payne and Wayne.

Frustrated because the authorities didn't
seem interested in their information, Wayne
talked to *Los Angeles Times* reporter Keith
Love. The front page of the B section of the
December 3, 1981, edition of the *Times* reports, "Heard Cries for Help Near Wagner
Boat, Woman Says." The story is eight col-
umns and identifies Wayne as a "commod-
ities broker."

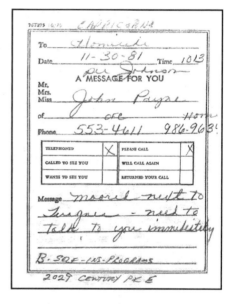

Figure 29: Message of the second phone
call from John Payne to the Homicide Bureau (Los Angeles County Sheriff's Department)

At 10:30 a.m. the day the story was published, Hamilton called Wayne. Out of the
presence of Payne, she provided details strikingly similar to what Payne had told Hamilton.
Hamilton's notes from his conversation with Wayne read:

> She was asleep on the Capricorn. Other person was John Payne. First
> time at Cataline (sic). At midnight John woke her and asked if she could
> hear something. I opened hatch and I could hear something. Woman
> yelling "Someone please help me, please help me." This was yelling
> coming from the direction of nine o'clock position from our boat. John
> asked me what I thought we should do and I said call the Coast Guard.
> He said he didn't want to go out there because they thought the wom-

an was from a drunken party that was on a boat that was at their one o'clock position (Vantage). Also, she heard someone from Vantage yelling back to her that they were coming to get her. She said John thought woman sounded drunk but I thought she was hysterical.

Yelling continued for 5 minutes and stopped. I thought someone from Vantage had picked her up. Didn't see dinghy. Didn't hear any noise from *Splendour* and didn't notice whether lights on.

It was very cold that night at midnight. It was "calm before the storm." About 1:45 it got very rough, thunder. Lightning.

Hamilton's notes of Wayne's call, however, were decidedly deficient, almost amateurish in detail. Saying Wayne heard yelling from the "nine o'clock position" told you nothing without identifying *Capricorn's* position in relation to the position of *Splendour*. *Was "nine o'clock" in the direction of Splendour? Was there, in fact, a drunken party on Vantage? Were the cries for help coming from the water?* It's almost as if the notes were written in an intentionally vague and confusing manner to leave the impression the witness was just as vague and unsure.

∽∾∽∾∽∾∽

In early 2016, I flew to Los Angeles to try to find Marilyn Wayne. Although I had her address, I had no way of knowing if it was accurate.

Based on my experience, the odds of finding Marilyn at home on my first attempt was slim. But, it's like fishing, "If you don't cast your lure in the water, you're guaranteed not to catch a fish."

Marilyn lived in Rancho Palos Verdes, about 23 miles from my hotel. When we arrived, I told my driver to park down the street because I didn't want Marilyn alarmed by a black town car sitting near her house. I walked up the hill and between two rows of condominiums with thoughts of how my presence would be received. I'll admit I was apprehensive as I knocked on the door.

Before I could knock again, the door opened. Even though she was in a sweat suit with her hair in a ponytail, I recognized her immediately from a TV interview. "Marilyn Wayne, my name is Sam Perroni. I'm writing a book about Natalie Wood and I was wondering if you could spare me a few minutes of your time," I said, expecting her to close the door in my face.

I could tell my presence dazed her, but to my surprise, she opened the screen door and said, "Sure, come on in." It was clear I had interrupted her, but Marilyn clicked off her computer and said, "Have a seat."

"Please excuse my appearance. I wasn't expecting anyone," she said, adjusting her hair. I apologized for showing up without an appointment and explained to her what I was trying to accomplish.

"I thought you came to kill me," she said gravely.

I was stunned. Thirty-seven years after Natalie's death, Marilyn genuinely feared for her life. She explained her fears by relating the tragic tale of her first and last trip to Catalina Island and the disheartening aftermath.

In 1981, Marilyn was employed as a securities broker at Shearson on 16 North Cañon Drive in Beverly Hills. As you know, Cañon Drive was also home to the Wagners, who lived at number 603. According to Marilyn, Shearson had a financial relationship with Robert Wagner and she believed Wagner's broker was Red Reeder. "He was that whole gang's stockbroker," she said. When I inquired what she meant by "whole gang," Marilyn told me Wagner and a few other actors and comedians were clients. "They all kind of ran around together and at times they would even come in together," she said.

Marilyn had seen Wagner in the office many times before November 1981. Her desk was stationed right before Red's office. "Wagner and the other celebrity clients had to go through my office to get to Red," she explained. Marilyn told me Wagner knew who she was and also knew Payne, her fiancé and a wealthy local businessman. As for Red, Marilyn saw him in the office almost daily.

After Marilyn become comfortable with me, she reminisced about her younger days before the securities business. Like many people in Los Angeles, she got involved in the acting business. "There was a short period in my life where I thought I wanted to do that. But I got out because people were too crazy," she said. I didn't follow up on that since I didn't want her to think I came for gossip.

But I needed to find out if she really was "someone seeking their name in the media," as Detective Rasure had described her in a 1981 newspaper article. Someone who was, perhaps, starstruck. So, I asked her the names of the movie stars and celebrities she had met. She listed Elvis Presley, Natalie Wood, John Wayne and more. "Really, I met more stars when I went into the business world than I ever did acting," she added emphatically.

I didn't ask Marilyn her age. But my researchers had learned her birth date during our background search, and from that, I extrapolated she was 38 years old in November 1981. That Thanksgiving weekend, she and her fiancé, along with Marilyn's handsome son, Anthony, decided to take John's sailboat to Two Harbors at the Isthmus. *Capricorn* was a 42-foot vessel, and this was its first trip to Catalina Island.

According to Marilyn, Payne loved his sailboat and they spent many weekends on the water, even when the weather was bad. *Capricorn* had two bedrooms, called berths. One was a double in the back of the boat, "I guess you would call that the master berth," she said, and her son slept in the smaller berth. It was "cold and rainy on Thanksgiving weekend," Marilyn recalled. But the boat was heated by a new, silent generator Payne had recently purchased.

After we became friends, I asked if she had any pictures from that weekend. Marilyn insisted on searching the boxes where she stored photos and sent several snapshots to me. As far as I know, they're the only photos in existence of the Isthmus the Saturday afternoon before Natalie drowned.

The photographs confirmed some of the weather conditions in the Isthmus, the moorings and the position of some of the boats. However, I anguished over one in particular. Marilyn is sitting in the sailboat's small inflatable dinghy. (See Page A-8.) *Capricorn* was moored facing Isthmus Pier. *Splendour* would have been on *Capricorn's* port (left) side approximately 100 feet across the fairway leading to the pier.

From Marilyn's position in the dinghy, *Splendour* would have been just outside of the picture to her right. But, Marilyn and Payne had no idea they were that close to the famous couple. They didn't recognize the boat or know that the Wagners owned it.

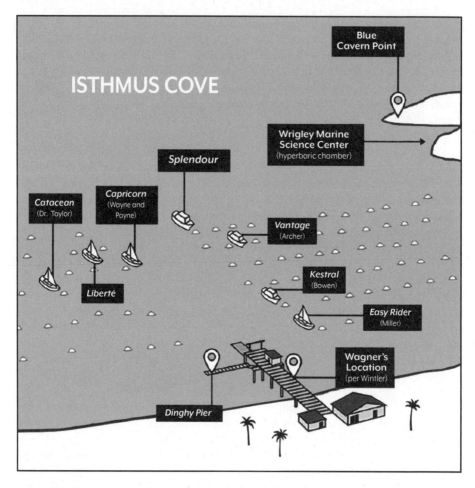

Figure 30: Illustration shows locations of watercraft moored in Isthmus Cove on Sunday morning, November 29, 1981. (Thoma Thoma)

I showed Marilyn an Isthmus mooring site map and explained the LASD's investigative file put *Splendour* at mooring site N-1, but that Oudin said he moored *Splendour* at mooring site O-1. Aerial news shots from the morning Natalie's body was found confirmed Oudin's memory. That would have placed *Capricorn* at site F-1. Marilyn told me a boat called *Liberté* was moored next to them at mooring site F-2, which would have been to the right or starboard side of *Capricorn*. There was no boat moored behind *Splendour*, because it was moored in the last row.

Marilyn, Payne and her son went to bed around 10 to 10:30 p.m. Saturday. Rain or shine, hot or cold, Marilyn opened a window for fresh air before she retired for the night. Saturday night aboard *Capricorn* was no exception. After they fell asleep, Payne woke Marilyn up saying, "Do you hear that?" Troubled, Marilyn said to me, "It alarmed me." She called out to Anthony, who said he heard it too.

I asked her the time this happened. She told me she knew it was 11:05 p.m. because Payne had recently given Anthony a new lighted digital watch and all three of them looked at it together.

"What did you hear?" I asked.

"We heard a woman calling for help. 'Help me, somebody please help me, I'm drowning,'" Marilyn said.

I could tell it was painful for Marilyn to recall. This had haunted her for over 35 years and the anguish was still there. Marilyn said Payne went out and switched on the high beam light and she went out on the deck. She said it was "very dark" and the water was "choppy." They couldn't see anything, but the cries continued.

"It was so confusing," she said. "It was very dark. We had already packed up to sail back to Newport Beach the next morning. There was no way to help unless I was to jump in and swim around blindly, which was not an option really, given the water temperature. I probably would have gotten hypothermia."

"To be clear, were the cries coming from the water?" I asked.

"Yes, for sure," she said, confidently. Then, she paused and looked up at me soberly. "I told John...I said, 'I'm going to jump in.' I had a bead on where the cries were coming from."

Marilyn explained she was a very strong swimmer at the time. Her dad, Marshall, was in the 1936 Olympics and won gold and silver medals in diving. His friend Johnny Weissmuller, an Olympic gold medalist who would go on to star in the movie *Tarzan*, taught her how to swim. "That's how I kept in shape," she said smiling.

After telling Payne she was going to jump in, Marilyn said he talked her out of it because he thought it was too dangerous. "I could be pulled under if she was drowning. I could be pulled under with her, and I had Anthony to think about. The whole thing was surreal... and so confusing," Marilyn lamented.

"What happened next?"

On edge, Marilyn replied, "We didn't know what to do. So, we did the logical thing. We radioed the Harbor Patrol, but nobody picked up. Then we called the sheriff's office in Avalon...that was 12 miles away. They said they would send a helicopter, but it never came."

"While you did this, did the cries continue?" I inquired.

"Yes, but we heard loud music...we thought there was a party on the *Liberté*. Then, we heard someone...it was slurred, as if the person were drunk...say something to the effect of 'Oh, hold on. We're coming to get you'...or...'We'll help you. Hold your hat. We're coming to get you.' But...the cries kept up. She was saying, 'Someone please help me. I'm drowning.'"

"Was the voice moving away from you or getting more distant sounding?" I asked.

"No, it was coming from the same direction. It was clear," Marilyn said.

"And, what direction was that? From which mooring?" I pressed.

"The mooring *Splendour* was tied to."

After all these years, Marilyn tensed up when she related the story of that fateful Saturday night. Her body language told me it was no act.

Marilyn recalled the cries for help lasted "25 minutes or so" and that she and Payne "felt helpless." During that time, Payne was on the radio and Marilyn was calling out to him. She explained it would have taken them at least half an hour to inflate their dinghy and "we thought a helicopter was coming any minute."

She said she yelled out, "Where are you? I'll come to help you. Keep talking." But she received no response.

"Can you describe the woman's calls for help? I mean, the sound of her voice," I asked.

"She sounded hysterical to me," Marilyn replied. So, they kept scanning the water with their light. They thought they might see the woman and the helicopter might see where they were. Marilyn then said sadly, "Then the cries stopped, and so did the music. I was very disturbed. I mean I still am…just talking about this. We could have helped her. We thought someone was coming for her."

Marilyn explained that when she said she had "a bead on where the cries were coming from," she meant they were coming from the boat next to them, somewhere around their nine o'clock position. I asked Marilyn whether she saw a dinghy tied to the back of *Splendour*. "I didn't really notice a dinghy because we weren't looking for a dinghy, and it was dark."

Marilyn said she and Payne did not learn the name of the boat until later that morning. "I didn't sleep the rest of the night. I was up by 5 a.m. and went right out on the deck… afraid that I would see something bad in the water. All I saw was water and *Splendour*. I jotted down the name because that was the area where the cries were coming from. Whoever it was crying out was between our boats, closer to *Splendour*, maybe 10 to 15 feet away [from it]."

Before they left for the mainland Sunday, Marilyn talked to "an official at the island," but didn't remember his name. But we know now from the *San Bernardino Sun* article she talked to Harbor Patrol's Curt Craig.

∽∾∽∾∽∾∽∾

After speaking with Craig, Marilyn and Payne finished packing up their things and sailed *Capricorn* back to Newport Beach. That's when they learned Natalie Wood had been found dead. "I felt numbness when I heard that…numbness and grief for her daughters. Just sick," Marilyn said. After realizing the importance of what they heard Saturday night, both she and Payne tried to make a report by calling the sheriff's department. "They never interviewed us," Marilyn emphasized.

Yet I knew each had been telephoned by CSI Hamilton on different days before Natalie's case was officially closed. Later, I realized the apparent inconsistency wasn't a lack of memory on that point, it was attributable to a lack of understanding as to what constitutes an "interview." People who are unfamiliar with criminal investigations think an interview must be in person. Otherwise, they feel the authorities believe their information to be unimportant, or worse, they're being dismissed. Marilyn and Payne weren't contacted in person by officials until 2012—31 years after the fact. And even then, they didn't ask Marilyn for photographs, show her a mooring map or learn her important background.

From a prosecutor's viewpoint, the content of the Payne and Wayne investigator notes, as incomplete as they were, suggested the couple didn't get together to fabricate their story. The fact there were now two witnesses to the event would tell a prosecutor there's a substantial likelihood the events described took place. Yet, what did Rasure do with the information from two highly credible witnesses at the scene? Nothing. Instead, according to the account in Finstad's book, here's how Rasure reacted:

Rasure discounted Payne's and Wayne's calls. "I'm not sure those people heard anything," he states, suggesting they were "making it up," or were remiss for not rescuing the woman in the water. Rasure claims he spoke to Payne and "got on his case pretty heavy…'Why didn't you get in your boat and try to save a woman helpless out there?'" Rasure does not remember whether he talked to Wayne, saying, "I don't believe her, either. She just wanted to keep it on the bandwagon."

With me, Marilyn was angry with Rasure. "How insulting. He didn't know us…never talked to us," she stressed.

If I had any doubts before, after examining the timeline of the Payne/Wayne matter, I was now convinced the fix was in within 24 hours of Natalie's death. It could well have been earlier, however. Perhaps when Wagner and Walken were chauffeured off the island by the very agency charged with the responsibility of investigating Natalie's unexplained death.

About two years after Natalie drowned, when Dr. Noguchi published his book, Marilyn called to tell him he was wrong about "his timeline." What has always been revealing to me about Dr. Noguchi is in his book he credited Marilyn with hearing Natalie crying for help before she drowned:

> She [Natalie] must have called out for help at that point. But her cries went unheard on *Splendour*, and on other vessels too. The rock music blaring from loudspeakers at the party ashore drowned out Natalie Wood's desperate calls from the surface of the dark sea. Yet there was still hope. Miss Wayne and her friend *did* hear her shouts. But when they looked outside, they could see nothing in the dark, and they thought they heard people on a neighboring boat say they were coming to her rescue.

Marilyn's involvement with Natalie's death didn't end with her brief phone conversation with CSI Hamilton. The same day the article with Marilyn's account appeared in the *LA Times*, her unrelenting fear of Wagner took shape.

"We came back to work on Monday and this happened on Thursday, four days after Natalie died," she recounted. "I went to my client box. The client boxes…they were designed for clients to drop off messages through a slot in front. The boxes were open in the back and labeled by broker name on each end. I found a scribbled message on a torn piece of paper in my box. It said, 'If you value your life, keep quiet about what you know.' Nothing made sense. Who wanted to keep me quiet? Why?"

Of course, I asked her what happened to the note. Marilyn told me she threw it away, but it disturbed her so much that she called her attorney.

"Did you tell John Payne about the note?" I asked.

"I don't remember, but I… I mean I must have. You should ask him," she replied, explaining she was no longer in touch with him.

I did try to ask Payne about the note and other details that the investigators in 1981 failed to explore. After numerous attempts over several months to obtain addresses or phone numbers for him, I was given a lead—his ex-wife's contact information. I sent Realtor Kerry Appleby Payne an email on February 12, 2018, introducing myself and explaining my mission. "I want to corroborate Marilyn's account of that Saturday night. I have what John told detectives in 1981, but there are several questions left unanswered," I wrote.

I was disappointed with the result. She replied that Payne was interviewed by LASD detectives after they had gone to Hawaii to look at *Splendour*, and the detectives would have notes of the interview. But Payne was not interested in discussing the matter with me.

It seemed he was comfortable with his public silence while Marilyn's credibility was being questioned. However, I knew one thing for sure: Payne didn't contradict Marilyn in his 2012 first-ever face-to-face interview with detectives. If he had, the current detectives would have had no hesitation in using that to discredit Marilyn further.

"Were you involved with anything else that you know of that would generate a threat like that note?" I inquired of Marilyn.

"Up to that night, I led a normal life. I just took care of my clients, John and my son. No, nothing I know of," Marilyn said, still troubled by the threatening missive.

⧼∾∾∾∾∾⧽

Marilyn and I have met and communicated continuously since our first meeting. She ended one of our sessions by confirming an incident that occurred in a restaurant a few weeks after Natalie's death. "We were having dinner at a Beverly Hills restaurant and Mr. Wagner walked in with his mother. Oddly, we were asked by the maître d' if we were uncomfortable and would we want to move to another room. We thought that strange and declined. Mr. Wagner looked over and saw us. He said nothing to us. Not then, not ever."

Twenty years passed before Marilyn spoke again for public consumption about Natalie. In 2000, Kashner, who had no background in criminal law, interviewed Marilyn for his *Vanity Fair* article. She also spoke to Finstad before Finstad's 2001 biography about Natalie was published.

"Why did you wait so long?" I inquired of Marilyn.

"My decision not to say anything to the press again…and, believe me, they tried…was based on [the question] would I want my son to read about his mother crying for help for 20 minutes and nobody doing anything? I kept quiet for the sake of her children, but it has seemed to have done more harm than good. Nobody seemed interested. I also had a certain fear. In fact, I was scared," Marilyn said.

Assuming she talked with CSI Hamilton over the phone, I asked Marilyn if she recalled telling him about the note.

Tensing up again, she replied, "Well, you have to understand that all of this made me very uncomfortable and nervous over the years. It was all just so surreal and confusing. Very confusing. But that doesn't change the fact that I got a threatening note. I know what we heard. You can ask my son. We heard a woman screaming for help near *Splendour*. We thought people on another boat were going to get her. We were wrong, and I am very sorry about that, because maybe we could have helped her."

⧼∾∾∾∾∾⧽

When I visited Isthmus Cove harbor and the mooring sites, I measured the distance between the mooring sites in the area of N-1 at about 100 feet. That's 10 feet further than the distance between home plate and first base on a big league baseball field. But the conditions on the day I was there were unlike those on that cold, rainy and windswept Saturday night in November 1981. Then, it was midnight with no moonlight or stars to help identify the location of the woman in the dark ocean. And, according to the many seamen I've talked to, sound travels differently over the water. So, it may have been a combination of *Capricorn's* position relative to *Splendour*, the weather, Marilyn's open porthole and Payne's silent generator that allowed them to hear the cries for help when other boaters couldn't.

In 2000 and 2001, both Kashner and Finstad gave credit to Marilyn's account. And in 2009's *Goodbye*, Davern and Rulli summed up Marilyn in glowing terms:

> The conviction in her voice left no doubt in my mind that I had talked to another witness to the death of Natalie—an honest one who had also received threats because of her connection with the death.
>
> Her time frame matched every single piece of Dennis's account.

Two years later, in an effort to encourage investigators to reopen Natalie's case, Rulli submitted typed statements to the LASD, including one from Marilyn recounting details of hearing screams for help near *Splendour* that Saturday night. It's obvious Rulli and Davern put a lot of stock in what Marilyn had to say in 2011.

Yet by July 2016, indoctrinated by the 2011 LASD detectives, Rulli disparaged Marilyn, a courageous soul, and claimed my "visit [with Marilyn] was a waste of time." My puzzlement at this contradiction was cleared up later when Lana stated that LASD Detective Hernandez had told her Marilyn "had no credibility."

Detective Hernandez, who had been improperly leaking information to Rulli and Finstad about the reopened investigation, had undoubtedly made the same remark to Rulli. *Why had Rulli made an about-face over a critical witness who had remained steadfast and unimpeached for over 30 years?* It was extremely disquieting to me. It still is.

The persistent attempt by the LASD to debilitate Marilyn's report of what she and Payne heard Saturday night continued as I concluded this book. During episode 11 of the 2018 podcast, Detective Hernandez and Davern questioned Marilyn's veracity:

> **Davern:** I was on the boat. I didn't hear anybody crying out for help. *And I didn't have the music that loud* [emphasis added]. I mean, if I would've heard somebody crying out for help, I would've heard it. I think the person that said they heard somebody crying out for help, I think that maybe they heard my music, or maybe they were just thinking they heard somebody. But I really, honestly don't think that they heard somebody crying out for help.

> **Hernandez:** In Dr. Lakshmanan [Sathyavagiswaran]'s report ... [he] explains that Natalie drowned within a short time of her entry into the water. It's supported by numerous details that he documents in his report. That would tend to make us believe that it was in fact someone else that was heard calling for help. It's also coupled with another witness's statement provided to the original investigators report about a party

that was going on in a nearby boat [and] substantiated with a detail that we're not providing, that's part of some of the holdback information [details the LASD allegedly withheld from the public].

To begin with, there were three people, including Marilyn's 8-year-old son, who heard the cries for help from someone in the water near *Splendour*, and none of them said it was Natalie. They didn't know who it was, but they not only heard a woman say she was drowning, they heard a drunken man reply, "Oh, hold on. We're coming to get you," or words to that effect. Payne and Marilyn put the event precisely when the circumstantial evidence shows Natalie disappeared and likely died.

Furthermore, Detective Hernandez's statement about Dr. L's report is misleading. Dr. L's exact statement was, "Also, given the temperature of the water and the time of death [around midnight] opined in the autopsy report [which he agreed with], it looks as though Ms. Wood drowned *within a short period of time of her entry into the water* [emphasis added]."

Of course, "short period of time" could mean minutes or hours. But it's clear to me that Dr. L's idea of "within a short period of time of her entry into the water" was governed by the pathologists' official time of death in 1981.

Davern has now made an about-face when it comes to Marilyn and his podcast comment that his music wasn't "that loud," demonstrating he's willing to be manipulated with the theory du jour. I leave you with the following excerpt from his signed statement in 2011 to encourage investigators to reopen Natalie's case: "I turned on the radio and *played music loudly* [emphasis added] to muffle the arguing."

Sure, there are minor discrepancies between the 1981 investigators' notes and Marilyn's account 20 and 30 years later—like the time the cries for help began and how long they lasted. But that's natural. What's important is the core event and that Marilyn is corroborated by two other steadfast witnesses and other confirmed evidence.

If Detective Hernandez believed Marilyn heard something, but it wasn't Natalie, why haven't we learned of a woman coming forward during the last four decades to say she was crying for help in the water near *Splendour*? Or a man coming forward to say he heard cries for help in the water and yelled, "Oh, hold on. We're coming to get you"? Or another body floating in the Isthmus? The LASD hasn't said.

CHAPTER 15

sister act

NATALIE'S YOUNGEST SISTER HAD BEEN ON MY "MOST WANTED" LIST for some time. I had read Finstad's *Natasha* and Lambert's biography. There were sections in each which addressed Lana's interactions with her famous sister and Wagner. In combination, it painted a sad portrait of a younger sibling's life in the shadows of a domineering mother and a sister who was Hollywood royalty.

Lambert, aided and abetted by Wagner, was particularly cruel in casting Lana as a money-grubbing backstabber. However, based on what I've learned, I don't put a lot of stock in what Wagner's biased friend had to say about Lana, her relationship with Natalie and Natalie's life in general.

Notwithstanding, comments by Natalie's former hairstylist troubled me the most. Ginger "Sugar" Blymyer wrote a touching memoir in 2000, aptly called *Hairdresser to the Stars*, that I carefully dissected. A lot of it details her work with Natalie. Over the years, she did Natalie's hair in many of her well-known movies. After Blymyer read Lana's memoir, she reacted this way in her book to a statement Lana made about Natalie:

> When I read in Lana's book that she was angry because Natalie didn't stay in contact with her, it made me angry at Lana. Actually, I think it was better for Natalie not to be with her family. They manipulated her in so many different ways. The only way she could escape was by staying out of reach.

Blymyer went on to add, "Natalie bailed Lana out time after time. In those days they didn't call it enabling, but it was."

After spending time with Lana, I can truthfully say at this point I'm conflicted when it comes to my feelings about her. It's hard for me to judge a person like her. How could I possibly know how a person would turn out growing up in an environment like hers? So, I'm doing my best to provide the facts necessary for an understanding of what motivates her and how that relates to her famous sister's life and death.

~~~~~~~~~

It was January 2017, and I was excited about my face-to-face meeting with Lana. Not because she was an actress, who among other roles played a legendary Bond Girl, but because I wanted to ask her questions like a prosecutor would if he was deciding whether to use her as a witness. As far as I could tell, her first contact with law enforcement regarding Natalie's death occurred in 2011 or thereabouts. I wasn't sure what they asked her, but I was quite sure they didn't question her about the things I wanted to know.

Looking back, I find it hard to believe she agreed to meet a man she didn't know in his suite at the Westin Bonaventure Hotel—alone. She must have checked up on me. It's the only reasonable explanation I can give. I guess that's why I'm so conflicted about her. I have an appreciation for her, notwithstanding the bumps in the road of our association. Let me explain.

As our meeting approached, I had everything carefully arranged. I gave Lana last-minute instructions on the door to enter and promised to meet her when she arrived. Three days before our meeting, I received a text that caught me completely off guard. "After discussions with my family, I will require an interview fee of $500, payable before I leave the meeting to return home. If this is acceptable, please let me know and I will help in any way I can." Frankly, I was stunned.

There had been no mention of money before that text. But, since I had incurred expenses to be there, I decided I wasn't going to let $500 stand in the way of my efforts to work with her.

It had now become a business proposition with Lana, fueled by years of living off the scraps of Bond Girl notoriety and being Natalie Wood's baby sister. But, little did I know how much that fee meant to her and her family. Ostracized by Wagner and his daughters, she was the primary provider for her adult daughter, Evan—a disabled cancer survivor with COPD—as well as her son-in-law and her three grandchildren, who were all living under the same roof with nine dogs and almost 30 cats.

∾∾∾∾∾∾∾

Leaning against the doorman's stand at the South Figueroa Street entrance of the hotel, I watched a shiny black car come to rest at the curb. My driver waved as he opened the passenger-side back door to reveal my celebrity witness. By the way she carefully eased herself out of the car, I could tell she was having knee or back problems. Dressed in a black turtleneck, jeans and a gray jacket, she reached out to greet me as I approached. I could see her resemblance to Natalie. She had the same petite features, dark eyes and some of the same mannerisms.

We took the long ride up the hotel's all-glass elevator to my floor. When we entered my room, I seated her across the center table facing me. As I sat down, I couldn't help but think this was as close as I would ever come to my boyhood fantasy of meeting Natalie Wood. Sadly, it took Natalie's death to bring about my meeting with Lana, and that wasn't exactly what I envisioned over 60 years ago.

∾∾∾∾∾∾∾

Lana told me she made her first film debut in 1956. She was 10. The film, *The Searchers*, included Natalie, John Wayne and Jeffrey Hunter. After that, Lana played bit parts in her sister's films, followed by television work. But, by far, her longest playing role was in the prime-time TV soap series *Peyton Place* as Sandy Webber, who falls in love with Rodney Harrington played by Ryan O'Neal.

Lana tastefully posed for *Playboy* magazine in 1971, causing a major stir in her family, and the same year played the character Plenty O'Toole in *Diamonds Are Forever*. Her scenes in that James Bond film lasted a little over three minutes, but the role placed her among a collection of beautiful women who have become worthy of veneration.

Lana has many other films and TV shows like *The Fugitive* and *Mission: Impossible* on her actress resume. But when that ended, she decided to try her hand as a producer. Then Natalie died.

"And suddenly I couldn't get another job. I was blacklisted," she said.

"Blacklisted!" I exclaimed.

Her answer was joined with Natalie's bequest to her. When Natalie died, her will contained several specific bequests. To Lana, Natalie gave "all of my furs and clothing." Wagner's books with Eyman and Lambert characterized Lana as ruthlessly demanding her gift a short time after Natalie's death.

After receiving carloads of beautiful clothes that she could never store in her two-bedroom apartment, she kept some and sold the remainder to a local store that specialized in selling clothing owned by celebrities after they tired of them. Wagner took great offense to that. So, we talked about Natalie's gift to her.

Figure 31: Lana Wood, Natalie's younger sister, doesn't limit her love of cats to the domestic type in this 1966 photo. (Courtesy of Lana Wood)

S.P.: I found Lambert's book interesting in this regard. He was almost brutal in his attacks of you. Your 1984 book doesn't attack Wagner. So, I couldn't figure out why they thought they needed to do that.

Lana: He's always been very scared of me. He considers me a loose cannon.

S.P.: Wagner?

Lana: Yes. I was working making a decent living—not wonderful, but a decent living—Natalie died—and suddenly I couldn't get another job. I had produced things, or I associated in production, or been involved in production at Universal Studios, and had been with Alan Landsburg in production, Jay Bernstein in production and suddenly the things I was promised fell apart and I couldn't get work. Then, I got a call from a gentleman by the name of Rowland Perkins—a very important agent at International Creative Management. He was my former agent. He said, "Lana, I'm calling you because I like you. I am going to tell you something." I said, "What?" He said, "R.J. has had you blacklisted and you're not going to be working." I couldn't get a production job. I couldn't get anything. Not anything. This was six or seven months after Natalie died.

S.P.: I'm sorry, Lana.

Lana: And what bothers me the most is that everything personal of Natalie's—the postcards she had written, letters she had received, awards—very, very personal things—mementos she kept, the Wagners put them up for auction and sold all of that recently. I heard Natasha said it's so she can stay at home and not have to work and just take care of her baby. That's the story.

Five days before the 34th anniversary of Natalie's death, *People* magazine featured a story on an upcoming auction of Natalie's possessions. The article was titled, "Robert Wagner and Daughters Put Natalie Wood's Personal Belongings Up for Auction." A subhead read, "The auction features items such as her 'International Stardom' Golden Globe Award, a bound screenplay of *Miracle on 34th Street*, a group of 1960s wardrobe test photos and more."

S.P.: I also saw where Davern was trying to auction off the coffee table that he took from *Splendour*. The one that had *Splendour* written across the top.

Lana: Was he?

S.P.: Yes, I don't know if he sold it. He wanted something like $8,000. He said in his book that he took it and some candles because they had significance to him. I don't understand why, if the table meant so much to him, he would auction it off.

Lana: I know. After Natalie passed away, I went on stage at the People's Choice Awards to accept her award for People's Choice, Favorite Actress. It was mine. I had it on my mantel. Natasha came over one time and said, "I would really like to have that. May I have that?" and I said, "Absolutely. Please take it." And she sold it.

After learning what Natalie left the girls in trust, many years before they were old enough to spend it, I couldn't wrap my mind around Natasha needing money badly enough to sell her mother's personal belongings and mementos. So, I changed the subject.

"Tell me a little about your mother, please."

Lana paused for a few seconds. "Our mother was…well, she was relentless. That's a good word for her…relentless."

I asked her in what way, and Lana's response was well-established.

"Mother had a fierce determination about her in everything she did. For example, she was determined to make my sister a star and she did. She was an immigrant from Russia… she and my father both. We were poor and she was ambitious and Natalie became her mission in life. When Natalie succeeded, Mother and the studios controlled her every move. And, Mother got my father a job at the studio as a carpenter and then in the special effects department. She ran our home and our lives. It drove my father to drink—literally."

"Did your father's drinking impact your home life?"

Lana's answer was short and sweet. "Very much so."

I followed up, "Was it accompanied by violence?"

Her answer was predictable. "My dad was a bad drinker and became very violent often...smashing the furniture and dishes. So, Natalie and I had a strong aversion to any violence. It just freaks us out."

> **S.P.:** So, please tell me about Natalie's personality in 1981.
>
> **Lana:** Well, where to start. First of all, Natalie was a good person and a great mother. But I think the best place to start for you to understand her would be her appearance. She never stopped being Natalie Wood. I mean, when she would go out in 1981—I mean, anywhere—she was always turned out. Groomed, dressed and jeweled for every occasion. But she also kept things in perspective and sensible. She was 43 and had been to therapy for years. It helped her very much in dealing with things.
>
> **S.P.:** How so?
>
> **Lana:** Well, let's take decisions. When Natalie decided to do something, it was done. Like with people who disappointed her or betrayed her trust. She made breaks fast and neat. Next, my sister was very straight-laced. Even prudish. Don't get me wrong, she wasn't judgmental. She respected people's choices. But, when it came to drugs or perverted things, she didn't want any part of it. And, she had an iron will...iron will. Very, very strong.
>
> **S.P.:** Let me follow up with your statement about being straight-laced. In his book, Wagner said Natalie liked bisexual men.
>
> **Lana:** He did? I don't read his books.
>
> **S.P.:** When I read that, I thought, *Does that mean that's why she liked you, because you were bisexual?*
>
> **Lana:** He was being very careful, because that's what broke up their first marriage. That's when she found him with another man.

Having a good appreciation for Natalie's personality, as it related to the manner of her death, I shifted the conversation at that point to the events leading up to Thanksgiving 1981. I wanted to know what was going on in Natalie's life professionally during that period. Lana told me Natalie made some very good movies and a lot of money up until she remarried Wagner. Natalie had a lot of success, but what she really wanted was a family.

So, for several years after that, she really didn't focus on the movie business. When she did, it was in movies with parts that weren't right for her or in movies that weren't written or directed well. So, she agreed to do some TV films and got some recognition for her acting, like the TV version of *From Here to Eternity*. Lana explained Natalie didn't just want to be an actress. She wanted to be a great actress and do quality things that allowed her to show people the extent of her talent. "It's not just a cliché to say that acting was Natalie's life…her whole life," Lana exclaimed. "And Natalie's coping mechanism was the stage. It was the film."

S.P.: So, where was she professionally about mid-1981?

Lana: I was worried about her insecurities for the future. But I underestimated her. While I was worrying, Natalie was getting busy. She found *Brainstorm* and got ready to go back to work. She was going to act with some excellent actors—Louise Fletcher and Christopher Walken, who was one of the hot young actors in Hollywood. And, she agreed to take a big risk…a very big risk.

S.P.: What was that?

Lana: She agreed to make her first appearance in the theater starring in the production of *Anastasia*. It was going to open in LA, and if it worked out, the play would move to Broadway in New York. It was the beginning of a whole new professional phase in her life.

As much as I hated to do it, I needed to confirm what I'd read about the conversations Lana had with Wagner after her sister's death. Her eyes told me it was still painful for her to talk about. Leaning back in her chair, she recited what she remembered.

Lana: It was after the funeral. I went to their home on Cañon Drive in Beverly Hills. There were a lot of people there. I was allowed to go upstairs to their bedroom. R.J. was sitting on the edge of the bed, and I said, "R.J., tell me what happened." He just kept saying, "I'm sorry. I'm sorry. I'm really sorry. Do you believe me? I'm sorry." And, then someone grabbed me by the arm and said, "Leave him alone." I said, "Fine," and walked away. He never sat me down and discussed anything with me. Never.

S.P.: Was Christopher Walken at the house after the funeral when you were there?

Lana: Yes.

S.P.: Did you talk to him?

Lana: Actually, my daughter had to use the bathroom. She was like 5 years old, and we're standing there waiting…and I finally started knocking saying, "Excuse me, but a little girl needs to use the powder room." And he exited without looking at me or speaking a word in a puff of smoke. I was like, "Wow, he was in there getting stoned." Back then, it usually wasn't what one does after a funeral in someone's home.

S.P.: Did you tell the publishers of your book about Walken exiting the powder room in a cloud of smoke?

Lana: Yes.

S.P.: So, I guess they didn't want to put that in there? They didn't mention the smoke. They said, "He emerged looking odd."

Lana: Oh, he reeked.

S.P.: Of marijuana?

Lana: Oh, yeah.

S.P.: Is that it?

Lana: That's it. He has never spoken to me.

~~~~~~~~~

To test the theories floated by Dr. Noguchi in *Coroner* and suggested by others that Natalie tried to board the dinghy by throwing her leg over the pontoon or attempted to climb in the dinghy backwards using the motor mount, I needed some accurate information about Natalie's physique. Lana told me she and Natalie were almost the same height—5-foot-2. While Lana was larger in the bust, in 1981 they weighed the same, around 115 pounds, and had the same body structure.

At my request, we measured Lana's right arm, from her shoulder to her wrist, at 18 inches; her forearm at 9-3/4 inches and her leg from her hip to the floor at 33 inches. Lana had a 26-inch inseam but said Natalie's was shorter. "I remember us trading slacks and hers hit me at the ankle," she said.

Then Lana added, "Natalie couldn't swim a lick." Lana, on the other hand, was a certified scuba diver. "It was a passion of mine. Lots of experience swimming and diving."

When I explained Natalie's autopsy report stated she had a fresh 4-inch by 1-inch bruise on her right forearm, and Dr. Noguchi suggested it got there when she tried to reach over the dinghy pontoon after going into the water, Lana bristled.

Lana: It couldn't be done. Unless you are kicking with your feet very, very hard, if you take your arm out of the water, you can't reach over anything. Particularly a dinghy pontoon. If she's not kicking her feet… if she's just doing a dog-paddle panicky thing, you can't reach anything. Unless you are propelling yourself out of the water with very strong legs and a strong kick, it cannot be done.

S.P.: What about Natalie throwing her legs over the side of a dinghy while in the water?

Lana: Oh, please. Oh, my. So, now she was really athletic, wasn't she?

S.P.: Was she?

Lana: Heavens, no! Natalie was a lot of things, but she was no athlete.

We discussed the frightening accident while filming that left Natalie with a deformed left wrist. "She was very self-conscious about it. She always kept it covered when she was around people," said Lana.

Over the years, people have said Natalie was drinking heavily around the time she was working on *Brainstorm*. I wanted to know what her sister observed in the weeks leading up to her death.

"Natalie wasn't a big drinker," Lana said. "She did love her glass of wine. She did. But, when she was working, she was dieting because she was always worried about how she looked on camera. On her tuna and lettuce trip." However, when Lana published her book, it said this about Natalie's drinking habits:

> Natalie once said she wouldn't be a true Russian if she didn't drink, and drinking certainly figured in our childhood. Hardly a night would go by that Natalie didn't have her cocktails or, in later years, wine. But when it came time to work, the drinking stopped. While everyone around her had wine with dinner, she would drink ice water and chew on fresh vegetables. Her refusal to drink while she was working held fast until *Brainstorm*, when she began staying around the set several afternoons a week and drinking with the crew. By the time she made *Brainstorm*, there had been several unsuccessful movies, her career was in jeopardy, and the pressure was obviously such that she dropped her ban on drinking at work.

While we spoke, Lana disavowed several book statements, including the alcohol consumption statement. She claimed the publishers had full authority to edit her manuscript as they saw fit and did so with abandon. I believed her on some of the items we talked about, but on this one, I had independent evidence to confirm Natalie was indeed drinking during *Brainstorm's* filming.

On October 18, 1981, Bill Morrison, Entertainment Editor of Raleigh, North Carolina's *The News and Observer*, wrote an article entitled "Playing Hooky from Life with Natalie Wood." The article stated: "'Making a movie,' said Natalie Wood *as she sipped wine* [emphasis added] in her elegantly appointed motor home, 'is like playing hooky from life. I mean within reason, not in a crazy way.'"

I wasn't troubled by the discrepancies. No case is without flaws. Time sometimes has a way of creating rough edges in a homicide case. Even when purportedly "solved," I've never seen a murder case that didn't have inconsistencies and mysteries. That's the reason our system of justice depends upon reasonable doubt, not certainty.

"Let me ask you about Dennis Davern," I said as Lana took a drink of tea. "Did you know him before your sister died?"

She responded immediately, almost sullenly. "While my side of her family wasn't included in Natalie and R.J.'s boating, I had met him several times at Natalie's house, the marina, coffee shop, you know around. But we weren't close friends, if that's what you want to know."

S.P.: Was there a time when Davern called you after Natalie's death?

Lana: Yes.

S.P.: When was that?

Lana: I'm so bad at time. Evie [Lana's daughter] was in high school…I remember that. I'd say 10 years after Natalie's death, and it was over a period of a month. He called three to four times. Suddenly, he just started calling me.

S.P.: What did he say to you, Lana?

Lana: OK. Well, first, when he called me, he was drunk and crying… weeping profusely. He was at times not able to finish his thought or sentence. He kept saying he felt guilty and felt he could have saved my sister. He said there were still things he couldn't bring himself to tell. Because it involved three or four calls, I may not have the order correct, but I remember him saying that R.J. and Walken fought in the kitchen…salon area and that R.J. broke a bottle. He said Chris left and went to his bedroom. Shortly after that, Natalie left to her bedroom. She was livid. After 10 minutes or so, R.J. followed her to the bedroom. Dennis said he could hear fighting and it sounded really bad…things hitting the walls and such. So, he went to the bedroom door and knocked. R.J. answered red-faced and he—Dennis—asked if there was anything he could do. Dennis said R.J. told him to leave. Dennis also said he turned on music for fear people would hear them fighting. When the fighting stopped, Dennis said he went to the back deck, where he saw R.J. At this point, Dennis broke down more and told me there were more bad things that happened, but he was crying and stumbling over words. That's when I told him he should go to the police or talk to an FBI agent friend of mine. He said he was afraid to go to the police.

S.P.: Is that all you can remember?

Lana: I think that was during the first call. During one of the calls, he said, "I'm responsible too. I'm responsible too." He said, "When Natalie went in the water, I said, 'R.J.?' and he said, 'Leave her there. Teach her a lesson.' And he wouldn't let me help her. I could have helped her, and I didn't help her." Then he said something about there are uglier things that I don't want to know. He said there wasn't just a fight in the salon, but when they went into the stateroom, he said, "R.J. would hurt Natalie." He said something about R.J. kept drinking and pouring him drinks. I began getting upset myself, and that's when he told me R.J. kept him like a prisoner in his home. I'm trying to think of what else he said, because he was so drunk and crying—weeping profusely. And then he would get off the phone very fast. "Oh, I've said too much. I'm getting off the phone." Boom. Gone.

S.P.: After those calls, did you hear from him again?

Lana: Not until Marti [Rulli] popped up.

As you can see, Lana's initial statements to me appeared inconsistent with her statement she didn't tell Finstad that Davern knew when Natalie went into the water. Over two decades later in her updated book, Finstad claimed for the first time that in 1999 Lana said Davern saw Wagner "push Natalie overboard." When I questioned Lana about it, she denied telling Finstad that.

I found it amazing that Lana kept quiet about the late-night calls from Davern for eight years, and that the disclosure was to Finstad for the 2001 version of her book. No doubt the claims inserted from Davern and Lana helped promote Finstad's books. Together, they were sizzling. So, I asked Lana about that.

"You have to understand something," she began. "For a long time, I didn't want to believe that a man I had known since I was 9 years old, who married my sister twice and to whom I was very attached, could have had something to do with my sister's death. That was horrible…the ugliest thing in the world. It had been very confusing to me. Very. Stories kept appearing with statements about arguments and smashing wine bottles and it was very upsetting. And, I felt Dennis was telling me these things in private, and I don't violate people's requests to keep things private. It wasn't for me to accuse R.J. or go to the police. That was something Dennis should have done. I even told him I had an acquaintance in the FBI he could talk to…or that he should go to the police. I told him to do it now. I think I did all I could."

When Davern talked to Finstad, I suppose Lana thought it was all right to talk about his phone calls. Because Davern's calls weren't taped by Lana, we will never know the exact words spoken by the obviously troubled boat captain. But the calls did happen. They were confirmed by Davern himself. Records would have been helpful to establish dates and times, but it's plain Davern was troubled by something that weighed heavily on his conscience.

⁓⁓⁓⁓⁓

In Lana's book, she was quoted as saying: "Late that afternoon [the day Natalie was found] we went to the house Natalie had loved so much. I went upstairs and found him [Wagner] sitting on the edge of their bed, weeping."

I inquired about that, because Lana had just told me she saw Wagner at the house on the day of Natalie's funeral, not the day Natalie's body was found. Lana said the editor got the "timing" in her book "all wrong" and added, "I don't recall ever seeing him weep. Ever."

I decided to end our first conversation by asking her something I had read concerning phone calls made from *Splendour* early Sunday morning. Based on what I knew about the way calls from yachts to the mainland were made in 1981, there had to be records of the day and time all calls were made from the yacht that weekend. I knew finding them would reveal some explosive actions on Wagner's part and further solidify the Fatal Gap timeline.

> **S.P.:** Do you know if any phone calls were made from *Splendour* to the mainland Saturday night?
>
> **Lana:** One of the things that always bothered me—the first call that came off the yacht *Splendour* that night was to Paul Ziffren. You call Harbor Patrol. You call the authorities. You don't call your attorney. It has

always stunned me. And now, of course, Paul is dead.

S.P.: How do you know that the first call was made to Ziffren?

Lana: I was told that by Dennis during one of his drunken calls. It's also in a log. It's in a log somewhere.

S.P.: In a log?

Lana: It's in a log. The calls have to get logged.

S.P.: When you say calls have to be logged, was this a radio call or a telephone call?

Lana: I believe it was a radio call.

Lana was right. It was a radio call through the AT&T yacht radio call switchboard. I knew the famous couple had the capability to make radio calls from the yacht. And it stands to reason. Both were busy entertainers with many business connections. They needed a radio call service. But I didn't have the log.

Did the investigators get the radio call records? I had some compelling evidence they may have tried. In the 1981 records I obtained from the sheriff's department, there was a telephone message slip dated December 22, 1981, to Detective Rasure from the "Phone Co." along with "975-4151. Mobile Phone #." On the back, in Rasure's handwriting, are notes on his conversation with Steve Bough with Pacific Telephone and Telegraph. The notes have an obvious relationship to questions Rasure had about a radio phone.

But, why did Rasure have this conversation nearly three weeks after he officially closed Natalie's case? I can only offer this explanation. In 1981, the phone companies were very cooperative with law enforcement—even without subpoenas. Someone had evidence of early morning telephone calls made from *Splendour* and was trying to trace them. Back then, it took a while to get the information, but initially, either Rasure or Hamilton was apparently inquisitive. He wanted to know when calls were made from *Splendour* after Natalie disappeared and who made them. It makes good detective sense when you're conducting a serious homicide investigation. But in this case, I suspect Rasure was only attempting to satisfy a celebrity-driven curiosity.

I was not given any records indicating detectives uncovered the existence of radio phone calls, and Rasure's official report did not mention tracing any calls. Furthermore, although Deputy Kroll and LASD investigators listed telephone numbers for Davern and Walken in their reports, Wagner's phone number was not included. The reason for that omission becomes one more item of evidence material to Natalie's death that may be buried in the sheriff's archives forever.

However, Wagner's friend Lambert—unwittingly perhaps—offered a clue for at least one call from the yacht. In his book, Lambert quotes Mart Crowley as saying that "shortly before seven a.m." Sunday, Wagner called him "distraught and hysterical," saying, "She's gone! She's gone!" before explaining that he and Walken were being taken by helicopter to Long Beach. And Wagner wanted Crowley to give him a ride home from there.

Davern also provided a second piece of the puzzle in *Goodbye*. He said Wagner made a "phone call" after Oudin called the Coast Guard. Oudin's call to the Coast Guard occurred at 3:26 a.m. Giving Davern's recollection credit, coupled with his statements to Lana, I believe a reasonable inference is Wagner's first call was indeed to Ziffren.

My first meeting with Lana was no doubt a fruitful discussion. I didn't get the impression she was holding back or intentionally sensationalizing things. She also agreed to send me a copy of an unpublished manuscript Natalie wrote for *Good Housekeeping* magazine in 1966. Then I walked her to the car. Waiting at the curb with a smile, my driver opened the door to the backseat and Lana waved goodbye.

∽◡∽◡◠◡∽◡∽

Two months later, I hadn't heard from Lana. I had a feeling something wasn't right. So, I sent a text asking about Natalie's manuscript. She replied she had been busy. I soon found out why.

In the past, I had always been the one to initiate communication with Lana, so when I received a text from her on March 22, it was rare. The message read:

> Sam…urgent and very serious situation. I need a loan against any future payment. I can sign anything necessary, and only have a limited amount of time. Five thousand dollars is what I need…I realize it's a fairly large sum, and I assure you in advance that if you must refuse, it will in no way affect our future working relationship in any manner.

For the second time, Lana had stunned me over money. *What could possibly have been so financially devastating in her life that she would ask someone she had just met for a $5,000 loan?*

Lana explained that she and her family were being evicted from their rented home after living there for seven years. She had seven days to raise enough money to pay rent for 30 more days, which would allow them time to move. Otherwise, they'd be forced to leave.

I was in anguish processing all of this. Her 42-year-old daughter had just been put on oxygen and her grandchildren were young, but how could she get in such a mess so fast? Once, she had been part of the court of Hollywood royalty. She traveled in limousines and private jets to faraway places, wore expensive clothes and jewelry, and ate at the best restaurants. She had fraternized with the elite in the entertainment business. Now, at 71 years old, she and her family were about to be put on the street. It was hard for me to grasp.

∽◡∽◡◠◡∽◡∽

The official eviction file confirmed Lana's situation wasn't new. My first meeting with her was on January 25, 2017, two days before a notice was served on her to pay in full or be evicted. That helped explain the "$500 interview fee." It also meant the case had been going on for two months before Lana asked for the loan. But I couldn't let this play out without extending a helping hand. So, I wired $2,000. "Bless you! Extremely grateful," was her reply to my loan. And I felt better, particularly for her grandchildren.

But it didn't stop the train wreck. Lana couldn't find a place to rent in time. As the court had ordered, the family was locked out of the home and the landlord moved all their possessions to the street. "People took lots of things as the landlord threw everything we didn't have time to pack up on the front lawn," Lana wrote.

The family stayed in a car the first night and then moved into a brassy motel outside LA. Her cats were taken by ASPCA, but her dogs made it to the motel.

"I know this is hard on everyone," I texted her.

"Tempers are uncontrolled, tears are the commonality. Exhaustion close by" was her heart-wrenching reply.

Lana and her family lived in the motel for nearly two weeks. The press got wind of it and were swarming like sharks. "Natalie Wood's Bond Girl sister is now homeless" read the Fox News headline. It would have been a calamity but for a friend setting up a GoFundMe page for the desperate movie star and her family. Faithful fans responded by contributing nearly $30,000, according to Fox News.

It was a wonderful display of generosity, but to me, it demonstrated much more. There was still an enormous amount of love in the public domain for the Wood sisters. Furthermore, Fox News added a much-needed postscript: "Many fans wondered why Robert Wagner, her sister's husband and a famous Hollywood actor, hasn't stepped in to help. Wood shared there hasn't been any contact between her and Wagner or any of Natalie's daughters."

But matters between Lana and I didn't end with her time living in a motel. I was on a mission and came up with an idea to get to the bottom of Natalie's death with Lana's help. In fact, she was the only person, outside of Wagner and Natalie's daughters, who could pull it off.

ᕫᕬᕫᕬᕫᕬᕫᕬ

In my quest to obtain copies of Natalie's autopsy photographs from the coroner, I had to deal with the provisions of a California statute prohibiting the "dissemination" of photographs taken by the coroner of any portion of a body at the "scene" of a death or during any "postmortem examination." The coroner's private lawyers in my lawsuit relied heavily on that statute for good reason.

I argued to the judge, and he agreed, that the statute wouldn't apply to photographs in the sheriff's department files, but it was very clear I was out of luck on photos in the possession of the coroner. I wanted to see the condition of Natalie's face and neck and close-ups of the scratches, scrapes and bruises on her body. I knew color photographs were taken during Natalie's postmortem because of a statement in Detective Rasure's official report.

Furthermore, because of the high-powered microscopes the coroner possessed, I was confident there were photographs made during the bruise tissue examination. I planned to give the photos to Dr. Stanley and Dr. Pozos for their review. I knew the photos, along with the bruise tissue slides, held a wealth of truth about how Natalie's injuries occurred.

Notwithstanding the legal roadblock, as one of my lawsuits progressed, I discovered that a bill was working its way through the California legislature to amend the troublesome statute. The amendment provided, among other things, that dissemination of the autopsy photographs was permitted: "(3) For *use or potential use* [emphasis added] in a civil action or proceeding in [California] that relates to the death of [a deceased person], if either of the following applies: (A) The coroner receives *written authorization from a legal heir* [emphasis added]…of that person before the action is filed or while the action is pending."

The amendment became law on January 1, 2017. My approach was going to be that under California law, Lana was a "legal heir" as the statute required. Not only was she a beneficiary to part of Natalie's estate, as Natalie's sister, she was an heir at law if Natalie had died intestate (without a will). As for the "civil action or proceeding" requirement, Lana could have been legitimately exploring a "potential" wrongful death suit against Wagner or building a case to request an official coroner's inquest—which California considers a special "civil proceeding." Either way, the photographs would have been for "potential use in a civil action or proceeding."

I knew it would work and finally expose what the coroner and sheriff had been hiding for nearly 40 years.

So, arrangements were made to meet with Lana again on May 16, 2017. I booked a room at the London West Hollywood at Beverly Hills to be close to where Lana was living.

When she arrived, I asked my follow-up questions and got more measurements. Then I told Lana about my idea to retrieve the autopsy photos. She listened intently as I explained why they were critical for getting to the truth in Natalie's case. My explanation included my opinion that Wagner might try to block our efforts. When I asked for her help, she agreed without hesitation.

At last, I believed I had an avenue to break through the government secrecy and reveal the truth through genuine forensic examination instead of relying on reports prepared under dubious circumstances. But after preparing the documents Lana needed, including an agreement on the use and ownership of the photographs, she changed her mind and her attitude.

On June 15, almost a month to the day of our second meeting, Lana wrote, "Do you have any idea what mental and emotional anguish seeing those photos would cause me? I no longer wish to attempt to attain the aforementioned photos."

Perplexed by the complete change of heart, I told her I would respect her decision and I moved on. We continued to text back and forth, but things never really felt the same between us. As in the beginning of our relationship, I only heard from her if I sent her a text—until the day her daughter died. At 6 p.m. on July 18, 2017, she wrote, "My daughter passed away." Evan was 42.

❧❧❧❧❧❧

I became immersed in writing and didn't communicate with Lana for months. Then, in February 2019, a reporter for the *National Enquirer* sent me a photograph and asked if I knew the identity of the people shown with a young Robert Wagner. (See *Figure 32*, next page).

When I examined the picture, the man in the suit and the older woman in the image looked very familiar. In fact, I did a double take when I first looked at the man. I told the reporter I didn't know and made a guess. Then I headed to my file on Peter Pitchess, the Los Angeles County sheriff when Natalie died. The resemblance was too great for me to discount the photograph. It sure looked like Pitchess, but the identity of the other people in the photograph seemed more crucial to me. If I could identify the setting, it might confirm not only the individuals in the photo, it might reveal why Wagner was with Pitchess if it was indeed the sheriff. And I would be able to confirm the date—although Wagner looks about 30 years old in the photo. So, I sent the picture to Lana.

Figure 32: Undated photo of Robert Wagner with unidentified guests (Provided to author by Douglas Montero)

She responded, "I do not recall who showed me the photo. I know it hangs in the sheriff's office." *Could that be true?* I set things in motion to find out.

Five months later, I was still trying to get to the bottom of the young Wagner picture. After I gave my LA research assistant, Kevin Brechner, his assignment, he headed to the LASD headquarters on West Ramona in Monterey Park. The officer at the lobby desk didn't recognize the photo, but he suggested Kevin try the old headquarters in downtown LA.

Before doing that, he went to the Los Angeles Sheriff's Museum in South Whittier, only to find it closed. However, two clerks at the South Whittier station gave him 19-year veteran Mike Fratantoni's phone number. Fratantoni is the LASD's historian and museum curator, and we reasoned if anyone would know about the photo, it would be Fratantoni. "I looked at the photo and I can assure you it was never hanging in the museum. I can't identify the people in the photo," Fratantoni replied in an email. But Kevin, who has vast experience in the history of Hollywood and LA County, did venture an educated guess that the young lady on Wagner's right was his second wife, Marion Marshall, and the elderly lady was Margaret Adams, a longtime sheriff's department employee.

But one thing was certain, the evidence was pointing toward a Pitchess/Wagner relationship years before Natalie's death.

CHAPTER 16

the fix

IN LOS ANGELES COUNTY, THE SHERIFF SERVES AS AN ELECTED
official. Until recently, candidates usually came from within the sheriff's department or
were experienced law enforcement officers from other walks of life. However, when sheriff
candidates run for office, they instantly turn into politicians who must raise money and support for their campaigns. In most cases, the motives of supporters are laudable, but some do
so to curry favor. And, for those supporters, calling in favors is an art form.

In 1953, Sheriff Eugene Biscailuz appointed Peter Pitchess as his undersheriff. For five
years, Pitchess reported directly to Biscailuz and made the contacts he needed to get elected
when his boss retired in 1958.

With a Bachelor of Science and law degree from the University of Utah, Pitchess kicked
off his career in law enforcement in 1940 as an FBI special agent. During his 12 years with
the bureau, Pitchess was stationed in three cities, before landing in Los Angeles. Along the
way, he rose to head the criminal investigation section of the FBI's LA field office.

Witnessing Pitchess' ascension through the ranks, I knew he was a good politician.
Agents without pull didn't get a plum position like his in the '50s without understanding
bureau politics and appeasing J. Edgar Hoover.

While heading the LA section, Pitchess maintained a large and active intelligence unit
that collected information on mafia activity in the county. That work necessitated developing informants and friendships with mobsters in order to obtain valuable information
on other criminals based on "mutual assistance," as Pitchess would describe it years later.
Simply put: a *quid pro quo*. According to Pitchess, some of his informants included mobsters
Benjamin "Bugsy" Siegel, Louis Tom Dragna and Jack Dragna, once dubbed the "Al Capone of Los Angeles."

〜〜〜〜〜〜〜

Historical materials say between January 1958 and January 1982, Pitchess was instrumental in making the LASD a modern-day police force. His many innovative advance-
ments in the department kept him in the public eye, enhanced his reputation in the community and made him popular with his troops.

But, and there's almost always a "but" in stories like this, there was a cancer growing in
the department that would be the downfall of its leadership in the years to come. Its genesis
was in the arena of excessive force, surfacing for the first time 14 years after Pitchess took
office.

In 1972, activist Caesar Echeveria and other citizens were arrested for committing bat-
tery against four deputy sheriffs. Awaiting trial, Echeveria claimed he was not guilty of the
charges because he acted in self-defense in response to the use of excessive force by the
deputies.

To prove this, Echeveria sought to obtain evidence of the deputies' propensity for violence by asking the judge to order the prosecution to produce records of several excessive force investigations by a sheriff's department internal affairs unit. The sheriff refused to cooperate and the case made it all the way to the California Supreme Court.

Pitchess claimed the information was confidential and secret, but the Supreme Court disagreed and created an unintended legacy for Pitchess, which continues to be a landmark decision in California excessive force cases.

But, as I learned from my CPRA lawsuit against the sheriff, the department learned nothing from its refusal to provide records. Official arrogance in refusing to furnish public records and violating the law in the process is the hallmark of an agency seeking to avoid accountability.

❧❧❧❧❧❧

Cognizant of how criminal law investigations should proceed, I began searching for a connection between Pitchess and Wagner's friend Sinatra. Sinatra was involved politically on both sides of the fence. So, it seemed far-fetched that Sinatra had not crossed paths with the sheriff during his time in office.

My initial search turned up a 1961 photograph of Pitchess on the set of the Sinatra-produced film *Sergeants 3*, starring all five members of the Rat Pack (*Figure 33*, below). Sinatra's performance contracts barred people from coming backstage or on his film sets. Since it wasn't an election year, the reasonable inference is Pitchess was on set because he was invited by Sinatra. But I knew a solitary photo wouldn't establish the connection that

Figure 33: Frank Sinatra, Sheriff Peter Pitchess and Sammy Davis Jr. on the set of the 1962 comedy *Sergeants 3* (Los Angeles County Sheriff's Department archives)

would prove my theory why the sheriff's office quickly closed Natalie's death investigation as an accident.

While devouring Kelley's biography of Sinatra, I found what I was looking for. After Pitchess became sheriff, but "years" before Kelley finished her book in 1986, Pitchess gave the singer "a special deputy badge." This privilege was right up Sinatra's alley.

And, when Sinatra died in 1998, four people gave eulogies at his funeral: his son, Frank Jr.; two giants of the film industry and longtime friends, Kirk Douglas and Gregory Peck; and Robert Wagner. *What happened to bring about Wagner's elevation in stature in Sinatra's world? Of all the hundreds of friends identified in Kelley's book, why Wagner?*

But like many things about Wagner, the mystery of his apparent closeness to Sinatra, in my opinion, came about because they not only shared the same women, they shared the same dark secret about Natalie's death. Here's my reasoning.

His Way is an intensely written story of Sinatra's life from his birth to May 23, 1985. It lays out in painstaking detail Sinatra's known marriages, high-profile affairs, brushes with the law, violent temper, friendships including the Rat Pack, career path, hate of the press, assaults and batteries, business deals, mafia associations and political connections. If even half the book is true, the reader comes away realizing Sinatra's legacy, outside of his voice, was how to create and maintain an image through stark fear and brute force intimidation.

Sinatra was 65 years old at the time Natalie died and had been in the entertainment business more than 40 years. His mother, "Dolly," whose birth name happened to be Natalie, was an Italian firecracker married to a Sicilian. She would come to describe a character trait of Frank this way: "My son is like me. You cross him and he never forgets."

Never forgetting a betrayal or dishonor is the very nature of the Sicilian mentality as well as that of many other Italians because the wrong is a moral offense. And Sinatra's life, built around violence and vendettas, sent a chilling message to the Hollywood community warning them not to cross him. And, the certainty of what happens when they did. "Folks in show business feared Sinatra the same way the folks in Communist Russia feared Stalin," said Sinatra's longtime personal valet. "He had a fear-inducing aura."

The event that likely molded the perception of Sinatra in the eyes of the public, particularly the Los Angeles community, was the outcome of his 1939 exclusive performance contract with famous bandleader Tommy Dorsey. After union membership dues, manager fees and Dorsey's cut, the contract left Sinatra with 10 percent of the gross. At the time, that was fine with Sinatra; he was working and a little of something was better than all of nothing.

However, as Sinatra's popularity grew, he became disgruntled with the deal. After unsuccessfully consulting lawyers and the artist unions, Sinatra went to Jules Stein, the mob-connected Chicagoan who founded MCA, the world's biggest theatrical agency.

With that, two conflicting stories emerged. The one that became part of popular gangster lore was that Dorsey refused a $60,000 (about $1 million today) buyout. Dorsey had grown to despise Sinatra and intended to hold on to the contract and drive Sinatra's career into the ground. Frustrated, Sinatra's hard-charging mother went to see her neighbor, mobster Guarino "Willie" Moretti, who controlled large sections of the East Coast entertainment industry.

According to John William Tuohy, an authority on the American mafia, "By the early 1940s, Moretti and the national syndicate still held a virtual lock on the entertainment business unions nationwide and mobsters were always looking to expand their control of the industry by managing the careers of promising entertainers."

Tuohy added:

> Working through Jules Stein, Moretti's first offer to Dorsey was $60,000 cash. When Dorsey turned that down, Moretti, who was considered in mob circles to be a madman, decided to take matters into his own hands, and make the band leader an offer he couldn't refuse.
>
> One night after a show, Moretti pushed his way into Dorsey's dressing room, put a gun in the band leader's mouth and told Dorsey to sell Sinatra's contract. Which he did. For one dollar.

Sinatra and Dorsey denied the Moretti story. But much later, after Moretti's October gangland-style murder, Dorsey told *The American Mercury* magazine when negotiations between he and Sinatra broke down and Sinatra wanted out of his performance contract, gangsters showed up and said, "sign it or else!" Whether it was true or not, it fixed the singer's image in the entertainment business as a man connected to the mob.

The dark side of Sinatra surfaced again on February 11, 1947, when he traveled to Havana, Cuba, with two Capone mobsters to meet with Sicilian mobster Charles "Lucky" Luciano, the founder of the seven family Mafia Commission and its first chairman. Sinatra and Luciano were followed by the FBI and within days, Scripps-Howard columnist Robert Ruark, who happened to be in Havana, broke a major story in the U.S.

Columnists Westbrook Pegler of the *New York Journal-American* and Lee Mortimer of the *New York Daily Mirror*, who had been bashing Sinatra for dodging the draft and being a communist, began to pound Sinatra for mobbing up. This culminated in an August 1951 article by Mortimer in *The American Mercury* reporting the Fischetti brothers delivered $2 million in cash on the trip "in the hand luggage of an entertainer." The information for the article was allegedly leaked by the Federal Bureau of Narcotics.

While the cash delivery was never proven, it was the perception that mattered. In fact, Sinatra reportedly idolized Joseph Kennedy, President John F. Kennedy's father, who once said shamelessly, "It's not what you are that counts, but what people think you are." Sinatra lived that philosophy to a T.

∿∿∿∿∿∿∿

Before John F. Kennedy was elected President in 1960, Sinatra had befriended Sicilian mobster Sam "Momo" Giancana. In *His Way*, Kelley said Giancana "ordered killings as easily as he ordered his linguine. Some of the victims were simply shot, while others were hung on meat hooks and tortured with electric cattle prods, ice picks, baseball bats, and blow torches."

Peter Lawford, a member of the Rat Pack, described Sinatra's relationship with Giancana to Kelley in chilling detail:

> "Frank never called him or any of his killers Mafia—they were always 'the Boys' or 'the Outfit,'" said Peter Lawford. "But they were Mafia all right. ... Because of Giancana, he kowtowed to the Chicago mob. Why

do you think Frank ended every one of his nightclub acts by singing 'My Kind of Town Chicago Is'? That was his tribute to Sam, who was really an awful guy with a gargoyle face and weasel nose. I couldn't stand him, but Frank idolized him because he was the Mafia's top gun. Frank loved to talk about 'hits' and guys getting 'rubbed out.' And you better believe that when the word got out around town [Hollywood] that Frank was a pal of Sam Giancana, nobody but nobody ever messed with Frank Sinatra. They were too scared. Concrete boots were no joke with this guy. He was a killer."

⌒⌒⌒⌒⌒⌒

Then in June 1975, in what could only be described as a syndicate don ordered slaying, Sinatra's friend Giancana was assassinated in the basement of his home. The following year, a stirring four-part series was published in the *Daily Mail,* the second biggest-selling London daily newspaper. It was titled, "The President, The Lady and The Godfather: A STORY OF INTRIGUE AND CORRUPTION AT THE CENTRE OF POLITICAL POWER."

"The Lady" was Judith Immoor Campbell, "the beautiful, restless daughter of a wealthy Irish-American family." "The President" was John F. Kennedy and "The Godfather" was Sam Giancana. However, the facilitator of this unimaginable tale was none other than Francis Albert Sinatra.

The headline on the second page read, "In the beginning there was Sinatra, king of the world where showbiz and politics meet." From there, the article chronicled how Sinatra introduced one of his mistresses, Campbell, to then presidential candidate John F. Kennedy. A few weeks later, Sinatra introduced her to Giancana. Both men began having an affair with her at the same time. And here, an early connection also surfaces between Robert Wagner and Sinatra.

The article stated "actor Robert Wagner was one of her [Campbell's] first boyfriends" when she was just out of high school. She later confirmed the relationship with Wagner in her 1977 autobiography, *Judith Exner: My Story.*

Along the way, Sinatra developed close ties with more than just President Kennedy. He became an important part of the political life of Presidents Richard Nixon and Ronald Reagan and cultivated close relationships with Vice President Spiro T. Agnew and First Ladies Jacqueline Kennedy and Nancy Reagan.

If Sinatra's power and influence, along with his halo of underworld ties, weren't firmly established internationally before the *Daily Mail* series, there was no doubt about them now.

⌒⌒⌒⌒⌒⌒

Just when I believed I had uncovered all I was going to find about the Pitchess/Sinatra connection, I learned Pitchess was a witness for Sinatra in a hearing before the Nevada State Gaming Control Board a few months before Natalie's death.

In January 1980, Sinatra filed an application to obtain a "non-restricted" license to work as an entertainment and public relations "consultant" with Caesars Palace after being banned in 1963 because of his association with Giancana.

My Nevada Public Records Act request netted a full transcript of several Nevada Gaming Control Board hearings. The transcripts included live testimonials from Kirk Douglas and Gregory Peck. But the first witness called by Sinatra's lawyer, Nevada state senator William J. Raggio, was the high sheriff—Peter Pitchess.

To appreciate the astounding import of the sheriff's voluntary testimony before the board, it's important to understand the timing of certain events leading up to Sinatra's application and impacting his public image. Besides the murders of friends Giancana and Moretti, Sinatra's image problems began to take on new meaning in 1978. The highest-ranking "made guy" in La Cosa Nostra ever to "turn" against the family—Jimmy "The Weasel" Fratianno—became a protected government witness.

According to Ovid Demaris in *The Last Mafioso*, the day Fratianno flipped, "not a single Mafia boss slept." And, neither did Frank Sinatra. Here's why:

In its day, the Westchester Premier Theater in Tarrytown, New York, about 30 miles from Times Square, was a topflight concert hall. Singer Diana Ross, who was at the peak of her career, opened the venue in 1975 and its early years included shows by many A-list performers, including Sinatra. He played at least 10 sold-out performances in the 3,600-seat theater between April 1976 and May 1977. The theater was raking in money, but controversy surrounded it from its very construction when evidence of mob involvement appeared.

According to Fratianno, as told by Demaris, he got involved in the Westchester when Tommy Marson, a neighbor of Sinatra's, wanted him to help retrieve $1,400,000 that Marson "represented" in theater investments. Fratianno, who first met Sinatra in 1947 in California, went to New York to see Sinatra at the Westchester and attend a private party after the performance.

Fratianno's idea was for Sinatra to add a few days to his appearance for four "benefit" shows to "help the family." According to Fratianno, Sinatra was to get money "under the table," much like the $50,000 cash [about $211,000 today] the family told Fratianno they had given Sinatra after a previous theater performance.

As was to be expected, after the gangsters skimmed all they could, the Westchester went bankrupt. And when Fratianno flipped, 10 businessmen and "goodfellas" were indicted. The trial lasted three months and ended in May 1979. Most of the defendants were convicted or pleaded guilty, but during the trial, Sinatra was featured over his alleged under-the-table payments, and Exhibit 181 (a picture of a smiling Sinatra with eight gangsters including Don Carlo Gambino, which is now part of Sinatra folklore) was introduced into evidence.

Its existence further solidified the public's belief in Sinatra's high-level mob connections. According to Kelley in *His Way*, and there's no reason to disbelieve her, the LASD was collecting organized crime intelligence in early 1981. I was confident Sinatra was privy to that intel because of what Sheriff Pitchess, the career law enforcement officer, said under oath before the Gaming Board. Pitchess began his testimony with reference to his official contacts with mobsters on the basis of providing "mutual assistance," giving some gangsters a pass on some of their provable criminal activities or forgoing an investigation of substantial allegations of criminal misconduct in exchange for information about the criminal activities of others. In other words, becoming a "confidential informant" (CI).

During the hearing, Pitchess testified he met Sinatra in the early 1940s when he was assigned to look into a kidnapping threat against the entertainer's daughter Nancy. At the time, Sinatra's popularity was cosmic, and Pitchess was working FBI mafia intelligence. It was no secret Sinatra was associating with organized criminals, and J. Edgar Hoover's men were hot on his trail. This, in my opinion, is where Pitchess seized an opportunity to cultivate Sinatra as a CI. And why Sinatra saw an opportunity to shield himself from his increasingly dangerous liaisons with his mafia friends by agreeing to become a snitch for Pitchess who, in turn, guaranteed his security.

During his testimony, Pitchess made it clear Sinatra was "a very good friend" and went into detail about their long and cozy relationship:

> **Pitchess:** As sheriff, I spent considerable time having my intelligence detail examine a large number of complaints, rumors, gossip, innuendoes, and outright charges against Mr. Sinatra.
>
> My reason for doing that was twofold. *He was my friend and I wanted to know for my own personal satisfaction if there were any truth to these things. Secondly, I did it because it was my responsibility as the chief law enforcement of Los Angeles County to know who was engaged in any such activities* [emphasis added].
>
> So, our investigation of Mr. Sinatra took—has continued over a long period of time.
>
> *I have spent many hours in discussing these matters with Mr. Sinatra on a very frank and outspoken level* [emphasis added].

Later in the hearing, Raggio asked if he used all available intelligence information when investigating Sinatra:

> **Pitchess:** Yes. I would say—I feel like I spent a lifetime in inquiring and investigating Sinatra, and at the same time enjoying *a very close personal relationship and friendship with him* [emphasis added]. And I say that for this reason: Because at no time did I ever hesitate to ask him direct questions and on no occasion did he ever avoid or evade any of the questions that I asked him.

I've seen a lot of incredible testimony in my long career, but nothing more incredible than Pitchess' testimony before the Gaming Control Board. Here was the head of a 7,800-employee law enforcement agency stating he was investigating a close friend's connections to organized crime by calling the friend up and asking the friend if the allegations were true. Then, when the friend said "no," the matter was summarily closed.

There are only two possible explanations for this bizarre and unethical behavior. The first is that Sheriff Pitchess was an arrogant, incompetent and starstruck fool. The second, and much more plausible, is that Sinatra was the sheriff's longtime CI, and while Pitchess was arrogant enough to disclose this sensitive arrangement in a public forum, his testimony for Sinatra was a trade-off.

Pitchess also maintained there was no link between Sinatra and organized crime. This explains why there were no charges ever brought against Sinatra for his malfeasance, including perjury. It wasn't just his power and influence, because there were plenty of folks in New York who didn't like him. It was because his "close friend" protected Sinatra by providing him with the cover he needed to shield himself from such events.

For his friend, the sheriff was even willing to disparage law enforcement who believed Fratianno:

> **Pitchess:** And I don't want to cast aspersions against my own profession—there is such a thing as police mentality where people in law enforcement like to accept as fact rumors that condemn other people. *And too often those rumors that are accepted by some of them as fact are not investigated thoroughly but just taken on the basis of the surface they appear on* [emphasis added].

Moreover, Pitchess was willing to publicly trash his own profession with testimony that could be used by the defense in Los Angeles County criminal cases to discredit the testimony of its criminal investigators. *Why would Pitchess be willing to do that?*

Perhaps, it was because he was on his way out and didn't need law enforcement anymore. Or, it may have been that the sheriff's arrogance was even greater than I suspected. But the sheriff wasn't finished, and when asked about Fratianno, he replied:

> **Pitchess:** *I wouldn't believe Fratianno in any of his allegations.* He is a confessed murderer. He has made statements and repudiated those statements over the years. *I wouldn't accept anything that Fratianno said even with corroboration* [emphasis added].

Federal prosecutors and grand juries from coast-to-coast were relying on the testimony of Fratianno in pursuit of an untold number of organized crime figures. Yet, Sheriff Pitchess was willing to become an adverse character witness for defense attorneys by discrediting Fratianno for Sinatra. It was hard for me to believe Pitchess didn't know he might jeopardize cases prosecutors had been working hard to make for years. I racked my brain trying to understand why he would stretch himself so thin for Sinatra. *Perhaps il padrone of Hollywood had something on the sheriff? Or maybe the sheriff was so in awe of Sinatra, he didn't mind prostrating himself? Or maybe both.*

Sinatra's lawyer wrapped up by giving Pitchess an opportunity to give an opinion as to whether Sinatra was "connected with, affiliated with in any capacity organized crime as that term is commonly understood."

> **Pitchess:** I am completely satisfied, my own personal satisfaction and the satisfaction of the people who work with me in this field, my subordinates in my department, that Frank Sinatra is not *a member of* any organized crime, any syndicated crime or the mafia. I can summarize it this way: In my opinion, after thirty-eight years of a rather close relationship with Mr. Sinatra, personally and officially, I can say this: If Mr. Sinatra is a *member of the mafia* [emphasis added], then I am the godfather.

Pitchess' last sentence was published in newspapers in Vegas and LA, but Ralph Seler-no, a Pitchess subordinate and LASD organized crime detective, wasn't buying it. He told a class for law enforcement officers, many of whom worked for Pitchess: "When you see Pete Pitchess, tell him I said, 'Hello, Godfather!'"

At the hearing's conclusion, Sinatra received his license. Six months later, Pitchess traveled to Bophuthatswana, South Africa, with his "close friend" Sinatra to witness a performance the entertainer was giving there. Knowing Sinatra and his largess, it was most likely an all-expenses-paid vacation for the elected official. The sheriff had done his duty.

〰〰〰〰

So, how does Sinatra's relationship with Pitchess factor into Sinatra's entrance into Natalie's death investigation?

Finstad was apparently able to interview Detective Rasure before he died. While failing to ask Rasure probing questions about the manner in which he spearheaded the investigation of Natalie's death, Finstad did manage to talk to him about the Wagner interviews he and Hamilton conducted on November 30 and December 4, 1981. In the following chapter, you will learn that the December 4 interview came about after Pitchess' direct intervention in Natalie's case.

〰〰〰〰

In his memoir *Pieces of My Heart*, Wagner bragged to Eyman about his long association with studio fixers whose job it was to clean up messes created by their contract actors, so the studios wouldn't take a hit at the theater box offices. In a 2014 book he published with Eyman, titled *You Must Remember This*, Wagner described his "freedom" and "license" this way:

> We who were lucky enough to be in the movie industry at that time lived in a cocoon of golden lace. We were protected from the consequences of our behavior by the vast studio apparatus and by a comprehensively different public attitude. We had freedom and, frankly, most of the time we also had license. If there was an arrest for drunk driving, there would be a nod, a wink, perhaps some modest amount of money changing hands, and that would be the end of it. No police record, let alone a trial. If an actor behaved the way that, say Tiger Woods did—and believe me, it was not unusual, it was covered up. No one knew, and no one would ever know...except the fixers at the studio.

Wagner first crossed paths with Harry Brand, Darryl F. Zanuck's confidant and head of publicity for Twentieth Century-Fox, in the early '50s. He described the notorious fixer in *Pieces* as being, "heavily connected. *He had an in with every police department in California* [emphasis added], knew everything that was going on, and could fix anything that needed to be fixed."

"An in with every police department" would certainly include the LASD and the celebrity-connected Sheriff Pitchess. Little is known about the reclusive and experienced fixer, but his influence was clearly acknowledged by Wagner after Natalie's death: "In due time,

Harry would fix a couple of things for me." Lambert revealed one of those instances in his book when he stated Wagner got Brand to fix a 1958 vehicular manslaughter charge filed against Natalie's father.

Brand retired from Twentieth Century-Fox in 1962 and continued as a "consultant" until 1982. Brand passed away in 1989. And, the secrets he held were buried forever.

∽∽∽∽∽∽∽∽

In his memoir, Dr. Noguchi wrote that after his news conference about Natalie's death, the controversy intensified as Wagner's allies in Hollywood rushed to defend the actor, making the coroner "the main target." In support of his claim, Dr. Noguchi said:

> Some Hollywood stars, still fretting over the William Holden report, struck hard at me, as well as at the *Times* for printing the remarks of the "stage-struck" coroner. *Frank Sinatra* [emphasis added] sent a letter to the Board of Supervisors which said, in effect, that coroners should be seen and not heard.

From everything I had read in Dr. Noguchi's Civil Service Commission file, he had failed miserably in his management of the coroner's department for years prior to Natalie's death without intervention by the LA County Board of Supervisors. Above all, Dr. Noguchi operated without negative oversight alerts from the supervisor assigned to the coroner's office—Michael Antonovich.

According to Dr. Noguchi, the day after his Natalie Wood news conference, this happened:

> [F]riends of Robert Wagner, who had been in seclusion ever since the accident, sought to still the rumors. They circulated word to reporters that there had been no dispute at all on the yacht. Instead, they said, Natalie Wood had been unable to sleep because the dinghy was knocking against the stern of the yacht. She had gone topside to adjust the line to the dinghy, had slipped while doing so, and fallen into the water.

No stranger to the movie industry's rumor mills, Dr. Noguchi continued:

> Hollywood was, of course, steaming with the news. And it seemed, from reports of the rumors that reached me, that many of the movie colony disbelieved Wagner—and actually thought that much more than an "argument" had taken place that night on the yacht. Scandalous stories and weird sexual allegations were spreading like brushfire.

Setting up the genesis of Dr. Noguchi's final days as chief coroner, Sinatra sent his letter to the Board of Supervisors in care of Antonovich, sometime between Monday afternoon, November 30, and Wednesday, December 2, 1981. The full text was not reported on by the media, but the *LA Times* did say it was critical of Dr. Noguchi and his methods. And there was no better shepherd for Dr. Noguchi's exit than the politically ambitious Antonovich.

~~~~~~

Antonovich was elected to the Board of Supervisors in 1980 and represented the Fifth District until he retired in 2016. The Fifth District, which covers a northern portion of Los Angeles County, currently has a population of 2 million.

As proof of Antonovich's efficiency in handling Sinatra's complaint, within four months of Natalie's death, the famous Dr. Noguchi lost his job.

I obtained a copy of his Civil Service Commission hearing file from the Executive Office of the Board of Supervisors to look for, among other things, a copy of the Sinatra letter. Although referenced in the file by Noguchi's lawyer, the letter was missing. I'd like to say I was surprised, but I had grown accustomed to man-made obstacles when it came to the truth in Natalie's case.

But, in reviewing the file, I stumbled upon excerpts from the hearing testimony of Antonovich. He was called as a witness by the county to testify about one of the board's grounds for relieving Dr. Noguchi of his position as Chief—his sensational news conferences in which he "demonstrated poor judgment and unprofessional speculation in [his] public statements regarding the recent local deaths of two movie celebrities [William Holden and Natalie Wood]."

Antonovich testified that after Dr. Noguchi's public discussions of the deaths of Holden and Natalie, his office received "telephone calls and letters" from members of the public "who were unhappy" about Dr. Noguchi's statements "of the possible circumstances" surrounding those deaths.

Strangely, however, not one letter was introduced into evidence and Antonovich "couldn't recall" the names of the members of the public. I found it extremely hard to believe that Antonovich couldn't recall receiving a letter about Dr. Noguchi from Sinatra, one of the most visible celebrities in the world. So, in January 2017, I dispatched my LA research assistant, Kevin Brechner, to the Executive Office of the Board of Supervisors to get to the bottom of the missing letter.

After an unsuccessful email to Bruce Crouchet, archivist for the Los Angeles County Board of Supervisors, explaining the puzzling absence of the Sinatra letter, Kevin contacted the office of the supervisor who had replaced Antonovich. After dealing with two assistants about his dilemma, it was relayed to Kevin that Antonovich had the Sinatra letter. Over the next several weeks, we pressed the Executive Office to retrieve the Sinatra letter from Antonovich. Getting nowhere, I filed my third lawsuit.

What followed was nothing short of astounding.

~~~~~~

After suit was filed, two private lawyers, on the taxpayers' dime, showed up defending the county. No explanation was given as to why they were needed to defend the county instead of one of the more than 300 lawyers on County Counsel's staff. But they claimed, among other things, the county lacked "information to admit or deny whether Mr. Antonovich communicated with the Executive Office and acknowledged possession of an alleged public record."

We prepared a notice of depositions for the Executive Office assistants and subpoena for

Antonovich. With that, it didn't take long for the deceit to begin. It started with a claim that the county couldn't "determine the identity" of the assistants. While that subterfuge continued, Antonovich was evading service of our deposition subpoena. Our first professional process server staked out Antonovich's home for six hours after no one answered the front door. Two SUVs were in the driveway, but the house remained dark, even though there "was evidence of activity in the residence."

Since the subpoena had to be served within a specified time before the deposition was scheduled, I hired a licensed private investigator to serve the subpoena. The PI caught Antonovich as he was about to board a private plane for a trip "out of town."

At our first hearing, on January 25, 2018, County Counsel finally admitted the accuracy of the legal proposition I had been advocating for the past 13 months. That should have been the end of the matter, but the defense attorneys continued their obfuscation. They filed a motion to prevent me from getting Antonovich under oath, attaching a sworn declaration (affidavit) from Antonovich that said, "I did not take any documents or files belonging to the county." But, the judge ordered Antonovich to testify.

⌒⌒⌒⌒⌒⌒

The LA Westin Bonaventure was chosen to host a round of depositions in *Perroni v. Los Angeles County*, Case No. 171171. This time a third attorney represented the county. Brian Chu, "principal deputy county counsel," entered his appearance a week before the depositions were scheduled.

Why Chu didn't save taxpayers some money by handling the deposition personally was a mystery.

I deposed the administrative assistants and got nowhere. Their memories seemed to have failed them. Such opacity of memory, however, was tame compared to what happened next.

After preliminary questions, I had this exchange with Antonovich:

> **S.P.:** Is it true or false that you had communications with someone in the supervisor's office about having possession of one of those letters?
>
> **Antonovich:** That's correct.
>
> **S.P.:** It's true?
>
> **Antonovich:** Yes, sir.
>
> **S.P.:** And did you tell them you had possession of one of the letters [the Sinatra letter]?
>
> **Antonovich:** I thought I had possession of the letter.

Following that came the bombshell, accompanied by fallacious objections from all three lawyers, with Antonovich (*Figure 34*, next page) relating the following:

> **S.P.:** Do you know what happened to that letter?

Antonovich: The letter I had received, *I had it framed on my wall* [emphasis added].

S.P.: So, what happened to it?

Antonovich: I don't know. Because if I knew, I would allow you to have a copy of it, because I have no pride in not having you see the letter.

S.P.: Well, why didn't you tell me that a year ago?

Lawyer No. 1: Objection.

Chu: Argumentative.

Lawyer No. 1: Argumentative.

S.P.: Are you following me here? You know, I didn't ask to come out here and sue everybody. Why didn't you pick up the phone or write me a letter and say, "Hey, I used to have this letter, but I don't have it anymore"?

After another barrage of objections, Antonovich just sat there, never responding to the question or apologizing for the disrespectful way he handled himself prior to the deposi-

Figure 34: Michael Antonovich testifies on the whereabouts of a letter Frank Sinatra wrote in 1981. (Habeas Videos)

tion. The letter hung on Antonovich's office wall as a cherished souvenir for 35 years until just before I sought its official disclosure, and then it vanished. How opportune.

$$\backsim\backsim\backsim\backsim\backsim\backsim$$

In *Pieces of My Heart*, Wagner expressed his feelings about Dr. Noguchi, and had this to say about Sinatra and the world-famous forensic pathologist:

> Thomas Noguchi, the Los Angeles coroner, got into the act and ventured some ridiculous speculations, just as he had with Bill Holden, and as he would when he reopened the investigation into the death of Marilyn Monroe. Noguchi was a camera-hog who felt that he had to stoke the publicity fire in order to maintain the level of attention he'd gotten used to. *Noguchi particularly enraged Frank Sinatra, who knew the truth* and, in any case, would never have allowed anybody who *harmed Natalie to survive* [emphasis added].

Sinatra knew Wagner's "truth" and "would never have allowed anybody who harmed" his former lover/comrade "Natalie to survive." Wagner had never spoken truer words. The reasonable inference is that after Wagner told Sinatra his "truth" about what happened that fateful Saturday night in November, Sinatra called his friend Pitchess. After assuring Pitchess he would help in facilitating the expedited closing of the LASD's investigation, the reasonable inference is that Sinatra put in a good word for his friend Wagner: *Hey, Pete, R.J.'s a good guy. Do what you can for him, will ya, pal?* The dutiful sheriff would have fallen all over himself to oblige.

Moreover, Wagner's comments about Sinatra's targeting Dr. Noguchi and Brand fixing things for him lead to the reasonable inference that Wagner also yelled "Hey, Rube!" after Natalie's death. When he did, his high-powered friends came rushing to rescue him. All they needed to hear was that Natalie's death was an accident and Wagner had nothing to do with it. And they believed him because not doing so was too horrible to comprehend.

A beautiful star was dead. A lot of money was going to be lost. No powerful friendship could be spared. So, the fixers and power brokers sought to head off a potentially salacious Hollywood-style scandal—a drunken argument between two male celebrities over a beautiful world-famous actress that ended in her death—with favors being called in, disinformation, misleading statements and outright falsities.

All of that and Jill St. John's long-standing connection with Sidney Korshak and Secretary of State Henry Kissinger. According to Walter Isaacson in *Kissinger*, his biography of the incomparable statesman, St. John told him he was "there when you needed him." And, Korshak? Well, his influence was golden.

All of this couldn't have fallen into place any better for Wagner in 1981. Now, all he had to do was keep Davern quiet. Wagner had no worries with Walken because he was never going to be man enough to tell the truth. As you will see, his career was entirely too precious for that to happen.

CHAPTER 17

marching orders

THE FIRST PHOTOGRAPH I SAW OF THE LEAD DETECTIVE IN THE 1981 investigation of Natalie's death was in Kashner's 2000 *Vanity Fair* article. In the prominently placed photo, retired detective Duane Rasure was wearing a blue denim, fleece-lined rancher's jacket and black cowboy hat wrapped with a sterling silver band.

While it doesn't show, the 70-year-old Rasure's slacks were undoubtedly held up by a wide, black belt with a silver buckle engraved with the number 187—the California Penal Code citation number for the crime of murder.

Rasure began working for the Los Angeles County Sheriff's Department in 1954. By the time Natalie died, Rasure had served 27 years and was a veteran detective close to retirement. Rasure had been credited with solving some major cases during his career and was apparently well liked. Having worked with Pitchess for so many years, Rasure was undeniably well-schooled in his way of doing things, i.e., by all means protect the rich and powerful from embarrassment or worse. For it was well known that Pitchess fawned over Hollywood celebrities.

Rasure passed away in 2014. According to the LASD, his partner in Natalie's case, Roy Hamilton, was also deceased. Had I been able to interview the lead investigators, I could have gained considerable insight into their "facts," both public and private. Now, I had to rely on their 1981 investigator notes and phone messages, Rasure's official report, and statements Rasure made to writers, journalists and biographers over the years.

In conversations with Finstad nearly 20 years after Natalie's death, Rasure left the impression he was assigned to Natalie's case by the "rotation" luck of the draw. He acted as though he was miffed because "90 percent of the workload was left on him." But I had my doubts. After all I've seen, I believe Rasure was handpicked for the assignment by his longtime boss, Peter Pitchess. Here's why.

To Finstad, he disclosed a direct and familiar connection with the sheriff during the first few days of the 1981 investigation. It occurred before the investigators' second interview of Wagner, five days after Natalie's death.

Rasure told Finstad that Paul Ziffren called him "wanting to know why I wanted to re-talk to Wagner." When Rasure told Ziffren he didn't get enough information in the first interview, Rasure claimed the prominent lawyer called Sheriff Pitchess.

Bypassing his chief of detectives, Homicide Bureau captain and supervising lieutenant, Sheriff Pitchess called Rasure "up to his office." Rasure claimed, "Pitchess got on the phone." He did not say who Pitchess called, but based on the timing and evidence, I'm convinced it was Wagner's friend Sinatra, who was well acquainted with the sheriff, or Harry Brand, who Wagner said was close to law enforcement and had "fixed a few things" for him in the past.

Finstad reported that Rasure told her, "the next day Wagner's attorney called me and said, 'you can have your meeting anytime you want it.' The sheriff pulled his power on that one."

Surely Finstad asked Rasure who the sheriff called and what he said to the person on the other end of the line, since Rasure claimed he was in the office when the call took place. I knew at the outset there was high-level LASD interest in Natalie's case from documents I discovered in her 1981 file. A telephone message was left for Rasure from the chief of detectives the day after Natalie's body was found (see *Figure I*, Page 266) at precisely the same time of day that investigator Hamilton called John Payne, one of the witnesses to the cries for help from a woman in the water near *Splendour*. And Sheriff Pitchess sent a December memo to the Homicide Bureau directing them to contact him about the "disposition" of Natalie's case. (See *Figure J*, also Page 266.)

From the context of Rasure's statements, we know Pitchess didn't call Ziffren. So, from what I knew about Wagner's connections, my money was on Sinatra or Brand, with Ziffren's change of heart being part of a deal to give Wagner a pass after Rasure got what he needed to close his file as an accident.

What's more, looking closely at Natalie's file, it seemed as though Hamilton assumed much of the workload when it came to interviewing witnesses. That conclusion was confirmed for me by the volume and detail of each investigator's notes. After Rasure and Hamilton left the island Sunday, it appeared from the notes as though Hamilton single-handedly conducted the remaining witness interviews by telephone—except for the remaining interviews of Walken, Wagner and Davern, which the duo handled together. In my opinion, that was a questionable division of labor on such a high-profile case since Hamilton had only recently been promoted to the position of crime scene investigator and his skills had not likely been fully tested in the field.

However, Rasure apparently did take the lead in preparation of the official report. If my hunch is correct, the official report in Natalie's case had to be finessed to distance Wagner from any culpability. After witnessing how Rasure directed the investigation and selected the information that was ultimately included in his report, my experience tells me he was an integral part of an LASD cover-up.

❦

It was standard operating procedure when a detective sought out a witness to take another investigator with him for backup. In the majority of garden-variety witness interviews, the lead detective, in this case Rasure, would question the witness while the second investigator would take notes. Sometimes, the lead detective would also take notes if his writing didn't distract him from interacting with and listening to the witness. As a result, the assisting investigator's notes would be, for the most part, more detailed. When comparing the notes of Rasure and Hamilton in Natalie's case, Hamilton's notes were more extensive and contained many important statements that were not found in Rasure's notes.

After a witness was interviewed, the detective responsible for the report would gather up both his and his partner's notes and dictate or handwrite a "memorandum of interview," which then would be typed for review and corrections, if needed. If a full report containing many interviews was required, the lead investigator would organize the memos or notes for the typist or dictate them chronologically to a stenographer for the full report. That transcript would thereafter be reviewed by the lead investigator, edited and crafted into a full report.

Because computers were not in common use in 1981, the process for preparing a lengthy report would sometimes take days, even when the typist was extraordinarily fast. It would have taken Rasure and the stenographer at least three days to organize the material, have it dictated, then correct the 22-page, single-spaced report before distribution to Rasure's supervisors. The final official report of Natalie's case, called a "Sheriff's Department—Supplemental Report," was dated December 11, 1981. To me, that suggested Rasure started preparing it well before that date.

The significance of the report's date to the overall timeline was that Rasure and Hamilton didn't interview Davern a second time until 11 a.m. on December 10, 1981. It's unlikely that any information from this interview could have been factored into the report in such a short time frame with the technology available. That means Davern's statements didn't affect Rasure's overall conclusion of accidental death.

Rasure's report itself was labeled a "Supplemental Report" because it was intended to be a codicil to Deputy Kroll's original "Complaint Report" that was handwritten by him on the island and completed for Rasure's review at precisely 9:37 a.m. the day Natalie's body was found.

‍

Rasure wrote in his report that he was "detailed" to the island at "0830 hours" Sunday, November 29, 1981, to investigate "the circumstances surrounding the death of Victim Natalie Wood Wagner." It had been presented to the investigators that "someone fell overboard and drowned," according to Rasure. Their trip to the island was to begin at the sheriff's heliport in Long Beach.

By all reliable accounts, Wagner and Walken were whisked off the island by the LASD rescue helicopter to meet the investigators in Long Beach a little more than an hour after Natalie's body was recovered. They landed at 9:45 a.m. and were brought to the sheriff's Long Beach headquarters. Davern had been left behind by Wagner to officially identify Natalie's body.

Because rescue helicopters were a pet project of Pitchess', I was confident he had something to do with requisitioning Wagner and Walken's highly unusual escort—even though the escort's authorization and use wasn't documented in Natalie's file.

In *Goodbye*, Rasure apparently told Rulli that Wagner appeared unstable when he got off the helicopter. "He could barely pull himself upright to walk" and was "shook up, *really* in bad shape." Wagner got some coffee as the investigators introduced themselves, and Rasure began to ask questions.

But in his notes at the time, all Rasure wrote about Wagner's behavior was that he was "quite shook." In his official report, Rasure wrote that Wagner "was in an emotional state." CSI Hamilton wrote nothing about the actor's outward appearance. There was no notation about Walken's demeanor in the investigators' notes and nothing to indicate whether either of the actors were examined or appeared intoxicated.

The investigators talked to Wagner for *six minutes* before Rasure let him leave.

Rasure had been around suspects in murder cases long enough to know the guilty, as well as the innocent, sometimes become emotional when law enforcement arrives. Some suspects are genuinely distraught, some are scared and some are acting. He also knew enough about the situation to know there were four people on the yacht—one actress, two actors and the captain. The death of the lone woman was unexplained, and Rasure's training had taught him all three men were homicide suspects until determined otherwise.

It was standard procedure to interview suspects without regard to their demeanor for as long as possible to get information to continue the investigation. It was highly unusual for the detective to voluntarily let two suspects go because one of them was "shook up." No one can convince me Rasure was following standard LASD Homicide Bureau operating procedure in doing so. This behavior on the investigator's part clearly pointed to a directive to go easy on these celebrities.

Sometime before Wagner entered his waiting car, he was intercepted by coroner's investigator Pamela Eaker, who asked the most probing question of the morning: "When was the last time you saw your wife?" Wagner said it was *10:45* Saturday night. Hamilton's notes, not Rasure's, also had Wagner making another critical statement that would later be debunked: "We were all in the boat—*Beautiful night.*" Natalie *"wanted to take dingy (sic) out."* And, "I started calling Harbor Patrol about *11:30* [emphasis added]."

Statements by suspects must be checked out by investigators. That's a fundamental procedure in homicide investigations, or any criminal investigation for that matter. If a suspect tells an investigator something to establish his innocence and the investigator determines later what the suspect said is untrue, you have learned in legal terms it's a "false exculpatory statement." That evidence then becomes proof of the suspect's "consciousness of guilt," which is used in trials daily by prosecutors across the country to prove criminal intent.

But those original statements by Wagner never made it into the official report because they quickly became inconsistent with accounts by other witnesses on the island and Walken's and Davern's later statements.

According to their notes, after talking to the restaurant's owner, night manager and employees as well as Wintler, the investigators learned the weather was cold, breezy and rainy on Saturday night, not a "beautiful night" as Wagner had said. Wagner's first contact requesting help in searching for Natalie had been between *1 a.m.* and *1:30 a.m.* Sunday, not 11:30 p.m. as Wagner had said. And the investigators debriefed Eaker before they left the island, undoubtedly learning Wagner told her he last saw his wife at 10:45 p.m.

The island interviews proved that of the three admissions made by Wagner recorded by Eaker and Hamilton, two were indisputably false. Not only that, the investigators talked to Davern and Walken on Sunday morning after they talked to Wagner, and they didn't ask either one if Natalie wanted to take the dinghy out after returning to the yacht from dinner. That simple question wasn't asked during Davern's and Walken's second interviews either. Why did this veteran investigator neglect to ask this and other questions in an effort to test Wagner's statements? Was it as intentional as the fact that the final report didn't include Wagner's damning false exculpatory statements?

∽∽∽∽∽∽∽

Rasure's official report for the file and his superiors had the outward appearance of being professional and thorough. Yet, despite having evidence establishing a 2-1/4-hour unexplained gap between the time Wagner said he last saw Natalie and the time he reached out for help, Rasure didn't mention that key detail in his report.

The entire report provided no times for events other than "safe times"—times that don't suggest an event is incriminating or suspicious of Wagner. Safe times include events like when a witness was interviewed or when Davern positively identified Natalie's body. The omission of important event times was manifestly deliberate. Rasure didn't want to call attention to the suspicious timeline.

∽∾∽∾∽∾∿

After the investigators' brief encounter with Wagner at Long Beach, they talked to Walken. Among other vague and unspecified statements, Walken told them that after the foursome returned to the yacht Saturday night, he and Wagner had a "small beef." There was no indication the detectives asked him what he meant by "small beef." Yet, by 10 a.m. Sunday, the investigators knew from an occupant on *Splendour* that all wasn't the friendly and peaceful evening aboard the yacht that Saturday night as Wagner had led the investigators to believe.

Immediately after Walken's "small beef" statement, Hamilton and Rasure wrote in their notes that Walken said he "ran out [the] door." Neither investigator apparently asked Walken what was so frightening that it caused him to run out the door. A reasonable person would suspect something much more significant than a "small beef" occurred to cause that reaction. But unsurprisingly, Walken's "ran out [the] door" statement didn't make it into Rasure's official report.

The only thing I was aware of that could have caused a reaction like Walken's was Davern's claims four years later to *Star* magazine that Wagner smashed a wine bottle on the yacht's coffee table after accusing Walken of wanting to have sex with his wife. Obviously, Rasure didn't have that information from Davern in 1981, but he was about to see something almost as incriminating. It was in *Splendour's* salon.

∽∾∽∾∽∾∿

After the Long Beach encounter with Wagner and Walken, the investigators and Eaker were transported by the department's helicopter to the sheriff's office in Avalon, arriving at 10:45 or 10:50 a.m., depending on which investigator's notes you use. The Avalon sheriff's office was approximately 18 miles by car and 12 miles by boat from Isthmus Cove and Blue Cavern Point, where Natalie's body was recovered.

While Eaker left the investigators to examine Natalie and take time-of-death parameters, Rasure and Hamilton debriefed Deputy Kroll. Kroll had interviewed Wagner, Davern and several other witnesses, searched the *Splendour* and accompanied Davern while he made a positive identification of Natalie's body.

Approximately 30 minutes after the debriefing, investigators interviewed Davern, who promptly lied about where Natalie spent Friday night and the reason for broken glass covering the yacht's salon floor. When questioned about the glass, both investigators' notes reported Davern said it was due to "rough seas." In fact, Hamilton's notes stated Davern said, "maybe six wine bottles were broken."

I believe the initial questioning of Davern by the investigators was prompted by suspicions Kroll had after searching the yacht with Wagner. Kroll saw a potential crime scene, and I believe he told the investigators as much.

When questioned about an argument between Wagner and Walken, Davern refused to answer. To any reasonable person, that would fuel speculation about what really happened during Wagner and Walken's "small beef." However, even this truncated question-and-answer exchange didn't make it into the official report. This omission was nothing less than an overt attempt by the detective to protect Wagner and Walken.

Given the information in the investigative notes, there were more than reasonable suspicions about what really happened on Saturday night after speaking with Davern, but there was more to come. At 12:45 Sunday afternoon, the investigators boarded *Splendour.* In the yacht's salon, there was physical evidence of an altercation recently occurring aboard the yacht. Initially, both investigators saw and noted broken glass on the salon floor, yet no close-up photographs of the broken glass were taken. That omission was highly irregular. Instead, the official report said, "there was no *real* [emphasis added] indication of any disturbance."

But there was a full-view photograph of the coffee table with the name "*Splendour*" embossed across its top. (See Page B-1.) I used my magnifying glass to examine what looked like damage on the edge of the table opposite the couch. After I had that area of the photo enlarged, the evidence I was looking for was staring me in the face.

The damage to the high-glossed table edge was clearly visible (also Page B-1). The small white specks in my enlargement were shards of glass. Again, no mention of this evidence was made in the official report or investigators' notes. The investigators had to have known the coffee table damage was caused by force. Under standard procedure, there would have been a request that the coffee table be secured for inspection by forensics. There is no record of a request, which again, was highly irregular.

Moving through the yacht, an LASD photographer snapped pictures of the galley, which was a mess, to say the least. (See two photos, Page B-2.) Among the photos was one that haunts me to this day. It showed that the tragedy unfolded in the presence of photographs of Natalie's daughters, Natasha and Courtney, which were displayed proudly on the galley wall. (See Page B-3.)

The photographer also snapped shots of a second coffee table and portside seating in the yacht's salon. (See Page B-3 and Page B-4.) On his way to the staterooms, the photographer took pictures of the galley floor area, including the trash containers. Yet no mention was made in the official reports or investigator notes of the empty wine and scotch bottles in plain view. (See Page A-6 and Page B-4.)

Where was the neck of the smashed wine bottle? Was it in the trash? Photos were taken of the trash cans, but no search was conducted of the contents. And, what about the remnants of the six broken wine bottles Davern reported? There was no record of them either. A wine bottle neck could have yielded finger and palm prints to show it was grabbed by a hand, and the breakage patterns could have been analyzed to determine if the bottle were broken with force exceeding that sustained when a wine bottle falls accidentally to a carpeted floor.

Furthermore, forensics could have established that a wine bottle produced the damage to the table by matching the curve of an identical bottle to the dent in the table. And, forensics could have identified the bottle's angle upon contact, perhaps ascertaining where the person wielding it had been standing or sitting. Finally, forensics could have measured the depth of the dent, leading to a possible determination of how much force it had taken to make it.

But, of course, none of that was done because the table wasn't seized as evidence and the trash cans were not inspected.

In essence, forensics could have yielded evidence to disprove the statement that wine bottles were broken during "rough seas" and, in fact, verify that the damage to the table was recently caused by a wine bottle being forcibly broken over its edge by a person standing up facing the couch where Natalie and Walken had been seated.

〰〰〰〰

The photographs of the master stateroom showed the bed in disarray, but the key to this room was not the messy bed. It was the wooden bed surround and the vanity area across the room where Natalie's clothes were left on a chair. (See Page B-5.) Designer blue jeans, a bra and what looked like a yellow sweater top were draped over the chair, and a red, white and blue purse was placed on the floor next to it. The clothing matched what witnesses told Deputy Kroll that Natalie was wearing in the restaurant Saturday night.

There was something else on top of the dressing table. Another photographic enlargement revealed an opened black pocketbook or wallet of some sort (also Page B-5). And, on the floor next to the vanity table chair was a brown travel bag with a yellow terry cloth robe tucked neatly between the carrying straps.

These personal items would cause any investigator to make two obvious conclusions. The first is that famous screen star Natalie Wood would not have "gone ashore to the bar," as Wagner told Kroll, dressed in a scanty nightshirt and without her wallet. Secondly, she would not have removed the clothing she wore to the restaurant and put on a nightshirt to "take the dingy (sic) out" for a cold late-night spin, as Wagner told the investigators a few hours earlier in Long Beach. There was no mention in the official report or investigators' notes about these conclusions nor the presence of a wallet on the dressing table.

As far as the wooden bed surround in the crime scene photo, it was a potential source of Natalie's lower leg bruises, bruises that were consistent with being compressed on a hard surface as Dr. Stanley suggested. (See Page B-6.) Yet there was no mention in investigators' notes or the report of measurements taken from the floor to the top of the wooden bed surround, measurements that could correspond to the location of the bruises on the back of Natalie's legs.

In fact, there was no mention in either of the investigators' notes as to the condition of *Splendour*. Hamilton's notes contained nothing about the yacht. Rasure's notes only said, "12:45 Exam Boat '*Splendour*.'" And Rasure's official report devoted only two sentences to the condition of the master stateroom:

> A more thorough examination showed the master stateroom to have a large double bed which appared (sic) to have been used, with the blankets in disarray. Clothing and other articles indicated occupancy by a woman.

The yacht had all the trappings of an altercation. Nevertheless, years later Rasure would tell Rulli in *Goodbye*, "No furniture was moved around. It didn't look like a fight or anything." Notably, it's standard that furniture on a seafaring pleasure boat is bolted down to prevent it from moving around during heavy seas or during movement from the marina to its destination. It's easy to spot when looking at the bases of tables and the bottoms of chair legs.

The official records of the LASD and coroner's office reflected that nothing on the yacht was secured as evidence—no glass shards from the broken wine bottle; no clothing, pocketbook, bedding or linens; no trash container contents, coffee table, carpet vacuuming evidence or potential trace blood evidence. In a proper homicide investigation, the evidence would be collected to have it available for forensics if it becomes needed.

According to the former director of the LASD Scientific Services Bureau, Barry A. J. Fisher, it's "better to have processed the scene more thoroughly than needed than to have overlooked something seemingly insignificant." Both investigators knew that; it's nothing but common investigative sense. Yet the yacht wasn't processed for any evidence.

After inspecting the yacht, Rasure also said they examined the Zodiac dinghy for scratches. In the report, Rasure described the "examination" as follows: "At 1245 hours on 11-29-81, investigators boarded the vessel *Splendour*. As investigators boarded the vessel they could observe the above described Zodiac tied up alongside the starboard side." That was the sum total of the detective's description of their inspection of the dinghy in the official report. Moreover, their investigative notes contained nothing about an examination of the dinghy.

The only meaningful inspection of the Zodiac was the one conducted by Paul Miller. From the LASD file, it appeared as though the investigators' examination of the Zodiac consisted of a photographer leaning over the side of the yacht to take a picture. (See Page B-6.) It also begged the question of why the dinghy, which had been discovered floating freely not far from the where Natalie's body was found, was not impounded for forensics as well. Instead, after the dinghy was towed from Perdition Cave (Page B-7), it was most likely deflated by Davern and stored on the bow of *Splendour*, covered with a blue tarp (also Page B-7).

The investigators spoke with Whiting early in the process. He told them, in his opinion, "the Zodiac as they [Whiting and Coleman] found it had never been started, it had just drifted to the position where it was found." Notwithstanding, there is no mention in the report of how the dinghy eventually came to be tied up to the starboard side of the yacht before the investigators boarded the yacht.

෨෨෨෨෨෨෨

According to Hamilton's notes, 25 minutes after "examining" *Splendour*, he and Rasure were at the USC marine lab at Catalina Island's Big Fisherman's Cove to view Natalie's body and meet Eaker. It probably took five to 10 minutes to travel by boat from Isthmus Cove to the marine lab. That leaves only 15 to 20 minutes for investigating *Splendour*. This establishes that the homicide investigators' examination of a potential homicide crime scene was cursory at best.

As for Rasure's official report, it contained the following description of the injuries the two investigators saw when they examined Natalie's body: "Additional visual examination revealed no signs of *heavy trauma* [emphasis added] other than light bruising on the lower portions of her legs."

No mention was made of the "small laceration" observed "on the bridge" of Natalie's nose and the "bruises" on her arms witnessed by Deputy Kroll a few hours earlier. Not a word about the large bruises on Natalie's left knee and right ankle or the right forearm contusion and throat scratch noted the following day during autopsy by Dr. Choi. Were they merely overlooked by the expert investigators? It seemed very unlikely. No doubt, these suspicious facts were deliberately left out of the official report.

Rasure's choice of words in reporting there was no "heavy trauma" was designed to dismiss Natalie's unexplained injuries. "Heavy trauma," whatever that might have meant to Rasure, was not the litmus test for suspecting a victim was involved in an altercation. However, if it were, Natalie's deep forearm, knee and ankle contusions would certainly have passed the test. Contusions are routinely characterized by forensic pathologists as a result of ruptured blood vessels caused by "blunt force injury, or pressure."

We knew from the autopsy report that Natalie had over 30 bruises, scratches, scrapes and contusions on her body. But here was what Rasure, who attended the autopsy, decided to include in his official report:

> Dr. Choi made a thorough examination of all *contusions and abrasions, and indicated to investigators that the majority of the abrasions* [emphasis added] appared (sic) to be 12 to 24 hours old. He stated there was a scraping type abrasion on her left cheek, and this abrasion appeared to have an upward direction to the scrape. When questioned exactly what Dr. Choi meant, he demonstrated this indicating that as one would fall down, one's head striking an object and the person going down over the object would create this upward scraping abrasion.

⌇⌇⌇⌇⌇

According to Hamilton's notes, Curt Craig approached the lead detective at 2:51 p.m. Sunday, November 29, with a report from passengers aboard *Capricorn*, a sailboat moored about 100 feet from *Splendour* on Saturday night. Craig told Rasure the people on the sailboat heard "a female screaming for help somewhere around midnight." Although troubling in and of itself, Rasure did nothing to follow up on this important account. Instead, he shamelessly questioned Wayne's and Payne's veracity in the local newspapers, and only directed Hamilton to telephone Wayne *after* she shared her account with the press.

In his official report, however, Rasure included his interview with Dennis Bowen, who told investigators he was with his girlfriend and family members on the vessel *Kestral* moored "85 to 95 yards" from *Splendour*. The report said Bowen "had his porthole open, which faced the vessel *Splendour*." It continued, "He stated he is a light sleeper and if someone had been yelling for help he would have heard it." The report also said Bowen checked with others aboard and they didn't hear anything either.

Ninety-five yards is nearly the length of a football field. Bowen would have needed to have superhuman hearing to hear screams from someone in the ocean from that distance away on a cold, windy night. He also reported he had gone to sleep "at approximately 11:30 p.m." According to the known forensic timeline, Natalie would have been unable to scream due to hypothermia symptoms by 11:30 p.m. Payne and Wayne, not Bowen, were close enough to hear Natalie's desperate cries for help. But Bowen's assertions were all Rasure needed to brush off Payne's and Wayne's accounts and lend credibility to his official position that there were no screams for help that night.

The day after Natalie's body was found, which was also the day of Natalie's autopsy, London's *Daily Mirror* quoted Rasure about the case. Contrary to evidence he had seen on *Splendour* the preceding day and before the official inquiry was completed, Rasure was pushing accident as the cause of Natalie's death, "Natalie may have fallen overboard from the yacht and knocked the rubber dinghy, which was moored alongside, adrift as she fell. Or she could have decided to take the dinghy out for a cruise."

The story concluded: "Police said Wagner was not alarmed when he first noticed the dinghy was missing because he knew Natalie liked to go off alone. The actress often sat quietly in the dinghy 'soaking up the silence', he told them."

These statements were not based on evidence and did not appear in the investigators' notes or in Rasure's official report. The only thing resembling a quote about Natalie going off alone was from Wagner's lawyer. In his press release the day her body was recovered, Ziffren said, "Since Mrs. Wagner often took the dinghy out alone, Mr. Wagner was not immediately concerned." It certainly looked like investigators were getting some of their "facts" from Wagner's lawyer or the newspaper instead of their own investigatory efforts, because they never checked into the validity of this statement.

∿∿∿∿∿∿

Rasure's deliberate manipulation of the "facts" in his official report was plain in his account of the December 4 interview of Wagner "in bed" at his home with his lawyer present. Wagner told investigators "15 minutes" after the foursome returned to the yacht from dinner Saturday night, Natalie went downstairs "to bed." And "15 minutes" later, he went down to check on her and noticed she was gone.

The investigators had already been told by at least three witnesses that the foursome left the restaurant between "10 and 10:30 p.m." As a consequence, Wagner admitted to investigators he knew Natalie was missing by 11 p.m., at most, and Wagner told the investigators in Long Beach that he started calling for help at 11:30 p.m. We knew Wagner didn't start the search for Natalie until 1 to 1:30 a.m. Rasure knew that as well. Yet, the veteran detective's official report contained no mention of the inconsistency and suspicious time gap.

But, the most compelling omission in his report was that Rasure didn't ask Wagner on December 4 what was happening aboard *Splendour* during that crucial period between the time Natalie disappeared and the time Wagner reached out for help. The foursome had been in a 60-foot yacht, and Wintler had told the investigators that Wagner "had possibly made a statement that he and his wife had a fight" when Wintler quizzed Wagner after Natalie disappeared.

Wagner reiterated his story about Natalie going back to the bar on her own on Sunday morning—until he was confronted with the way Natalie was dressed when found. Rasure had been informed Wagner searched the yacht with Deputy Kroll, so he knew Wagner saw Natalie's clothing and pocketbook in the master stateroom. Rasure portrayed Wagner's change of position in his official report this way without any hint of skepticism: "*Having knowledge* [emphasis added] of what she was wearing when she was recovered from the sea, he [Wagner] added 'She would not have gone out in the dinghy dressed that way.'" Rasure massaged the context to keep Wagner's narrative change from being readily apparent.

When the investigators interviewed Walken the second time, his statement was clearly inconsistent with his narrative Sunday morning. Summing up on December 3, Walken said when he woke up Sunday morning, *before Natalie's body was discovered*, Wagner and Davern were together in the salon and Wagner stated, "She may have drowned." A reasonable investigator would have reacted with immense suspicion at that untoward statement by the husband of the victim, but Rasure's official report contained no mention of the remark.

∽∽∽∽∾∾∾

Then there was captain Dennis Davern. As mentioned, he was interviewed a second time in the law offices of his criminal defense attorney six days after Wagner's second interview. In fact, Davern was accompanied by two criminal defense attorneys. That was a great deal of legal power for a regular citizen who denied having much knowledge of the events that night. What could Davern know that required a criminal defense team? That question had to have crossed the experienced detective's mind before the interview began.

In the official report, however, there was something very subtle indicating something unusual was afoot. The report stated:

> Prior to the interview of Mr. Davern, investigators met with Attorney Steven Miller and Attorney Mark Beck, where investigators advised both attorneys and gave them a review of the original [Davern] interview conducted on Catalina Island. Both attorneys agreed to all questions posed by investigators.

It's classic criminal defense work to determine a client's status in an investigation before the client ever talks to law enforcement and to hopefully gain insight into what the investigators intend to ask. However, what Rasure was doing in this meeting was telegraphing in an official report that he and Hamilton told Davern's lawyers that Davern wasn't a suspect or target of the investigation, despite Davern's culpability for making false statements to investigators on November 29. With that assurance, and armed with knowledge of the questions, Davern's lawyers let him talk, and he offered nothing specific about Natalie's disappearance. The substance of Davern's story was Natalie went to bed and he didn't see her again. Rasure recorded it without question or analysis. Years later, he admitted to Finstad that Davern "was always a bit evasive" and "he was suspicious" of him at the time. Yet, nothing like that appeared in Rasure's official report.

∽∽∽∽∾∾∾

In any unexplained death, detectives must assume the death is a homicide until the physical and forensic evidence demonstrates otherwise. It's basic and elementary. Failing to do so is so contrary to a homicide detective's instincts that it signals a deliberate purpose to do otherwise. And that failure is disastrous to crime scene evidence, which must be gathered immediately, particularly where the death occurs on the sea and the clock instantaneously begins ticking on the availability of many forms of evidence.

As we know, the coroner's file did not substantiate claims that Wagner, Walken and Davern were examined for bruises, scratches or scrapes. And no attempt was made by Rasure or Hamilton—at any time after they arrived on the scene—to check the men for injuries and glass shards or to collect fingernail clippings from them or Natalie. Not doing so ensured the evidence was lost forever.

Motive—the reason for killing someone—is paramount in cases of unexplained death. As mentioned earlier, every unexplained death case needs to be treated by investigators like it was a homicide. Jealousy, love-triangle situations, anger and money are all motives commonly found to be the basis for many marital homicide cases. Yet, there was no effort made by the LASD Homicide Bureau to determine if anyone had a motive to kill Natalie. In fact, as we'll see later, when damning motive evidence was presented to Rasure about Natalie's stay in a North Carolina hotel while shooting *Brainstorm*, he simply filed it away and made no mention of it in his official report.

～～～～～～

Over the last 40 years, reporters and authors have tried to explain away the numerous items of detective work in 1981 that were either omitted or handled with disregard as the product of negligence, incompetence or carelessness. I don't subscribe to that conclusion.

Years later, Rasure was still maintaining the party line. He confessed to Finstad 20 years after Natalie's death, that after spending six minutes with Wagner in Long Beach on Sunday morning, he was already of the opinion that "it was an accident." Finstad continued, "According to Rasure, the Sheriff's Department viewed Natalie's death that morning as 'nothing more than a big-time [accidental] celebrity drowning.'"

In another passage, Rasure told Finstad: I didn't have any suspicions that anybody had injured or killed her, none whatsoever. … I think that Dennis Davern is exaggerating this whole incident to sell his book."

And in 2011, Rasure told *48 Hours* that he wasn't changing his mind because he didn't believe Davern.

Given the great weight of evidence available to him at the time, it was unlikely a veteran investigator like Rasure would come to this conclusion. It suggested Rasure was told to go to the island and close the case as an accidental death as quickly as possible to prevent any official scrutiny of Wagner's involvement. And it worked for nearly 30 years.

CHAPTER 18

decades of denial

ONLY TWO PEOPLE WERE ABOARD THE YACHT WITH DAVERN THE Saturday night Natalie drowned. Walken—with the exception of his less-than-candid statements to investigators on November 29 and December 3, 1981—had kept his public silence about what happened that night for three years, claiming he hadn't talked about Natalie's death "out of respect for the family."

On the third anniversary of Natalie's death, Walken spoke with a reporter affiliated with *The Face* magazine. Launched in London by British journalist Nick Logan, *The Face* was billed as "a well-produced, well-designed and well-written monthly with music at its core but with expanding coverage of the subjects that informed it, from fashion and film to nightclubbing and social issues." *The Face* reporter Neil Norman must have been salivating at the potential bombshell Walken could have handed this upstart magazine.

Dr. Noguchi had already cashed in on Natalie's death with his best-selling version of the facts in *Coroner*. According to *People* magazine, Lana was given a $50,000 advance (about $128,000 today) for her 1984 memoir about Natalie.

A couple weeks after Lana's book came out, Davern's ex-girlfriend was interviewed by *Star* magazine. What she was paid for her little bit of gossip is unknown. In the article, Alanis claimed after Davern identified Natalie's lifeless body, "The memory and nightmare that experience gave him just tore him apart as a man. For a while, Dennis turned to drink to get through it. In just a few weeks he lost forty pounds. Eventually, we broke apart. He became someone else."

In February 1985, when Walken's interview was finally published in *The Face*, it was now his turn to publicly deal with the night Natalie died.

To start with, it was curious to me that Walken chose a relatively new British magazine for his first interview about Natalie's death. Perhaps he did so because of the fee he received. Possibly he didn't trust the American media. Or maybe it was the need for some positive media exposure.

You see, his career had sputtered since his first big break in 1978 cast opposite Robert De Niro in *The Deer Hunter*. Critics praised his acting and delivery, and the role earned him the Academy Award for Best Supporting Actor.

His next film, *Last Embrace*, cast Walken as a supervisor of a spy agency. Critics rated it 29 percent or "Rotten" on Rotten Tomatoes, a movie and television review-aggregation website. The 1980 *Heaven's Gate* was expected to be a blockbuster but became one of the biggest box-office bombs of all time. Walken followed up with *The Dogs of War*, which lost money and had received mixed reviews. His next role was as a dancer in the comedy *Pennies from Heaven*. Released shortly after Natalie's death, it was another commercial failure.

When *Brainstorm* eventually arrived in theaters in September 1983, it received less-than-stellar reviews and didn't prove to be the film that established Walken as a lead actor at the box office.

The Face article was titled "Walken Talks" and a photo of the actor with an impassive expression took up the entire adjoining page. Whether the magazine knew what he was going to say in advance was certainly a vexing question.

Walken began by saying his silence for three years had simply been a "silence of ignorance." Claiming they "were all having a great weekend" and "a very, very good time," he added: "[W]e were not the only people having a good time. It always sounds like we were all alone out on the high seas. We were actually fifty feet off the shore in a Catalina harbor with many, many boats around us. The weather was shitty. Everybody was locked inside. There was a sort of cold drizzle. We were partying, there's no question about it...." But, he added, they were partying "very conservatively."

Figure 35: Photo of Christopher Walken from 1985 issue of *The Face* magazine (Derek Ridgers)

From that point on, if readers thought they were going to learn the truth about the infamous Thanksgiving weekend in 1981, they were sorely disappointed. Walken claimed he was "asleep when it happened." Norman called it the "perfect alibi."

〰〰〰〰

After *The Face* interview, Walken, for an undisclosed sum of money, consented to an interview with *Star* that was published on June 18, 1985. The front-page article was titled "Natalie Wood, Wagner and Me—Christopher Walken Tells Own Story of Drowning" with a subhead that read, "Star Denies Rumors That Nearly Wrecked Career." It begins with Walken saying, "I wish with all my heart I could have saved her." *Did Walken have an opportunity to save Natalie?* He told *The Face* he was "asleep when it happened."

The timing of the publication of the two Walken articles is important to understanding the strength of Davern's credibility. It's also important for an understanding of Walken's purported absence from the scene shortly before Natalie died.

Walken complained in the June 1985 *Star* interview that when he returned to New York after Natalie's death, there was no work for him. "The press had a field day. They crucified me. The less I said about it, the more people filled in the missing pieces themselves. But their assumptions were wrong," he asserted.

As far as his knowledge of the events leading up to Natalie's death, Walken said this to *Star:* "Natalie was tired. She wanted to go to bed. R.J. and I were not having an argument. It had been a very pleasant evening until..." At that point, the article caustically notes that Walken's voice "trailed away."

For emphasis, Walken repeated himself: "But I want to stress there was no argument between R.J. and me. The family was very good to me."

I knew that both the "pleasant evening" and "no argument" statements were patently false from my reading of Davern's book, Wagner's *Pieces of My Heart* and Lambert's *Natalie Wood: A Life*. Davern and Wagner both admitted the weekend was anything but pleasant, and there was indeed a violent scene between Wagner and Walken, triggered by Walken's disagreement with Wagner over Natalie's career.

After Walken's interview ran in *Star*, a battle was waged within the magazine's pages. A little over a month later, an enraged Davern shot back at Walken by offering a scoop to *Star*, which resulted in a lengthy article based on an extensive interview with the *Splendour* captain.

It was a bombshell and worthy of front-page billing, but Davern would later claim he "didn't tell them everything." Davern said in his 2011 statement to the LASD that he gave the interview because of Walken's statements in the June *Star* article: "I was angry because what he said was a lie."

I was also intrigued by the amount Davern received: *$26,000*. It appeared to be a ne-gotiated amount—an amount that would be agreed upon when an agent is involved. *Did Davern have a publicity agent by 1985?* He has never said, but he has an agent now, and every time he opens his mouth with the agent organizing things, he gets paid.

෩෩෩෩෩෩

As far as I could tell, in the early '80s, Wagner had not spoken publicly about Natalie's untimely death since he issued two press statements through his lawyer on November 29 and December 1, 1981, and then a third through a "close friend" on December 26, 1981.

I knew from experience Wagner had been wisely counseled by his lawyers to make no public statements about the facts of the case—ever. Anything Wagner said could be used against him, including his comments in magazine interviews and books. The lawyers knew many criminal suspects think they can talk themselves out of jail. But, in fact, most talk themselves *into* jail. And celebrities, in particular, take discipline to stay silent. Their image, ego, family and friends make it extremely difficult for them to remain quiet when they are getting hammered in the press.

In spite of the legal advice, Wagner's concern about his public image likely prompted the third press statement published in the New York *Daily News* on December 26, 1981. This one started a new narrative—the "kiss her good night" story. As told by a Wagner friend, reporter Bob Lardine wrote [emphasis added]:

> "*We reached the boat in a happy frame of mind* after spending a few hours at the restaurant eating and drinking.

> "During dinner, I got into a *political debate* with Walken and we continued it aboard the yacht. There was *no fight, no anger*. Just a lot of words thrown around like you hear in most political discussions such as 'You don't know what you're talking about!'

> "Natalie sat there, not saying much of anything, and looking bored.

> "She left us after about a half hour, and we sat there talking for almost

another hour. Then *I went down to kiss her good night* and found her missing. *I wasn't alarmed*, and *casually* went looking for her throughout the boat.

"During my search for her, I noticed the dinghy was missing. *I thought perhaps she had gotten moody and gone to shore*, though that wasn't at all like her. The idea that any harm had come to her never entered my mind. *I got into my speedboat* and went to look for her near the shore. I couldn't find her or the dinghy, and then I became worried after returning to the yacht and discovering she hadn't returned."

Wagner's friend also shared details to introduce the "banging dinghy" theory as the reason for Natalie's death. With that, Wagner held steadfast and kept quiet about his wife's death until the Walken and Davern interviews were made public. But then, he folded under the pressure—and probably the lure of a nice fee—and joined the war of words.

On August 27, 1985, *Star* published an interview with Wagner, which was largely a promotional piece for his new TV show *Lime Street*. Referring to the movie Natalie was making when she died, the story included this telling quote from Wagner:

"I never did see *Brainstorm* and—I doubt I ever will," he says. As for Christopher Walken, Wagner says: "I don't socialize with him. He was at the funeral, which I suppose was only right, but I was very uncomfortable with him being there."

The article closed discussion of his wife's death this way: "Of the past, he says: 'There is nothing to talk about. I know what happened and I keep saying it was an accident.'"

A few months later, in May 1986, Walken stunned readers in a *People* magazine article when he snapped out that having a conversation about Natalie's death was "a --ing [fucking] bore." A disrespectable comment like that wouldn't have been uttered if a district attorney had placed him under oath. He would have answered every question, or a judge would have sent him to jail.

〰〰〰〰

The following year, Wagner assisted Maychick and Borgo with their book. It was publicized as "a rare glimpse into the private and stormy life of a Hollywood legend." While "Hollywood legend" is debatable, the authors were billed to have drawn "on their in-depth interviews with Robert Wagner." What Wagner was paid for these "interviews" is again unknown. But, contrasting the inconsistencies between his first press release and the Maychick and Borgo book representations exposes an attempt to change the narrative.

〰〰〰〰

By 1988, Davern's story was still for sale. He and Steve Dunleavy with Fox TV's *A Current Affair* discussed a deal to get Davern's story on the air. Davern claimed that during the negotiations, Dunleavy accused him of having sex with Natalie the Friday night he spent with her in the Pavilion Lodge. He and Rulli claim there was to be no pay for his appearance on the show, but they felt his appearance would enhance the appeal of their book. The show didn't materialize.

Then, around 1991, Lana started receiving phone calls from an intoxicated Davern about "knowing what really happened." She told me in 2017, "…his conversations…were always fraught with despair."

I guess I'm just suspicious by nature. The timing of Davern's calls led me to believe Wagner and his grapevine learned about Davern's loose lips and attempted to preempt any new Davern stories with another sympathy story of their own.

On November 12, 1991, *Star* magazine published another interview with Wagner. The front-page headlines blared, "Robert Wagner's 10 Years of Torment." If *Star* thought it was finally going to get a blockbuster statement from Wagner, it could have saved some money. Wagner only repeated what he had told the *Heart to Heart* authors five years earlier. But it was another profitable tabloid teaser, and Wagner was able to tug on the heartstrings of those who still believed in him and get paid in the process.

⌒⌒⌒⌒⌒⌒

With that backdrop and timeline, I could already see that a skilled criminal defense attorney could "make some hay" with Davern's alcohol abuse and ever-expanding pronouncements of his and Rulli's "truth." My examination began, however, with the process used to get Davern's "whole" story out there.

As far as I could discern, Rulli, who claims she is a freelance writer, had spent the 12 years since the book was published waiting for the sheriff's department to do something it never intended to do—arrest Robert Wagner for killing his wife.

In the 1985 *Star* interview, Davern, for the first time, revealed that Wagner, in an accusatory rant toward Walken shortly after the foursome reached the yacht Saturday night, grabbed a wine bottle by the neck and violently smashed it on a coffee table in front of Natalie and Walken.

But Davern has said he did not divulge all of what he knew in 1985 because he was afraid for his life. I believe he had good reason to be afraid. Sinatra had lost Giancana and several more of his mafia pals to assassinations and prison by 1985, but he and the muscle that surrounded him were still a force to be reckoned with. And Davern knew Wagner and Sinatra were friends.

The first public blow to Davern's credibility came on January 26, 1992. Rulli and Davern had been trying to get a book published for years. In an attempt to gain the attention Rulli thought they needed to get their book widely distributed, they accepted an invitation to appear on Geraldo Rivera's TV show *Now It Can Be Told*. The award-winning journalist hosted the investigative news program on Fox in 1991 and 1992. Rivera was known for a take-no-prisoners reporting style that had earned him exclusive interviews with big-name players in matters of major cover-ups and government scandals.

Rivera and his producer, Susan Levit, convinced Rulli, who in turn convinced Davern, that "Rivera could help publish [their] manuscript" by claiming that releasing Rulli and Davern's "high-profile story" on Rivera's popular show could "draw millions." Rulli admitted in *Goodbye*, "The possibility of publishing drew me in. Dennis's account was lost to the public without a book."

With no written agreement as to the format of the show or the assistance that Rivera would provide to help with the book's publication, Rulli took the bait.

The format for the Natalie Wood episode was a three-person panel of legal experts who would review the evidence in Natalie's case and jointly determine whether foul play was involved. Rivera, who never pulled punches, began asking some pointed questions on behalf of the panel. After the cameras were rolling, the duo began to hesitate on telling Davern's story. At that point, the producer asked the million-dollar question: "How did Natalie get into the water?"

After a period of extreme discomfort, Davern asked for time to consult with Rulli. Out of what they believed was earshot and camera exposure, the two discussed whether to answer the question, according to transcripts quoted in Texas' *Houston Chronicle* and Georgia's *Atlanta Constitution*. But the cameras and microphones were rolling, and the entire conversation was being recorded.

Davern began by saying, "They were yelling and screaming at each other to get off the boat…oh God, I don't know if I can tell them that or not."

Rulli responded, "We have to say how she got in the water, Den…saying it right, but saying it to protect ourselves, too. See, I don't want to…he pushed her in…I know…I know…"

Then, Davern said, "I don't wanna tell them."

To which Rulli replied, "Don't you tell them how she got in the water…we put that into the book and we'll make billions from it…we won't tell them."

When the program aired, the duo's credibility exploded like it was hit by an IED, and they've been fighting off claims of greed and self-promotion ever since.

When *Goodbye* was finally published 17 years after the Rivera TV episode aired, Rulli attempted to distance herself from the "billions" remark, saying it was hyperbole. But it was too late. Their public image of trying to sell books and pump up their own profile was cast. And the image haunts them to this day. Although Davern didn't make the comment, his credibility was damaged before *Goodbye* was published. But somewhere in that time frame, in my opinion, Davern completely sold out.

◇◇◇◇◇◇◇◇

The next blow to Davern's credibility came in 2011 with Rulli's attempt to get the LASD to reopen Natalie's case. On Rulli's blog, she posted four typed and signed statements she claimed were submitted to the sheriff in 2011, along with a signed petition she orchestrated online. One of those statements was from Davern. Comparing them revealed material inconsistencies between the narrative in Davern's statement and the public claims he made over the years.

In addition, some of the signed statement facts were obviously embellished or intentionally tailored to appear consistent with other witness statements. For example, in his 2011 statement to reopen Natalie's case, Davern boldly said in the second paragraph, "I did not lie to anyone, including the authorities or the attorney. I simply obeyed what was asked of me and offered no details." In his book *Goodbye*, Davern admitted he lied to investigators about Friday night.

If Rulli was genuinely trying to help prosecute Wagner, she was going about it the wrong way. A defense attorney dreams about multiple witness statements in a criminal case because there will invariably be inconsistencies. By creating multiple witness statements for Davern, Rulli was unwittingly helping Wagner. Davern, according to his book and Finstad's *Natasha*, said he gave two statements to the LASD in 1981. One on November 29 and one on December 10. But you now know he gave three—the last one being March 5, 1982. Thereafter, he spoke to the *Star,* Geraldo Rivera, Nancy Grace and countless other representatives of the media between 1984 and 2018. In each, he left a discernable trail of inconsistencies.

Anything generated by witnesses or the prosecution that can help a criminal defense attorney cast doubt on the credibility of a key witness is ammunition to create reasonable doubt. And, when assessing a case, a good prosecutor weighs those factors in deciding whether to prosecute.

This didn't mean the core of Davern's story was untruthful. It just meant that it was going to be a harder sell in an already difficult case. *So, what could be done about his credibility? How could a prosecutor use him in trial?* There's only one tried-and-true way to repair Davern's believability, and that is corroboration of every material thing Davern said happened that Thanksgiving weekend in 1981. Rulli didn't have the skills to understand that. She tried using polygraphs, questionable experiments and re-creations. But in the end, it fell far short of what could have been.

◇◇◇◇◇◇◇◇

I needed to ask Davern some tough questions. I needed to look him in the eye and study his mannerisms and emotions while answering me. That's how I determined if a jury would believe a key prosecution witness—that and corroboration. So, I set out to arrange a meeting with Rulli.

My first email to Rulli was sent December 29, 2015, about six weeks after filing my CPRA lawsuit against the sheriff and coroner. A few days after my email to Rulli, the *National Enquirer* got wind of my lawsuit and featured an article about it titled, "Wagner Protected by Conspiracy of Silence." The article quoted me on the stonewalling I had experienced at the hands of the sheriff and coroner. It also quoted me on the potential importance of the Miller report.

It was helpful press that let everyone know I was out there sniffing around, and the article eventually led to the discovery of witnesses and important leads.

I had my doubts whether I would hear from Rulli, but to my surprise, on January 3, 2016, I had a reply in my inbox. However, the first few lines of her email told me all I needed to know about the freelance writer and where my attempt to forge a working relationship with her was headed [emphasis added]:

> Dear Sam, Thank you for reaching out to me. *There is no one who knows more about the Wood case than I do*, and what I know is fact, and I also know all about the fiction. *I deal with facts.* The only value of the Miller report is its contribution to all of the rubbish included in this decades-long saga. … The new lead detectives in this case cooperate with me to this day. With NO pompousness intended, *I AM "the nobody" who got the Natalie Wood case reopened.* Spent my life on it and no one wants true justice for Natalie more than I do. … Sincerely, Marti Rulli

Rulli also told me she was working on another book that was to be finished "by March 2016" and that she had "attorneys and prosecutors helping [her] with this project." In other words, Rulli knew everything there was to know about Natalie's case and had all the help she needed. Moreover, even though she hadn't read it, the Miller report was "rubbish." *How do you deal with someone in her frame of mind?* I asked myself. But I wasn't ready to give up on her.

In reply to my next email, Rulli told me she had read my CPRA complaint. She questioned whether I could prevail and stated the Miller report had "nothing of value in it." She ended by saying she would discuss things more "in a few weeks" and assured me "all answers to this NON-mystery now, will soon be told."

After politely challenging her assertions, I asked if we could meet and discuss things to determine if we could help each other. This time, Rulli seemed different in her reply. More conciliatory, she hinted at a possible meeting and surprisingly asked my advice on how to get Wagner "arrested." It had been five years since Natalie's case was reopened and nothing substantive had happened.

Rulli continued to tout her knowledge of Davern's story and the polygraphs, which she claimed were "hard—damn hard—to beat." Then, without provocation she said this:

> Lesser evidence in other cases has put many killers away for life. Wagner is getting away with this because of his celebrity and because the LASD is embarrassed. *The two lead detectives in the new investigation are disgusted about that* [emphasis added]!

After admitting she was talking to the detectives, Rulli was now confirming for me there was dissension in the LASD ranks over Natalie's case. But was their hesitation to act solely because of celebrity and embarrassment? As you will see, that's questionable.

∽∾∽∾∽∾∽∾

In my investigation, I learned Walken, with his criminal defense attorney in tow, worked out an arrangement to participate in another interview with the new detectives in early 2012. Understanding the process, I also knew that Walken's attorney had obtained an agreement from the detectives that if Walken gave a statement, he would be treated as a "witness" and not a "suspect" or "target." So, I told Rulli I knew about the statement but didn't know what it said. She replied: "I know everything Walken said in his statement for the new investigation. *He reluctantly told the truth in it* [emphasis added], if that helps."

Of course, I didn't know what the truth was at that point, but I surmised what Rulli was saying was a detective told her Walken corroborated Davern's story but continued with his "alibi"—he was "asleep when it happened." That was the position he staked out in his second LASD interview. And that he repeated in a 1997 *Playboy* interview, saying his "story" about sleeping through the events of Saturday night was "the absolute truth."

I've never believed Walken's alibi. Based on the known timeline, it would mean Walken, in the span of 15 minutes at most, fell so sound asleep after Wagner smashed a wine bottle in his face and accused him of wanted to sleep with his wife, that he didn't hear a cussing, screaming, banging fight between Natalie and Wagner that occurred no more than 25 feet from his cabin. And I was sure the detectives didn't press the Academy Award-winning actor on that point. But, if I got the chance, I would.

One effect of my lawsuit was LASD leaks to Rulli were now cut off, causing her to abruptly end communication with me. Rulli and Detective Hernandez had been constantly communicating about the LASD's activity in its claimed investigation of Natalie's death. When it became obvious to LASD investigators that under the law they would have to give me what they were giving Rulli, they shut the information pipeline down.

～～～～～～

A couple of years later, I discovered the name of the agent who negotiated Davern's appearances and speaking fees. I wrote to him requesting an opportunity to talk to Davern. Before I finished my work, I wanted to give Davern an opportunity to field the type of questions a prosecutor would pose if Davern were a witness in an actual homicide case. I had been forewarned that the agent, Stuart Miller, was "a self-important, most objectionable man," and he lived up to his reputation by replying that Davern did not have "any interest in being interviewed by you." He ended by implying that out of the three men on the yacht, only Davern could be believed.

I wasn't surprised by Miller's rude response, given my communications with Rulli and the fact that I dangled no prospect of money in front of him. But a few things the agent said and insinuated underscored the inconsistencies and dogmatic approach Team Davern has taken over the last few years.

To begin with, Rulli and Davern are now joined at the hip. Apparently, you don't get to speak with Davern unless you pay both. Because Stuart Miller only copied Rulli in his emailed response to me, I was convinced he hadn't told Davern about my request. Secondly, it looks like Rulli has now changed her tune about Walken. According to Rulli's 2016 email, Walken *was telling the truth* when he last spoke about Natalie's death to LASD investigators in 2012. But according to Rulli's agent in 2018, Walken *never told the truth*.

～～～～～～

People haven't made billions off Natalie's death, but some have most likely made millions. Capitalizing on mystery and sensation, some people have tortured the truth to the point that it is barely discernable. Yet two constants remain: the forensic evidence and documented timeline of events. While the living can lie, dead bodies don't, and no amount of money and fame can change that.

CHAPTER 19

politics as usual

ON FRIDAY, NOVEMBER 18, 2011, THE DAY LT. CORINA, AN IMPRESSIVE, smooth-talking officer, announced to the world the LASD was reopening Natalie Wood's death investigation, it was big news.

The scheduled press conference followed the distribution of five press releases the day before. Upon receipt, the *Los Angeles Times* immediately contacted Sheriff Baca. The following morning, on the front page of the LATExtra section, a five-column article appeared with a 1972 photograph of Natalie and Wagner at the London premiere of *The Godfather*. The article was titled: "Natalie Wood case is reopened" and included a quote from the sheriff:

> Sheriff Lee Baca said detectives want to talk to the captain of the boat
> after learning of comments he recently made about what happened on
> board. Baca did not provide further details, adding only that the captain
> "made comments worthy of exploring."

But the sheriff's in-house spin doctors had already been in touch with the folks at CBS' *48 Hours*, who just happened to be working on "a special [Natalie Wood] segment with *Vanity Fair* magazine" scheduled to air Saturday, November 26. The *Times* reported, "they [*48 Hours*] contacted the sheriff's department after learning that detectives had new information in the case." To clarify, the Natalie Wood press conference was timed to immediately precede the *48 Hours* retrospective segment on Natalie's case.

Lt. Corina's sensational press conference, in front of "more than 40 journalists" from as far away as Japan, offered no reasons for the timing of the announcement.

But few were questioning, *Why now?* What was it that caused the LASD, obviously with Sheriff Baca's blessing, to reopen a 30-year-old death case with such great fanfare? In one of the press releases, the LASD attempted to explain what led up to the official action:

> Recently, Sheriff's Homicide Investigators were contacted by persons
> who stated they had additional information about the Natalie Wood
> Wagner drowning. Due to the additional information, Sheriff's Homi-
> cide Bureau has decided to take another look at the case.

The "persons" were Marti Rulli, Dennis Davern and Roger Smith. The "additional information" was Davern's revelation of an argument between Wagner and Walken in the yacht's salon followed by a fight on *Splendour's* back deck between Natalie and Wagner shortly before she disappeared. But that information had been in the public domain for years.

With signatures and statements from Smith, Davern and others, Rulli presented the LASD with the same claims she and Davern made in their 2009 book. While Rulli is convinced that she, and she alone, was the impetus for the LASD reopening Natalie's case, I doubt it. Let me explain.

Based on the 2011 *LA Times* article, we begin with the knowledge that Natalie's case was dusted off the shelf with Sheriff Baca's approval. In June 2016, Captain David Smith, retired Homicide Bureau commander, told me in a sworn deposition that in 2011 he reported to William McSweeney, the chief of detectives, who in turn reported directly to the high sheriff. The chain of command continued with Lt. Corina reporting to Smith, and Detective Hernandez reporting to Corina.

During Captain Smith's deposition, I attempted to learn who authorized the reopened investigation, but Smith's attorney, who was also representing the current sheriff, instructed Smith not to answer my question. Sheriff Baca had resigned by the time of Smith's deposition. The reason will soon become self-evident.

∿∿∿∿∿∿

Here's what was happening at the LASD in the months leading up to the press conference.

In July 2011, an LASD deputy took a bribe from an inmate at the LA County jail. Reports and grapevine talk of corruption and abuse had convinced the U.S. Department of Justice the transaction was a common occurrence. However, in this particular instance, the deputy had been bribed by a confidential federal informant in a setup named "Operation Pandora's Box."

Before becoming sheriff, Baca was a captain under Sheriff Pitchess. When Pitchess retired in 1981, he handpicked successor Sherman Block. While Block was sheriff, Baca was one of his division chiefs. Block was in poor health before his fourth-term reelection bid in 1998, and Baca smelled blood.

Baca retired and ran against his boss, making Block—the highest paid elected official in the nation—the first incumbent in more than a century to draw an opponent. Sadly, Block died before the election, and Baca was elected sheriff.

Not long after the election, things started going south for the "first political sheriff," as his lead campaign consultant described him. After a flurry of negative media, Baca was forced to shut down his controversial "badge and gun club" for celebrities and wealthy donors to his campaign. Following in the footsteps of Sheriff Pitchess, donors were issued "juice badges," becoming honorary uniform deputies authorized to carry Beretta 9mm semi-automatic pistols.

This followed unfavorable publicity over Baca's coziness with campaign supporters connected to Asian organized crime (following an FBI warning); his request of President Bill Clinton to pardon a cocaine smuggler whose father was a campaign contributor; and his receipt of a zero-down-payment sweetheart home loan of $750,000 from a broker with whom Baca helped promote home loans directly to law enforcement officers.

Controversy continued to swirl around the sheriff into the mid-2000s when he spawned more bad press for the LASD after going easy on two celebrities. Authorized to release inmates from the county jail, Baca commuted actor Mel Gibson's and socialite Paris Hilton's jail sentences, bringing on claims of favoritism.

Between 2009 and 2011, the ACLU informed Baca "of and published reports about allegations of pervasive [jail system] abuse, violence, and retaliation by the sheriff's deputies against inmates." Baca and his department generally responded to the allegations with denials and internal investigations that "almost always concluded that the allegations were 'unfounded.'"

Baca's reelection was looming and by spring 2011, sheriff's department scandals involving drugs, money and deputy abuses began to dominate the news. Three federal investigations and civil suits were filed, including one case in which the jury awarded $100,000 in punitive damages against Sheriff Baca personally.

Through at least July 2011, allegations also surfaced about deputies who engaged in "gang-like violent behavior, used excessive force against inmates, and falsified reports to cover up wrongdoing." Not to mention a federal investigation of racial discrimination by deputies in Antelope Valley in northern LA County.

According to the federal conspiracy indictment in the case of *United States v. Gregory Thompson, et al*, beginning around July 13, 2011, the LASD began receiving federal grand jury subpoenas for records. On August 8, 2011, according to the indictment, "internal affairs investigators," also charged as co-conspirators, learned about the federal investigation, "found out about a bribe," and discovered the "identity of [the] federal informant" who set up the deputy.

Within days, the indictment claimed Baca and his chief deputy became totally aware of the calamity.

Between August 18 and October 3, 2011, the *Thompson* indictment recited that the internal affairs investigators hid the jail bribe informant's "records jacket"; made "false entries in computer databases" to make it appear the informant had been released; "rebooked the informant under a fictitious name"; moved the informant "so the FBI couldn't get him"; caused the LASD to "conduct surveillance" of one of the FBI agents; and performed other acts to "obstruct the federal investigation," including trying to get a Superior Court judge to "compel the FBI to disclose what they were investigating."

On August 25, 2011, a federal judge ordered the appearance of the federal informant before the grand jury. And, by "no later than September 2011," according to the indictment, Baca "knew the extent of the jail abuses."

On September 26, 2011, Baca appeared on television and claimed the FBI may have "committed a crime" by setting up the jail bribe and investigating the sheriff's department. The appearance backfired. Then, a few weeks later, while the department was in the crosshairs of the federal criminal investigation, Corina presided over the Natalie Wood press conference.

As for Sheriff Baca, in 2013, he unwisely consented to an FBI interview about the jail investigation. According to a federal indictment returned against Baca in 2015, the sheriff "knowingly and willfully made" materially "false and fictitious statements" to the FBI about his knowledge of the federal investigation. In addition, it was alleged he tried to hide the informant to thwart the FBI agents' interview of the informant and facilitated the contact and intimidation of an FBI agent working on the bribery investigation. Sheriff Baca eventually resigned from the department in disgrace, was convicted and sentenced to federal prison.

So, either it was a colossal coincidence that the reopening of Natalie's case occurred at a time when Baca needed something positive to emerge from the department or Natalie's investigation was inspired to create a much-needed, positive public diversion from the jail abuse and corruption headache.

As I've said before, I don't believe in coincidences in cases like this. Not when cover-ups seem to be the LASD's *modus operandi.*

∽∽∽∾∾∾∾

In 2018, more than six years after the LASD reopened Natalie's case, CBS surprised everyone with a remarkable TV announcement about "new" evidence surfacing. Their lead-up to the Saturday, February 3, episode of *48 Hours* was a *coup de main* of sensational headlines claiming that LASD sheriff's department investigators would "reveal new clues, new witnesses and a shocking revelation." Even if you knew nothing about Natalie Wood, you couldn't help but think, *I have to see what this is all about.* Of course, that's obviously what the network planned.

I had just finished my lawsuit against the sheriff and knew the players in the sheriff's department, so I was immediately suspicious of the timing and content of this presentation. But I wasn't about to miss it. *CBS can produce a show like this in a week or less,* I thought. *So, that means the investigators must have talked to CBS around late January 2018. What new witnesses could they possibly have? And why announce it now?*

Those questions and more can be answered with another confirmed timeline.

On November 24, 2014, the *National Enquirer* reported that Lt. Corina repeated Wagner was not a suspect in Natalie's death. In late 2015, I sued the sheriff and successfully obtained hundreds of records hidden away in the department's archives. During my litigation, Detective Hernandez testified he had a little more than three years of homicide investigation experience when the LASD reactivated Natalie's case. And as of the day of his first 2016 deposition, almost four and a half years into the "investigation," he still had not seen coroner investigator Eaker's official report, a report that contains a crucial timeline statement by Wagner, or Natalie's probate file.

Within a few months of filing my lawsuit, I was also told Natalie's file had not been sent to the district attorney. But Detective Hernandez and several evidence technicians did manage at least one, maybe two, trips to Hawaii in 2012 to perform some "tests" on *Splendour.* While there, they also found time to pose for photographs that appeared in a *National Enquirer* "World Exclusive" piece.

On September 27 and October 20, 2016, the Superior Court judge in my CPRA case stated and thereafter found that despite the conclusory statements by the sheriff's department—specifically Detective Hernandez—he "didn't believe there was a live investigation" in Natalie's case "even though the detectives said there was." Moreover, the judge added that despite conclusory statements to the contrary, "there was no prospect of criminal enforcement in the Natalie Wood matter."

On October 27, 2017, I wrote to New York attorney Mathew Rosengart, Walken's current criminal defense lawyer, asking if his client would agree to speak with me. I emphasized that I was nearly finished with my manuscript and wanted Walken to have a chance to correct the inconsistencies uttered by him over the years when asked about Natalie's death. I also explained I knew his client had been interviewed again after the case was reopened in 2011 and that I generally knew what his client said.

My purpose for writing Rosengart was to give Walken a chance to talk to me before I went to publishers and to provide proof that I gave Walken that chance. Of course, I didn't receive the professional courtesy of a response from Rosengart.

Likewise, on January 4, 2018, I wrote to Wagner's Los Angeles criminal defense attorney, Blair Berk. I told Ms. Berk I was nearly finished with my work and wanted to give Wagner an opportunity to talk with me. Again, I knew Wagner would decline, but I expected to receive a kind response from Ms. Berk telling me that. I was wrong.

At this point, Corina, Hernandez and their superiors knew I was nearly finished with my investigation. And what I believed would happen happened. Four weeks after my letter to Wagner's attorney, the latest CBS *48 Hours* episode was scheduled to air.

✺✺✺✺✺

When Saturday rolled around, I was in front of the TV. The show begins with Lt. Corina stating the case was suspicious enough for the LASD to "think that something happened." He added that he believed Robert Wagner "absolutely" knew a lot more about what happened to his wife than he's ever said, because "he's the last one to see her."

The LASD Homicide Bureau knew over six years earlier Wagner was "the last one to see her." But perhaps Corina, who passed away suddenly in 2019, didn't know what Davern said in his 2009 book and 2011 signed statement. And, by spring 2016, five years after the case was reopened, Corina confessed to me under oath he had still not reviewed the entire 1981 file in Natalie's case.

As the episode of *48 Hours* continued, Corina was joined by Detective Hernandez. After Corina's enlightening remarks, Hernandez was asked about the Homicide Bureau's activities over the last six years.

> **Reporter:** So, for the last six years, have you been able to get even more evidence that makes you question that this was an accident?
>
> **Hernandez:** We have. There are witnesses who were nearby the *Splendour* that evening.

I was waiting with bated breath. You see, in my lawsuit against the sheriff, I had subpoenaed Chief McSweeney to testify about an interview he gave to the *Los Angeles Times* on January 10, 2012, a little short of two months after the Homicide Bureau reopened Natalie's case.

McSweeney arrogantly failed to appear for his deposition, so while I was preparing to file a motion for McSweeney to "show cause" why he shouldn't be held in contempt of court, the sheriff's private lawyers agreed to stipulate to three material factual matters to avoid having McSweeney forcibly brought before the judge to face contempt charges.

The sheriff stipulated McSweeney *truthfully* told the *Times* in 2012 that "several weeks of new interviews and other investigative work had *uncovered no new evidence* [emphasis added] at this time that Natalie Wood's death was a homicide;" that "Natalie Wood's death is an accidental death and nothing had been discovered to suggest changing that at this time;" and that McSweeney "was doubtful that more investigating will change the overall conclusion that her death was an accident."

After Sheriff Baca took full advantage of the nonstop publicity generated by Natalie's case, McSweeney made his statements to the *Los Angeles Times*. A few weeks later, Corina confirmed for the press that Walken had spoken to the detectives about the circumstances surrounding Natalie's death, and after the latest inquiry, "authorities have not identified any suspects."

As the *48 Hours* episode rolled on, recycling old file footage and often-repeated quotes, Corina and Hernandez were just getting cranked up.

> **Corina:** Because of the [November 18, 2011] press conference, we found a lot more clues, a lot more evidence on the witnesses.

> **Narrator:** For the last six years, veteran homicide detective Ralph Hernandez and Lt. John Corina have doggedly pursued this case.

> **Corina:** Six years later, we've followed up on all the clues…over 150 clues we got followed up on, talked to a lot of people.

> **Narrator:** For the first time, they are speaking publicly about evidence they've uncovered, and there's a lot to tell. Does that evidence lead you to believe that whatever happened to Natalie Wood was not an accident?

> **Corina:** It does. It actually confirms my suspicions even more that what was originally reported isn't exactly what happened.

> **Narrator:** They point to the numerous bruises on Natalie Wood's body that were photographed and noted in the autopsy report. It's some of those bruises and where they were located that played a big part in convincing a medical examiner to change the manner of death. Why are those bruises suspicious to you?

> **Hernandez:** Because she looked like the victim of an assault.

The 1981 files for both the sheriff's and coroner's departments contained photographs taken by the coroner's staff during Natalie's autopsy. I knew, without any doubt, close-up color photographs were taken of the bruises, scrapes and scratches on Natalie's body based on my experience and because Rasure said so in his official report. The sheriff's lawyers fought me tooth and nail on releasing the LASD's autopsy photographs, claiming in 2016 they were secret and confidential. The Superior Court judge sided with the officials. But it was confirmed in Superior Court on the record that photographs of Natalie's body on Catalina Island and during autopsy still, in fact, existed in the sheriff's 1981 files.

The photographs had not changed in 36 years. Neither had the autopsy report's full-body anterior and posterior diagrams showing the precise position of at least 30 bruises on Natalie's body, in addition to other unexplained scratches and scrapes. *So, why was it that Natalie's body looked like she had been "the victim of an assault" in 2018, but not in 1981 or 2011?*

Hernandez knew everything about the bruises by January 24, 2012, inasmuch as he and two other detectives attended a meeting in Dr. L's office, before Dr. L. changed the coroner's conclusions in Natalie's case. The foundation for his 2012 Supplemental Report was undoubtedly due to the injuries to Natalie's body. *So, why the dramatic revelation by the sheriff's office in 2018?*

Undaunted, Corina continued.

> **Narrator:** All three [Wagner, Walken and Davern] told the police that they assumed Natalie had left the *Splendour* on the yacht's dinghy despite the late hour and stormy weather.
>
> **Corina:** That didn't make any sense to me. Why would Natalie Wood, this big movie star, try to go out on the dinghy in the middle of the night in her socks and her pajamas and at midnight in rough seas?

Had it made sense to him and Hernandez in 2011? If it had, what changed his mind? If it hadn't made sense, why the sudden clarity in 2018?

Then, the captain of *Splendour* added more to the mix.

> **Davern:** The jealousy was under the surface until there was so much drinking that it started to come out. And it was obvious.
>
> **Narrator:** Once back on the *Splendour* [Friday, November 27], Davern says that the tension escalated, and now for the first time, investigators say they have a new witness corroborating Davern's account. That Friday, someone on a nearby boat claims to have been close enough to see and hear a fight between the couple.
>
> **Hernandez:** Natalie, to this witness, appeared to be the aggressor in the argument, appeared to be intoxicated. Robert Wagner appeared to try and walk away from the argument. At the point that he's walking away, she actually fell down to one knee.
>
> **Narrator:** Davern says the couple was fighting over whether to move the *Splendour* to the other side of Catalina Island.

If it's true that the detectives have a "new witness" about *Friday night*, it contradicts many statements Davern has made since 1981.

At no point has Davern, or Walken for that matter, said that Natalie and Wagner had a fight on the yacht's back deck Friday night. To the contrary, Davern has said Natalie was waiting impatiently for him in the master stateroom and Wagner was in the wheelhouse gunning the engines when the decision was made for Davern to take Natalie ashore to spend the night in an Avalon hotel. *Furthermore, why would this mysterious new witness wait more than three decades to come forward in a case that has garnered worldwide public attention? And, why would the detectives believe a witness who made an appearance like that?*

Witnesses Wayne and Payne were discounted out of hand 38 years ago by Detective Rasure. *Yet, the LASD now wants the public to believe it has a "new witness" who claims they saw something Davern has never stated happened?* I personally believe the detectives either fabricated this witness or the new witness is not to be believed.

But for the show, the detectives didn't stop there. They claimed two more people witnessed a fight on the back deck on *Saturday* night:

> **Narrator:** Until now, Davern has been the only person to put both Robert Wagner and Natalie Wood outside on the back of the boat arguing Saturday night before she died.
>
> But *after the press conference reopening the case* [emphasis added], investigators got a huge break. Two new witnesses told detectives they not only heard the fight, one of them says she saw it.
>
> **Hernandez:** She saw the figures in the back of the *Splendour*...a male and a female...whose voices they recognized as being Robert Wagner and Natalie Wood arguing on the back of the boat.
>
> **Narrator:** And how credible are these new witnesses?
>
> **Corina:** They're very credible. They have no reason to lie. Their story matches what Dennis Davern says.

~~~~~~~~~

The two new mysterious *Saturday night* "witnesses" allegedly came forward "after the press conference" on November 18, 2011. Again, I don't believe they exist, since Chief McSweeney completely contradicted this claim in his truthful press statements reported less than two months after Corina's press conference.

Moreover, Corina said one of the two witnesses was close enough to recognize voices and see figures, yet there was no mention of their mooring location or the name of their craft.

I went to the scene. I saw the distance between the moorings. It was approximately 100 feet between each mooring. The vessels in the cove were facing into the wind in the direction of the pier. Based on the mooring map and witnesses at the scene, no vessel was identified as being tied behind *Splendour*. One of the diagrams in Miller's report showed his schooner *Easy Rider* as being moored several rows ahead of *Splendour* at J-1, but he saw and heard nothing when the fight between Wagner and Natalie took place.

Acting Harbormaster Oudin told a *Times* reporter that "only one other boat was nearby [*Splendour*]." He didn't say it was *Capricorn*, but Oudin's quote was in the same article that reported Wayne's account of hearing "cries for help." The careful reporter was obviously checking out Wayne's story, and Payne's *Capricorn* was the only boat near *Splendour* Saturday night in the Isthmus.

Facing the pier, *Capricorn* was identified by Payne as being on the starboard side of *Splendour*, at mooring F-1, a little ahead of *Splendour*. That leaves *Splendour's* port side mooring—O-2. Again, no vessel has been identified as being next to *Splendour's* port side.

What about the weather? Between 10:45 p.m. and 11 p.m., it was cold and windy with no moon or stars. Small choppy waves buffeted the boats and the harsh wind whipped through the wind funnel at Isthmus Cove.

For someone to claim he or she could recognize voices and people on the back of a yacht from more than 100 feet away in the pitch-black dark with the weather conditions that existed that Saturday night in the Isthmus is incredulous.

In spite of that, the real test of a witness' veracity in matters like this is most often defined by the timing of his or her revelation. The thought of someone waiting more than 30 years to come forward with this type of miraculous identification in a controversial case involving the death of an internationally known movie star is hard to swallow. *Who are these witnesses? And why did the detectives decide to share their new "evidence" in February 2018 when they claim they had it more than six years earlier?* Instead of trying Robert Wagner in the media with phantom witnesses, they should have brought them forward for the world to see.

But that wasn't even *48 Hours'* crescendo.

> **Narrator:** Six years of investigation, four new key witnesses, two determined investigators with a lot of questions for Robert Wagner.
>
> **Corina:** As we've investigated the case over the last six years, I think he's more of a *person of interest* [emphasis added] now. We know now that he was the last person to be with Natalie before she disappeared.
>
> **Narrator:** For the first time in more than 36 years since Natalie Wood drowned off Catalina Island, investigators are calling her husband a person of interest. But they stop short of calling him a suspect.
>
> **Hernandez:** We have not been able to prove that this was a homicide, and we haven't been able to prove that this was an accident either. The ultimate problem is we don't know how she ended up in the water.
>
> **Reporter:** The statutes of limitation have run out on all crimes, except one…murder. And to prove murder, there has to be evidence that someone intentionally put Natalie in the water. Falling in by accident wouldn't count. If people knew that Natalie was in the water and they didn't save her…they could have saved her and they didn't save her, will that be enough to bring charges in this case?
>
> **Hernandez:** No. Believe it or not, there is no duty to act.

I was truly stunned when I witnessed this exchange. To begin with, in any investigation of alleged malfeasance, only one conclusion really matters. It's whether the investigation produced prosecutable evidence. I may not have a lot of sympathy for Robert Wagner in the matter of Natalie's death. But Corina's pronouncement shattered a primordial rule of investigatory justice—"put up or shut up." As a law enforcement investigator, if you're not going to charge someone with a crime, then you shouldn't turn around and convict him in the media with innuendo.

Next, the phrase "person of interest," according to my homicide detective friends, is just a cryptic way of saying "suspect." Why the LASD feels the need to shy away from the truth is beyond me. But one thing is certain—the LASD has been playing games with Natalie's case since 2011.

Finally, the final dialogue between the *48 Hours* reporter and Hernandez punctuates a fundamental misunderstanding the detective has of California murder law. Detective Hernandez lacks sufficient understanding of *corpus delicti*, implied malice and circumstantial evidence to comprehend the level of proof required in the prosecution in a second-degree murder case. And as far as I can tell from my lawsuit against the sheriff, Hernandez never sought out schooling on these legal principles from the DA.

You now have the tools to understand a prosecutor's burden of proof in a case like Natalie's. But educating the sheriff's department investigators at this point would be a waste of time. Too many critical witnesses have died or become incompetent by age or illness, and too much evidence has been lost to prosecute Wagner now.

ᘒᘒᘒᘒᘒᘒᘒ

I could only shake my head in disbelief as I searched for the "off" button on the TV remote. The upshot was, more than six years after the case was reopened, the LASD wanted the public to believe it had actually done something to advance the investigation. And to further sensationalize things, it claimed Wagner was now a "person of interest."

You can now understand why I believe the 2011 reopening of Natalie's case was done to give the department a much-needed image boost. Furthermore, I believe the "new witnesses" claim by the LASD is bogus. If that's not so, the witnesses should be publicly identified. Moreover, I'm convinced the sheriff's investigators contacted *48 Hours* to demonstrate to the public they were still "digging" and to control the narrative in advance of this book, which they were worried would expose them.

In a case suffocating in coincidences, new eyewitnesses allegedly coming forward more than 30 years after Natalie's death as a result of a press conference in 2011, when the chief of detectives announced there was no new evidence, is simply not credible. Sensationally stating Wagner was now "a person of interest" within a few weeks of my letters to Rosengart and Beck, and seven years after 2011, is the work of a Homicide Bureau trying to save face. But you be the judge of that.

As a postscript, there hasn't been one official word out of the sheriff's department concerning Natalie's investigation since it generated the *48 Hours* news story. I rest my case when it comes to their motives.

CHAPTER 20

follow the money

WAGNER HAD A LIFE PLAN THAT INCLUDED A WEALTHY EXISTENCE. IN *Pieces of My Heart*, Wagner told Eyman that when he chose to become an actor, his father was not going to be a source of financial assistance to him. And he wasn't. So, let's look at the state of Wagner's financial condition during the nine years between his divorce from Natalie in 1963 to the day he remarried her in July 1972.

To begin with, Wagner had been fighting the IRS over a delinquent tax lien the service was trying to collect. I searched to determine if it was for unpaid personal income taxes or some other assessment. We couldn't confirm what caused the lien to be placed on Wagner, but it was there. At some point, Wagner borrowed $40,000 (worth about $335,000 today) from a friend, after his father declined the loan, and used those funds to either pay off the tax lien or to make a property acquisition of some sort. Wagner was broke, and his 1963 marriage to Marion Marshall, who had amassed a net worth of $72,000 (about $600,000 today) because of her divorce from Stanley Donen, didn't appear to improve his personal financial worth. In fact, it may have damaged it.

Before Wagner and Marion were married, a custody battle erupted between Marion and her ex-husband over their two children. It raged on for over two years, with Wagner's personal lifestyle being dragged into the messy mix. The custody battle began in London, England, and later surfaced in Los Angeles County, with both courts claiming jurisdiction of the matter.

According to the Superior Court clerk's file, Marion and Stanley were divorced in Los Angeles in July 1959, and Marion, among other things, was awarded custody of their two boys, ages 9 and 7; $10,800 per year (about $94,300 today) in child support; other valuable assets and alimony ranging from $14,000 to $42,000 per year (about $122,300 to $366,900 today). Before the ink was dry on the settlement, Marion moved the children to an apartment in Rome, Italy, so she could be near her boyfriend, Sheldon Reynolds. Stanley moved to London and remarried.

The custody dispute centered around Marion's lifestyle, including the fact Sheldon and later Wagner spent the night under the same roof with Marion and the children. There was also proof before Marion's relationship with Wagner began, a gay friend lived with Marion and the children for six weeks. In sum, it was claimed Marion neglected the children while she entertained her boyfriends and gay associates overnight.

In those days, being a divorced woman with children was difficult at best, but entertaining boyfriends and gay men under the same roof with the children was taboo, particularly if the boyfriends slept with the mother. In the Superior Court clerk's file is a letter Stanley wrote to Marion on January 29, 1962. After stating his deep concern for their sons' welfare, he wrote, "You are entitled to live your own life no matter how reprehensible others may think your conduct to be, as long as your moral standards and behavior do not adversely affect the boys." He concluded, "I feel that your behavior endangers the boys' moral and emotional health and jeopardizes their future happiness."

After a preliminary hearing in London, the court ordered that the children remain with their mother in Rome until the final hearing, but Wagner "shall not live at or spend any night at her [Marion's] apartment or at any other place at which she may be residing with the said infants." When the proceedings concluded in London, however, the presiding judge awarded custody to Stanley.

Wagner and Marion were quickly married, and following years of court battles in both London and Los Angeles and the legal bills that ensued, the couple turned the situation around.

In *Pieces*, Wagner described the financial impact of the litigation this way: "The trial transcripts were eventually five feet high, and defending the case cost me a great deal of money. Between the court case and the purchase of the Tarzana property, I was financially strapped and very much on the edge."

The Tarzana property was a developed 8-acre ranch Wagner bought in California in October 1963 after he married Marion, so they could "have dogs and horses for the children." The couple apparently traveled back and forth from Marion's place in Rome to the Tarzana ranch. Nice life, but expensive, and Marion, a struggling actress, didn't contribute to the marriage financially like Natalie did during Wagner's first marriage.

You have already learned Marion and Wagner had a child, Katie. When Katie was 7 years old, Wagner cheated on Marion. Marion counterpunched in the fidelity department, and the combination resulted in the couple's separation in June 1970. The divorce decree was filed December 10, 1971. Two months later, Wagner and Natalie reunited, much to the chagrin of Lana. Lana told me she asked Natalie why they got back together. Natalie replied with resolve, "Sometimes the devil you know is better than the devil you don't."

∽∾∽∾∽∾∽∾

Natalie's divorce from Richard Gregson was finalized in April 1972, after their separation the previous August. At that point, Wagner wrote in *Pieces* that about the time he got back together with Natalie, he was "cleaned out" with an "income tax matter" hanging over his head.

We couldn't confirm the source of the income tax matter because the court file in *Robert Wagner v. Marion Marshall Wagner* was conveniently sealed by the judge. It was a practice in those days for lawyers to ask for special concessions for their celebrity clients by sealing the files from public view. But the tax problem appeared to be from unpaid income taxes. If so, that meant Wagner was actually underwater financially. And the income stream from his TV series *It Takes a Thief* ended in March 1970 after three seasons.

Before Wagner and Natalie remarried, here's how Wagner described Natalie's finances in *Pieces*: "Because of her percentage of the profits of *Bob & Carol & Ted & Alice*, Natalie was in fine financial shape. She couldn't have cared less about the financial disparity between us."

And on his wedding day, Wagner penned in *Pieces*, "It was the most deeply emotional time of my life, and I don't think there was a day when I didn't spend every waking hour in a state somewhere between contentment and jubilation. My money troubles didn't really faze me because I knew that with Natalie at my side, good luck would surely follow."

With that last sentence, Wagner had never spoken truer words. His luck was about to skyrocket.

∿∿∿∿∿∿

A long time ago, as a young prosecutor, I learned you could tell a lot about what a person has been doing and thinking by looking at how they spend their money. An investigator can accomplish that in a variety of ways. One is by examining a probate file. Another is scrutinizing credit card statements or checking bank account records. Those records will tell a story if you let them speak.

Notwithstanding having records that had been "sequestered" for decades, I knew my expertise in trusts, wills and probate was minimal. So, I enlisted the assistance of a fellow attorney who I respected for his unmatched knowledge in the field. I hired him many years ago to help me with my personal estate planning, and he has assisted me with that matter ever since.

As I expected, the probate file did indeed contain a story of Natalie's life shortly before her death. But, a tutorial in estate planning is necessary to appreciate some of the details I uncovered within the archived probate file for Natalie Wood Wagner.

Probate law, in a nutshell, concerns the administration of an estate when a person dies, whether the person has a will or not. Administration includes paying bills and distributing the remaining assets of the deceased. It all needs to be managed, both from an accounting standpoint and legally.

The concept of wills is complex. Briefly, a will is a legal document that sets forth someone's wishes regarding the distribution of his or her property and care of his or her family at death. A will gives the person the ability to decide how the property will be distributed, can help with taxes and also provide for trusts.

Trusts are complicated as well, but a trust is usually used to minimize taxes and can offer a fiduciary arrangement allowing a trustee to hold assets on behalf of a beneficiary or beneficiaries. It can also be used to specify exactly how and when an asset is passed to a beneficiary, like a son, daughter or grandchild. Although a trust is similar to a will, a trust usually avoids probate.

In reviewing Natalie's probate file, I saw the petition to probate her estate was filed at 5:14 p.m., December 8, 1981—nine days after her death. The petition was signed by attorney William Stinehart Jr. and Robert Wagner Jr., as petitioner and the executor and trustee under the will. However, as you have learned, Wagner signed the petition December 1, 1981, *two days* after Natalie's death.

There is no way to know why it took seven days from the date Wagner signed the petition to file it with the clerk. Perhaps it was a matter of gathering records together. Or, a matter of timing, so it wouldn't look bad. Either way, money was on Wagner's mind the day Natalie was buried, just like the day he married her the second time.

Attached to the petition was a list of the names and ages of "heirs devisees...legatees" and a copy of Natalie's "Last Will and Testament," signed on April 17, 1980, 19 months before her death. She was 41 years old at the time. On the last page of the will were the signatures of Natalie and two witnesses. The will was 19 pages long. I read it very carefully. Several items jumped out at me, but the first was something that told me a lot about Natalie's state of mind in April 1980. On Page 17, the 16th paragraph of the will read, in part:

> *It is my further request that my said daughters be permitted to reside in* **my residence** *located in Beverly Hills, California, and that, for so long as said WILLIE MAE WORTHEN is caring for my said daughters* [emphasis added], *or for either of them, my Executor or Trustee, as the case may be, permit her to reside in the same residence, free of charge to her, and that my Executor or Trustee compensate her for her services in rendering such care, out of my share or shares of the Residuary Fund set aside for my daughter or daughters for whom she is caring.*

Natalie purchased the couple's Beverly Hills home on October 1, 1974, from famous singer Patti Page for $350,000. Natalie's love for her home was deep, indeed. She obviously wanted the girls to grow up together in the house she decorated herself. But Wagner put her home up for sale a year after her death and eventually used the proceeds—$1.75 million (about $4.3 million today)—and Natalie's other assets to buy a horse farm and expensive Arabian horses to fill the barn. Jeff Jarvis of *People* magazine wrote in July 1983, "Last fall [1982] Wagner bought her [Natasha] a gelding named Fad-a-lei, and plunked down around $50,000 apiece [approximately $265,000 each today] for two mares of his own: Fadjur's Margie and Fadjur's Heidi, both offspring of Black Stallion stand-in Fadjur."

Natalie's will also contained a trust and other language to create a marital deduction fund. Under the Internal Revenue Code, because of the way her will was written, her estate got the benefit of a marital deduction to help reduce the estate taxes. The significance of the marital deduction fund in Natalie's case was this: California is a community property state, meaning each spouse in a marriage is treated as owning half of all marital property. So, if during a marriage, the parties acquire a piece of land worth $50,000, for example, as a general proposition, half would belong to the wife and half to the husband. If one dies, $25,000 in value would be included in that spouse's estate.

The marital deduction for estate tax purposes would then apply to that $25,000 as well as all nonmarital property. Nonmarital property is property a spouse brings into the marriage that does not become community property. For example, if two people get married and one owns a $10,000 bank account, the full amount would be included in that spouse's estate as nonmarital property when he or she dies.

Natalie owned both marital and nonmarital property at the time of her death. In 1981, California provided for an "inheritance tax referee," which is currently called a "probate referee." Inheritance tax referees were people paid to appraise all of the probate property other than cash and cash equivalents. The file indicated Natalie had assets, according to the inheritance tax referee's report, with a clear market value totaling $5,939,925 (approximately $16 million today).

The referee's report is prepared after all bills are paid and expenses are deducted. According to the report, deductions of $734,621 (about $2.07 million today) were paid out of Natalie's estate, including a mysterious, undocumented $30,032 (about $89,000 today) "lien." While I was unable to confirm all of the items that made up the total, from reviewing the entire file, it appeared that some of Wagner's debts were run through her estate. As far as I could determine, Natalie had no liens filed against her property.

Wagner also used Natalie's estate to pay out thousands of dollars for his personal credit card bills, thousands of dollars of liquor store charges (many incurred after Natalie's death), yacht club fees, the diamond necklace purchased on Catalina Island and even a parking ticket.

Now, you might be thinking, *What difference did it make who paid Wagner's bills? Wasn't it his money to spend now that Natalie was gone?* In fact, it wasn't. Every dollar he spent on himself reduced the amount that went into trust for Natalie's daughters, Natasha and Courtney.

The report also provided the value of assets that went through probate to her half-sister, Olga Viripaeff, who received $15,319 in cash; Lana Gurdin (Lana Wood), who received $25,000 in value from a specific bequest of furs and clothing; and Natalie's mother, Maria Gurdin, who received $99,182 in value that was assigned to a bequest of $1,000 per month for the remainder of her life. Probate assets that didn't go into the marital fund were divided into three shares for Natalie's girls. Stepdaughter Katharine Wagner received $56,786 in cash, and daughters Natasha and Courtney, who were minors at the time, each received $1,239,815 (nearly $3.5 million today) in estimated asset value to be held in a residuary trust for them or their children. Both girls were taxed $150,000 (about $419,000 today) on her share of the assets. Finally, Robert Wagner received $3,263,007 (over $9 million today) in estimated asset value, tax-free, because of the marital deduction.

In order to qualify for the marital deduction, the property passing to Wagner had to be owned by him in such a way that it will be included in his estate at death. So, in reality, the estate taxes were deferred on Wagner's share rather than avoided at Natalie's death. When property is left in trust for the surviving spouse's benefit—like in Natalie's will—rather than outright ownership, it can qualify for the marital deduction as long as the surviving spouse—Wagner in this example—has sufficient authority over the property so that he almost has outright ownership.

To establish that, Wagner must be paid all income from the trust at least annually. In addition, Wagner must have a "general power of appointment," so that he can transfer the property to whomever he pleases during his lifetime or at his death. That would include transferring it to himself while he was alive.

Natalie's will also provided that Wagner could pay himself such amounts up to the whole amount as he might demand of himself. So, there was really no limit on the amount he could take out of his marital deduction trust. Furthermore, if the net income of the trust was insufficient to meet Wagner's needs for his "health, support and maintenance in accordance with the standard of living to which he is accustomed," Wagner could draw principal from the trust to meet those needs. And Wagner was the person who decided if the situation met the "standard of living to which he was accustomed."

Moreover, under another article of the will, it provided that Wagner was entitled to take distributions from the principal of *the girls' residuary funds*, to the extent necessary for his "continued health, support and/or maintenance." Natalie may not have appreciated this, but under her will, Wagner was the trustee of the children's trust and also the person who decided what was needed for his "health, support and maintenance." So, at Natalie's death, even though he didn't own it outright, Wagner had access to *all* of Natalie's assets, including the girls' trusts, if "necessary."

⁓⁓⁓⁓⁓⁓⁓

At this point, you need to understand something about the real value of Natalie's estate. Except for cash and cash equivalents, Natalie's probate file contained no *independent ap-*

praisals for any of the assets for probate purposes. The values for Natalie's assets came from the inheritance tax referee.

The referee in Natalie's case was Esther N. Peck. Peck signed the bottom of eight inventory and appraisement declaration forms purporting to contain the clear market value of certain assets. The forms were also signed by Wagner as petitioner. All of the forms stated that Wagner and Peck had "truly and honestly appraised the property" described on the forms. Presently, probate referees have to take a class in appraisals and receive other education, but in my attorney friend's opinion and experience, Peck most likely accepted the values Wagner gave her for several items in Natalie's estate—unless she had expertise in entertainment contracts, pro forma income projections, fine art and the like.

One of the inventory and appraisement forms signed by Peck and Wagner related to "profit participations" Natalie owned at her death. A profit participation is an agreement between parties to a contract to divide profits—usually net profits—on a project. Profit participations can be used with a real estate development, a film or TV production, or even a business, if the parties so agree.

Natalie owned three profit participations at her death, according to the probate file: one for the film *Bob & Carol & Ted & Alice*, a second for the film *Love with the Proper Stranger*, and the third for the television series *Charlie's Angels*. (See *Figures K* and *L*, Pages 267-268.)

Keep in mind the values attached to the profit participations were someone's opinion of *future earnings*. Moreover, the value was for estate purposes. So, the higher the value, the higher the possible taxes. According to my lawyer friend, while a referee can't be "ridiculous about it," the object is to try to be on the low side of values with big estates. The reason is obvious.

The profit participation for *Bob & Carol & Ted & Alice* was valued at $48,622 (about $130,000 today). That film was released in 1969, so Natalie had been receiving income from the film for 12 years before she died. In December 1981, Natalie's estate received a check for $11,591 (about $34,500 today) from the *Bob* profit participation. Generally, entertainment profit participations are paid annually, sometimes semi-annually. *Bob* was a big hit, receiving four Academy Award nominations. In all likelihood, Wagner is still collecting money from that contract.

The *Love with the Proper Stranger* profit participation was valued at $14,415 (about $40,300 today). *Proper Stranger*, released in 1963, was nominated for five Academy Awards, including Natalie's nomination for Best Actress. Both Natalie and costar Steve McQueen were also nominated for Golden Globes for Best Actress and Best Actor, respectively. *Proper Stranger* was also nominated for the American Film Institute's top 100 greatest love stories of all time.

In February 1982, Natalie's estate received $1,530 (about $4,600 today) from her profit participation in *Proper Stranger*. That was 19 years after the movie was released.

The final profit participation was for the TV series *Charlie's Angels*. My research, and Wagner's admissions, indicated that Natalie and Wagner owned a 50 percent interest in the net profits of *Charlie's Angels*. So, at her death, Natalie owned one-half, or 25 percent, of this community property asset. The other 25 percent was owned by Wagner. Natalie's portion of *Charlie's Angels*, for probate purposes, was valued at $2,300,620 (about $6.1 million today).

The hit series featured Farrah Fawcett, Kate Jackson and Jaclyn Smith and was released in 1976. It ran through June 1981 with a total of 110 episodes. Obviously, this was a very lucrative venture for the Wagners. Most everyone, even children, have heard of *Charlie's Angels.*

In a nutshell, the *Love Song/Charlie's Angels* contract, executed in 1973, with a supplemental contract in December 1977, provided for an agreement between Natalie and Wagner with Spelling-Goldberg Productions to do a TV movie together called *Love Song,* which was later released as *The Affair.* (See *Figures M–P,* Pages 269-272.) Natalie received $65,000 (about $160,000 today) to appear in the TV movie. Wagner received $21,000 (about $50,000 today). The first contract was executed with the producers, Spelling-Goldberg Productions, 11 months after Natalie and Wagner remarried.

Paragraph 11 of the 1973 *Love Song/Charlie's Angels* contract provided that each party— the Wagners and Spelling-Goldberg Productions—was to submit up to five ideas to ABC for a pilot script for the 1974 season. If anything hit, the Wagners and Spelling-Goldberg Productions would split the profits. *Charlie's Angels* hit, and after some legal wrangling, another contract was signed in 1977.

According to the accounting in Natalie's file, her estate received $859,250 (about $2.3 million today) on January 12, 1982, from the *Charlie's Angels* profit participation. Of course, the income didn't stop because the series ended. That series was syndicated, and there were subsequent DVD releases and TV film remakes. Network syndication for a series like *Charlie's Angels* means the series was first shown on ABC and then, when the show stopped, the distributor sold the program to other networks or stations, so they could show the episodes. Profits for a television hit like *Charlie's Angels* become enormous when the show is sold for syndication. Syndication profits were included in the contract Natalie and Wagner executed with Spelling-Goldberg Productions. And Wagner himself confirmed the high dollar value of syndications in *Pieces.*

As for *Charlie's Angels,* it continues to have a pop culture promoting it and to this day is aired on television networks in the U.S. and abroad, including MeTV and Cozi TV. It is literally a gold mine spinning off a fortune each year.

Of course, without tax returns, there's no way to compute the amount of money generated from the profit participation contract for *Charlie's Angels* since November 29, 1981. But, to give you a point of reference as to the potential value of this contract, in 2007, Wagner sued Columbia Pictures Industries and others over whether the contract he and Natalie negotiated in 1973 covered two *Charlie's Angels* movies that made—not grossed—almost $200 million dollars. Wagner lost the suit because the California Court of Appeal said Spelling-Goldberg Productions had not contracted with the Wagners for the movie rights that Spelling-Goldberg sold Columbia Pictures. But through syndication, the TV series alone has been aired in more than 90 countries over the years.

Notwithstanding all of this, the estate value put on that community property contract by Peck and Wagner was a little less than three times what Natalie's estate received in 1982. In my opinion, the contract was worth significantly more. However, because of Natalie's death, Wagner has collected 100 percent of their *Love Song/Charlie's Angels* profit participation contract from the date of her death until the present. And, without question, the Wagners' *Love Song/Charlie's Angels* contract was the direct result of Natalie's agreement to participate in projects produced by Spelling-Goldberg Productions.

I can confidently say that, because at the time the contract was signed, Wagner, individually, had nothing to offer the extraordinary producers who had become immensely wealthy from their trade. They wanted Natalie involved in their business, but to get her, they had to take Wagner as well.

〜〜〜〜〜〜

A detailed analysis of Natalie's estate is also critical in understanding what would have happened financially if Natalie and Wagner were divorced a second time. That potential event was not idle speculation after Wagner embarrassed Natalie with his drunken, violent displays of jealousy Friday and Saturday nights off Catalina Island. Natalie told Davern as much in their hotel room Friday night.

As you may recall, according to Davern, Natalie was still very angry when they checked into the Pavilion Lodge. She had been enjoying her conversation with Walken when Wagner "ruined it." She was upset he didn't respect her professional relationship with Walken the way she did with his costar Stefanie Powers.

Natalie told Davern she knew Wagner's mid-October to visit her in North Carolina was to check up on her, and she would not "tolerate" Wagner's jealousy and out-of-control behavior, which she attributed to alcohol. Natalie warned Davern that Wagner would have to "face the music" on Monday, even if she had to "see a lawyer" to send him "the message loud and clear."

If the Wagners had divorced, the *Charlie's Angels* profit participation would have been divided equally. The family's Cañon Drive home would have stayed with Natalie. And there is little doubt the girls would have stayed in the house with her, particularly if alcohol and uncontrolled rage were grounds. The same would have occurred for the remaining millions in nonmarital assets Natalie owned at her death, including the profit participations in *Bob* and *Proper Stranger*, a condo, some real estate, fine artwork, annuities, and other properties and assets Natalie owned separately.

On top of that, Natalie would have been entitled to one-half of all marital property she owned together with Wagner. In my research, I discovered the existence of a profit participation for *Hart to Hart* through Wagner's admissions, a federal Freedom of Information Act request to the FBI for a file opened on Spelling-Goldberg in August 1980 and a memoir written by Tom Mankiewicz, creative consultant for *Hart to Hart*. Jeff Jarvis reported in *People* that Wagner owned "about half" of *Hart to Hart*, but Mankiewicz, who had become the Wagners' close friend, was more precise in his book when he said Wagner owned "50%."

With a divorce, Natalie would have been entitled to one-half of any profit participations Wagner acquired during their marriage. Yet, the *Hart to Hart* profit participation was not specifically identified in Natalie's estate. The only indication such an agreement was included was found on the last page of an asset appraisal signed by Wagner on July 19, 1982. (See *Figure 36*, next page.) It reflected a value of $9,761.50 (about $29,000 today) as the marital one-half interest of Natalie's right "to receive residuals from all motion pictures and/or television programs completed by Robert J. Wagner after July 16, 1972, which are payable to Robert J. Wagner."

That means the total value placed on Wagner's residuals was a mere $19,523 (about $58,000 today), calculated by doubling the 50 percent figure of $9,761.50.

That was difficult for me to swallow. *Hart to Hart* was a big hit and has also been syndi-

```
Community one-half interest in right to
receive residuals from all motion pictures
and/or television programs completed by
Robert J. Wagner after July 16, 1972, which
are payable to Robert J. Wagner

     Value of Entire
     Community Property:

          Decedent's Community            9,761.50
          One-Half Interest:
```

Figure 36: Probate appraisal of Wagner's residuals (Natalie Wood Wagner probate file)

cated. In all likelihood, millions of dollars have been generated from the series syndication. Stefanie Powers appeared to lament in a 1998 interview with *The New York Times* that the "less than $1 million" she negotiated for a share of the profits of *Hart to Hart* was lacking. Considering the disparity in entertainment fees between males and females in 1981, Powers probably had reason to gripe.

But the appraisal carries this significance. According to my expert, because of the language in Natalie's will, any omitted community property asset meant less money to Natalie's daughters. For example, if the true value of the *Hart to Hart* profit participation was $1 million (equal to Powers' share), $500,000 would have been included in the residual trust, and the girls would have received their share of that amount, minus taxes. I am disposed to believe that Wagner, with his high-powered tax lawyers, would have known of that result.

As for the yacht *Splendour*, according to the probate file, it was listed as marital property and valued at $250,000. However, the file stated the yacht was "sold" for $250,000. If it was indeed given away, as Davern claimed, the probability is Wagner used it as a $250,000 deduction on his personal tax return.

But there is one more element of benefit that was most likely reaped by Wagner as a result of Natalie's death—life insurance, the proceeds of which are generally not counted in a decedent's estate. It's hard to fathom that the Wagners didn't have life insurance.

Even an untrained eye would be lifted in skepticism at the mountain of evidence of financial gain/loss motive evidence available to the detectives in 2011. If the truth be told, I have only scratched the surface. They had the ability to obtain financial records, including tax returns and bank records, with legal processes that were unavailable to me. I tried to find out in my CPRA case against the sheriff's department whether it used the resources available to it since 2011 to uncover financial motive evidence, but the defense refused to cooperate and the judiciary sided with the LASD. However, based on what I did learn about their work, I feel confident the LASD failed to follow the leads on this important motive evidence.

CHAPTER 21

person of interest

THE DECISION TO PROSECUTE SOMEONE FOR MURDER ALMOST ALWAYS includes some questionable action and evidence of an admission, confession or false exculpatory statement by a loose-lipped suspect. So, let's look at the questionable actions and false, misleading and strange statements made by Wagner over the years that were available to detectives in 1981 and 2011, and see what reasonable inferences can be made.

Recall that, after leaving Davern on Catalina Island to identify Natalie's body, Wagner said, according to CSI Hamilton's notes, "We were all in the boat—*Beautiful night. She wanted to take dingy* (sic) *out*" and he *"started calling Harbor Patrol about 11:30* [emphasis added]."

Later that same day, in the comfort of his home and under the protection of his well-connected personal attorney, Wagner talked to friends who came to pay their respects, including Army Archerd, who wrote a legendary gossip column, *Just for Variety*, that was devoured by the public, including celebrities, for its titillating details about the steps and missteps of the Who's Who of Hollywood.

Archerd was given exclusive passage through the throngs of press and onlookers scrambling to breech police barricades at the Wagners' iron gates after Natalie's death.

Apparently, Wagner was composed enough to walk from room to room acknowledging guests, with Archerd describing him as having eyes "wet with old and new tears." He reported that a few guests asked Wagner questions, including "Why did Natalie go out in the dinghy?" Wagner's "murmured" response was: *"She often did and the water was smooth as glass."*

❦❦❦❦❦

You may remember Wagner issued three press releases after Natalie's death. In the second one, the day of her funeral, Wagner said he thought Natalie went to the master stateroom to go to sleep. When he went down *"ten or fifteen minutes later,"* he discovered she was gone and noticed the Zodiac was gone. He claimed *"he went out with his boat to try to find her. And then he immediately called the Coast Guard."*

Wagner didn't speak about the events again until investigators Rasure and Hamilton went to his home to question him Friday, December 4.

With respect to Friday, November 27, Rasure wrote in his interview notes that Wagner "talked" of "going home" because "the sea was rough." And wrote further that Wagner moved the boat, but "told" Natalie and Davern to "go ashore and stay in a hotel."

In Hamilton's contemporary notes, he reported that Wagner said that Saturday night at Doug's Harbor Reef they had an early dinner, then returned to the boat. *Fifteen minutes later,* according to Wagner, Natalie "went down below." *Fifteen minutes* after that, Wagner said he "went down." Wagner claimed Natalie wasn't there, so he "got a boat [and] went to shore to look for her." As for that Saturday afternoon, Rasure's notes agreed with Hamilton's that Wagner said Natalie left a note and took Walken to the bar "on the Zodiac."

The investigators also asked about the broken glass. According to Hamilton's notes, Wagner told them: "*Don't recall when bottles got broken* [emphasis added]." Detective Rasure wrote that Wagner said the broken glass was from "*rough seas* [emphasis added]" and that Wagner "was in bed" when they interviewed him with Ziffren "present."

∽∽∽∽∽∽∽

Between 1 a.m. and at least 2:30 a.m. Sunday, Wagner managed to direct searchers away from the open sea and toward the Isthmus Cove shore, specifically Doug's restaurant and bar. He continued the "she went back to the bar" narrative with investigators for four days. But Wagner had apparently forgotten about Natalie's Saturday night clothing, underwear and purse in the master stateroom. The same stateroom he admitted during his December 4 statement he searched with Deputy Kroll after Natalie disappeared.

It was clothing the always "turned out" actress would never have been without while enjoying a public outing at midnight. Not to mention her money or credit cards. Wagner's story had to change to make sense, and most importantly, to be believed. Moreover, Rasure's concluding notes contained the only concern voiced by Wagner during the second interview. A concern focused on the whereabouts of jewelry.

The December 4, 1981, interview was Wagner's last official interview, 40 years ago and counting. Yet, since 2011, his criminal defense lawyers have spun a disputed tale of cooperation with the authorities. However, from a defense standpoint, the truth is Wagner had already talked to law enforcement two times too many.

If Wagner had been charged in the '80s, his false exculpatory statements to investigators on November 29 and December 4, coupled with his many questionable statements and actions, could have been used against him as evidence of consciousness of guilt with great prosecutorial fanfare.

∽∽∽∽∽∽∽

By all accounts, with the exception of a puff interview appearing in the July 4, 1983, issue of *People* magazine, Wagner stayed exceptionally quiet about Natalie's death until August 1985. In a *Star* magazine article, Wagner denied her death involved a "love triangle." However, we now know in truth it was indeed a *love triangle* fueled by Wagner's suspicious jealousy of Natalie and Walken.

A year passed before Wagner was quoted again about Natalie and the tragic weekend she died. In *Heart to Heart*, the authors discussed Wagner's relationship with St. John, whom he was dating at the time. Wagner told them he stayed in his bed for days before recovering enough to start seeing her.

As for Wagner's story to Maychick and Borgo about the night Natalie died, Wagner stuck with the same storyline he neatly presented in his third press release to a close friend on December 26, 1981, with the exception of telling the authors they paid their check at Doug's restaurant "*at 10:30 p.m.*" and he went down to kiss Natalie good night "*toward 1:30 a.m.*"

Recall that Eaker reported that Wagner told her the last time he saw Natalie was at *10:45 p.m.* and in his December 4 statement he said "15 minutes" later he went down to check on her. With Wagner's own words, we now have a clear falsehood about his discovery of Natalie missing and a timeline bracket to work with. The foursome left Doug's around

10:30 p.m. Wagner last saw Natalie at *10:45 p.m.*, 15 minutes later Wagner went down to check on her, and Wayne and Payne heard cries for help from a woman in the water near *Splendour* between *11:05 p.m.* and *"around midnight."*

Armed with the evidence from my experts and forensic pathologists that the time of death was "around midnight," it's now been reasonably established that Natalie was in the ocean sometime between *11 p.m.* and *around midnight.* At this point, an investigator couldn't ask for much more in the way of a suspect's admissions.

⌁⌁⌁⌁⌁⌁⌁

In one of Wagner's interviews with the authors of *Heart to Heart*, Wagner claimed after he went down to the master stateroom to "kiss her good night," "[t]he idea that any harm had come to her never entered my mind. *I got into my speedboat* [emphasis added] and went to look for her near the shore." After saying he couldn't find Natalie or the dinghy, he went back to the yacht and "became worried" that she hadn't returned. He concluded by telling the authors this:

> "It was only after I was later told she was dressed in a sleeping gown, heavy socks and a parka that it dawned on me what really occurred.

> "Natalie obviously had trouble sleeping with that dinghy slamming up against the boat. It had happened many times before, and I had always gone out and pulled the ropes tighter to keep the dinghy flush against the yacht.

> *"She probably skidded on one of the steps after untying the ropes. The steps are slick as ice because of the algae and seaweed that is always clinging to them* [emphasis added]."

Of course, Wagner didn't own a speedboat, and there was no evidence the swim step was coated with algae and seaweed. In fact, there was evidence to the contrary from Miller. But "a lie begets a lie."

⌁⌁⌁⌁⌁⌁⌁

Wagner's next attempt at a credible narrative was in Lambert's 2004 biography of Natalie. Citing hundreds of Wagner's friends as sources, Wagner wanted his friend Lambert to clear the air for him concerning his wife's death. After Davern, Kashner and Finstad, Wagner had a definite image problem. Unflattering doubts about his veracity had soared, so what better way to subdue them than to have reputable friends come to his rescue *again*?

Lambert claimed that Wagner "talked very openly" to him during his research. So, let's explore the truthfulness of Wagner's purported transparency.

Apparently, Wagner told Lambert that in mid-October he took a break from filming *Hart to Hart* and flew to Raleigh, North Carolina, "where he became uneasy about the situation with Natalie and Christopher Walken." Lambert quoted Wagner as saying, *"It crossed my mind that they were having an affair, but I wasn't sure, and didn't say anything about it to Natalie* [emphasis added]."

Wagner also told Lambert he was away "on location in Hawaii shooting *Hart to Hart*" the weekend before the yacht trip with Walken—the weekend of November 20, 1981. From the records and witnesses I discovered, coupled with statements made by Stefanie Powers in her memoir, *One from the Hart*, the evidence strongly suggests Wagner's representation is false.

Natalie had agreed to perform the lead role in a Los Angeles produced play about the Russian Grand Duchess, *Anastasia*, after she finished *Brainstorm*. Wagner apparently told Lambert that originally there was "no conflict" about leaving Los Angeles to go to New York if the play made it to Broadway. And then Lambert quoted Wagner as saying, "When Natalie first planned to do *Anastasia*, and before she met Walken, we'd talked of buying a farm in upstate New York, and it had nothing to do with *what we argued about later* [emphasis added]." *What argument came later?* Lambert didn't enlighten us.

Addressing Friday evening, Lambert related, "*He agrees that his suspicion of an affair between Natalie and Walken, and Natalie's anger with him for being suspicious, fueled all their later arguments* [emphasis added]." Again, Lambert didn't identify the "later arguments," but both Davern and Wintler did—a fight between Wagner and Natalie before she disappeared Saturday night.

Wagner told Lambert that Saturday afternoon Natalie and Walken got up from their naps before everyone else and took the "dinghy to shore, leaving a note." When he and Davern got up, they took a shore boat to Doug's "around 4 and they drank—all four of them—until 7 when they moved to the dining area for dinner." After dinner, Wagner told Lambert they went back to *Splendour* and continued drinking in the salon.

At that point, Lambert reported that Wagner said:

> Walken kept encouraging Natalie to pursue her career as an actress, to follow her own desires and needs. He talked about his "total pursuit of a career," which was more important to him than his personal life. It was obvious I didn't share his point of view. *It struck me as some kind of put-down, and I got really angry.* I told him to stay out of it, *then picked up a wine bottle, slammed it on the table, and smashed it to pieces* [emphasis added].

After 23 years of denying an argument with Walken, claiming "rough seas" broke the wine bottle and saying Davern couldn't be believed, Wagner admitted to Lambert a violent scene occurred, after believing he was being "put-down." While Davern had told *Star* magazine that very thing in July 1985, Wagner had never mentioned it to investigators, reporters or book authors—until Lambert's book.

Wagner went on to tell Lambert that Walken told him to "Let Natalie do what she wanted to do." And Wagner replied, "I complained that doing what she wanted to do took her away from home and the kids too often." With that, Lambert wrote, "Natalie got up, turned her back on both of them and left for the master stateroom."

The sequence of events is important because Wagner told Lambert that *Natalie was present* when he angrily smashed the wine bottle in front of her guest. Witnessing that event is a defining moment when assessing the depth of Natalie's anger and humiliation. Notwithstanding his position with Lambert, Wagner later claimed in *Pieces* that Natalie *wasn't* present when the violent scene unfolded.

Wagner continued by telling Lambert that once Natalie and Walken left the salon, he and Davern stayed up drinking "*until at least 1:30 in the morning.*" And sometime thereafter, he "went down to the master stateroom" to "*make sure Natalie was all right*" and discovered she wasn't there.

Wagner's reaction after discovering Natalie and the dinghy were gone, according to Lambert, was:

> In my totally fuddled state, *I wondered if she'd taken it and gone off because we'd started arguing again* [emphasis added]. Then I thought, surely not. Natalie was terrified of being alone on dark water, and besides, when you started the dinghy engine, it fired very quickly and we'd certainly have heard it.

But now the narrative changes again. Contrary to what Davern told investigators on March 5, 1982, and something never before mentioned by Wagner, he told Lambert that the Zodiac dinghy was "*tied to port*"—the left side of the yacht. (See Page B-8.) And, he hadn't checked the "dinghy *ropes*" by the time Natalie went to the stateroom.

That setup would result in the dinghy and the yacht floating parallel to each other in the water facing the pier. The perfect scenario for the "banging dinghy" theory, if it were true.

Then came the *coup de grace*. Wagner advised Lambert that sometimes the dinghy would come loose and "*Natalie would open the door to the swim step and step on it to untie the rope, then retie the dinghy to a brass ring beside the step.*" Of course, Lambert was no investigator. If he had been, he would have looked at photographs of the *Splendour's* stern before the yacht was disposed of to determine if there was, in fact, a "brass ring beside the step." Had he done so, he would have discovered that no such brass ring existed. (See Page A-7.) Furthermore, Miller inspected the swim step and its brackets, at Dr. Noguchi's request, for signs of Natalie trying to re-board the yacht from the water, and he identified no brass ring under, attached to or near the swim step. (See *Figure 26*, Page 109.)

The sheriff's department's March 3, 1982, photograph of *Splendour's* transom, taken at Detective Rasure's request, depicted the swim step and closed swim step door with a chrome eye-ring near the starboard (right) side transom of the yacht. (See Page A-2.) That photograph was indisputable evidence that there was no need to go onto the swim step to retie the dinghy if it were tied to the chrome eye-ring like Davern told Rasure on March 5, 1982.

～～～～～～～

Wagner's next version of the events came four years after Lambert's book with the publication of his memoir *Pieces*. Eyman, a former book editor and art critic from West Palm Beach, Florida, penned the book for Wagner. But the obscene language used is vintage Wagner.

As far as Thanksgiving weekend 1981, Wagner had wrecked any chance of salvaging Natalie's forgiveness for his conduct Friday night and had humiliated her beyond repair Saturday evening. Based on what he knew about Natalie, Wagner knew he was going to pay. And the logical inference is Natalie told him in the stateroom she had had enough. She was going to her lawyer. So, a banging, cussing, screaming fight between the two stars is not only more than probable, it is practically a certainty.

In *Pieces*, Eyman used four and a half pages to describe Wagner's version of the events that weekend. Here's part of what Wagner claimed happened Friday night:

> By this time [after returning from shopping] we had had slightly too much to drink, and *things were getting combative* [emphasis added]. When I suggested moving the *Splendour* closer to shore to avoid having to ride out the swells, Natalie gave me an argument, and I gave her an argument right back. She got angry and told Dennis Davern, who took care of the *Splendour* for us, to take her to Avalon in the dinghy. She spent the night at the Pavilion Lodge. Chris just shrugged and went below to his cabin. I secured the boat and went to sleep myself.

Wagner didn't explain what "things" were "getting combative." But he noted, "The next morning Natalie came back to the boat and everything was fine." He made no mention of Davern spending the night with Natalie or being present when the foursome made its way to the Isthmus Saturday.

Wagner described events after he woke from his nap Saturday afternoon this way [emphasis added]:

> When I woke up, I found a note from Natalie saying that she and Chris had taken the dinghy and gone to the island. They went to Doug's Harbor Reef for about two hours. I wasn't angry, but *I was agitated*. I called the shore boat and joined them. *It would be fair to say that I was upset*, but not so much that I let on.

The narrative continued with Wagner omitting any of the events at dinner, opting instead to discuss the level of drinking and his state of mind:

> Again, we had had quite a bit of wine with dinner, but I would categorize our condition as tipsy; certainly, nobody was anywhere near drunk. We got back to the salon of the *Splendour* and had some more drinks. *And it was at that point that I got pissed off* [emphasis added].

Once again, Wagner omitted a critical time, the time he "got pissed off."

Then Wagner confessed—using his favorite four-letter word—"I finally had had enough. '*Why the fuck don't you stay out of her career?*' I said. 'She's got enough people telling her what to do without you.' Walken and I got into an argument. *At one point I picked up a wine bottle, slammed it on the table, and broke it into pieces* [emphasis added]."

Furthermore, Wagner claimed, "*Natalie was already belowdecks at that point* [emphasis added]." Exactly the opposite of what he told Lambert four years earlier and contrary to what Walken told the detectives Sunday morning.

Wagner's four-letter word alone created the link between the violent bottle-smashing incident and the truth of what happened next.

After saying Natalie was already belowdecks, Wagner told Eyman:

> She had gotten up during our argument—she didn't rush out, she just got up—and went down the three steps from the salon of the boat to

the master cabin to go to the bathroom. *The last time I saw my wife she was fixing her hair at a little vanity in the bathroom while I was arguing with Chris Walken* [emphasis added]. I saw her shut the door. She was going to bed.

The crime scene photographs establish that you can't see the master stateroom bathroom from the salon. (See Page B-8.) You would have to be in the stateroom to see someone in the bathroom. Once again, this assertion could have been confirmed, but apparently no one bothered to check.

However, if the stateroom door is open, you can see the chair in front of the vanity table from that vantage point. That's where Natalie's clothing from Saturday evening was placed when Natalie was undressing. But it's highly unlikely after Natalie left the salon angry and humiliated, she kept the stateroom door open while she stripped naked to slip on her nightshirt for bed.

At this point, Wagner found it necessary to explain to Eyman how he and Walken interacted after Natalie left, but Wagner's genius failed him as he contradicted what he told his friend Lambert four years earlier:

> About fifteen minutes after Natalie closed the door, *Chris and I moved from the salon up the three steps that led out onto the deck. If I had to categorize the emotional temperature, I would say things were threatening to get physical* [emphasis added], but the fact is that they never did.

Things were now threatening to get physical? You can't look at that admission and not come away with the conclusion that over 25 years after Natalie's death, Wagner was still angry with Walken and violence was still on his mind. However, Wagner stopped short of saying things escalated after he and Walken went out of the yacht's salon and onto the deck. According to Wagner, they came back into the salon, sat there awhile and then "Chris went to bed."

An astounding piece of evidence was revealed for the first time in the 2020 HBO documentary *Natalie Wood: What Remains Behind.* I caught it on my second pass through the feature. In a brief segment of a conversation between Natasha Gregson Wagner and Mart Crowley, Crowley related that he was asked to go on the Thanksgiving weekend cruise and declined. Obviously tormented, Crowley said, "R.J. and Chris were arguing all the time. I didn't want any part of it." Now, from an unimpeached source, we know there were disagreements between Wagner and Walken leading up to the trip to Catalina. A fact I would corroborate in my investigation with a clue hidden in plain view in Natalie's 1981 LASD file.

How Wagner explained in *Pieces* what happened next and his state of mind are simply beyond odd to me [emphasis added except for the words "No way"]:

> I went below, and Natalie wasn't there. *Strange.* I went back up on deck

and looked around for her and noticed the dinghy was gone. *Stranger.* I remember wondering if she'd taken the dinghy because of the argument, and then I thought, *No way,* because she was terrified of dark water, and besides that, the dinghy fired up very loudly, and we would have heard it, whether we were in the salon or on deck.

Your wife disappears from your yacht, moored in the cold Pacific Ocean in the middle of the night, and all you can say to yourself is "strange" and "stranger"? Most would find *that* strange. Yet, Wagner ended with another startling revelation: *Davern,* not Wagner, radioed for help "on the Harbor Channel" at 1:30 a.m.

The preceding entries in *Pieces* were Wagner's last discussion of the details of his wife's death until HBO's 2020 documentary. And most people who know anything about Natalie's case, or who look it up online, believe *Wagner* called for help on the yacht radio around 1:30 a.m., and that call was intercepted by the night restaurant manager, who was relaxing on his boat in Catalina Harbor. But, Wagner dispelled any notion it was he who made the call by admitting it was *Davern.*

On this score, I believe we finally have a small dose of the truth. Davern did make the call while Wagner was completing his charade with Wintler, riding back and forth between the rows of boats looking for Natalie and the dinghy. I believe Davern knew Natalie didn't take the dinghy back to the bar, so in Wagner's absence, he made the desperate radio call. But, as Miller reported to Noguchi, the precise time of the call was *1:50 a.m.*

∽∽∽∽∽∽∽

In my earlier chapter *Corpus Delicti,* I introduced you to the circumstantial evidence murder case of Eric Bechler, the man convicted of murdering his wife after she disappeared while the couple was boating off the California coast. The similarity between the facts in *People v. Bechler* and Natalie's case is not a coincidence.

Murder cases like Bechler's are tried regularly in California state courts, and a very high percentage of the defendants are convicted. Every murder case has components similar to *Bechler,* including jealousy, envy, financial gain and marital discord. Those motives for murder have been used by prosecutors to obtain convictions since the inception of our republic. It's nothing new, and neither is the proposition that in any domestic death investigation, the spouse or lover is always the first to be suspected.

In 1982, Martin Daly, Margo Wilson and Suzanne Weghorst, in a study for the journal *Ethology and Sociobiology,* announced what every homicide detective knows: "Male jealousy may be the major source of conflict in an overwhelming majority of spousal homicides in North America."

The LASD investigators knew that in 1981, and they knew it in 2011. But they would never admit it. In 1981, the investigators were turning their heads from suspicious evidence. Since 2011, the detectives continue to protect Wagner by dancing around his status in Natalie's case.

While you mull over the question of the need to protect Wagner's status as a suspect since 2011, let's see what kind of evidence existed in 2011 to establish *corpus delicti* in the death case of Natalie Wood Wagner.

~~~~~~~~

Wagner's intense jealousy of Natalie can be traced back to before they were married the first time, and it intensified after they separated in 1961. All you need to convince yourself of that is to examine what Wagner confessed to Lambert and Eyman.

When Wagner decided to press for marriage, he dropped an engagement ring in a champagne glass and swept a teenager off her feet with his sophisticated charm. It was a whirlwind affair that culminated in a small ceremony on December 28, 1957.

A couple of years later, Natalie began making the film *Splendor in the Grass* with the terribly handsome Warren Beatty. Wagner and Natalie rented an apartment in New York state while she was shooting on location. He told Lambert he was with her because a movie of his had been "postponed."

Wagner felt the need to describe Natalie's feelings about New York and New York actors in *Pieces*: "Natalie's fascination with New York translated into a fascination with young Method actors, guys who played the same brooding notes as Brando and Monty Clift but didn't actually have their talent. Scott Marlow, for instance. In Natalie's mind, New York was always sort of acting promised land."

After college, Beatty moved to New York City to study acting, and Walken, who was born in Queens, studied dancing and dramatic acting in the city. As for Natalie, when the movie *Splendor* started, Wagner quoted the film's director, Elia Kazan, and exposed his sensitivity toward being married to someone who dedicated herself to her profession and was successful in her own right. Kazan said, "With Natalie, acting was her whole life." Agreeing with Kazan, Wagner said in his autobiography: "At this point in her career, I think Kazan was right—Natalie's success or failure as an actress was more important to her than anything else. Including me."

In *The Psychology of Jealousy & Envy*, a collaborative scientific study of the subjects, Boston University assistant professor of psychology Richard H. Smith opened his chapter "Envy and the Sense of Injustice" by saying, "envy typically involves both feelings of discontent" and "a measure of hostility directed at the envied person." The discontentment, according to Smith "seems a natural result of noticing another's superiority."

And, so the love/hate feelings Wagner had for Natalie began. He had a beautiful, celebrated wife who was achieving amazing success—financially and professionally—without him, and he was feeling both inferior and hostile toward her superiority. Moreover, Wagner's insecurities fueled his long-lasting mindset of suspicious jealousy.

When the film *Splendor* came upon the scene, the evidence suggested Wagner's suspicions became more intense. He said in *Pieces*, "There was an added sense of fear. When such a fear is combined with the feeling that you're not being responded to in the way you expect, things can get very edgy, very fast."

Wagner admitted by February 1961, he and Natalie were quarreling a great deal, noting: "My insecurities were mounting." Natalie's movies were getting bigger and bigger and Wagner claimed he "was excluded from almost everything that was happening to her, and I was jealous." With that, Wagner admitted he was not only jealous of other men, he was envious of Natalie's success.

Much to the dismay of Hollywood and the famous couple's adoring fans, Natalie and Wagner separated in June 1961. Wagner confessed in *Pieces* they "got into a terrible, terrible argument. There was a lot of yelling that ascended to screaming." And Natalie left the house.

The split occurred before *Splendor* was released October 10, 1961. Although it had to be an emotional time for her, Natalie was beyond outstanding in her performance in the film, and it resulted in an Academy Award nomination for Best Actress. Natalie attended the awards ceremony with Beatty.

But according to Wagner in his memoir, he didn't relish in her joy. He said, "I was totally humiliated, in a way I'd never felt before and, thank God, have never felt since. *Life* magazine was calling Beatty 'the most exciting American male in movies,' and my last four or five pictures had been flops."

In the next paragraph, he exposed his state of mind: "I was hanging around outside his house with a gun, hoping he would walk out. I not only wanted to kill him. I was prepared to kill him."

Although Wagner conceded in *Pieces* that Beatty didn't break up his marriage to Natalie, in his warped mind, her costar did exactly that. But this was not an isolated instance of potential violent jealousy on Wagner's part. In *Goodbye*, Davern recalled that Wagner on one occasion "decked a guy...for flirting with Natalie."

ᗢᗢᗢᗢᗢ

In February 1979, a little more than two years before Natalie's death, NBC released the three-part, six-hour television miniseries *From Here to Eternity*. It was a remake of the 1953 Academy Award-winning movie of the same name. The miniseries starred Natalie, William Devane, Kim Basinger, Steve Railsback and Joe Pantoliano. In one of the subplots, Natalie's character, Karen Holmes, has an ongoing affair with Sgt. Milt Warden, played by Devane, whose commanding officer is Karen's husband in the movie. Because of this subplot, there were a number of lovemaking scenes featuring Natalie and Devane.

A great deal of the production was shot in Hawaii and Wagner accompanied Natalie to Hawaii on this part of the filming. So did their friend Mart Crowley and his partner.

One evening in the hotel room, after several of the romantic scenes had been filmed, an intoxicated Wagner, who told Lambert that Natalie was "swishing her tail" at Devane, accused Natalie of having an affair with her costar. As the accusations escalated, Lambert wrote in his book Wagner ran to a terrace balcony screaming Devane was "fucking his wife," and claimed he was going to jump and kill himself. Crowley and others pulled him back into the hotel room.

When she returned from Hawaii, Natalie appeared in two films before beginning *The Memory of Eva Ryker*. During its filming, part of Natalie's entourage was hairstylist Ginger Blymyer, known to her friends as "Sugar." Blymyer, who credits Natalie with jump-starting her career, worked with Natalie in several films over the course of their 17-year relationship and they became good friends. Natalie trusted Sugar, and Sugar loved the famous actress.

Remarkably, Blymyer, a perfect prosecution witness, has never been interviewed by LASD investigators. Articulate, smart and a close friend of the victim, what better witness than a likable hairdresser?

Blymyer was very gracious and spent a good deal of time going over sections of her book with my research assistant Jan, answering questions I had prepared in advance. Blymyer recounted that in October 1979 she got a call to work with Natalie in *Eva Ryker*. When

Figure 37: Hairstylist Ginger "Sugar" Blymyer with Natalie in 1966 on the set of the film
This Property Is Condemned (Courtesy of Ginger Blymyer)

they got together, Natalie told Blymyer about her life since they had last visited. "Natalie adored [her] kids and loved being a mother. They were always her first priority," Blymyer wrote in her memoir.

During the filming of *Eva Ryker*, Blymyer explained in her book she "felt so close to her in that movie. We talked about our lives and our mutual distress. She was under a lot of stress…home stress." Blymyer related to Jan that Natalie was frustrated over Wagner's drinking…"That it had been getting worse and had gotten out of hand."

According to Blymyer's memoir, in which she confirmed its accuracy to Jan, Natalie confided in her because the hairstylist was going through the same thing. "My husband eventually sobered up. Mr. Wagner did not. However, he was always nice to me and seemed to be nice to Natalie. He was often unreasonable when drinking. He didn't want her doing plays or TV shows or other projects. Natalie wanted to do new things but he didn't support her in that."

Blymyer also shared further about Natalie's therapy sessions. "Natalie said she had learned in therapy you have to be firm with alcoholics. That was the reason, she said, that she locked the liquor cabinet when her daddy was alive and came to their house. …. And she said she once paid for her friend to get therapy for his drinking. That was after she told him to stay away until he got a grip on his problems." The friend was Mart Crowley.

Blymyer's statements also tied in perfectly with a revelation in Lambert's book from Wagner's stepson Josh Donen, who was staying with Natalie while Wagner was on location in Hawaii. Lambert quoted Donen as saying, "jealousy made RJ drink too much. A very kind and thoughtful man, but his demons came out when he was drunk."

This motive evidence was available to the detectives in 2011. But, astonishingly, it was overlooked.

〰〰〰〰〰

During my meticulous examination of the 1981 sheriff's file, I was stunned to find two phone messages containing potentially explosive motive evidence connected with Natalie's location shooting in Raleigh-Durham. Natalie was filming *Brainstorm* in the charming twin cities beginning in September 1981. As noted earlier, after a short period of location shooting, rumors started flying in Hollywood that Natalie and Walken were having an affair.

The timeline revealed auditions for *Brainstorm* local extras took place in Raleigh-Durham on September 2, 1981, and Natalie arrived with movie producer John Foreman on September 15.

She checked into the upscale Governor's Inn Hotel and was assigned its finest room, the Governor's Suite. After an appearance by the film's lead stars at a press conference with Gov. Jim Hunt, the crew started shooting on September 28. Natalie flew home for daughter Natasha's birthday on September 29 and immediately returned to North Carolina. The affair rumors began during the first two weeks of October.

Wagner admitted that concerned about the rumor, he flew to Raleigh to determine if it was true. When he returned, he claimed he was satisfied Natalie was not having an affair with Walken. But I'm confident—very confident— Wagner *wasn't* convinced there was no affair. Here's why.

On Sunday, December 6, 1981, exactly one week after Natalie drowned, a person identified in a Homicide Bureau phone message as Carolyn O'Brien from North Carolina called Detective Rasure at the Los Angeles County Sheriff's Department at 11:10 p.m. Eastern Time. There were several Durham and local newspapers with front-page Associated Press articles quoting Rasure and Dr. Noguchi, among others. From those stories, O'Brien would have in all likelihood learned Rasure was the lead detective on Natalie's case.

On the message slip, Deputy Charles G. Guenther entered O'Brien's name, a North Carolina phone number, the date, the local

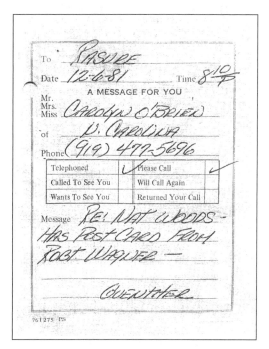

Figure 38: Message of the phone call to Detective Rasure from Carolyn O'Brien (Los Angeles County Sheriff's Department)

time (8:10 p.m.) and a short message. "RE: NAT WOODS—HAS POSTCARD FROM ROBT. WAGNER." But that wasn't all.

I'll address O'Brien in more detail shortly, but first I want to discuss another phone message in the official file.

The day of Natalie's funeral, December 1, 1981, a person who identified himself as Ronald Woods called the Homicide Bureau at 2:08 p.m. local time. The number left by Woods was a local number. The message read, "RES OF ING—FROM GUY IN N. CAR," followed by a phone number, name: "DANNY TOLER," location: "REIDSVILLE, N.C.," and the notation: "CALLED COLLECT."

There's no evidence in the file Rasure called Ronald Woods or Danny Toler, but there really wouldn't be if my educated theory is correct.

With the help of a former homicide detective, we deduced that "RES OF ING" stood for "resident of Inglewood," and based on our experience, we found it reasonable to conclude Woods had some sort of connection with law enforcement in California. Furthermore, only confidential informants (CI) call law enforcement officers collect. The reason is simple. A CI knows he can and his call will be accepted. It looked like a law enforcement officer in North Carolina told Toler, who had information about Natalie's case, to call someone in law enforcement in Inglewood because the officer trusted that person to get a message to Rasure.

But, what could Danny Toler of Reidsville, North Carolina—a town of less than 10,000 people located 90 miles from Raleigh-Durham—know about film star Natalie Wood's death investigation? I knew one thing—it was important enough for Ronald Woods to accept Toler's collect call and then for Woods to call Rasure. *So, why are there no notes of a call from Rasure to Woods or Toler?*

Rasure's handwritten file notes associated with his return call to Carolyn O'Brien answered the question for me.

After studying Rasure's notes (see *Figures 39* and *40*, next two pages), I gleaned these key points:

- ♦ Carolyn O'Brien had a friend named Mary Ann who staffed the front desk at the Governor's Inn.

- ♦ Mary Ann stated Robert Wagner sent a threatening postcard, and Mary Ann read it.

- ♦ Wagner was jealous of Natalie and Walken and kept tabs on her.

- ♦ Wagner came to the hotel and got in a fight with Natalie at the restaurant.

- ♦ Wagner called Natalie often, one time every 10 minutes.

- ♦ Mary Ann may have remarked that Wagner was badgering Natalie.

There was no indication Rasure or any other detective followed the lead, by going to North Carolina and attempting to make contact with Carolyn O'Brien or locate "Mary Ann." There was also nothing in Rasure's 22-page official report about O'Brien, Toler, Mary Ann or North Carolina. But the scribble at the end of his notes from the conversation with O'Brien led me to believe Rasure pondered the gravity of what he heard during the return call.

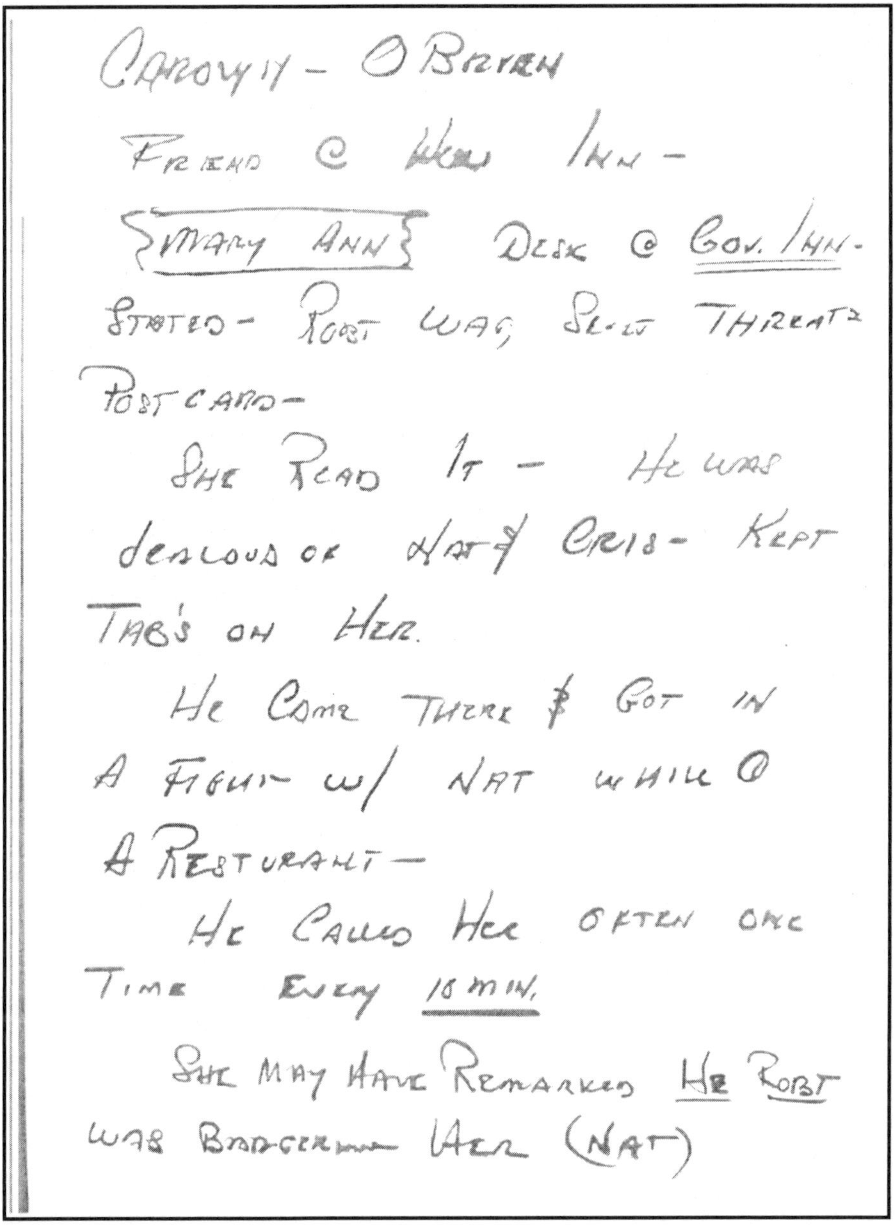

Carolyn - O'Brien

Friend @ ____ Inn -

{Mary Ann} Desk @ Gov. Inn.

Stated - Robt was, Sent threats

Post card -

She Read It - He was

jealous of Nat & Cris - Kept

Tabs on Her.

He came there & got in

a fight w/ Nat while @

a Resturant -

He called Her often one

time every 15 min.

She may have remarked He Robt

was badgering Her (Nat)

Figure 39: First page of Detective Rasure's notes from his phone conversation with Carolyn O'Brien (Los Angeles County Sheriff's Department)

I was awestruck by this information right under the nose of the 2011 detectives. My mind was racing over the value of this evidence, but first, we needed confirmation that witnesses could corroborate the notes and what I believed transpired at the luxury hotel.

From the notes, it was reasonable to believe Wagner was angry that Natalie was in North Carolina with her leading man. Having to deal with rumors of an affair that were taking hold like a California wildfire, Wagner intended to do something about it.

First, the O'Brien notes suggested Wagner forged a relationship with a desk clerk, and perhaps others at the Governor's Inn, to spy on Natalie and Walken. Next, in all probability, with the help of his friend Sinatra, Wagner made inquiries of people who could intimidate or frighten Natalie, Walken or both. Keep in mind intimidation wouldn't necessarily mean threatening physical harm. It could mean making subtle threats of violence or other criminal activity. Perhaps something that could harm Walken's career or frighten him into distancing himself from Natalie.

In the past, according to Kelley's book, Sinatra had done something similar for Joe DiMaggio when he tried to get dirt on Marilyn Monroe during the couple's contentious divorce. If it was good enough for Joe, it was good enough for Wagner. In my opinion, that was the reason for the collect call from Danny Toler to Ronald Woods. Toler knew something about Wagner's efforts in North Carolina, and he was trying to get the information to Rasure. Of course, this effort would not have been altruistic on Toler's part. It's common practice to pay CIs for this type of information. And, Toler would undoubtedly think this information deserved a big payday, inasmuch as it involved Natalie Wood.

With the efforts of two retired homicide detectives, two private investigators and three research assistants over a period of two years, here's what I learned about the two mystery witnesses after four decades.

The phone number left in the Ronald Woods message was traced to Emma C. Toler, the mother of Danny Lee Toler, who died in 1989. Danny Lee was 63 years old by the time we

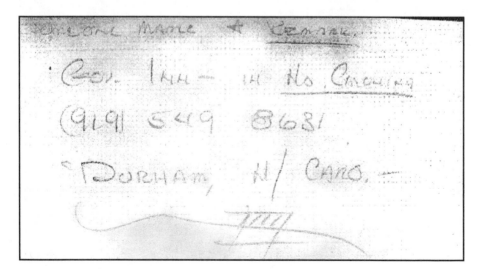

Figure 40: Second page of Detective Rasure's notes from his phone conversation with Carolyn O'Brien (Los Angeles County Sheriff's Department)

started our search, making him 28 in 1981. According to our criminal background check, Danny Lee had a healthy criminal record with arrests for driving while impaired (DWI), bad check writing, threatening phone calls, assault with a deadly weapon, possession of Schedule II narcotics, and breaking and entering, among others. He served time on some of them, and a relative we tracked down confirmed Danny Lee "had been in trouble in the past."

This is precisely the type of person who gets targeted by law enforcement to become a CI. In exchange for information on others, the confidential informant gets a break on his criminal malfeasance, money or both. But my excitement over Toler was short-lived. The relative said Danny Lee had moved and was "possibly committed to a mental institution."

It was a frustrating blow, but I wanted to confirm whether Danny Lee was so incompetent as to be unable to tell us why a small-town boy from Reidsville could have information for a LASD detective investigating the mysterious death of an international film star. And why he chose Ronald Woods as his emissary. With additional information from relatives, we located a likely and suitable facility, serving those with mental illness, in Rockingham County, North Carolina. But with the receptionist citing HIPAA privacy and security provisions, my investigator never got past the check-in desk. It was August 2018, and I was out of ideas on Danny Lee.

So, I decided to focus my attention on Ronald Woods. There were dozens of men by that name in California and other parts of the country. Because I was confident our subject was affiliated with law enforcement in 1981, we directed our attention to retired law enforcement officers in the Inglewood area. One of my private detectives struck pay dirt. He found an article about a retired police lieutenant, Ron Wood, who had sued Inglewood for reverse discrimination in 2002. He was 55 years old at the time of his successful jury award, making him 70 at the time of our search and 34 in 1981. His name was spelled "Wood" without the "s" at the end as it was written on the message slip, but it seemed like too much of a coincidence not to be the person we were looking for.

I struggled for months trying to come up with a good address. Retired law enforcement officers are very careful about keeping information like that private, and for good reason. Furthermore, personnel records are not subject to release under the law as public records in California. In the end, my efforts to contact Ron Wood were unsuccessful.

However, even though I was unable to completely solve the mystery of Ronald Woods and Danny Lee Toler, I did establish what I believe to be a connection between the Woods/Toler call and the Carolyn O'Brien call.

~~~~~~~~~

At the outset, here's what my experience told me about the call from O'Brien and the notes from the return call by Detective Rasure. First, and foremost, it was 11:10 Sunday night in North Carolina, exactly one week after Natalie's death and nearly the exact same time of day Natalie drowned. O'Brien would have known that from the North Carolina newspaper accounts.

North Carolina is part of the "Bible Belt," the region of the country in which evangelical Protestantism plays a vigorous role in society. Surely O'Brien knew Rasure wouldn't be in his LA office on Sunday at 8:10 p.m. Pacific Time. But I believe something was bothering O'Brien. Something she knew created a moral, if not legal, obligation to report. Something so damning in Natalie's case it took a week for her to work up the courage to call the Homicide Bureau. And it was Sunday, a day when many reflect on what's wrong in the world and what's right in their hearts. So, the devoutly religious Carolyn O'Brien called when she could no longer deny doing what was right.

Furthermore, O'Brien told the deputy who answered that she possessed something from Robert Wagner—a postcard. At least, that's all the deputy wrote. In my opinion, having a postcard from Robert Wagner would have hardly qualified to get Rasure's attention. Payne and Wayne couldn't get his attention when they reported hearing screams for help near *Splendour* in the middle of the night, so O'Brien had to have told the deputy something more. Something more problematic for Rasure that ran counter to closing Natalie's case as an accident. So, Rasure called O'Brien, fearing another front-page article similar to Wayne's if he didn't.

Finally, the evidence that "threats" and "jealousy"—as well as a confrontation, obsessiveness and "badgering" involving Natalie and Wagner—was *documented*. The notes read: "Robt Wag Sent Threats Postcard—She Read It." Knowing the message O'Brien left said she "has postcard" from Wagner, I'm of the opinion that meant she possessed it and likely read it aloud to Rasure. It would stretch credulity to believe Rasure didn't question O'Brien as she read this damning information.

Rasure's notes contained no date, but based on their placement in the file with other telephone messages, the return call appeared to have been made Monday, December 7, 1981. Yet, there was nothing else in the file about North Carolina. No follow-up. Nothing. Rasure's official report is dated December 11, 1981, giving Rasure plenty of time to include something about his conversation with O'Brien. But it didn't happen.

You might be asking yourself about now, *If there was a cover-up, why didn't Rasure throw away his Carolyn O'Brien notes?* I asked myself that question as well. The answer is, *I don't know.* Maybe he hesitated in throwing them away because O'Brien might have tape-recorded the conversation and would have proof she called. However, with the notes in the file, Rasure could claim he didn't believe her if confronted later. We know he had no qualms about doing that, and more, with witnesses who got in the way of his official conclusion of accident in Natalie's case.

∽∽∽∽∽∽∽∽∽

So, we began our search in earnest for O'Brien and the "Mary Ann" mentioned in the telephone message. We started with the person who took the message, Deputy Guenther. I felt if we could find him, perhaps he would tell us more about the message. Unfortunately, Deputy Guenther passed away on August 2, 2014. His death pushed the death count to 13 key witnesses lost due to the passage of time. But he was available in 2011.

The callback number left by O'Brien was a Durham, North Carolina residential number. We traced the number to numerous individuals, and one business, but no affiliations were found with any person named O'Brien. Of course, we had no idea if the caller was going by the same name. And we didn't know if O'Brien was a married name in 1981 or if she still lived in North Carolina. The area code and prefix of the callback number were most predominately found in the 27705 ZIP code area of Durham. Now, we knew the number wasn't fictitious and the call wasn't made from another city.

Next, by using the 1981 City Directory for Durham, we confirmed that the second number O'Brien gave Rasure was a 1981 number for the Governor's Inn Hotel at Research Triangle Park. The nonprofit Research Triangle Institute is headquartered in the Park and served as the location for some *Brainstorm* filming.

The Governor's Inn opened its doors in 1972. Sandra Thomas Sailer was head of house-keeping for 15 years. When Jan contacted her in 2018, Sailer happily reminisced for hours about the 128-room hotel, which had expanded to 203 rooms before it closed in 2013.

"Very classy" was the only way to describe the hotel, according to Sailer.

After opening, the Governor's Inn quickly became well known for its professionally de-signed golf course, which hosted many famous golf tournaments over the years. And the "renowned" Golden Nugget Supper Club, on the third floor of the hotel, was open 7 p.m. to 3 a.m. nightly. With its live entertainment, the club was "a very popular" night spot for hotel guests and the public. As for the Governor's Suite, Sailer had the details etched into her mind: "It was actually one huge room with a beautiful mahogany king-size, four-poster bed being the focal point."

Karl H. Lack was hired as the Governor's Inn first general manager. Lack managed the Governor's Inn for nearly 18 years. Jan located the 66-year-old's contact information and made a cold call. When Jan reached Lack, she explained the reason for her call and he enthusiastically confirmed he was manager of the hotel in 1981. Launching right into the subject of Natalie Wood, Lack acknowledged, "Yeah, she was there with that guy in the movie with her…that Walken guy, the director, I forget his name, and the crew were all there for two or three weeks."

After denying knowledge of a postcard from Robert Wagner, Lack volunteered there was "a lot of partying going on with that bunch." And Natalie spent a lot of time with Walken, "everybody knew what was going on there." He then added, "Wagner visited her a *couple of times* while she was there." When Jan said, "Yeah, I hear they had a big argument in a restaurant," Lack laughed and confirmed that event. "Yes…that was very true…heard other people had to calm him down," he said. "I wasn't a partyer, so I wasn't around for any of that stuff."

Jan continued by commenting, "I heard he also called her often, one time about every 10 minutes." Lack replied he definitely remembered that. He then volunteered, "Oh yeah! Robert was always checking up on her because he knew there was a lot of drinking going on and thought she was having a fling with Walken."

After that exchange, Lack said his resident manager, Ron Hunter, would probably have more information "because he had more contact with the guests." He shared Hunter's current place of employment.

While the iron was hot, Jan called Hunter. Hunter said he didn't remember a front desk clerk named Mary Ann. But when Jan said to him, "I heard that Wagner visited Natalie a couple of times," Hunter confirmed that Wagner had been at the hotel. Then Hunter vol-unteered, "*He was there the weekend before she died.* When I heard about it [her death], I couldn't believe it—he was just here!"

To double-check, Jan repeated, "He was there the weekend before she died? He was there toward the end of November?"

Hunter replied, "Yes, the weekend before she died." Hunter also confirmed the argu-ment between Natalie and Wagner at the Golden Nugget Supper Club.

Wagner visited Natalie the first time when they were filming *Brainstorm's* wedding scenes.

The Chronicle, a Duke University paper, reported the scenes were shot at Duke Gardens on October 14. Three days later, Natalie, her costars, director and crew left Durham for nearby Pinehurst for several days of shooting, and Natalie stayed at the famous Pinehurst Hotel, according to Raleigh's *The News and Observer.* The director finished shooting the North Carolina location scenes the evening of October 27, 1981.

After talking with Hunter, Jan made a follow-up call to Lack because I had some specific questions for him. Lack confirmed the public argument between Natalie and Wagner took place in the hotel's supper club. Jan asked Lack if Walken was present during the argument and Lack responded, "Yes, she and Walken were together in the restaurant. It was a surprise all right!"

At my request, Jan told Lack I was going to be in the area and asked if he would meet with me. He said he would be happy to, but it turned out to be a mistake asking him. After the Christmas holidays, I emailed Lack to set up a time to talk to him in person. I received the following reply: "I must respectfully decline due to possible liability litigation. Respectfully Yours, Karl Lack." Over 35 years after Natalie's death, the fear factor had raised its ugly head in Natalie's case once again.

But in a subsequent call to Hunter, Jan managed to clear up the "Mary Ann" question. It turned out a "Mary Ann" was indeed working the hotel's front desk in November 1981. Hunter told Jan that Mary Ann was a "young college girl" who only worked there about a year. In response to a final question about him seeing Natalie at the hotel, Hunter said, "They were all drinking and just having a good time."

The significance of Jan's conversations with Lack and Hunter established one unshakable fact. O'Brien's telephone call was no hoax. Three things in the note were confirmed by two credible witnesses. First, a young Mary Ann did, in fact, work the front desk of the Governor's Inn when Natalie was there. Next, there was an argument in the hotel restaurant and, finally, Wagner called Natalie repeatedly, once "every 10 minutes." O'Brien could not have known that without a hotel employee telling her. Only an insider could have known about Wagner's calls to the hotel.

But, Jan wasn't done with this long-standing mystery. She located Marian Cheshire, the hotel's former reservations manager, in Durham and learned Marian and Mary Ann were "still friends." Cheshire said Mary Ann, who never married, currently lived in Dillsboro, North Carolina, and Jan talked Cheshire out of Mary Ann's current phone number.

Researching, Jan determined the phone number was registered to Gladys Clark, who Jan believed was Mary Ann's mother. She also discovered Mary Ann was born in 1959, making her 22 in 1981. Our Mary Ann subject was the perfect age to be dazzled by a handsome movie and television star. So, Jan called the number and left several messages. Her calls went unanswered.

Digging further, Jan was able to confirm Gladys Clark did, in fact, live in Dillsboro. With that information, Jan ran a background check and located her address. We didn't know if Mary Ann was living there, but I was determined to find out.

෬෬෬෬෬෬

With the holidays on the horizon, I booked a ticket to Raleigh-Durham and stayed at Ron Hunter's place of business. Hunter, a self-made man, worked for the Governor's Inn from the day it opened until the day it closed—41 years. "When it closed, it was like losing my right arm," Hunter later told me.

During my interview with this crisp, sharp-looking gentleman, Hunter told me he spent the first 17 years or so as a waiter and unofficial "resident manager" at the hotel. He officially became the hotel's assistant manager in 1982 and its general manager in 1995. He said the turnover was pretty regular for the Golden Nugget waitstaff, so he didn't remember particular employee names. Since he appeared to be a hands-on manager, I thought that statement strange, but it had been a long time ago.

Hunter recalled working the day Natalie arrived. He said *Brainstorm* costars Louise Fletcher, Cliff Robertson and Christopher Walken also stayed at the hotel and all of them ate frequently in the supper club. Then we discussed the matter of Wagner's visits and Hunter told me, "I only recall one [Wagner] visit" and that was "the weekend prior to her death."

Hunter was adamant, but I sensed a little hesitation in his delivery. My gut told me he had talked to Lack and was now becoming nervous about what he had told Jan and now me. His statements to me were seemingly inconsistent with his statements to Jan about two trips. I knew Jan hadn't misunderstood him. Without talking to each other, however, Lack and Hunter had told consistent stories about the same unforgettable events.

My suspicions about Lack talking with Hunter were confirmed after I returned to Arkansas. Several emails to Hunter about employee names went unreturned. Jan called and her calls went unanswered, even after leaving phone messages. At this point, we had now been shut out by two former high-ranking Governor's Inn employees. But the stonewalling didn't end there.

∽∾∽∾∽∾∽∾

After meeting with Hunter, I decided to track down Marian Cheshire. Arriving unannounced, I rang the front doorbell. Cheshire came out of the carport door behind me, I turned around and greeted her, saying, "Hello, I'm Sam Perroni. I was wondering if you might be willing to visit with me for a couple of minutes." I could tell she was nervous and surprised to see me.

Backing away, Cheshire replied, "Mr. Perroni, I can tell you what I know, and that's really all I can tell you. She stayed there and Robert Wagner came to visit. I know nothing."

Walking to the car, I said, "OK, I want you to do me a favor. I want you to call Mary Ann and tell her I've got something I want to ask her."

Cheshire hesitated, then said, "I'll give her a call and tell her that. But she is a very private individual. She lives six to seven hours away from here. She's not in town. She has Jan's number." Now we knew Mary Ann had been getting Jan's messages.

Keep in mind, Cheshire had no idea what I wanted to talk to Mary Ann about. Yet, after freely talking to Jan, she was now guarding Mary Ann's privacy. I strongly suspected she knew something. That she and Mary Ann had talked about something that happened at the Governor's Inn involving Mary Ann, and Mary Ann didn't want to talk about it.

∽∾∽∾∽∾∽∾

For my attempt to interview Mary Ann, I enlisted the help of a former homicide detective in the area who had started her own private detective business. I thought having an experienced female beside me might make Mary Ann feel more at ease. I also asked her to help me with Danny Toler.

My driver escorted us to Dillsboro and we quickly located the residence of Gladys Clark. We walked to the front door of the small, well-appointed home. As I knocked on the frame of the storm door, I saw someone duck out of sight. After a few seconds, an elderly female with a serious expression opened the door. I could see another woman behind her holding her hands up in a defensive position and pacing back and forth in the living area of the home. I had interviewed hundreds of witnesses in my career, but I'd never seen anyone who acted more defensive. It instantly convinced me I had the right person.

I was standing on the doorstep when Mary Ann walked toward me shielding herself with the elderly female.

> **S.P.:** Are you Mary Ann Clark?
>
> **Mary Ann:** Yes.
>
> **S.P.:** I'm Sam Perroni. I was wondering if I might be able to spend a few minutes with you and visit about your time working at the Governor's Inn.
>
> **Mary Ann:** I don't have any knowledge or any information. I don't.
>
> **S.P.:** We won't be very long if you will let us come in and sit down and let me show you a couple of things and tell you why I've come all this way.
>
> **Mary Ann:** I don't have any knowledge. I can't help you. I am not interested in what you all are doing. I'm sorry…we didn't know you were coming. I'm on a project right now.
>
> **S.P.:** We can come back in a little while.
>
> **Mary Ann:** No. I'm making myself clear, and you're not hearing me. I don't know anything. You're kind of barking up the wrong tree. That was so long ago.
>
> **S.P.:** I know, but…
>
> **Mary Ann:** But what do you not understand?
>
> **S.P.:** I wanted to know if you knew a lady by the name of Carolyn O'Brien.
>
> **Mary Ann:** No. No.
>
> **S.P.:** If you will let me show you something…
>
> **Mary Ann:** No. I'm not interested in it. I feel sorry it happened to her.

Mary Ann's last sentence struck a nerve with me. There was a touch of guilt in her expression of sympathy. Furthermore, in my experience, a witness claiming not to know about something someone hasn't explained is generally withholding information.

Without warning, my investigator snatched Rasure's notes from my folio and began reading them while Mary Ann repeatedly claimed no knowledge and struggled to get her to stop. In the end, Mary Ann admitted she worked at the front desk, there were no other Mary Anns working there and she had just graduated from college when she started at the hotel job.

We both left there believing Mary Ann wasn't being completely honest with us, but we had no way of exploring things further. A California prosecutor could employ a process to obtain a sworn deposition from Mary Ann in North Carolina. The process of being under oath and subject to the penalties of perjury will many times result in witnesses coming clean. But I had no such process, so there were no other options for me. Instead, I switched my focus to Carolyn O'Brien.

༄༅༄༅༄༅༄

The search for the elusive Carolyn O'Brien had me convinced we should be looking for a married Caucasian female between 65 and 70 years old who had a strong religious affiliation as well as connections with Research Triangle Institute. We searched for months trying to identify females who fit that description.

Up to that point, the O'Brien ordeal had been very discouraging, and I was about to give up when a prospect was located by Linda Hudson, a former Little Rock police officer I've known for many years.

A Facebook page for a female reflected all the right profile attributes. Born in 1950, making her 31 years old when Natalie drowned, she was married and living in Raleigh in 1981. Educated at the Baptist Women's University—now Meredith College—in Raleigh in the 1970s, she retired from Research Triangle Institute, affiliated with the Governor's Inn.

It would have been a monumental coincidence for all of the pieces to fall together— both from the note's details and O'Brien's personal characteristics and background—and this person *not* be our subject. So, in January 2018, two years after we had first started looking for her and almost 37 years after Natalie's death, I sent Linda's husband, Tommy, to Raleigh to talk to Carolyn O'Brien.

Mr. O'Brien answered the residence front door. Tommy identified himself, and Mr. O'Brien "graciously" invited him in. A short time later, Carolyn O'Brien entered the room, looking perplexed. After Tommy showed her the LASD phone message, he asked if she knew anyone named Mary Ann. "Sir, I don't know anything about this. You've got the wrong Carolyn O'Brien," she said, adding she was never associated with the number on the message slip.

Tommy's interviewed thousands of witnesses, including a good many bald-faced liars. He knows how to size people up and he believed Mrs. O'Brien. But I wasn't convinced. I don't believe in multiple connecting coincidences. To me, if it looks like a duck and quacks like a duck, it's most likely a duck. If this was an elaborate hoax to distract Rasure from closing Natalie's case, the female schemer must have been as shrewd as Matty Walker, the "relentless" character in the neo-noir thriller *Body Heat*.

Yet, notwithstanding the last chapter of Carolyn O'Brien, several things were made clear through my efforts to locate O'Brien and Mary Ann. According to credible witnesses and documents as well as Wagner's own admissions, Wagner traveled to North Carolina because of rumors of an affair between Natalie and Walken in mid-October. He said in *Pieces*, "*I chose not to confront her with my feelings* [emphasis added]. I flew back to my series, and Natalie continued production on *Brainstorm*."

But the reasonable inferences suggest he did, in fact, confront her during his first trip to North Carolina. He got in a "fight" with Natalie in the Golden Nugget Supper Club after his surprise visit. The "big argument" was so intense, people had to "calm him down." Finally, when Wagner was not at the hotel, he was "badgering" Natalie with repeated phone calls, one time "every 10 minutes."

⌁⌁⌁⌁⌁⌁

But it's Wagner's second trip that adds even more fuel to the jealousy fire. As I have reported, at the same time Natalie was in Los Angeles working on *Brainstorm*, Wagner was in Hawaii working on *Hart to Hart*. His location shooting was between November 2 and 12, 1981, at the Hyatt Regency Maui.

According to Powers in *One from the Hart*, the cast returned to LA from Hawaii on Thursday, November 12, and began shooting in Los Angeles the following day, Friday, November 13. The dates are firmly recalled by Powers due to the discovery of her boyfriend William Holden's body on Monday, November 16, and the farewell gathering she hosted for him at her home November 22. There's no evidence the cast returned to Hawaii at any time after November 12. Moreover, according to Lana Wood, a former producer's assistant, cast members wouldn't be in Hawaii the weekend before Thanksgiving because "they go on hiatus for the holidays" and the crew overtime is prohibitive.

Yet, in *Natalie Wood: A Life*, Wagner told Lambert, after admitting it crossed his mind that his wife and Walken "were having an affair," that he was on location shooting a *Hart to Hart* episode in Hawaii the weekend before Natalie's death (Friday, November 20, through Sunday, November 22). Then Lambert added this: "He was supposed to take Natalie to dinner to Roddy [McDowall]'s house, but because he [Wagner] was out of town, she took *Walken* instead."

I've never been able to confirm Lambert's supplemental statement about Natalie attending a party at McDowall's home with Walken. It certainly didn't sound like Natalie to take Walken in her husband's place, but McDowall and Lambert are deceased, and Walken and Wagner aren't talking. I don't know where Lambert got his information, and without knowing whether there was actually a party at McDowall's that weekend and who was there, I was stumped. When I asked Lana about that passage, she laughed and said, "Bullshit. She wouldn't do anything like that. She'd been in therapy too many years."

There was no mistaking the fact, however, that Wagner wasn't in Hawaii shooting *Hart to Hart* the weekend before Natalie's death. *So, if he wasn't in Los Angeles, where was he?* According to the managerial staff at the Governor's Inn, Wagner was in North Carolina. And I believe the circumstantial evidence pointed to Wagner, in advance of the Catalina trip with Walken and Natalie, meeting with the people he enlisted in North Carolina who kept tabs on Natalie, as Rasure's notes about his conversation with Carolyn O'Brien reflected. That could have included private detectives, employees or people of questionable repute.

By 2011, LASD detectives not only had Wagner's copious false, misleading and incriminating admissions that I have reviewed, they also had the following questionable actions:

1. Wagner's 2-1/4-hour delay in calling attention to Natalie's disappearance.

2. Wagner's efforts to steer searchers away from *Splendour* and the open sea and instead toward the shore, pier and cove moorings.

3. Wagner's calls from *Splendour* to Crowley and his lawyer before Natalie's body was found.

4. Wagner's failure to call his children when Natalie's body was found.

5. Wagner's departure from Catalina Island without identifying Natalie's body.

6. Wagner becoming "quite shook" when the investigators wanted to interview him yet able to talk to Kroll and Eaker without any reported problems.

7. Wagner telling Davern he wasn't going to Natalie's funeral.

8. Wagner, during his claimed "catatonic" state, calling Dr. Choi to expedite Natalie's autopsy.

9. Wagner, during his catatonic state, signing a Petition to Probate Natalie's lucrative estate on the day of her funeral.

10. Wagner's 45-minute visit with St. John during his claimed catatonic state.

11. Wagner's dating of St. John, his future third wife, within two months of Natalie's death.

My observations amount to a listing of the obvious items of bothersome behavior exhibited by Wagner within the first eight weeks of Natalie's death. But only one reasonable conclusion can be formulated. Wagner's actions demonstrated a consciousness of guilt, making out a solid case for the only legitimate suspect in Natalie's death.

CHAPTER 22

summation

THERE'S NO MAN-MADE INSTITUTION I RESPECT MORE THAN A JURY trial. As a prosecutor, I learned early on that sometimes a case cries out for a public airing of legally admissible evidence before an impartial judge and a jury, with the evidence challenged by the greatest engine ever devised for testing the truth—cross-examination. And, personally, I've never seen any case more suited for a jury trial than the death case of Natalie Wood Wagner.

But, since that will never happen, I want you to imagine that you are a juror listening to the prosecutor's closing argument in the second-degree murder case of *People of the State of California v. Robert John Wagner Jr.* As I speak for the prosecution, check me against what you have learned in this book, keeping in mind that Wagner would be cloaked with the presumption of innocence throughout the actual trial, including the summation.

∽∼∽∼∽∼∽

Ladies and gentlemen, the law on murder with malice aforethought, circumstantial evidence and consciousness of guilt in California is not unique. Its foundation is based on nearly 250 years of cases across the United States that decided and developed the law for one reason—to help jurors speak the truth through their verdict.

At the end of a criminal case, the judge instructs the jury on the law. Armed with those instructions, jurors are asked to apply the law to the facts to arrive at their verdict. A juror simply can't make an honest judgment about a criminal case without understanding the law. So, I suppose it could reasonably be said that jury instructions are like a blueprint, a blueprint for justice. A guide to help ordinary citizens determine the truth as they make their way through the evidence.

But, *how do you use the blueprint?* To answer this question, jurors should ask themselves this: *Who has the burden of proof? How must the party with that burden prove the case? What must be proved by the party who has the burden of proof?*

The prosecution has the burden of proof in a second-degree murder case. And a defendant's presumption of innocence requires proof of the defendant's guilt beyond a reasonable doubt. *What is "beyond a reasonable doubt"?* Following established law, the blueprint says:

> Beyond a reasonable doubt means proof that leaves you [a juror] with an abiding conviction that a charge is true. But the evidence the People present does not need to eliminate all possible doubt. Because everything in life is open to some possible or imaginary doubt.

With that instruction, the law recognizes that nothing can be proved beyond all possible doubt. *Nothing.* So, courts in their wisdom created a *reasonable* burden for the prosecution.

As for what kind of proof can be used, the blueprint says:

> There are two types of evidence which you may use to properly find a
> person guilty of a crime. One is direct evidence—such as the testimony
> of an eyewitness. The other is circumstantial evidence—the proof of a
> chain of circumstances pointing to the commission of the offense.

For example, if a person sees a man push his wife off a cliff to her death, that's direct evidence. But, if the same man isn't seen pushing the wife, but has a $5 million life insurance policy on her, a secret girlfriend and is seen speeding away from the area shortly after witnesses watch her tumble to her death, you could reasonably conclude that he pushed her. That's circumstantial evidence.

A "chain of circumstances pointing to the commission" of a murder. A logical inference. "A deduction of fact that may logically and reasonably be drawn from another fact or group of facts established by the evidence." And, it's not an all or nothing proposition. You can use both direct evidence (what people saw or heard) and circumstantial evidence (logical inferences) in combination to prove guilt.

That very simply means this to Natalie's case: A prosecutor doesn't need to have a witness who saw Robert Wagner push Natalie Wood into the Pacific Ocean to establish guilt.

The prosecution also has the burden of proving three elements to establish the offense of murder. "First, that a human being was killed by another. Second, that the killing was unlawful, and third, that the killing was done with malice aforethought."

In Natalie's case, the blueprint tells you that "malice may be either express or implied." Malice "is express when there is a manifested intention to unlawfully kill a human being." As an example, Wagner admitted in his memoir that he wanted to kill Warren Beatty with a gun. If Wagner had killed Beatty, the homicide would have been committed with express malice aforethought.

But the blueprint also recognizes that a prosecutor can't always prove an accused's expressed intention to kill. So, the law provides that "malice aforethought is implied when the killing resulted from an intentional act—where the natural consequences of the act are dangerous to human life and the act was deliberately performed with conscious disregard for human life."

That means this, if you should find from the evidence that a screaming, physical fight between Wagner and Natalie on the back deck of *Splendour* was the cause of Natalie ending up in the ocean, and Wagner, an accomplished swimmer and diver, knowingly allowed her—when he knew she couldn't swim—to drift away from the yacht and drown, he killed her with malice aforethought, just as sure as if he had put a gun to her head. That would be so, because the natural consequences of Wagner's actions were dangerous to Natalie's life, and the act—knowingly causing her to fall into the water and failing to provide assistance—was deliberately performed with conscious disregard for her survival.

Moreover, "the word *aforethought* does not imply deliberation or the lapse of considerable time and does not require any ill will or hatred of the person killed." Simply put, you can formulate an intention to kill within seconds, and you can love the person and still have the mental state necessary to be guilty of murder.

What are the facts? Let's begin with Natalie, a petite woman at 5-foot-2 and 115 pounds, she would have been easy to push around. Her forearm measured less than 10 inches, and she had an inseam less than 26 inches. And, Natalie, who was terrified of dark ocean water, would quiver and shake in even the safest water scene environments. That much about her is completely undebatable.

Lana said Natalie was always "turned out" when she was in public, never going out without her left wrist covered. Natalie was right-handed, and the coroner's report noted injuries on the top of her right hand and the underside of her right forearm, which she would instinctively use to defend herself. And, finally, we know that when Natalie decided to do something, it was done. That is also beyond controversy.

By all accounts, Natalie was a serious professional actress who lived for quality work and performances. But we know that after her second marriage to Wagner and a second child, Courtney, she immersed herself in motherhood, causing her work to lose velocity. However, after her father passed away and her girls began to get older, she longed to return to the profession that was her life. And, Natalie pursued nothing halfway.

In the late '70s, Natalie began making film and TV movies and even agreed to star in a stage play, *Anastasia,* that was to begin rehearsals a few weeks after her death. She took a big risk agreeing to perform live in front of an audience—something she had never done before. If it was successful in Los Angeles, the plan was to take *Anastasia* to Broadway in New York.

But I submit Natalie was being held back by a self-centered, possessive and insecure husband who gave her no encouragement and regularly weighed her down with drunken, jealous rants over her male costars. Wagner's drinking was so much of a problem that during *Eva Ryker,* Natalie even shared her dismay with her longtime hairdresser, Ginger Blymyer.

And, what about Wagner and his state of mind after he first wed the 19-year-old Natalie? Because of his resentful envy of her career and suspicious jealousy of her leading men, he demonstrated a pattern of violence, shamelessly admitted to in his memoir where he coolly confessed that after his separation from Natalie, he was prepared to gun down one of Natalie's costars.

It's no wonder Walken has claimed he slept while Natalie and Wagner engaged in a lengthy screaming, cussing, physical fight and why Davern waited 30 years to purportedly tell *all* he knew. Wagner—a powerfully connected potential killer and perhaps now an actual killer—was out there watching and sending subtle messages about what he was capable of doing while associating with violent people who hung around with notorious gangsters. *Who wouldn't be afraid?*

Also, by his own admission, Wagner's first divorce from Natalie totally humiliated him like nothing he had ever experienced. And, I submit to you, the facts and inferences show he wasn't going to let it happen again.

An only child from a well-to-do family, Wagner always wanted to be a big-time actor like his idols Spencer Tracy, Clark Gable and Sir Lawrence Olivier. But by 1981, resolved that films were no longer in his future, Wagner wanted to be like Jonathan Hart in his TV series—suave, debonair, smart, rich and married to a beautiful woman who wanted nothing more than to stay at home or by his side and adore him.

And, Wagner, obsessed over money, had IRS problems and was broke the second time he married Natalie in 1972. Remarkably, he confessed that one of his first thoughts after his second marriage to Natalie was about money: "My money troubles didn't really faze me because I knew that with Natalie at my side, good luck would surely follow."

Sure enough, 11 months into his second marriage to Natalie, this broke, washed-up film actor was given an opportunity to partner with the biggest names in TV—Spelling and Goldberg—all because of his wife's reputation. And that opportunity allowed him to share in the *Charlie's Angels* profit participation that has paid him millions since Natalie's death. Moreover, a year after signing the contract with Spelling and Goldberg, Natalie bought the couple a home in Beverly Hills and 12 months later, the Wagners were cruising to Catalina Island on a recently acquired 60-foot yacht.

And, what was the couple's relative financial worth at the time of Natalie's death?

Natalie's estate, excluding life insurance if she had any, was conservatively valued for tax purposes at nearly $6 million—about $17.8 million today—and her separate, nonmarital property was valued at more than $4 million or nearly $11.9 million today. The only community property of Wagner's that was identified—even though there's an abundance of evidence he agreed to a valuable profit participation for *Hart to Hart*—was appraised by him, under oath, at a little over $19,000—around $58,000 today.

So, what does that tell you? Practically everything Wagner owned or inherited because of Natalie's death was the result of his second marriage to her. But, if she had divorced him a second time, Wagner would have been forced to leave Natalie's home—which he eventually sold for $1,750,000, lose millions of dollars—including Natalie's share of the *Charlie's Angels* profit participation and the two film profit participations she owned outright, and lose Natalie's one-half community property interest in his *Hart to Hart* profit participation. Furthermore, the man with a violent temper and alcohol problem would have more than likely lost custody of Courtney and Natasha, at least.

It would have been bad for him, very, very bad. And, humiliating. Indescribably humiliating.

∾∾∾∾∾∾∾

The law provides that the prosecution doesn't have to prove a defendant had a motive for murder. But, if the prosecutor proves a motive or motives, the blueprint tells you this: "Having a motive may be a factor tending to show that the defendant is guilty."

It's as old as the Bible. Jealousy, envy and financial gain have been motives for murder for thousands of years. "For where jealousy and selfish ambition exist, there will be disorder and every vile practice," and "For the love of money is the root of all evil."

Wagner was violently jealous of Natalie and envious of the careers of both Natalie and Walken. And, he stood to lose tens of millions of dollars and the children if Natalie divorced him a second time. The evidence is almost overwhelming on these points, beginning with Wagner's own admissions about his financial condition before the couple's second marriage. And, then there was the likelihood of another woman, a motive that is substantiated by the logical inferences, Wagner's admissions and his history of infidelity.

At this point, I want to address Dennis Davern, a young, impressionable Navy man who fell into a sailor's dream job as captain of a yacht owned by two of the biggest names in Hollywood. No doubt, the Wagners gave the inexperienced sailor a chance offered to very few.

Rapidly becoming Natalie's personal attendant when they were on the water, he also became the couple's loyal friend. Invited to their home and the famous parties they hosted for their closest friends, he took care of their children and became part of the family. And there was no denying it until he began talking about what happened on the back deck of *Splendour* the evening Natalie died.

Davern was a man who was so trusted by Natalie that he was allowed, without question, to spend the night in a hotel room with her, comfortably sleeping beside the famous star the last night she spent on this earth. He was the young man who would be told to identify Natalie's body, retrieve the yacht and box up the memories of the good times everyone had on the Pacific Ocean with *Splendour* before November 27, 1981.

Now, some consider him a drunk who was hallucinating that night or a profiteer who is boldly fabricating facts for money. But, in doing so, Davern's detractors are ignoring the overwhelming evidence corroborating every *material statement* he has made about what happened that weekend. Sure, Davern made some mistakes, gave some inconsistent statements, and certainly misstated and exaggerated facts. *So, do I think he has told all he knows?* No. But, the core of his story has never changed and has a ring of truth.

There was an argument Friday night, precipitated by Wagner, that caused Natalie, embarrassed and fed up, to leave the yacht. The truth is Wagner didn't mind his superstar wife being seen with another man checking into an Avalon hotel room in the middle of the night. All he cared about was his ego.

But here's where Wagner proves by his own words his state of mind Friday night. He told Gavin Lambert in 2004 that there was an argument, that he tried to talk Natalie out of leaving, and that the scene was a replay of the one over Natalie's costar in *From Here to Eternity*, except Natalie "was 'swishing her tail' at Walken far more insistently than she'd swished it at William Devane."

Swishing her tail. That's what Wagner thought of his wife. *What better proof of Wagner's unbounded suspicious jealousy of Walken and contempt for the woman he claims he loved dearly?*

Finally, Davern said Natalie was steamed Friday night, exhausted over Wagner's drinking and jealousy of her leading men, and she said, "I can't tolerate this kind of nonsense from R.J." She continued: "Come Monday, R.J. will face the music on this. And he knows it!" And when Davern asked what she meant, Natalie responded by saying Wagner's jealousy and drinking was unacceptable and she would see a lawyer if she had to.

Wagner, on the other hand, lied about Friday night. He knew his actions would look incriminating, so he lied about Friday night in 1981 and he has lied about it ever since. Those lies establish his consciousness of guilt.

There's no doubt that Davern stayed with Natalie in an Avalon hotel room Friday night. *Can there really be any doubt they talked?* And, based on what you now know really happened, *can there be any doubt what they talked about?* If you believe the evidence supports what Davern has said about Natalie's bedtime intentions Friday night, then you also have a foundation for what happened Saturday night on the back deck of *Splendour.*

There was the violent, jealous wine bottle scene between Wagner and Walken, giving way to the reasonable inference that Natalie was embarrassed so deeply that she angrily left the salon for the master stateroom, reminded of experiences with her alcohol-abusing father.

Wagner followed her, by his own admission in his memoir, and became the last person to be with Natalie before she was found dead. Finally, we know for a fact that Wagner delayed any search for Natalie from about 11 p.m. to 1 a.m. at a bare minimum. And during that time, based on the forensics, Natalie, weakened by the effects of hypothermia, drowned.

The blueprint says, "To constitute the crime of second-degree murder, there must be in addition to the death, an unlawful *act or omission* which was a cause of that death." Cause is defined in criminal law as "an *act or omission* that sets in motion a chain of events that produces, as a direct, natural and probable consequence of the act or omission, the death and without which the death would not occur."

Let me explain. From the facts, you can reasonably conclude that during a physical struggle between Natalie and Wagner on the back deck of *Splendour*, Wagner either pushed or intimidated Natalie toward the open swim step door and dinghy, or Natalie moved to that location to avoid him. Next, you can reasonably conclude that as a direct result of that act, Natalie slipped and fell into the cold ocean.

Armed with those deductions, even if Wagner didn't mean to kill Natalie by that point, by knowing she couldn't swim, deserting her in the darkness to fight for her life in the frigid ocean and obstructing efforts to help her until it was too late, you can reasonably find an "act or omission" that caused Natalie's death.

And under the blueprint, "If the circumstantial evidence permits two reasonable interpretations, one of which points to the defendant's guilt and the other to his innocence, you must adopt the interpretation that points to the defendant's innocence and reject that interpretation that points to his guilt. If, on the other hand, one interpretation of the evidence appears to you to be reasonable and the other interpretation to be unreasonable, you must accept the reasonable interpretation and reject the unreasonable."

In other words, if you find as unreasonable, an interpretation of the circumstantial evidence that while intoxicated, Natalie, partially jeweled, got up from bed in the middle of the night because of a banging rubber dinghy. Then she put her down jacket on over her nightshirt, and with Davern in the salon only about 18 feet away, walked from the back deck to the swim step in her wool socks to retie the dinghy, where she slipped and fell into the water and drowned without anyone on board hearing her cries for help. According to the blueprint, you would be required to reject that interpretation and accept any reasonable interpretation of the circumstantial evidence.

So, what is the reasonable interpretation of the direct and circumstantial evidence? First, Wagner had an abiding desire to move the yacht from the busy harbor in Avalon, the main city of Catalina, to Isthmus Cove in Two Harbors, a rugged, desolate part of the island Friday night. He told the authorities in 1981 it was because of "rough seas" in Avalon. But when Davern asked him why they were at the Isthmus, Wagner's response was, "Because Natalie wants a weekend with Christopher Walken, and Natalie will get more than what she came for."

When you consider that statement with the evidence of Wagner's trip to North Carolina the week before Natalie's death, the fight in the North Carolina restaurant, his threats and obsessive telephone calls to her hotel, his lie about being in Hawaii filming *Hart to Hart* the week before Natalie died and, according to Crowley, his arguments with Walken before the trip, I submit you can reasonably conclude that he was still highly suspicious, if not convinced, there was an ongoing affair, or the potential of an affair, between Walken and Natalie. Wagner said in his memoir he was satisfied there was no affair after his first trip in October. But the truth is, on Saturday, November 28, the evidence suggests he wanted them both on the yacht where he could confront them in a location where there were no people to witness his actions.

By Wagner's own admission to Lambert, Saturday evening started out with Wagner agitated and upset that Natalie left while he was sleeping to go to the bar with Walken. You don't need Davern to tell you the truth about dinner at Doug's Harbor Reef. The witnesses who saw the foursome described Wagner as "irate and upset with Natalie"—according to Don Whiting. And, according to Dr. Taylor, an expert in linguistics, he recognized bitter anger in Wagner's eyes that night.

And we don't need Davern to know the truth about the established timeline. Curt Craig, a Harbor Patrol officer, watched the Wagner party get in their dinghy before he went off duty at 10:30 p.m., and Whiting, Wagner, Walken and Davern said the foursome returned to the yacht about 10:30 p.m.

But at this point, it's noteworthy that there is a material discrepancy in one of Davern's more current statements. In his book, Davern was adamant that he tied the dinghy—with two ropes—to the stern cleats. However, on December 10, 1981, and March 5, 1982, Davern told the detectives that *Wagner* tied the dinghy to the rear of the yacht. We can reasonably conclude this meant at the eye-ring tie as identified by Paul Miller and the LASD photograph.

Of course, both of Davern's statements can't be true. But *who* tied the dinghy is not as important as *where* it was tied. Tied to the stern of the yacht at the eye-ring tie, the dinghy would be trailing behind with the prevailing winds pushing it away from the yacht like a balloon. The swim step has a rubber bumper, and according to Miller, there's no banging and little noise with rubber against rubber.

Next, if the dinghy were tied to the eye-ring tie or even the rear side cleats and it came loose, it could be easily tightened from the back deck with no need to walk out onto the swim step. And, finally, the photographs of the yacht taken by the LASD establish that the headboard for the master stateroom was against the port side of the yacht.

What does all of this mean? I submit it created an "uh-oh" moment, and Wagner tried to fix it in 2004 with Lambert's book. Wagner had never said this before, but he told Lambert that he tied the dinghy with "ropes"—plural—to the "port side of the yacht." Of course, this conveniently creates a situation in which the dinghy could rub against the yacht—right next to Natalie's head to keep her from sleeping. Wagner needed it tied there. Otherwise, with the dinghy tied to the stern, any so-called banging couldn't be heard with the doors closed on a cold night. A fabrication like that also demonstrates consciousness of guilt.

So, what's the timeline of events after the foursome returned to the yacht? Again, on December 4, 1981, Wagner told both Rasure and Hamilton in his bedroom interview with his lawyer present that after the group returned to the yacht, Natalie went downstairs, and 15 minutes after that, he went to check on her and she was gone.

Wagner had six days between the day Natalie's body was found and the interview to get his story straight. You can easily infer he talked with his lawyer, Mr. Ziffren, before he gave the statement. And, we know his lawyer became his official spokesman the day Natalie was found. You can also easily infer that Davern's lawyers, paid by Wagner, and Walken's lawyer, most likely a referral from Ziffren, talked with Ziffren before Wagner appeared for his December 4 interview. As a consequence, Wagner should have been well-schooled on everyone's stories by the time he spoke to investigators.

Furthermore, there's absolutely no doubt that a statement by Walken triggered the defendant's jealousy and rage. Up to this point in time, Wagner's misrepresentations about that event included telling the *Star* there was "no love triangle" and "no argument." It took Wagner nearly 25 years to admit it, but he finally did, after Davern exposed it years earlier. Wagner told Lambert that his suspicion of an affair between Natalie and Walken, and Natalie's anger with him for his suspicions, "fueled all their later arguments" and led him to admit, "I got really angry. I told him to stay out of it, then picked up a wine bottle, slammed it on the table, and smashed it to pieces."

But, what did Wagner tell investigators about the broken wine bottle in 1981? It was broken by rough seas. He looked the law enforcement officers right in the eye and lied—again. This is more evidence of consciousness of guilt.

But the falsehoods don't stop there. Wagner said in his memoir when the bottle-smashing occurred, "Natalie was already belowdecks." This was after telling his old friend Lambert, just a few years earlier, Natalie was present and "turned her back on both of them" after the display of violence occurred. Now, Wagner wants everyone to believe Natalie didn't witness, or hear, his violent explosion.

Wagner wants everyone to believe Natalie didn't witness the bottle-smashing because that fact leads to one unmistakable conclusion. Natalie was horrified, embarrassed and shocked at that dangerous display of jealousy. After that, the Natalie we've come to know through the evidence was *done*. She was finished with his drunken rages and relentless jealousy. And, Wagner knew it.

This also supports the two things Davern said happened next.

First, Davern said after glass and wine flew everywhere, Walken, his hands shaking, got up and walked out the side door and stood there for a few minutes. Walken, who downplayed the scene and intentionally failed to tell the detectives the whole truth about the argument in 1981, confirms that after the "beef" happened, he went outside. Davern also said when Walken returned, he went straight to his room without a word. Walken wants everyone to believe that after he returned from the yacht's side deck, he and Wagner had a hugfest in which they reconciled and then he went downstairs. *Which one rings true to you?*

After a husband, in a rage, smashes a wine bottle on the table in front of you and screams about you wanting to have sex with his wife, you are going to be frightened—particularly if the husband is still holding the jagged neck of the wine bottle. Walken was afraid, and he did what most sane people would do—he extricated himself from the scene, de-escalated the tension with Wagner and got out of there.

In 1981, Walken didn't tell investigators the whole truth about the argument with Wagner and the wine bottle, because he knew what happened next between Wagner and Natalie. And a couple of years later, he flat-out lied when he told *The Face* magazine that everyone was having a great weekend and lied again to *Star* magazine in 1985 when he said—twice—there was "no argument."

But I submit Walken's big untruth was when he said he slept through the events that occurred that night. He told LASD investigators in 1981 that they all thought Natalie had gone ashore, probably to the restaurant, when she disappeared from the yacht. So, Walken said it didn't mean much to him because the night before Natalie had stayed in Avalon. Unconcerned, Walken said, "I just went to my stateroom and went to sleep."

Walken wants you to believe that in minutes, according to our established timeline, he was so sound asleep that he didn't hear what Davern said happened—a screaming, cussing, banging fight that spilled out onto the back deck not 25 feet from Walken's cabin. Even now, it looks like Walken is sticking with that storyline. *Why?* I submit it's because he's still afraid of hurting his image and, probably more so, looking like a coward. He said to *Star* magazine in 1985, "I wish with all my heart I could have saved her." Maybe he could have if it weren't for that jealous mistress career of his.

⌒⌒⌒⌒⌒⌒

Davern's detractors also say you only have the word of a money-hungry, drug-abusing drunk that there was a fight on the back deck of *Splendour*. But they are wrong.

To begin with, there's the testimony of Paul Wintler, the Santa Catalina Island Company maintenance man. He was the first civilian to speak to Wagner face-to-face early Sunday morning. He recalled that Wagner said he had a fight with his wife and now she was "gone."

Then, there's the forensic evidence. The full body diagrams in the official autopsy report show Natalie had a big fresh bruise on her right forearm, fresh bruises on her right ankle and left knee, many fresh low-body bruises, and a scratch in the middle of her throat precisely where a thumbnail impression or scratch from a throat grab would cause such an injury. The wounds on Natalie's right forearm and top of her right hand are classic defensive injuries. The back leg bruises are consistent with being compressed on the yacht's wooden bed surround. The Tardieu spots on Natalie's lungs are consistent with a violent, screaming scene. A small laceration on the bridge of Natalie's nose was documented by Deputy Kroll. And, there were cries for help from a woman in the water near *Splendour* at the precise time of Natalie's disappearance.

All of these things create, in combination, a chain of circumstances pointing to a physical confrontation between Natalie and Wagner, confirming what Davern said he saw and heard before Natalie disappeared.

How does the time of death in this case impact the offense of second-degree murder?

Dr. Choi, Dr. Kornblum, Dr. Noguchi, and my experts, Dr. Pozos and Jonathan Unwer, all place the time of death around midnight.

The uncontradicted evidence is that even though Wagner last saw his wife at 10:45 p.m. and noticed her missing 15 minutes later, no effort was made by him to search for Natalie between 11 p.m. and at least 1 a.m.—a two-hour gap in time. By that time, Natalie was surely gone. And, you could reasonably infer, that's exactly what Wagner intended.

Over the years, Wagner has tried to narrow the Fatal Gap in books and interviews by claiming he was drinking with the boys until midnight, or later, before discovering Natalie was missing. That was done purely because he realized he made another unforeseen error. By leaving a substantial gap between the time he said he discovered Natalie missing and the time he first reached out for help, Wagner made his biggest mistake of all. For that's when Natalie perished.

⌒⌒⌒⌒⌒⌒

The evidence establishes Wagner directed everyone toward the other yachts, the shore, the restaurant bar, and away from *Splendour* and the open sea when the search began.

During his second interview with investigators, Wagner said his first thought when Natalie went missing was that she had taken the dinghy and gone back to the bar. He also told them in his first interview he started calling the bar and people on shore at 11:30 p.m. When investigators informed Wagner how Natalie was dressed when she was found during his second interview, he remembered the clothes she had worn at dinner were still in plain view in the master stateroom, and he had been in that stateroom after she was gone, looking for her, by his own admission.

So Wagner said, "She would not have gone out in the dinghy dressed that way." And a short time later, his lawyer and spin doctors started spreading the "banging dinghy" theory—the unreasonable and unbelievable theory Wagner has relied on every time he's been quoted since his second interview with investigators on December 4, 1981.

We know Wagner, without any consideration of the effect it would have on his young employee, sent Davern to perform the traumatic chore of identifying Natalie's body. Then, he got the LASD to whisk him back to Long Beach in its helicopter where he had a brief encounter with investigators.

According to their notes, Wagner told them it was a "beautiful night" and Natalie wanted to take the dinghy out.

That six-minute interview in Long Beach was the beginning of Wagner's greatest and longest acting performance. He was cool enough on the yacht with Davern when he pulled out a bottle of scotch and drank while Natalie fought in vain for her life, but suddenly with the investigators in Long Beach, he was "shook up" with his thoughts on the children. Wagner said in his book *Pieces of My Heart* that he didn't want the children learning about Natalie's death on television. But it was already 10 a.m. Sunday, and Natalie's body was found at 7:44 a.m., more than two hours earlier. By that time, the media was in high gear, and Natasha learned about her mother's death from the radio.

In *Pieces,* Wagner said he went home to bed and was "catatonic" for over a week, "maybe up to eight days." But during his catatonic state, Wagner managed to get his lawyer to the house for a fabricated press release, have a 45-minute conversation with Jill St. John—the woman he would start dating within two months of Natalie's death, and tell friends like Army Archerd that Natalie "often" took the dinghy out at night and the ocean "was smooth as glass."

And what else was this catatonic man able to do during the week after Natalie's death? He managed to call the deputy coroner, Dr. Choi, on November 29, the day Natalie was found, to request an expedited autopsy so he could have her funeral December 1. He managed to meet with Davern on the day Natalie was found to tell him to keep his mouth shut and see a lawyer he had arranged for him. He managed to meet with Davern the following day, November 30, to tell him to call his lawyer and to use a driver he had hired to transport Davern to the appointment. And also November 30, he managed to use his credit card to buy some jewelry for someone.

On the day of Natalie's funeral—two days after her death—Wagner also managed to revise his earlier press release and sign the petition to probate Natalie's entire estate.

Finally, during his December 4 bedroom interview with investigators, Wagner—who three days earlier had buried his wife—managed to ask only one question they considered important enough to record in their notes. The question was, *What happened to Natalie's jewelry?* I suppose he was worried about the whereabouts of the expensive diamond necklace, the same necklace that was selected in front of Walken and ended up being paid for by Natalie's estate. Or, he may have been worried about the expensive pendant and ivory horsehead and bead bracelet he purchased for someone.

I submit you can infer that innocent people don't act that way, which is more evidence of Wagner's consciousness of guilt.

As for Davern's overall credibility, I suggest you consider this. Wagner and his supporters have been trying to take advantage of Wagner's own wrongdoing when it comes to Davern's 1981 falsehoods. Wagner got Davern drunk after Natalie disappeared and convinced him to lie for him. He subjected Davern to unspeakable psychological trauma by directing him to identify Natalie's body, fueling Davern's abuse of alcohol. He intimidated Davern with threats of prosecution and kept him close, paying him for his silence, until things cooled off. Wagner didn't try that with Walken because he knew Walken would go to his grave with the knowledge about that night to save his career. Now, those people want you to believe Davern can't be trusted to tell the truth, because he once told the very lies that he and Wagner agreed upon.

So, what happened after the Wagner party left Doug's on Saturday, November 28, 1981? When you consider the totality of this case, not just Davern's declarations standing alone, here's what you can infer that the complete body of evidence establishes beyond a reasonable doubt:

The early evening of Saturday, November 28, began with Wagner agitated and jealous after Natalie and Walken went to the bar without him. As the evening wore on, he became more angry, jealous and intoxicated—to the point that he eventually put a stop to the evening. Around 10:30 p.m., the foursome returned to *Splendour* in the Zodiac, which Wagner tied with one painter line to the stern transom eye-ring. The group stepped out of the dinghy, went through the yacht's open swim step door and walked to the salon where they continued their evening.

Natalie was enjoying Walken's company when her costar injected something in response to Wagner's complaint about Natalie's absence while filming that ignited Wagner's suspicious jealousy and rage. Wagner accused Walken of wanting to have sex with Natalie and followed that accusation by taking a wine bottle by the neck and smashing it on the coffee table. Walken, now afraid for his life in the yacht's small salon, did the best and most prudent thing he could. He went outside. After a few minutes, Walken returned and went straight to his cabin.

Walken locked his door. But when the fight between Natalie and Wagner was taking place, Walken unlocked the door to get a better feel for what was going on and to, perhaps, intervene. But fear overcame valor and he retreated, forgetting to relock the door.

After Walken went to his room without a word, poor Natalie—shocked, embarrassed and humiliated to tears—did exactly what Davern said she did. She stood up, said Wagner's outburst was outrageous, then turned and went directly to her bedroom, slamming the door behind her.

At that point, Wagner's mind must have been spinning with countless abysmal thoughts. He knew Natalie, and this wasn't the first time his jealousy and drinking had embarrassed and humiliated her. He also knew the consequences when Natalie had had enough and that his image would be irreparably damaged if the bottle-breaking incident hit the press.

So, Wagner did the only thing he could think to do. He told Davern he was going down to patch things up, even though he didn't "really expect her to accept his apology." He went downstairs, and he was right. By then, Natalie had taken her Antivert and Darvon, as prescribed, and was getting ready for bed. Wagner interrupted her as she was taking off her jewelry…obviously the last thing Natalie did before bed.

We know she was partially jeweled when found because of the absence of her left wrist bracelet, necklace and earrings. Natalie wasn't going anywhere voluntarily. And, she hadn't been to bed with a gold chain around her waist.

After the interruption and first words out of Wagner's mouth, Natalie let him have it with both barrels, including what she told Davern on Friday night. She was going to see her lawyer. At this point, more grim thoughts were rushing through Wagner's mind. Thoughts of the press headlines to begin with. Then, the house, the boat, the money and the girls. All of it was in jeopardy. Even his TV career, bankrolled by Natalie's friends Spelling and Goldberg, was at risk.

That's when the screaming, cussing fight begins. It escalated into pushing and shoving. Remember, they're not fighting in their Beverly Hills home. They're in the tight quarters of their yacht's master stateroom, where everything is bolted to the floor. Natalie's legs are hitting the vanity chair and table and being pressed against the wooden bed surround. Maybe things are thrown…who knows? But during this time, Natalie used her right arm to shield herself from a blow. The big right forearm bruise didn't happen when she was in the water with her down jacket on, and there's no evidence connecting that bruise to anything on the dinghy. But, suffice to say, the fight scared Davern so badly that he ran up to the flybridge and turned on the music loud enough to drown out the noise.

After the fight spilled onto the boat's back deck, more angry words were hurled. Now, the following will always be one of the mysteries of this case. How, when and why did Natalie come to be wearing her red down jacket? No one really knows. She was only wearing a nightshirt, so perhaps she grabbed it to keep warm during the fight. It was cold out. We may never know the answer, but she was probably wearing it when Wagner screamed, "Get off my fucking boat!"

Natalie wouldn't take an order like that kindly. So, she yelled back and that's when Wagner lunged at her. He reached for her neck and she instinctively put up her hands to protect herself. As he grabbed her throat, he scratched it and injured the back of her right hand as he began pushing her toward the open swim step door. Natalie slipped, hitting her left knee on the wooden step, accounting for the big bruise in that location. That slip also caused the big bruise on her right ankle, perhaps from striking the frame of the swim step door. But, as she fell, she reached for the dinghy to catch herself and her face brushed the side of the rubber pontoon as she fell into the water, causing the upward abrasion on her cheek and forehead.

When Natalie hit the cold water, her torso reflex took her breath away. Then, panic set in. Flailing away at the water, thinking of nothing but the need for oxygen, Natalie was unable to see in the darkness. The only thing that kept her from drowning within minutes was her down jacket. It gave her a brief chance to do the only thing she knew how to do before the shivering suppressed her voice—scream for help.

Terrible images, thoughts and emotions created an overwhelming whirlwind in Wagner's mind. The headlines would include intoxication, violence, spousal abuse and jealousy! The press would crucify the suave Jonathan Hart wannabe. He couldn't stand the thought of the humiliation and financial collapse that would follow another divorce from Natalie.

So, he did what he thought he had to do.

He untied the dinghy painter line from the eye-ring and threw it in Natalie's direction saying, "Hold on. We're coming to get you." Natalie grabbed the line and her flailing entangled it around her down-jacket-covered arms. She cried out for only a few minutes until the effects of shivering and hypothermia silenced her and drained her strength. With the stamina she had left, Natalie held onto the painter line until the cold sapped her remaining energy. Pushed by the wind and tide, she and the Zodiac moved toward the open sea with Natalie's light body guiding the dinghy until they hit the island currents, sweeping them toward Blue Cavern Point.

The air bubble caused by Natalie's jacket being unzipped held her up until hypothermia overtook her and her face fell forward into the water. At that point, Natalie became untangled from the painter line, separating her from the Zodiac, which drifted like a balloon to the rocky shore.

The circumstantial evidence, combined with the hard, scientific evidence, proves Natalie died around midnight. The delay in rescuing her was her death sentence, and Wagner knew it. That's why he didn't call for help, why he got Davern drunk, why he lied to the investigators about events and times, and why he got Davern to lie for him. Combine that with the North Carolina evidence, Wagner's suspicious jealousy of Walken and resentment of Natalie's career, what he stood to lose from a second divorce, and what he stood to gain financially and personally from Natalie's death, and you have a recipe for murder.

Just like my fictional scene at the top of the cliff. You didn't see it, but the woman was ushered off the cliff to her death by someone with a motive to kill. It's the same way with Natalie ending up dead in the cold Pacific Ocean. You didn't see it, but the strong circumstantial evidence points to murder.

Ladies and gentlemen, now it's time for you to decide.

additional documents

Figure A: Phone message from Robert Wagner requesting early post mortem (Los Angeles County Department of Medical Examiner-Coroner)

MEDICATION & EVIDENCE RECORD

COUNTY OF LOS ANGELES

THOMAS T. NOGUCHI, M.D.
CHIEF MEDICAL EXAMINER-CORONER

3 A

FIREARMS ☐ GUNSHOT RESIDUE TEST-KIT # _____

HANDGUNS   *OTHERS*

☐ Automatic ☐ Revolver   ☐ Rifle ☐ Shotgun

Cal. or

Guage _____ lake _____ Model _____

Serial _____ Spent _____ Live _____

Case No.   81-15167

Case Name

WAGNER/Aka: WOOD, NATALIE

Found 11-29-81

Aco.   Page No. _____ 1

☐ LIGATURES — TYPE _____ Evidence Bin No. _____

☐ PARAPHERNALIA OR KIT — Describe _____ Evidence Bin No. _____

☐ OTHER — Describe _____ Evidence Bin No. _____

No.	Rx NUMBER	NAME OF PHARMACY	PHONE No.	DOCTOR
1.	320168	Schwab's	016-1212	Rudnick
2.	347017	"	"	"
3.	709135	Beverly HillsBourely	271-5721	Satnick
4.	334250	Schwab's		Rudnick
5.	339933	"		Sutnick
6.	3371198	"		Rudnick
7.	319969	"		"
8.	364700	Thrifty	273-3561	Shulman
9.				
10.				
11.				
12.				

CONTINUE INFORMATION BELOW USING THE SAME PRESCRIPTION FOR THE SAME NUMBER

No.	DATE	MEDICATION NAME	No. Issued	No. Left	INSTRUCTIONS ON PRESCRIPTION LABEL
1.	11-15-81	Darvon Comp.	65	37	As Directed
2.	10-30-81	Placidyl 500mg.	30	2-80	As Directed ✗ (1) Pill Stuck to bottom of bottle. PE 12-8-81
3.	11-24-81	Optimine 1mg.	12	11	1 Tablet Twice a Day
4.	9-14-81	Metahydrin 4mg.	50	38	1 Tablet As Directed
5.	7-25-80	Antivert 12.5mg.	20	17	As Directed
6.	4-8-80	Dalmane 30mg.	7	0	1 Capsule @ Bedtime
7.	3-7a-80	Synthroid .15	100	17	1 Tablet Daily
8.	11-03-81	Bactrim DS	20	7	1 Tablet Every 12 hrs.
9.					
10			Also **		4½ 10mg Valium
11.					1 Red Capsule ✗ Placidyl Per PDR
12.					PE 12-8-81

WHEN MORE THAN TWELVE MEDICATIONS ON A CASE USE ADDITIONAL SHEETS AND MARK THE PAGE NUMBER

Pamela K Eaker

INVESTIGATOR   11-29-81
Pamela K. Eaker   DATE

WHITE · FILE
YELLOW · LABORATORIES
PINK · INVESTIGATIONS

76M(18V-7-78- PG B 78

Figure B: Natalie Wood's medication list prepared by coroner's office investigator Pamela Eaker (Los Angeles County Department of Medical Examiner-Coroner)

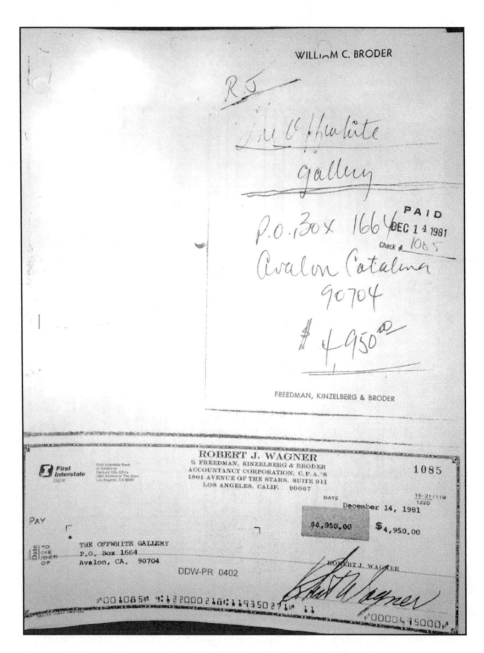

Figure C: Robert Wagner's probate check written to Off White Gallery (Natalie Wood Wagner probate file)

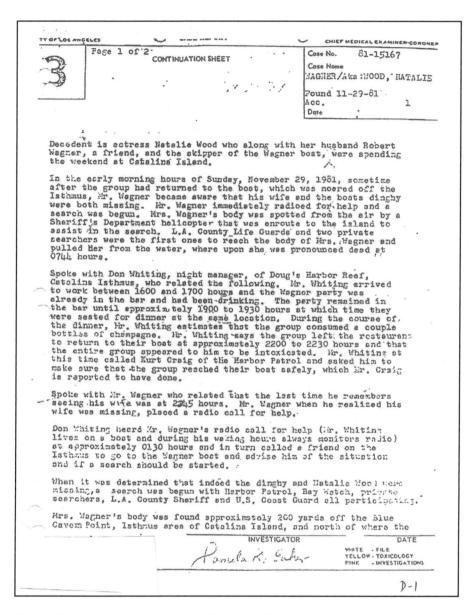

Page 1 of 2
CONTINUATION SHEET

Case No.   81-15167
Case Name
WAGNER/aka:WOOD, NATALIE
Found 11-29-81
Acc.   1
Date

Decedent is actress Natalie Wood who along with her husband Robert
Wagner, a friend, and the skipper of the Wagner boat, were spending
the weekend at Catalina Island.

In the early morning hours of Sunday, November 29, 1981, sometime
after the group had returned to the boat, which was moored off the
Isthmus, Mr. Wagner became aware that his wife and the boats dinghy
were both missing. Mr. Wagner immediately radioed for help and a
search was begun. Mrs. Wagner's body was spotted from the air by a
Sheriff's Department helicopter that was enroute to the island to
assist in the search. L.A. County Life Guards and two private
searchers were the first ones to reach the body of Mrs. Wagner and
pulled Her from the water, where upon she was pronounced dead at
0744 hours.

Spoke with Don Whiting, night manager, of Doug's Harbor Reef,
Catalina Isthmus, who related the following. Mr. Whiting arrived
to work between 1600 and 1700 hours and the Wagner party was
already in the bar and had been drinking. The party remained in
the bar until approximately 1900 to 1930 hours at which time they
were seated for dinner at the same location. During the course of
the dinner, Mr. Whiting estimates that the group consumed a couple
bottles of champagne. Mr. Whiting says the group left the restaurant
to return to their boat at approximately 2200 to 2230 hours and that
the entire group appeared to him to be intoxicated. Mr. Whiting at
this time called Kurt Craig of the Harbor Patrol and asked him to
make sure that the group reached their boat safely, which Mr. Craig
is reported to have done.

Spoke with Mr. Wagner who related that the last time he remembers
seeing his wife was at 2245 hours. Mr. Wagner when he realized his
wife was missing, placed a radio call for help.

Don Whiting heard Mr. Wagner's radio call for help (Mr. Whiting
lives on a boat and during his waking hours always monitors radio)
at approximately 0130 hours and in turn called a friend on the
Isthmus to go to the Wagner boat and advise him of the situation
and if a search should be started.

When it was determined that indeed the dinghy and Natalie Wood were
missing, a search was begun with Harbor Patrol, Bay Watch, private
searchers, L.A. County Sheriff and U.S. Coast Guard all participating.

Mrs. Wagner's body was found approximately 200 yards off the Blue
Cavern Point, Isthmus area of Catalina Island, and north of where the

INVESTIGATOR   DATE

Pamela K. Eaker

WHITE - FILE
YELLOW - TOXICOLOGY
PINK - INVESTIGATIONS

D-1

Figure D: Page 1 of the report prepared by Pamela Eaker, coroner's office investigator
(Los Angeles County Department of Medical Examiner-Coroner)

Page 2 of 2 CONTINUATION SHEET

Case No. 81-1516(

Case Name

WAGNER/Aka:WOOD, NATALIE

Found 11-29-81

Loc. Date. 1

dinghy was found, near the shoreline, a couple hours earlier.

Mr. Wagner was also questioned regarding the possibility of suicide, however he states that wife was not suicidal.

Don Whiting was one of the private searches who located the dinghy and says that key was in the ignition, which was in the off position. The gear was in neutral and the oars tied down, and it appeared as if the boat had not even been used.

Decedent's body had been taken from the ocean and placed in the Hyperbaric Chamber building for safe keeping. Upon this investigators arrival at location, decedent observed lying in "stokes litter". Decedent is wrapped in plastic sheet, she herself is dressed in flannel nightgown and socks. The jacket that she was wearing when found floating, is no longer on the body, having come off when she was pulled from the water. At time decedent was pulled from the water, sheriff's personnel says that body was absent of any rigor and they noted foam coming from mouth. Decedent still has foam coming from mouth. Rigor is now present of a 3 to 4+ throughout her entire body. Decedent has numerous bruises to legs and arms. Decedent's eyes are also a bit cloudy appearing. No other trauma noted and foul play is not suspected at this time.

Skipper of the Wagner boat, Dennis Davern, identified body to sheriff's deputies.

Please notify Detectives Rasher and Hamilton 1-HOUR PRIOR TO POST AT 974-4341.

PE

DDW 037

INVESTIGATOR

Pamela K. Eaker

11-29-81

DATE

WHITE - FILE
YELLOW - TOXICOLOGY
PINK - INVESTIGATIONS

Figure E: Page 2 of the report prepared by Pamela Eaker, coroner's office investigator

(Los Angeles County Department of Medical Examiner-Coroner)

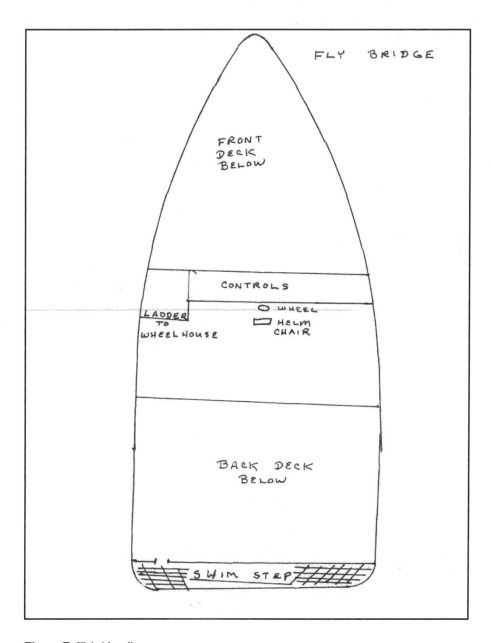

Figure F: Flybridge diagram (Courtesy of Ron Nelson)

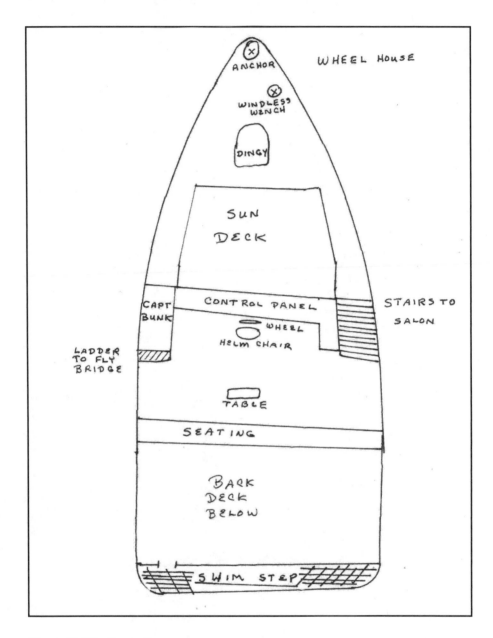

Figure G: Wheelhouse diagram (Courtesy of Ron Nelson)

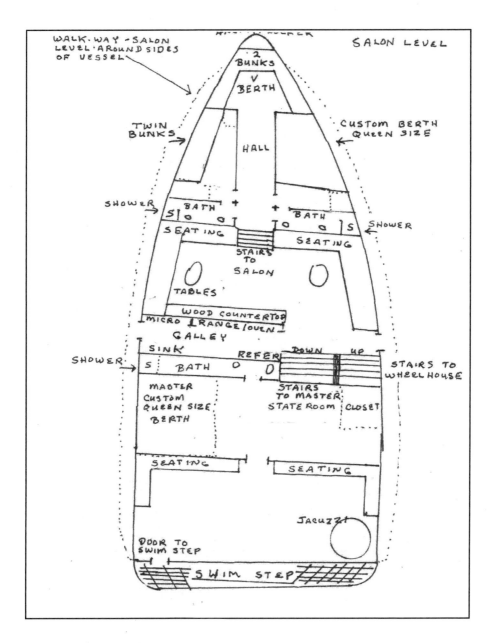

Figure H: Salon level diagram (Courtesy of Ron Nelson)

76T273 10/79

To Rasure

Date 11-30-81 Time 1115

A MESSAGE FOR YOU

Mr.
Mrs.
Miss Chief Stimerick

of

Phone 974-4301

TELEPHONED	X	PLEASE CALL	X
CALLED TO SEE YOU		WILL CALL AGAIN	
WANTS TO SEE YOU		RETURNED YOUR CALL	

Message

Figure I: Phone message left for Detective Rasure from Chief Stimerick, chief of detectives (Los Angeles County Sheriff's Department)

LOS ANGELES COUNTY SHERIFF'S DEPARTMENT

FROM: PETER J. PITCHESS, SHERIFF DATE DEC 21 1981

TO:
- [ ] UNDERSHERIFF BLOCK
- [ ] ASSISTANT SHERIFF VON MINDEN
- [ ] ASSISTANT SHERIFF EDMONDS
- [x] CHIEF
- [ ] INSPECTOR
- [ ] CAPTAIN
- [ ] MEDICAL DIRECTOR
- [ ] ______

PREPARE REPLY FOR:
- [ ] MY SIGNATURE
- [ ] YOUR SIGNATURE

UNIT:
- [ ] ADMINISTRATIVE DIVISION
- [ ] COURT SERVICES DIVISION
- [ ] CUSTODY DIVISION
- [x] DETECTIVE DIVISION
- [ ] FIELD OPERATIONS DIVISION EAST
- [ ] FIELD OPERATIONS DIVISION NORTH
- [ ] FIELD OPERATIONS DIVISION WEST
- [ ] TECHNICAL SERVICES DIVISION
- [ ] SPECIAL OPERATIONS
- [ ] FISCAL SERVICES BUREAU
- [ ] INFORMATION BUREAU
- [ ] INTERNAL INVESTIGATIONS BUREAU
- [ ] PERSONNEL BUREAU
- [ ] TRAINING BUREAU
- [ ] CONTRACT LAW ENFORCEMENT BUREAU
- [ ] INDUSTRIAL RELATIONS BUREAU

DISPOSITION
- [ ] YOUR RECOMMENDATION
- [ ] YOUR INFORMATION
- [x] YOUR DISPOSITION
- [ ] FILE
- [ ] INVESTIGATION
- [ ] PLEASE SEE ME
- [ ] PLEASE HANDLE
- [ ] PREPARE AND RETURN
- [ ] REVIEW AND COMMENT
- [ ] DO YOU CONCUR?
- [ ] PLEASE CALL ME

REMARKS: HOMICIDE BUREAU PLEASE CONTACT

SH-AD-510 (REV. 11/80)

Figure J: Message from Sheriff Pitchess to chief of the LASD's Detective Division regarding the disposition of Natalie's investigation (Los Angeles County Sheriff's Department)

Estate of Natalie Wood
a/k/a Natalie Wagner

Case No. P 669 545

Attachment 2

Profit Participations

Item	Description	Value
1.	Decedent's right to receive income from Profit Participation Agreement with respect to "Bob & Carol & Ted & Alice"	48,622.00
	Decedent's Separate Property:	
2.	Decedent's right to receive income from Profit Participation Agreement with respect to "Love With The Proper Stranger"	14,415.00
	Decedent's Separate Property:	
3.	Decedent's community one-half interest in the right to receive one-half of the net profits from the television picture pilot and television series entitled "Charlie's Angels" pursuant to that certain document entitled "AGREEMENT" entered into by Spelling-Goldberg Productions and Natalie Wood and Robert Wagner and dated as of December 1, 1977, as modified by that certain document entitled "SUPPLEMENTAL AGREEMENT CONCERNING 'CHARLIE'S ANGELS' PROFIT PARTICIPATION BY NATALIE WOOD AND ROBERT WAGNER" entered into by Spelling-Goldberg Productions and Natalie Wood and Robert Wagner and dated as of December 29, 1980	
	Value of Entire Community Property:	
	Decedent's Community One-half Interest:	2,300,620.00

Figure K: Probate documents reveal the assessed value of Natalie Wood's profit participations
(Natalie Wood Wagner probate file)

Residuals

Item	Description	Value
1.	Right to receive residuals from all motion pictures and television programs completed by Natalie Wood prior to July 16, 1972 which are payable to Natalie Wood	
	Decedent's Separate Property:	1,549.00
2.	Right to receive one-half of all deferred compensation payable to Robert J. Wagner by Columbia Pictures Corporation, dated January 4, 1961 with respect to the motion picture entitled "Sail A Crooked Ship" (Separate property as a result of severance of community property)	
	Decedent's Separate Property:	12.50
3.	Right to receive one-half of all deferred compensation payable to Natalie Wood by Harold Mirisch Company under and pursuant to an agreement between Natalie Wood and Beta Productions, a joint venture, dated August 29, 1960 with respect to the motion picture entitled "West Side Story" (Separate property as a result of severance of community property)	
	Decedent's Separate Property:	297.00
4.	Community one-half interest in right to receive residuals from all motion pictures, and/or television programs which were completed by Natalie Wood after July 16, 1972 which are payable to Natalie Wood	
	Value of Entire Community Property:	
	Decedent's Community One-half Interest:	1,890.50

2

Figure L: Probate documents include more details about Natalie Wood's assets

(Natalie Wood Wagner probate file)

JUL-16-2003 10:15 FROM:LITIGATION   3102441557   TO:213 620 1398   P.14/42

A G R E E M E N T

THIS AGREEMENT executed as of the twenty-eighth day of June, 1973 between SPELLING-GOLDBERG PRODUCTIONS (hereinafter referred to as the "Producer"), and NATALIE WOOD and ROBERT WAGNER (hereinafter referred to as the "Artists").

In consideration of the covenants and conditions herein contained and other good and valuable consideration, the parties agree as follows:

1. The Producer has employed the Artists to render their services as actors to portray the roles of "Courtney Patterson" and "Marcus Simon", respectively, in the motion picture photoplay entitled "LOVE SONG", which is first to be exhibited on national network television in the United States and Canada.

2. The term of Artists employment hereunder shall be deemed to have commenced on July 16, 1973 and Artists have rendered services thereafter for such time as Producer required their services in connection with the production of the photoplay.

3. As full consideration for all services rendered and all rights granted and agreed to be granted by Artists to Producer hereunder, and subject to all of Producer's rights under this agreement, employer has paid to Artists the following sums:

    a. Sixty-Five Thousand Dollars ($65,000.00) for the services of Miss Natalie Wood;

    b. Twenty-One Thousand Dollars ($21,000.00) for the services of Mr. Robert Wagner.

The payment entitles Producer to 1) as many pre-recording and rehearsal days as are necessary; 2) as many days of principal photography that are set forth in the pre-approved shooting schedule plus two free days and 3) two free non-consecutive days for looping.

    Other than stated above, Artist shall not be entitled to any additional compensation for any of their services which shall be rendered by Artists as provided for under this paragraph.

-1-

Doc# 1 Page# 53 - Doc ID = 1480432291 - Doc Type = Case File

Figure M: Page 1 of the 11-page 1973 *Love Song/Charlie's Angels* profit participation contract with Spelling-Goldberg Productions (Natalie Wood Wagner probate file)

(Page 56 of 287)

JUL-16-2003 10:16 FROM:LITIGATION   3102441557   TO:213 620 1398   P.17/42

above unless they otherwise direct Producer in writing signed
by all such persons or unless otherwise required by any applicable
collective bargaining agreement to which Producer is a sig-
natory. Such persons represent and warrant that they agreed
with each other in good faith (and without suggestion or direction
by Producer) prior to offering themselves for employment hereunder to collaborate as a team.

11. Producer and Artist will jointly submit up to five
(5) ideas to ABC for the basis of a pilot script for the 1974-
1975 television season. The two parties will work together
to obtain five (5) ideas to present to the network. These
ideas can be for a 30-minute or a 60-minute pilot. If approved,
ABC would spend up to $25,000.00 for such script and the writing
thereof must commence within twelve (12) months from the start
of the principal photography of the photoplay.

If the submission made to ABC goes forward, then Producer and Artists or Artists' designated corporation shall enter
into a business relationship the form of which will be negotiated
in good faith by the parties and where the profits therefrom are
shared equally between the parties. The Artist shall have the
right to consult with Producer as to the creativity, production
and business management of such pilot and/or any such series
which may be resulting therefrom, but, Producer shall have the
final decision with respect thereto in the event of any dispute.
Any relationship entered into between the parties shall be subject to Producer's exclusive arrangement with ABC.

Producer shall submit to Artist true copies of the network agreement, relating to such pilot and series, when same is
available.

If either of the Artists decide to perform in the
pilot and/or the series, the fees payable to such Artists for
the pilot and/or the series will be negotiated in good faith
by the parties.

12. All notices from the Producer to the Artist under or in
connection with this agreement may be given by mail
addressed to the Artist as hereinabove specified (or at
such other address as may from time to time be designated
by a written notice from the Artist to the Producer) and
by depositing the same, so addressed, postage fully prepaid, in the United States mail, or by sending the same
so addressed by telegraph or cable or, at its option,
the Producer may deliver such notice to the Artist personally, either in writing or, unless otherwise specified

-4-

Doc# 1 Page# 56 - Doc ID = 1480432291 - Doc Type = Case File

Figure N: Author's emphasis on paragraph 11 on fourth page of the 11-page *Love Song/
Charlie's Angels* profit participation contract (Natalie Wood Wagner probate file)

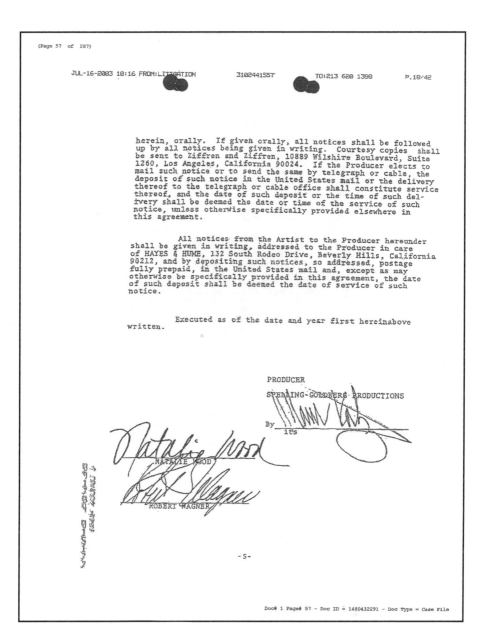

(Page 57 of 287)

Figure O: Page 5 of the 11-page *Love Song/Charlie's Angels* profit participation contract
(Natalie Wood Wagner probate file)

JUL-16-2003 10:17 FROM:LITIGATION ●● 3102441557 ●● TO:213 620 1398   P.26/42

AGREEMENT

Reference is hereby made to that certain Agreement dated as of June 28, 1973 between SPELLING-GOLDBERG PRODUCTIONS (hereinafter referred to as the "Producer") and NATALIE WOOD and ROBERT WAGNER (hereinafter referred to as the "Artist") for their services in the motion picture photoplay entitled "LOVE SONG". In consideration of the covenants and conditions herein contained and other good and valuable consideration, the receipt of which is hereby acknowledged, the parties hereby agree as follows:

1.   Pursuant to Paragraph 11 of said Agreement, the television motion picture pilot and television series entitled "CHARLIE'S ANGELS" falls under the provisions of said Paragraph 11 and, therefore, Exhibit "I" attached hereto and incorporated herein by reference is deemed to apply in connection with the net profits relating to said series. All profit participations to third parties shall be deducted "off the top" prior to payment of net profits to Artist and Producer hereunder.

2.   All notices from the Producer to the Artist hereunder shall be given in writing, addressed to Artist in care of International Creative Management, 8899 Beverly Boulevard, Los Angeles, California 90048, and by depositing such notices, so addressed, postage fully prepaid in the United States mail, the date of such deposit being deemed the date of service of such notice.

All notices from the Artist to the Producer hereunder shall be given in writing, addressed to the Producer in care of Hayes & Hume, A Professional Corporation, 132 South Rodeo Drive, Beverly Hills, California 90212, and by depositing such notices, so addressed, postage prepaid, in the United States mail and the date of such deposit shall be deemed the date of service of such notice.

Dated as of December 1, 1977.

ARTIST:

_____
(NATALIE WOOD)

_____
ROBERT WAGNER

PRODUCER:
SPELLING-GOLDBERG PRODUCTIONS

BY:_____
ITS

Doc# 1 Page# 65 - Doc ID = 1480432291 - Doc Type = Case File

Figure P: 1977 supplement to the *Love Song/Charlie's Angels* profit participation contract
(Natalie Wood Wagner probate file)

author's note on index

My website features an index for this book to help readers easily find locations for important facts about the critical players and events. Please go to: **www.nataliewood brainstorm.com**.

The website also includes additional details about my ongoing investigation into the handling of the Natalie Wood case by the Los Angeles County Sheriff's Department and Los Angeles County Department of Medical Examiner-Coroner.

❧❧❧❧❧❧❧❧

author's chapter notes
on resources

For those of you seeking verification of the many substantive factual representations contained in this book, an extensive listing of my resources has been compiled and organized by chapter. This section also contains additional material on matters of interest, including narratives on subjects germane to my investigation.

The following notes identify many of the sources I used in writing each chapter of the book, including the people interviewed, the records and documents examined, the legal authorities consulted, and the published sources referenced. It is by no means exhaustive, but it is intended to give the reader a detailed list of some of the research used to back up my claims. In the interest of brevity, the following references will be abbreviated:

Natasha (Finstad) — *Natasha: The Biography of Natalie Wood*, Suzanne Finstad (Three Rivers Press paperback 2001)

Natalie Wood (Finstad) — *Natalie Wood: The Complete Biography* (previously published as *Natasha*), Suzanne Finstad (B/D/W/Y Broadway Books paperback 2020)

Goodbye (Rulli with Davern) — *Goodbye Natalie, Goodbye Splendour*, Marti Rulli with Dennis Davern (Medallion Publishing, Inc. hardcover 2009)

Natalie Wood (Lambert) — *Natalie Wood: A Life*, Gavin Lambert (Doubleday large print home library edition 2004)

Pieces (Wagner) — *Pieces of My Heart: A Life*, Robert J. Wagner with Scott Eyman (Harper Collins 2008)

Natalie (Lana Wood) — *Natalie: A Memoir by Her Sister*, Lana Wood (G.P. Putnam's Sons hardcover 1984)

Heart to Heart (Maychick) — *Heart to Heart with Robert Wagner,* Diana Maychick and L. Avon Borgo (St. Martin's Press 1986)

Coroner (Noguchi) — *Coroner,* Thomas T. Noguchi, M.D. with Joseph DiMona (Simon and Schuster hardcover 1983)

One (Powers) — *One from the Hart,* Stefanie Powers (Gallery Books paperback 2010)

His Way (Kelley) — *His Way: The Unauthorized Biography of Frank Sinatra,* Kitty Kelley (Bantam Books 1986)

Handbook (Eliopulos) — *Death Investigator's Handbook: A Field Guide to Crime Scene Processing, Forensic Evaluations, and Investigative Techniques,* Louis N. Eliopulos (Paladin Press paperback 1993)

Techniques (Fisher) — *Techniques of Crime Scene Investigation (Forensic and Criminal Justice)* Eighth Edition, Barry A. J. Fisher and David R. Fisher (CRC Press hardcover 2012)

Vanity Fair (Kashner) — Vanity Fair magazine, *Natalie Wood's Fatal Voyage,* Sam Kashner (3/2000)

Probate file — Natalie Wood Wagner probate file number P669545

Eaker report — Pamela K. Eaker's official investigator report dated 11/29/1981

Kroll report — Dep. R.W. "Bill" Kroll's official report dated 11/29/1981 in LASD file case number 081-00898-1873-490

Miller report — Paul J. Miller's official report to the LA County Medical Examiner-Coroner Dr. Thomas Noguchi dated 1/28/1982

LASD 1981 file — LASD file case number 081-00898-1873-496, including Det. Duane P. Rasure's official report dated 12/11/1981, pp. 1-22, and official notes of Det. Duane P. Rasure and investigator Roy D. Hamilton

Coroner 1981 file — LA County Medical Examiner-Coroner file case number 81-15167, including official autopsy report for Natalie Wood Wagner dated 12/4/1981

Noguchi and Wilson 1981 videos — CNN report of Dr. Thomas Noguchi's news conference on Natalie Wood's death, https://www.youtube.com/watch?v=WVyQ8h6KaY8, and Entertainment Tonight's coverage of Richard Wilson comments re: Natalie Wood's death, https://www.youtube.com/watch?v=0tptZZaGmQg

Rulli blog — Marti Rulli author blog, signed witness statements of Roger Smith, Marilyn Wayne, Dennis Davern and Marti Rulli submitted to LASD in 2011, http://martirulli.blogspot.com (statements have since been removed)

Dr. L supplemental report — Official supplemental autopsy report dated 5/20/2012 signed by Lakshmanan Sathyavagiswaran, M.D., Chief Medical Examiner-Coroner/Interim Director

Dr. L amendment — Official physician's coroner death certificate amendment for Natalie Wood Wagner dated 8/1/2012 signed by Lakshmanan Sathyavagiswaran, M.D., Chief Medical Examiner-Coroner/Interim Director

Hernandez deposition — Deposition of Det. Ralph Hernandez dated 5/3/2016 in *Perroni v. Fajardo, et al* (Superior Court for County of Los Angeles case number BS159430)

Corina deposition — Deposition of Lt. John Corina dated 5/3/2016 in *Perroni v. Fajardo, et al* (Superior Court for County of Los Angeles case number BS159430)

Noguchi deposition — Deposition of Thomas T. Noguchi, M.D., dated 6/1/2016 in *Perroni v. Fajardo, et al* (Superior Court for County of Los Angeles case number BS159430)

Howard podcast — Transcript of *Fatal Voyage: The Mysterious Death of Natalie Wood* podcast, Dylan Howard (2018)

HBO documentary — HBO documentary *Natalie Wood: What Remains Behind* (May 2020)

Perroni v. Fajardo — *Perroni v. Mark A. Fajardo, et al* (Superior Court for County of Los Angeles case number BS159430)

Inflation Calculator — US Inflation Calculator, https://www.usinflationcalculator.com/

Chapter 1: Star-Studded Cruise

Books: *Natasha* (Finstad) pp. 3-4, 27, 31-32 (Maria's personality), 10-11 (superstitions), 16-21 (family history), 29-33 (alter ego), 35-44 (*Tomorrow Is Forever*), 57 ("One-Take Natalie"), 69 (contract), 74-79 (*Green Promise*), 141-144 (Frank Sinatra), 153 (emotionally immature), 166-169 (Nicholas Ray), 272-274 (Wagner with another man), 334-340 (first divorce, Wagner dating, "bailed me out"), 337 (Hollywood Reporter 1972), 455 (Maria resources), 501-502 (remarriage and resources); *Natalie Wood* (Lambert) p. 237 ("glittered among the bubbles"), 515 (*Brainstorm* in LA); *Natalie* (Lana Wood) pp. 149-150 (back together); *One* (Powers) p. 188 (Hawaii episode); *Pieces* (Wagner) pp. 3-5 (starstruck), 11 (father), 31 (Henry Willson), 53-54 (Susan Zanuck), 172, 177 (Marion and Katie), 182-183 (Wasserman), 184-186 (Wagner's career moves), 196-198 (Marion divorce), 199 ("a light went on"), 202, 204 (Wagner debt, bailed out), 203 (*Ramblin' Rose*), 229 (*Valiant* and *Splendour* names), 249 (south of France, *Brainstorm* call), 249-250 (October trip to NC, location shooting in Hawaii); *Goodbye* (Rulli with Davern) pp. 29-30 (*Challenger*); *My Life as a Mankiewicz: An Insider's Journey Through Hollywood*, Tom Mankiewicz and Robert Crane (University Press of Kentucky 2012) p. 20 (Zodiac), 219 ("one of the greatest friends"), 222-223 (*Hart to Hart* pilot), 294-295 (Wagner's stardom), 305-306 (meets Natalie), 309 (*Anastasia*); *Christopher Walken A to Z: The Man, The Movies, The Legend*, Robert Schnakenberg (Quirk Books) pp. 43-44 (*Brainstorm* rumors)

Court documents and records: Property Settlement Agreement, *Robert Wagner v. Marion Marshall Wagner*, Superior Court of Los Angeles County case number D 786834

Magazines: Photoplay, *Don't Sell Natalie Short*, Richard Gehman (8/1957) pp. 52-53; Photoplay, *Don't Sell Natalie Short, Part II*, Richard Gehman (9/1957) pp. 60-61; Movie Life, *I Learned to Let Natalie Have Her Own Way*, Maria Gurdin (7/1958) pp. 48-49, 54-55; Hollywood Life Stories, *Love Is Worth Fighting For* (Vol. 1, No. 9 1959) pp. 2-7; Movie Life, *Cupid Does It Again! Nat & Bob remarry...This time it's for ever and ever*, Cheryl Jamison (11/1972) pp. 42, 58, 60, 62; GQ, *Robert Wagner: Heart to Heart*, Mark Goodman (3/1986) pp. 268-269, 366-371

Newspapers: The Salemite (Salem, N.C.) *Actors Are People Too; Salem Student Observes Film Take* (11/6/1981); The News and Observer (Raleigh, N.C.) *'Brainstorm' back on West Coast* (10/29/1981)

Online sources: Natalie Wood blog by Paco Granados, BOXOFFICE and Parents' Magazine awards, https://natalie43wood.blogspot.com/2013/03/natalie-wood-galery.html

Television: HBO documentary, .09 ("I wish that I could marry him"), .10 (reservations at Romanoff's), .17 (pressure on career caused divorce), .19 ("broke two engagements"), .25 (Natasha arrives), .26 (Gregson affair), .28 (honeymoon in Isthmus), .59 ("eight years in Freudian analysis")

Wagner also uses this documentary to claim that Natalie's death was an accident and his first divorce from Natalie happened because of "the pressure on her and her career." (.17) The last claim, of course, is inconsistent with the great weight of evidence.

Chapter 2: The "Official" Account

Some sources erroneously list December 2 or 3, 1981, as the date of Natalie's funeral, but December 1 is correct, per Lana Wood and official autopsy records.

Mention needs to be made at this point of Suzanne Finstad's 2020 remake of *Natasha*, called *Natalie Wood: The Complete Biography*, containing so-called "explosive new chapters and insider details," according to its cover. In a peculiar format and presentation unbecoming an author of her stature, Finstad purportedly resurrects her file notes from 21 years ago and combines them with "revelations" from alleged "new witnesses" in a desperate attempt to crown herself "the authority" on how Natalie met her death. Where pertinent to the overall facts and conclusions of this book, I will note and comment upon some of her claims.

To begin, on Page 463, Finstad reports she "tracked down" Deputy R.W. Kroll's widow, who said Kroll was "troubled" when Natalie's case was closed as an accident. Vagueness aside, if Kroll indicated to his wife that he disagreed with the official result, he didn't make it known in his 10-page report. As I have noted in this book, however, there are signs Kroll suspected there was something more to Natalie's death than what was reported by Wagner and Davern.

Finstad states on Page 459 that Kroll "classified" Natalie's death as a homicide. She's wrong on that score. Every LASD criminal case opened in 1981 was assigned a classification code. In his report, Kroll assigned code number "490," followed by "Person Dead/ Apparent Accidental Drowning." When the case was officially closed by the LASD, it was classified as a "496," followed by "Person Dead/Accidental Drowning." Code 496 was "unknown death" in 1981. The classification for "criminal homicide" in 1981 was "011" and a "suspicious" death was "444."

Finstad also claims on Page 459 that Wagner explained the broken glass on the salon floor to Kroll by saying the wine bottle "must have fallen." Those three words are not in the report of Kroll's interview of Wagner. Moreover, since Kroll was deceased by the time Finstad started her research, he could not have said that to her.

Finally, on Page 481, Finstad claims a "confidential source" told her in 2019 that Walken said he heard the Saturday night fight between Wagner and Natalie. In works like Finstad's, statements from confidential sources should be avoided at all cost because they are unverifiable. Even though I personally believe Walken did hear the master stateroom fight, anyone allegedly saying Walken confessed should step forward, particularly when the individual makes the claim nearly 39 years after the fact.

Books: *Goodbye* (Rulli with Davern) p. 158 (Wagner's and Ziffren's directives to Davern), 159 (call lawyer, use driver); *Heart to Heart* (Maychick) Acknowledgments, pp. 140-142 (45 minutes with St. John); *Coroner* (Noguchi) p. 21 (Eaker skilled investigator), 23 (first duty to suspect murder); *Natalie Wood* (Lambert) p. 545 (Wagner call to Crowley); *Between Two Harbors: Reflections of a Catalina Island Harbormaster*, Doug Oudin (iUniverse 2013) pp. 46-55 (Oudin's narrative), 48 (weather Saturday night), 50 (Coast Guard call)

Court documents and records: Probate file; Hernandez deposition, pp. 32-34 (codes "490" and "496")

Investigatory records: Eaker report; Kroll report; LASD 1981 file; Coroner 1981 file

Magazines: National Enquirer, *Medical Expert's Shocker: Natalie Didn't Drown* (12/1982) p. 29, 31; Variety, *Just for Variety*, Army Archerd (12/1/1981)

Newspapers: Daily Mirror (London) *Natalie's Last Hours*, Barry Wigmore (12/1/1981); Los Angeles Times, *Drowning Called Accidental: Natalie Wood Fell From Yacht, Coroner Believes*, Jones and Belcher (12/1/1981); Los Angeles Times, *Dispute Before Wood's Death Now in Doubt*, Jones and Harris (12/2/1981); Los Angeles Times, *Natalie Wood's Death Accidental Drowning: Coroner Says Actress Apparently Slipped While Leaving Yacht as Her Husband, Co-Star Argued*, Jones and Belcher (12/1/1981); Los Angeles Times, Richard W. Kroll funeral notice (4/25/1996)

Online sources: Noguchi and Wilson 1981 videos

Television: HBO documentary, .01 (Natasha learns of death), .36 ("She's gone," Wagner phone call to Crowley)

Transcripts: 12/1/1981 press release by Paul Ziffren for Robert Wagner as reported by Catherine Mann, *Entertainment Tonight*

Witnesses: Pamela Eaker and Paul Wintler to SP; memo to SP regarding retired LASD detective Louis Danoff from SP's lawyer Brandon Cate

Chapter 3: Unresolved and Unsettling

Books: *Handbook* (Eliopulos) pp. 1-9 (crime scene protocol), 15-21 (crime scene drawings), 23-27 (photographing a death scene), 45 (fingernail scrapings), 101-119 (crime scene canvass, interviewing, suspect interrogation), 121-124 (truthful vs. deceptive behavior), 127-151 (homicide investigations, altercation homicides), 139, 195-196 (motive and opportunity), 231 (ethanol concentrations), 233-243 (strangulation and choking), 253-267 (blunt trauma investigations), 275-278 (drowning deaths); *Techniques* (Fisher) Preface, p. 15 ("duty to the truth"), 35-38 (recording times, entering and protecting crime scene), 55-56 (objectives of crime scene investigations), 58 (healthy skepticism), 96-99 (collecting evidence), 380 ("suspect the worst"), 412-413 (time of death), 426-427 (defensive wounds); *Goodbye* (Rulli with Davern) pp. 213-216, ("came up behind R.J.," "poured me a drink," "she's gone" and Oudin called Coast Guard), 262 (didn't see Natalie in the water), 262 (Davern's 2008 rendition, quarrel between Wagner and Natalie); *Pieces* (Wagner) p. 229 (Willie Mae Worthen); *Natasha* (Finstad) pp. 367-448 (*Act Five*), 506-512 (references to "official notes" and "official file")

California law: California Penal Code §§ 192 (manslaughter; involuntary, voluntary, vehicular); 799 (offenses punishable by death or life imprisonment); 800 (offenses punishable by imprisonment for eight years or more); 801 (offenses punishable by imprisonment); 187 (murder, defined); 188 (implied malice, defined); 189 (murder, degrees); 939.2 (subpoena of witnesses; issuance); 1326 (subpoena; persons authorized to issue); 1523 (definition of search warrant); 1528 (issuance); California Jury Instructions–Criminal 2.00 (direct and circumstantial evidence inferences); 2.01 (sufficiency of circumstantial evidence, generally); 2.02 (sufficiency of circumstantial evidence to prove specific intent or mental state); California Government Code §§ 11180 (subjects of investigations and actions); 11181(e)(powers in connection with investigations and actions); 26500 (public prosecutor); California Government Code §§ 27511, 27491 (coroner duties), 27491.6, 27491.7, 27493, 27492, 27499 (summoning witnesses), 27499.1, 27498, 27499, 27491.8 (confidential communications of deceased), 27497, 27504, 27504.1 and 27502.2 (inquest authorization and procedures)

Court citations: *Brovelli v. Superior Court* (1961) 56 Cal. 2d 524

Court documents and records: Corina deposition

Investigatory records: Dr. L supplemental report

Magazines: Star, *Natalie Mystery Solved: Yacht skipper breaks his silence...at last* (7/23/1985); Vanity Fair (Kashner) pp. 214-233

Newspapers: Los Angeles Times, *Natalie Wood Found Dead Off Catalina*, Ted Thackrey Jr. (11/30/1981); Canyon News (Beverly Hills, Calif.) *Natalie Wood's Case Reopened* (9/27/2011); Los Angeles Times, *Mystery of the reopened case*, Allen, Winton and Goffard (11/19/2011)

Online sources: aerial photos of Catalina Island Isthmus, https://www.islapedia.com/index.php?title=Isthmus,_Santa_Catalina_Island

Witnesses: Lana Wood to SP

Chapter 4: Corpus Delicti

California law: California Evidence Code §§ 210 (relevant evidence), 1101, subds. (b) and (c) (evidence of character to prove conduct); California Jury Instructions–Criminal 2.72 (*corpus delicti* must be proved independent of admission or confession)

Court citations: *People v. Eric Christopher Bechler*, 2003 WL 2268395 (11/14/2003) (circumstantial evidence murder conviction); *People v. Jacobson* (1965) 63 Cal. 2d 319, 327 (*corpus delicti* proved inferentially; circumstantial evidence); *People v. Ochoa* (1998) 19 Cal. 4th 353, 406-407 (*corpus delicti* has two elements; noncriminal cause); *People v. Cullen* (1951) 37 Cal. 2d 614, 624 (*corpus delicti* and criminal agency; extra-judicial admissions); *People v. Bolinski* (1968) 260 Cal. App. 2d 705, 714-715 (*corpus delicti* proved by slight or *prima facie* showing; degree of crime by extra-judicial statements); *People v. Cartier* (1960) 54 Cal. 2d 300, 311 (murder proved by circumstantial evidence)

Court documents and records: Hernandez deposition

Investigatory records: LASD 1981 file

Witnesses: Lana Wood and Dave Nath to SP

My quest to get records from the U.S. Coast Guard spanned, on and off, over four years.

I started my Freedom of Information Act (FOIA) journey one day in 2017 by going to the Coast Guard office in Long Beach, California, without an appointment. But, at 4 p.m., the office was closed. So I sent a FOIA request to the office's commandant for a written report on the search and rescue effort for Natalie Wood during the early morning hours of November 29, 1981. I knew it was a long shot, but I had to try. Months later, I was told records were discarded after 20 years, so I abandoned the effort.

Then, in February 2020, after reading the details of a California criminal case concerning the Coast Guard's involvement with a death on the high seas, I had an idea. I sent an FOIA request to the commandant in Washington, D.C., asking for every document I could think of that the Coast Guard might have generated in Natalie's case. Five months later, after receiving no reply, I contacted a lawyer to make some inquiries. In October 2020, that effort yielded a letter from Lt. K. L. Moore, the "FOIA Coordinator Sector Los Angeles—Long Beach," explaining that records going back to 1981 should have been sent to the National Archives and Records Administration's records center in Washington, D.C., and suggesting I "submit [my] request directly to that agency."

If it looks like I was going in circles, it's because I was. However, I wasn't giving up. Instead, I sent a letter to the "Special Access and FOIA Staff" asking for the same things I had asked for months earlier. But God must have decided to spare me further anguish, because in January 2021, He sent me Adebo Adetona, Archives Specialist, A1 Reference Branch, who took pity on me. Specialist Adetona took the time to respond in detail like a public servant should. The response clearly set out who I should contact and where the records might be located. And, those instructions hit pay dirt. But because of COVID-19, the National Archives Building in Washington, D.C., and Research Room in Riverside, California, were closed.

I still have not gotten access to the record facilities. But one day I will.

Adetona also suggested I make a request for the ship logs for the U.S. Coast Guard cutter *Point Camden* for November 29, 1981, that were apparently kept in the Riverside, California, archives.

If you recall, Deputy Kroll wrote in his report that he was contacted at 5:55 a.m. that day by Avalon Sergeant J. Dyer and advised that Baywatch Isthmus lifeguards and the *Point Camden* were conducting a search for Natalie.

So I followed Adetona's thoughtful suggestion and requested the logs.

To my surprise, four years after I was told any records involving Natalie Wood's death no longer existed, Archive Specialist James Huntoon emailed me *Point Camden*'s logs covering November 27, 1981, to November 30, 1981.

With the arrival of Huntoon's email, I thought, *Now, I am getting somewhere.*

You can imagine my grave disappointment when my examination of the records revealed no information relating to Natalie's drowning death. Not only that, the records contained blank lines from 1 a.m. to 4 a.m. November 29, 1981, and at 4 a.m., the records state, "moored calm."

After racking my brain on why the records would contain no information about the search for Natalie, I decided to send them to William Peterson, the former Coast Guard officer and shore boat operator who was on duty Saturday, November 28, 1981. What he told me was further confirmation of the conclusion I drew from the evidence about the LASD preventing the Coast Guard from getting involved in Natalie's case.

Peterson said the records the Coast Guard had sent me were "operations weather logs," not "navigation logs." He said there should have been both if the Coast Guard dispatched the *Point Camden* on a mission to find Natalie.

In 1981, the actual navigation was done using radar, radio direction finder and hopefully Loran-C. GPS was not available at the time.

Navigation logs would typically list the time the cutter got underway, the initial course and speed to the search area, every change in course and speed made while covering the search area, any sightings, any changes in the search plan and notes about the mission. Peterson even sent me an example, which is posted on my website, **www.nataliewood brainstorm.com**.

In examining the operations weather logs, Peterson noticed that during the times in question, *Point Camden* was in San Pedro at "condition YOKE"—meaning "portholes and watertight doors set for getting underway" —and on "Law Enforcement and SAR (Search and Rescue) Standby." That indicated to Peterson that *Point Camden* was "at berth standing by with a crew aboard and conditions set for getting underway if called for a SAR assignment." According to Peterson, "there is no indication from the two operations weather log pages that *Point Camden* ever went out."

So, Deputy Kroll was seriously misinformed. And we have further evidence of an LASD cover-up now that we know the sheriff's department left the Coast Guard cutter cooling its heels in San Pedro. No wonder Coast Guard officials were trying to contact Rasure the following day.

Chapter 5: A Second Opinion

Much of the information in this chapter comes from the training and experience of forensic pathologist Dr. Christina Stanley and former coroner's investigator Pamela Eaker combined with Dr. Noguchi's official autopsy report and results of toxicological and microscopic tests for Natalie Wood Wagner.

On Pages 481-483 in *Natalie Wood*, Finstad claims to have discovered a new witness, Dr. Michael Franco, a family medicine specialist in Los Angeles, who told her, nearly four decades after the fact, that he was a "volunteer intern" in the coroner's office, was present during Natalie's autopsy and saw "friction burns" on the "anterior thighs and shins and ankles" of both legs. Those injuries led Dr. Franco to believe that because of the "striations," it was "almost like somebody being *pushed off*" [emphasis added]. The official autopsy diagrams depict no such "friction burns," and, most significantly, Interim Chief Coroner and Medical Examiner, Dr. Lakshmanan Sathyavagiswaran, who examined the undisclosed autopsy photographs before drawing his conclusions in 2012, reported no such "friction burns." Our attempts to locate Dr. Franco were in vain. We could find no record of him currently practicing family medicine in Los Angeles. Like so many of Finstad's "resources," the claim is unverifiable.

Before publication of this book, I filed my fourth California Public Records Act case *Perroni v. Villanueva* (Superior Court of Los Angeles County No. 21STCP00108) to obtain access to the Natalie Wood autopsy photographs to close the book on the amount, severity and location of bruises, scrapes and scratches on Natalie's body, including the scratch on her throat. The Superior Court judge has yet to rule.

Books: *Coroner* (Noguchi) pp. 14-16, 18-20, 23-24, 32-33, 37-38 (Paul Miller), 24, 26 (Choi), 25 (bruises, no deep skull trauma, "conscious in the water"), 26 (Kornblum), 32 ("fingernail scratches" on dinghy); *Goodbye* (Rulli with Davern) p. 146 (Natalie had seafood)

Investigatory records: LASD 1981 file; Coroner 1981 file; Eaker report

Newspapers: The Washington Post, *Ronald Kornblum; Did Stars' Autopsies* (9/29/2008); Los Angeles Times, Joseph Choi obituary (1/19/2012)

Online sources: Rulli blog; National Oceanic and Atmospheric Administration historical tide chart for Santa Catalina Island, Calif., for November 28, 1981, and November 29, 1981, https://tidesandcurrents.noaa.gov/noaatidepredictions.html?id=9410079&units= standard&bdate=19811128&edate=19811129&timezone=LST/LDT&clock=12hour& datum=MLLW&interval=hilo&action=data; *Measurements of the forearm in inhabitants of the Lublin region*, Zarzycka and Zaluska, *Annales Universitatis Mariae Curie-Sklodowska*, 1989; 44:85-92, https://www.ncbi.nlm.nih.gov/pubmed/2562693

Television: HBO documentary, .45 (mid-1970s interview of Natalie with Rona Barrett about fear of "dark water, sea water")

Witnesses: Lana Wood, Pamela Eaker and Sherry Joyce to SP

Chapter 6: Half-Life

Books: *2010 Physicians' Desk Reference* re: Bactrim DS (PDR Network LLC, 11/2009); *Natasha* (Finstad) p. 252 (nightly sleeping pill); *Natalie Wood* (Lambert) p. 521 (nightly sleeping pill), 507-510, 539 (abusing drugs); *Natalie* (Lana Wood) p. 205 (nightly sleeping pill)

Investigatory records: Coroner 1981 file; Eaker report

Newspapers: Los Angeles Times, *Medication Found in Body of Actress Reported Harmless* (12/4/1981)

Online sources: Lilly H03 Darvon (Darvon 65 mg) https://www.drugs.com/imprints/ lilly-h03-darvon-14801.html; Janet Carleton's Hollywood, *Quaaludes Probably Killed Natalie Wood, Not Robert Wagner*, http://www.janetcharltonshollywood.com/?s=Natalie +wood+NOt+Robert+Wagner; Radar Online, *Never-Before-Heard Tape: Natalie Wood Admits to Boozing, Pill Popping & Smoking Weed* (2/7/2018) https://radaronline.com/videos/natalie-wood-death-admitted-pills-weed-secret-recording/

Professional journals: *The Effect of Therapeutic Hypothermia on Drug Metabolism and Drug Response: Cellular Mechanisms to Organ Function*, Zhou and Poloyac, *Expert Opinion on Drug Metabolism & Toxicology*, 7/2011, 7(7):803-816; *Effects of Hypothermia on Pharmacokinetics and Pharmacodynamics: A Systematic Review of Preclinical and Clinical Studies*, van den Broek, Groenendaal, Egberts and Rademaker, *Clinical Pharmacokinetics*, 5/2010; 49(5):277-294; *Meclizine Metabolism and Pharmacokinetics: Formulation on Its Absorption*, Wang, Lee, Pearce, Qian,

Wang, Zhang and Chow, *Journal of Clinical Pharmacology*, 9/2012, 52(9):1343-1349; *Postmortem Drug Concentration Intervals for the Non-Intoxicated State – A Review*, Linnet, *Journal of Forensic and Legal Medicine*, 7/2012, 19(5):245-249; *Hydroxyzine Distribution in Postmortem Cases and Potential for Redistribution*, McIntyre, Mallett, Trochta and Morhaime, *Forensic Science International*, 7/10/2013, 231(1-3):28-33; *Drug Concentrations in Post-Mortem Femoral Blood Compared with Therapeutic Concentrations in Plasma*, Launiainen and Ojanpera, *Drug Test Analysis*, 4/2014, 6(4):308-316

Television: Reelz *Autopsy: The Last Hours of Natalie Wood*, Season 6, Episode 1, 1/30/2016 (medication susceptible to bruising)

Witnesses: Jonathan Unwer and Dr. Christina Stanley to SP; communications with Eli Lilly about Darvon capsules

Chapter 7: Cold Water

Books: *The Nature and Treatment of Hypothermia*, Robert S. Pozos, Ph. D., and Lorentz E. Withers, Jr., Ph.D. (University of Minnesota Press Minneapolis 1983) pp. 3-19 (immersion hypothermia), 61-68 (cerebral circulation), 121-129 (shivering/respiratory parameters), 182-194 (accidental hypothermia); *Hypothermia: Causes, Effects, Prevention*, Robert S. Pozos, Ph. D. And David O. Born (New Century Publishers, Inc. 1982) pp. 1-8 (the human experience), 9-22 (hypothermia and thermoregulation), 23-42 (biology of body heat), 43-68 (hypothermia: what really happens), 52-53 (cold-induced gasps), 55-56 (cold-induced diuresis); *Human Performance in the Cold*, Gary A. Laursen, Robert S. Pozos and Franklin G. Hempel (Undersea Medical Society, Inc. 1982) p. 2 (muscle strength and shivering), 7-28 (pain), 25 (effects of cold stress), 26 (cold shock vs. hypothermia), 29 (brain cooling), 30-31 (shivering), 31-32 (alcohol minimizes shivering); *Handbook of Forensic Pathology*, Second Edition, Vincent DiMaio and Suzanna Dana (CRC Press 2007) p. 216 (drowning victims sinking); *Goodbye* (Rulli with Davern) p. 18 (adjusting the heat), 261-263 (Wayne); *Coroner* (Noguchi) Preface, pp. 9-12, 13-41 (Natalie Wood chapter); *Hypothermia, Frostbite and other Cold Injuries*, Gordon Giesbrecht Ph.D. and James A. Wilkerson M.D. (The Mountaineers Books 2006); *Natasha* (Finstad) p. 432 (Wayne said "twenty minutes"); *Natalie Wood* (Finstad) p. 479 ("struck unconscious," what Dr. Lakshmanan Sathyavagiswaran believes), 481 (Herrera, significant head wounds)

On Vidal Herrera's LinkedIn page, he calls himself a former "Deputy Medical Investigator." In fact, he started in the coroner's office as an autopsy technician and became a coroner investigator sometime around Natalie's death. Finstad calls him a "photographer" in *Natalie Wood*, but according to Pamela Eaker, the lab had full-time photographers in November 1981, and Herrera wasn't one of them. When Herrera left the coroner's office, he started a business, 1-800-AUTOPSY, performing private autopsies. I learned that over the years, the coroner's office has been troubled over Herrera charging families for performing autopsies that should have been performed for free by the coroner. So, I contacted Eaker about Herrera and his allegation in Finstad's *Natalie Wood* that he saw "significant" wounds on Natalie's head that weren't documented. Eaker, who was present during the autopsy and witnessed no such injuries, was understandably offended by Herrera's 39-year delayed revelation.

Court documents and records: Hernandez deposition

Investigatory records: LASD 1981 file; Coroner 1981 file; Miller report; Eaker report; Dr. L supplemental report

Online sources: Noguchi and Wilson 1981 videos; weather station data for November 28, 1981, at Naval Auxiliary Landing Field (NALF) Sherman Field weather on San Clemente Island, Calif., https://www.almanac.com/weather/history/zipcode/90704/1981-11-28#; CBS *48 Hours* interview of Doug Bombard (2011) https://www.cbsnews.com/video/doug-bombard-on-finding-natalie-woods-body/

Professional journals: Abstract, *Effect of alcohol on thermal balance of man in cold water,* Fox, Hayward and Hobson, *Canadian Journal of Physiology and Pharmacology,* 8/1979; *Shivering and pathological and physiological clinic oscillations of the human ankle,* Pozos and Iaizzo, Department of Physiology, School of Medicine, University of Minnesota, *Journal of Applied Physiology,* 11/1991, 71(5):1929-1932; *Current concepts: Accidental hypothermia,* Danzl and Pozos, *The New England Journal of Medicine* 12/29/1994, 331(26):1756-1760

Transcripts: Howard podcast

Witnesses: Doug Bombard to Jan Morris; Dr. Robert Pozos, Doug Bombard, Dr. Christina Stanley, Pamela Eaker and Lana Wood to SP

Chapter 8: First Contact

Books: *Natasha* (Finstad) pp. 415-417 (Wintler and Whiting); *Poor Little Rich Girl: The Life and Legend of Barbara Hutton,* C. David Heymann (Lyle Stuart, Inc. 1983) p. 283 (Egyptian scarab beetle)

Court documents and records: Probate file

Investigatory records: LASD 1981 file; Kroll report

Magazines: Reminisce, *Ma Bell on the Line: Switchboard operators connected callers across the board* (9/2018)

Newspapers: Los Angeles Times, Richard W. Kroll funeral notice (4/25/1996)

Online sources: Isthmus Cove mooring map, https://assets.simpleviewinc.com/simpleview/image/upload/c_pad,q_75,w_1600/v1/clients/catalinaisland/Isthmus_dee3cbdb-1088-4c43-8501-e3034f678b24.jpg; scarab beetle gold rings, https://www.ross-simons.com/14kt-yellow-gold-scarab-beetle-ring-915470.html

Witnesses: Paul Wintler to SP; SP's interview with "old-timer" in Catalina bar; Sherry Joyce to SP

Chapter 9: The Bond Girl

Books: *Natasha* (Finstad) pp. 141-144 (Natalie and Sinatra), 389-390, 393 (Louise Fletcher); *His Way* (Kelley) p. 226 ("real good to his girls"), 243 (hired Korshak), 439 (Bea Korshak maid of honor), 529 (Capone and Korshak); *Mr. S: My Life with Frank Sinatra,* George Jacobs and William Stadiem (HarperCollins 2003) p. 11 (Wagner crazy about St. John), 70 ("conducted in top secret"), 70-71 ("very protective;" encouraged Natalie to marry Wagner), 72 (forgave Wagner for Tina; gave blessing to marry St. John), 109 (Korshak most feared fixer), 256 (Barbara best friends with Bea Korshak); *Goodbye* (Rulli with Davern) p. 82 (Jill St. John and Stefanie Powers), 127, 136 (pieces of eight necklace); *Pieces* (Wagner) pp. 197-200 ("extramarital gopher holes"), 198 (Wasserman), 202-204 (financial disparity), 214-215 (Ziffren), 264 ("catatonic"), 276-279 (St. John); *Heart to Heart* (Maychick) Acknowledgments, pp. 140-142 (St. John); *Natalie Wood* (Lambert) p. 96 (St. John ballet classmate); *Kissinger: A Biography*, Walter Isaacson (Simon & Schuster 1992) pp. 360-361 (St. John relationship), 365 (holding hands with Kissinger); *My Life as a Mankiewicz: An Insider's Journey Through Hollywood*, Tom Mankiewicz and Robert Crane (University Press of Kentucky 2012) pp. 81-82 (*Diamonds Are Forever* roles), 145 (St. John's roommate), 223 (St. John in *Hart to Hart* pilot); *Supermob: How Sidney Korshak and His Criminal Associates Became America's Hidden Power Brokers*, Gus Russo (Bloomsbury 2007) p. 329 (St. John was Korshak's "weakness," her "alleged 162 IQ"), 330 (met Korshak in 1962), 331 (Korshak "keeping" St John, apartment in Beverly Hills, "passion" for jewelry, home in Aspen), 333 (St. John and Kissinger), 335 (Korshak-St. John affair ended), 399-400 (Cubby Broccoli like a brother; St. John gets Tiffany Case role); *Poor Little Rich Girl: The Life and Legend of Barbara Hutton*, C. David Heymann (Lyle Stuart, Inc. 1983) p. 283 (St. John and Reventlow, her high IQ and passion for jewelry), 290 (Reventlow to advance St. John's career), 296 (St. John ambitious), 300-301 (St. John 1963 divorce from Reventlow, seeing Sinatra)

Court documents and records: Probate file

Investigatory records: LASD 1981 file

Magazines: Playboy, *The Scarab Formula One* (March 1960); People, *Friends Say It's Love* (8/28/1982); Globe, *Robert Wagner and Sinatra Loved Same Three Women* (6/9/1998); Rustler, *Jill St. John: Her Nips Are The Pips* (July 1981); Popular Mechanics, *The True Story of the Lost Sci-Fi Movie 'Brainstorm,' Natalie Wood's Last Film* (12/21/2018); Vanity Fair, *The Man Who Kept The Secrets* (April 1997); This Week, *Too Many Jacks for Jill* (1/5/1964); Saturday Evening Post, *Hollywood's Carefree Child* (5/9/1964)

Newspapers: The News and Observer (Raleigh, N.C.) *'Brainstorm' back on West Coast* (10/29/1981); Los Angeles Times, *Jill St. John: A Return To Show Biz*, Roderick Mann (10/15/1981); Democrat and Chronicle (Rochester, N.Y.) *JILL ST. JOHN: Daughter of a construction worker, today she takes luxury for granted in everything from her huge collection of jewelry to her huge set of electric trains'* (7/26/1970); The Miami News, *Jill St. John survives in really fine style* (8/9/1971); The New York Times, *What's Doing on Hawaii's Neighbor Islands*, Robert Trumbull, 12/19/1982; Washington Post, *Sean Penn, El Chapo and Hollywood's Mutual Fascination with Big Crime* (1/11/2016); Los Angeles Times, *SHARE's Boomtown Blast* (5/22/1979); The Honolulu Advertiser, *Hawaii Report*, Don Chapman (11/4/1981)

Online sources: Inflation Calculator; Jill St. John biography, https://www.imdb.com/name/nm0001762/bio?ref_=nm_ov_bio_sm; Hawaii Tourism Authority, https://www.gohawaii.com/islands/maui/regions/west-maui/kaanapali-beach; Plantation Course, https://www.golfatkapalua.com/plantation-course/; Golf magazine, https://golf.com/travel/maui-golf-trip-play-plantation-course/; Rome2rio travel planning, https://www.rome2rio.com/s/Hyatt-Regency-Maui-Resort-Spa-Lahaina/K%C4%ABhei

Television: HBO documentary, 1.26 (Natasha states that when "Daddy Wagner and

Jill" started dating, she told him more than once that, "it was painful and I didn't like it." Natasha didn't say when Wagner and Jill started dating, but the implication was that it was shortly after her mother died. Nevertheless, Wagner apparently wasn't bothered enough by Natasha's pain to stop.)

Witnesses: Barbara Sherman to SP

The *Hart to Hart* episode Wagner was filming in Hawaii in November 1981 was "Harts and Palms," which aired in February 1982. The plot: On a restful trip to Maui, the Harts become involved in a murder mystery when Jennifer hears the wife of Jonathan's business associate scheming to murder her husband.

Chapter 10: Red Flags

Books: *Coroner* (Noguchi) pp. 21-22 (Eaker skilled investigator, what Noguchi said Eaker reported), 26-27 (Noguchi meeting before news conference, learns of Wagner/Walken quarrel); *Natasha* (Finstad) pp. 415-417 (Wintler, Oudin and Whiting), 419 (Smith found dinghy), 421 (Eaker), 436 (Smith reports fingernail scratches), 438 (breaking rules); *Goodbye* (Rulli with Davern) p. 281 (Eaker), 328 (Smith); *Goodbye Natalie, Goodbye Splendour,* Marti Rulli with Dennis Davern (E-Rights/E-Reads, Ltd. Publishers, paperback 2009) Epilogue, p. 373 (Smith the victim), 374 (Wagner said argument transpired), 375 ("boat-hopping"), 378 (examined Natalie's body), 379 (saw scratches on the dinghy)

Investigatory records: Coroner 1981 file; Eaker report; Dr. L supplemental report; Kroll report; LASD 1981 file

Newspapers: Los Angeles Times, *Natalie Wood Found Dead Off Catalina*, Ted Thackrey Jr. (11/30/1981)

Online sources: Rulli blog

Transcripts: Howard podcast

Witnesses: Pamela Eaker to SP; John Claude Stonier to Jade Vinson

Chapter 11: Coroner to the Stars

Books: *Coroner* (Noguchi) p. 16 ("match his expert findings"), 23 (first duty to suspect murder), 27-32 (news conference re: Natalie), 28 (alcohol level), 34-36 (believed Wagner), 45-46 (father's case), 47 (law school), 47-49 (medical background), 48 ("break new barriers"), 68 (board certified), 163 ("psychological autopsies"), 173-194 (DeFreeze), 196 (requests to solve mysterious homicides), 220-222 (Holden), 242-244 (demotion); *Goodbye* (Rulli with Davern) pp. 209, 211-212 (screaming, cussing argument); *Handbook of Forensic Pathology,* Second Edition, Vincent DiMaio and Suzanna Dana (CRC Press 2007) pp. 7-8 (autopsy photographs), 13 (speculation should be absent), 17-18 (fingernails), 23 (TOD factors), 26-27 (stomach contents), 74 (abrasions), 156-158 (choking and strangulation), 213-217 (drowning victims sinking), 220 (hypothermia), 257 (collect blood from femoral vessels), 258 (routine testing); *Handbook* (Eliopulos) p. 24 (photographing a death scene), 45 (fingernail scrapings), 101 (factors that solve crimes), 125 (witness appraisal), 127-151 (homicide investigations, altercation homicides), 195-196 (motive and opportunity), 231 (alcohol-related death); *Gia Scala: The First Gia*, Tina Scala with Sterling St. James (Parhelion House 2012) p. 7 (blood on her pillow)

On Pages 455-457 of *Natalie Wood*, Finstad attempts to create linkage between Noguchi's mention of a psychological autopsy at the news conference on Natalie's autopsy findings and the subsequent intervention of Frank Sinatra. However, Noguchi in *Coroner* touches on the subject in passing as a less than serious idea to distract reporters from his Wagner/Walken "argument" statements.

California law: California Health & Safety Code §102875 (death certificate requirements of coroner); California Government Code §§ 27511, 27491 (Coroner duties), 27491.6, 27491.7, 27493, 27492, 27499 (summoning witnesses), 27499.1, 27498, 27499, 27491.8 (confidential communications of deceased), 27497, 27504, 27504.1 and 27502.2 (inquest authorization and procedures)

Court citations: *Thomas T. Noguchi, M.D. v. Board of Supervisors of the County of Los Angeles, et al* No. C457707; *Morris v. Noguchi* (1983) 141 Cal. App. 3d 521; *Huntly v. Zurich General A. L. Ins. Co.* (1929) 100 Cal. App. 201; *Mar Shee v. Maryland Assurance Corp.* (1922) 190 Cal. 1; *Noguchi v. Civil Service Commission of the County of Los Angeles* (1986) 187 Cal. App 3d 1521; respondent's brief dated 5/30/1984 in *Thomas T. Noguchi, M.D. v. Board of Supervisors of the County of Los Angeles, et al* No. C457707, pp. 40-41; *Bock v. County of Los Angeles*, Court of Appeal, Second District, Division 5, California (Civ. No. 66916, 12/22/1983); *Brymer v. Sheriff* (1976) 92 Nev. 598 (Oscar Bonavena); findings of fact and conclusions of law issued 2/2/1983 by Sara Adler, hearing officer, Civil Service Commission, in *Thomas T. Noguchi, M.D. v. Board of Supervisors of the County of Los Angeles, et al* No. C457707, pp. 35-36; respondent's brief prepared by William A. Masterson 5/23/1983 in *Thomas T. Noguchi, M.D. v. Board of Supervisors of the County of Los Angeles, et al* No. C457707; *Bock v. County of Los Angeles* (1983) 150 Cal. App. 3d 65; *Noguchi v. Civil Service Commission of the County of Los Angeles* (1986) 187 Cal. App. 3d 1521; Respondents' brief filed on 6/18/1986 in *Noguchi v. Civil Service Commission of the County of Los Angeles, et al* Court of Appeal, Second Appellate District, case number B009475; findings of fact and conclusions of law recommendation, clerk's transcript, *Thomas T. Noguchi, M.D. v. Board of Supervisors of the County of Los Angeles, et al* No. C457707 (8/16/1984)

Court documents and records: Noguchi deposition

Investigatory records: Coroner 1981 file; Miller report; Dr. L supplemental report and Dr. L amendment; certificate of death for Natalie Wood Wagner; LASD 1981 file

Magazines: National Enquirer, *Enquirer Exclusive: Blistering Best-Seller That's Rubbing the Raw Nerve of Hollywood* (3/1983)

Newspapers/Noguchi: Los Angeles Times, *New twist in Wood's death: Coroner adds 'other undetermined factors' to drowning as cause*, Goffard, Mather and Winton (1/14/2013); The New York Times, *A Chastised 'Coroner to the Stars,'* Robert Lindsey (3/12/1982); The Bulletin (Bend, Ore.) *Sinatra wants Noguchi fired: 'Coroner of the stars' suspended*, Roger Bennett (3/12/1982); Los Angeles Times, *L.A. Coroner Draws a Reprimand: Comments on Holden and Wood Termed 'Sensationalism'* (1/20/1982); Los Angeles Times, *Need to Be 'Big Cheese': Ego Problem Seen as Noguchi's Flaw*, Laurie Becklund (12/28/1981); Los Angeles Times, *Coroner's Office Errors Trigger Criticism: Serious Mistakes Affect Inquiries, Trials, Insurance Settlements*, Laurie Becklund (12/27/1981); The Hanford Sentinel (Hanford, Calif.) *L.A. clears Noguchi* (11/9/1983); Los Angeles Times, *Noguchi Blends Job With Pet Projects,* Laurie Becklund (12/28/1981); The Muncie Star (Muncie, Ind.) *Officials Order Investigation of L.A. Coronor (sic)* (12/30/1981); Daily Journal (Franklin, Ind.) *'Quincy' model: Coroner's Office Investigated* (12/30/1981); Los Angeles Times, editorial, *A Sloppy Ship* (12/29/1981); Los Angeles Times, *7,000 Sign Scroll, Ask Just Ruling on Noguchi Dismissal,* Ray Zeman (7/16/1969); Los Angeles Times ad, *A Plea For Justice* (7/11/1969)

Newspapers/1981 death: Los Angeles Times, *Drowning Called Accidental: Natalie Wood Fell From Yacht, Coroner Believes,* Jones and Belcher (12/1/1981); Los Angeles Times, *Heard Cries for Help Near Wagner Boat, Woman Says,* Love and Klunder (12/3/1981); The Sun (San Bernardino County, Calif.) *Sheriff winding up Wood drowning case* (12/2/1981); Los Angeles Times, *Dispute Before Wood's Death Now in Doubt,* Jones and Harris (12/2/1981); Los Angeles Herald Examiner, *Some Drinks, a Fight, a Death. Natalie Wood Left Yacht While Husband and Co-Star Argued, Coroner Says,* Schorr and Furillo (12/1/1981)

Newspapers/other: Progress Bulletin (Pomona, Calif.) *Patricia Hearst, Harris couple drop from sight* (5/26/1974); Los Angeles Times, *Suspected SLA Hideout Stormed, 5 Die: Fire Destroys House; Victims Burned Beyond Recognition* (5/18/1974); Independent (Long Beach, Calif.) *Saga of 'two Patty Hearsts' quite intriguing* (6/27/1974); The Times (San Mateo, Calif.) *Coroner's Team Rules: Marilyn 'Probable Suicide'* (8/17/1962); Oakland Tribune (Oakland, Calif.) *Some Believe Marilyn Met 'Foul Play'* (11/3/1962); Tulare Advance-Register (Tulare, Calif.) *Mystery Phone Call Clouds Marilyn Monroe's Death* (8/7/1962); The San Francisco Examiner, *Marilyn -- Poison Ruled Out* (8/16/1962)

Online sources: Noguchi and Wilson 1981 videos; *Omni* magazine, *Interview: Thomas Noguchi, M.D.*, Douglas Stein (11/1986) pp. 47-50, 77-80 of PDF: http://www.housevampyr. com/training/library/books/omni/OMNI_1986_11.pdf; *Death and Resurrection: The Tale of Coroner Noguchi,* Daniel J. B. Mitchell, UCLA, https://escholarship.org/uc/item/6vn0p89z

Professional journals: *Strangulation: A Full Spectrum of Blunt Neck Trauma,* Line, Stanley and Choi, *The Annals of Otology, Rhinology and Laryngology,* 11/1985, 94(6):542-546; *Ambroise Tardieu: The man and his work on child maltreatment a century before Kempe,* Labbe, *Child Abuse & Neglect,* 4/2005, 29(4):311-324; *Asphyxial Deaths and Petechiae: A Review,* Ely and Hirsch, *Journal of Forensic Sciences,* 11/2000, 45(6):1274-1277; *Types of Injuries and Interrelated Conditions of Victims and Assailants in Attempted and Homicidal Strangulation,* Harm and Rajs, *Forensic Science International,* 9/1981, 18(2):101-23

Transcripts: Testimony transcript of Thomas Noguchi in *United States of America v. Leonard Peltier* (Dist. Ct. of North Dakota, CR No. C77-3003, 1977, Vol. IV, pp. 36-83); transcript of appearance of Thomas T. Noguchi, M.D. on 8/28/1988 episode of *The Late Show* with Ross Shafer

Chapter 12: Overboard

Books: *Coroner* (Noguchi) p. 15 (perfectly positioned expert), 18 (saw Natalie alone in the dinghy), 20 ("It was Robert Wagner"), 20 ("cruising in the vicinity"), 23 ("would be conclusive," "special investigation"), 23 (directives to Miller), 32 ("fingernail scratches" on dinghy), 32-33 (radio check), 36 (Miller report filed away); *Natalie Wood* (Lambert), pp. 535-536 (dinghy tied to *Splendour's* port, called Coast Guard); *Natasha* (Finstad) pp. 435-439 (Noguchi and Miller), 437 (body and dinghy "close together")

Court documents and records: Respondent's answers to requests for admission, First Set, Nos. 2 and 3 filed 4/8/2016 and Noguchi deposition in *Perroni v. Fajardo*

Investigatory records: Eaker report; Miller report; LASD 1981 file; Dr. L supplemental report

Magazines: National Enquirer, *Wagner Protected by 'Conspiracy of Silence'* (1/4/2016); National Enquirer, *Natalie Wood Probe Stalls as Cops Refuse to Talk* (5/23/2016)

Newspapers: Daily News (New York, N.Y.*) How Natalie Wood died: Her husband, bitter over stories, gives his views*, Bob Lardine (12/26/1981)

Online sources: California Sailing Academy website, http://www.californiasailing academy.com/CSA_Paul_Miller.php (site was removed sometime before the summer 2019); California Sailing Academy Inc., http://showgirlltd.com/CSA-1.html; Healthline, *Managing the Fear of Water (Aquaphobia)* Sara Lindberg (3/15/2018) https://www.healthline. com/health/aquaphobia#causes; Atlas Obscura, *The People Who Suffer From Thalassophobia, or Fear of the Sea*, Eric Grundhauser (7/21/2016) https://www.atlasobscura.com/articles/ the-people-who-suffer-from-thalassophobia-or-fear-of-the-sea

Witnesses: FOI communications with Hawa A. Wehelie, U.S. Coast Guard, Office of Information Management (EFOIA@uscg.mil) concerning transcripts of radio communications from the Isthmus, Catalina Island, from 10 p.m. November 28, 1981, to 10 a.m. November 29, 1981; Robert Pozos, Paul Wintler and William D. Peterson to SP

Additional material: SP's inspection of Isthmus Cove, Santa Catalina Island, California

For me, it was plain to see that Paul Miller had suspicions about the story and time line of Natalie's disappearance. He wanted Dr. Noguchi to get the Coast Guard transcripts of radio transmissions so he could verify the back end of the time line on Natalie being officially declared missing. The transcripts would have unquestionably done that as well as identify the person who called the Coast Guard and the time of the call. Dr. Noguchi ignored Miller's suggestion. In addition, I saw no evidence that the LASD attempted to secure this important evidence.

Chapter 13: Down with the Ship

On Page 274 in his book *Pieces*, Wagner claims that everything Davern removed from *Splendour* and stored in the Cañon Drive pool house was placed in a storage building that was completely destroyed by the Northridge earthquake that hit Los Angeles in 1994. The peak ground acceleration of the earthquake was the highest ever instrumentally recorded in an urban area in North America. It caused billions of dollars of damage and killed 60 people. Due to the passage of time, I was unable to confirm Wagner's assertion that the *Splendour* items were wiped out. So, whatever evidentiary value they could offer was now lost forever.

Books: *Goodbye* (Rulli with Davern) pp. 7, 9-10, 50 (a drunk), 18 (tasks, "menial or large"), 21-23 (military service, background), 26 (scotch), 29-33 (*Dizzy Izzy*, meeting the Wagners), 38 (Walken's wisdom), 45 (call me R.J., met Wille Mae Worthen), 50 (Crowley, Natalie's best friend), 67-75 ("prisoner"), 92-94 (invitations to Cañon Drive), 96 (moved to *Splendour*), 107-109 (Yolanda), 112 (afraid for his life), 117-123 (Quaaludes), 125-148 (Friday and Saturday morning), 151 (collusion with Wagner), 153 (getting stories straight), 156-166 (Sunday morning), 173-174 (in the movies), 190-191 (leaving LA), 195 ("swish"), 209-216 (Davern's rendition of events), 242 ("bitter anger"), 253-254 ("tied lines tight"), 271 (Kroll sees broken glass), 288 (Lambert's mission), 313-316 (polygraphs), 321-323 ("forensic hypnotist"); *Natasha* (Finstad) pp. 372-373 (fear of water, drinking on the job), 443 (Davern's "funds depleted"); *Pieces* (Wagner) p. 131 ("that fucking cunt"), 173 ("the beautiful Marion"), 229 (Willie Mae Worthen); *The Westmores of Hollywood*, Frank Westmore and Muriel Davidson (J.B. Lippincott Company 1976); *His Way* (Kelley) p. 503 ("control"); *Natalie Wood* (Lambert) p. 530 ("a terrible fight")

Court documents and records: Probate file

Investigatory records: LASD 1981 file; Kroll report; Dr. L supplemental report and Dr. L amendment; Coroner 1981 file; Eaker report

Magazines: National Enquirer, *Wagner Lies Over Night Natalie Died* (8/31/2015); Star, *The Untold Secrets of Natalie Wood's Life With Robert Wagner* (1/17/1984); Star, *Natalie Mystery Solved: Yacht skipper breaks his silence…at last* (7/23/1985); Star, *Natalie Wood, Wagner and me– Christopher Walken tells own story of drowning* (6/18/1985); Vanity Fair (Kashner) pp. 214-233

Newspapers: Los Angeles Times, *Entertainment Industry Under Inquiry by FBI* (10/2/1980); Los Angeles Times, *Walter Grauman "Columbo" TV Director Dies*, David Colker (3/29/2015); Honolulu Star-Advertiser, *Yacht tied to Natalie Wood's drowning removed from harbor* (1/30/2020)

Online sources: Rulli blog; Television Academy Foundation, Archive of America Television interview with Walter Grauman, https://interviews.televisionacademy.com/interviews/walter-e-grauman?clip=97408#people-clips; Beck Law website, https://www.markbecklaw.com/who-we-are; Frank Westmore obituary (5/16/1985) https://www.nytimes.com/1985/05/16/arts/frank-westmore-62-a-film-makeup-artist.html; Tommy Thompson biography, http://www.tv.com/people/tommy-thompson-v/biography/; Edwin James Butterworth Jr. obituary (12/17/2018) https://www.legacy.com/obituaries/name/edwin-butterworth-jr-obituary?pid=191037028; November, 1981 moon phases, https://www.predicalendar.com/moon/phases/1981/november/

Television: HBO documentary, .13 (Hollywood royalty); Geraldo Rivera TV show, *Now It Can Be Told* (1/26/1992); Episode 4 of British documentary, *The Final Day:* Natalie Wood (7/8/2000)

Transcripts: Howard podcast; TV episode of *Nancy Grace* (11/18/2011) http://transcripts.cnn.com/TRANSCRIPTS/1111/18/ng.01.html

Witnesses: Marti Rulli, Paul Wintler, Lana Wood, Jonathan Unwer and Ron Nelson to SP

Additional material: SP's inspection of mooring sites, pier, Harbor Reef Restaurant and Harbor Reef Saloon at Two Harbors, Santa Catalina Island, California; Robert Wagner Instagram, 12/1/2020 (date of Willie Mae Worthen's death)

Chapter 14: Out of the Shadows

There is nothing more illuminating than visiting the scene of a crime. The Isthmus at Santa Catalina Island has changed very little in the last 40 years. Viewing the terrain, feeling the wind and observing the distances in person are certainly more beneficial than reading about them. While the weather and time of day cannot be perfectly duplicated with conditions on Saturday, November 28, 1981, if I were prosecuting a case involving Natalie's death, I would ask the judge to allow the jury to visit the scene to observe it for themselves.

Books: *Natasha* (Finstad) pp. 413-414 (Payne and Wayne), 431-432 (Rasure's doubts); *Coroner* (Noguchi) p. 39 (Wayne did hear shouts for help); *Goodbye* (Rulli with Davern) p. 266 (Wayne "conscientious and honest")

Investigatory records: LASD 1981 file; Kroll report; Dr. L supplemental report

Magazines: Vanity Fair (Kashner) p. 218

Newspapers: Los Angeles Times, *Heard Cries for Help Near Wagner Boat, Woman Says,* Love and Klunder (12/3/1981); The Sun (San Bernardino County, Calif.) *Witness says she heard screams from direction of Wood's yacht* (12/4/1981) (Curt Craig quotes); Canyon News (Beverly Hills, Calif.) '*I Heard Natalie Wood's Cries*' (10/19/2011); The Guardian (London) *Natalie Wood case: witness feared for life* (11/21/2011)

Online sources: Rulli blog; Isthmus Cove mooring map, https://assets.simpleviewinc .com/simpleview/image/upload/c_pad,q_75,w_1600/v1/clients/catalinaisland/Isthmus _dee3cbdb-1088-4c43-8501-e3034f678b24.jpg; Avon inflatable boats, https://www. penninemarine.com/boat-fleet/zodiac-bombard-avon-zodiac-milpro-brands-explained; Marshall Wayne (identification material only) https://en.wikipedia.org/wiki/Marshall_ Wayne

Television: HBO documentary, .35 (TV news station helicopter shot of Isthmus Sunday morning, November 29, 1981, after Natalie's body was discovered)

Transcripts: Howard podcast

Witnesses: Lana Wood, Marilyn Wayne, Kerri Appleby Payne, Marti Rulli, William Peterson, Paul Wintler and Curt Craig to SP

William Peterson said Warren Archer, who was obviously three sheets to the wind, called him at "approximately 1:00 a.m." asking if the bar was still open. After Peterson said no, Archer called back five minutes later to ask if Peterson would call *Splendour* and invite the group over for a drink. Peterson declined. After being rebuffed by Peterson, Archer states he called *Splendour* to personally invite them over for a drink. On Pages 463-464 in *Natalie Wood*, Finstad boldly claims Archer told investigators that when he called, he overheard "R.J. and Natalie fighting *shortly before 11 p.m.* [emphasis added.]" In fact, the official report and Rasure's notes give no time for the call and reflect an uncertainty about what he heard. Rasure's notes state, "He [Archer] *got the impression* Bob and Natalie *or someone* [emphasis added] was arguing or fighting (noise in the background)." Based on the known timing of the call to Peterson, Archer's call to *Splendour* had to be much later than 11 p.m. and if it was around 1 a.m. like Peterson said, Natalie was most likely deceased.

Additional material: SP's inspection of Isthmus Cove, Harbor Reef Restaurant, Harbor Reef Saloon and Blue Cavern Point, Santa Catalina Island, California

Chapter 15: Sister Act

Books: *Natalie* (Lana Wood) pp. 199-204 (call from Wagner, Walken "looking odd"), 69, 205 (Natalie's drinking); *Natalie Wood* (Lambert) p. 267 ("I got the tits"), 441 (honeymoon), 489 (credit card charges by Lana), 525-26 (Lana and Davern's avarice), 556-58 (Lana inherits clothes), 564 (Lana keeps Maria close), 545 (Wagner call to Crowley); *Goodbye* (Rulli with Davern) p. 216 (Wagner's phone call); *Hairdresser to the Stars: A Hollywood Memoir*, Ginger "Sugar" Blymyer (www.InfinityPublishing.com 2000) pp. 218-224 (*Memory of Ava Ryker*, "bailed Lana out"); *Pieces* (Wagner) p. 269 (Lana's inheritance); *Coroner* (Noguchi) pp. 38-39 (Noguchi's theory); *Natasha* (Finstad) pp. 445-448 (Davern's drunken calls); *Natalie Wood* (Finstad) p. 464 ("push Natalie overboard"), 466 (Wagner and Lambert), 476 (Davern "did nothing"), 478 (Davern's alleged confession)

California law: California Civil Code of Procedure §129 (photographs, etc. taken in course of post-mortem examination or autopsy)

Court citations: official file in *Patino v. Edward Maldonado, Evan Maldonado and Lana Wood* case number 56-2017-00492713-CL-UD-VTA

Investigatory records: LASD 1981 file; Coroner 1981 file

Magazines: Playboy, *The Well-Versed Lana Wood* (4/1971) pp. 100-103; People, *Robert Wagner and Daughters Put Natalie Wood's Personal Belongings Up For Auction* (11/23/2015); Reminisce, *Ma Bell on the Line: Switchboard operators connected callers across the board* (9/2018); National Enquirer, *Natalie Wood's Secret Diaries: My Loveless Marriage to Robert Wagner*, Simpson, Herz and Bell (4/15/2015); People, *Natalie Wood's Secrets Revealed in New Book: Her Intimate Thoughts on Dating Warren Beatty and the Death of Marilyn Monroe*, Liz McNeil (10/10/2016); People, *Natalie Wood: At last, the startling story of her life, loves and mysterious death–by her sister, Lana*, David Wallace (10/10/1983); People, *Her Final Moments: Captain Who Witnessed Natalie Wood's Last Hours Is Auctioning Off Items from Yacht*, Jodi Gugliemi (1/26/2016)

Newspapers: The News and Observer (Raleigh, N.C.) *Playing hooky from life with Natalie Wood*, Bill Morrison (10/18/1981)

Online sources: *Splendour* coffee table and plaque auction website, https://natedsanders .com/mobile/lotdetail.aspx?inventoryid=41049; Bonhams Auctions' sale of Natalie Wood awards from *The Harvard Lampoon* and *The Harvard Crimson* (11/23/2015) https://www. bonhams.com/auctions/22486/lot/34/; DailyMail.com, *Former Bond girl Lana Wood, 71, is given $30,000 by her fans after she was left homeless and living in a cramped motel room*, Crane and Parry (7/12/2017) https://www.dailymail.co.uk/news/article-4690084/Lana-Wood-given-30k-fans-left-homeless.html; FoxNews.com, *Former Bond Girl and Natalie Wood's sister Lana now homeless*, Stephanie Nolasco (4/27/2017) https://www.foxnews.com/entertainment /former-bond-girl-and-natalie-woods-sister-lana-now-homeless; FoxNews.com, *Bond Girl Lana Wood on surviving homelessness: My life was 'rapidly falling apart'*, Stephanie Nolasco (7/12/2017) https://www.foxnews.com/entertainment/bond-girl-lana-wood-on-surviving

-homelessness-my-life-was-rapidly-falling-apart

Television: HBO documentary .25 (Richard Gregson, Natalie's second husband, was arguably the most honest participant in the presentation. He admitted she caught him cheating on her and confirmed Natalie's personality as described by Lana, "She had a pretty good temper, I must say. When she let go, she let go.")

Witnesses: Lana Wood to SP; Kevin Brechner research on suspected Peter Pitchess photo

Chapter 16: The Fix

Books: *Coroner* (Noguchi) pp. 33-36 (Sinatra letter, "I became the main target"); *The Last Mafioso: The Treacherous World of Jimmy Fratianno*, Ovid Demaris (Bantam Books 1981); *The Mafia Encyclopedia*, Third Edition, Carl Sifakis (Checkmark Books, 2005); *My Story*, Judith Exner as told by Ovid Demaris (Grove Press, Inc. paperback 1977) p. 27 (dated Wagner); *His Way* (Kelley) pp. 25-26, 29 (mother), 61-64 (Tommy Dorsey), 262-269 (fear and Giancana), 281 (Frank's victory for JFK), 396 (Ronald Reagan), 410-412 (Richard Nixon), 405-406, 492-495, 436, 452 (Agnew, first ladies), 448-452 (Westchester Premier Theater), 467-484 (Pitchess, deputy badge, "Hello, Godfather," South Africa, Nevada Gaming Commission); *Kissinger: A Biography*, Walter Isaacson (Simon & Schuster 1992) pp. 360-361 (St. John relationship), 366 ("there when you needed him"); *Mr. S: My Life with Frank Sinatra*, George Jacobs and William Stadiem (HarperCollins 2003) p. 134 ("fear inducing aura"); *The Godfather*, Mario Puzo (G.P. Putnam's Sons 1969); *Natasha* (Finstad) pp. 421-422 (after Wagner's first interview, "Rasure had "what he needed"), 430-432 (Pitchess steps in), 441-443 (Walken and Davern); *Pieces* (Wagner) pp. 38-39 (fixer Harry Brand), 266 (Noguchi enrages Sinatra); *You Must Remember This*, Robert J. Wagner with Scott Eyman (Plume 2014) p. 14 ("fixers at the studio"); *Natalie Wood* (Lambert) p. 250 (Nick Gurdin manslaughter charge)

Court documents and records: letter dated 3/15/1982 from Isaac Godfrey on behalf of Thomas T. Noguchi, M.D. to Harry L. Hufford, chief administrative officer, County of Los Angeles, regarding complaints against Noguchi by Frank Sinatra and others; findings of fact and conclusions of law issued 2/2/1983 by Sara Adler, hearing officer, Civil Service Commission, in *Thomas T. Noguchi, M.D. v. Board of Supervisors of the County of Los Angeles, et al* No. C457707, p. 54; *Pitchess v. Superior Court* (1974) 11 Cal. 3d 531; declaration of Michael D. Antonovich dated 4/16/2018 and deposition of Michael D. Antonovich dated 4/25/2018 in *Perroni v. County of Los Angeles, et al* case number BS171171; CPRA request from SP dated 2/23/2017 to Kathryn Barger, supervisor, Los Angeles County Executive Office; pleadings and documents filed 10/16/2017 in *Perroni v. County of Los Angeles, et al* case number BS171171; emails from Anna Birenbaum to SP regarding identity of assistants in *Perroni v. County of Los Angeles, et al* case number BS171171; report from Nationwide Legal, LLC regarding service of subpoena process on Michael D. Antonovich in *Perroni v. County of Los Angeles, et al* case number BS171171; report from Kevin Childs, private investigator, to SP containing photo of Michael Antonovich being served a deposition subpoena in *Perroni v. County of Los Angeles, et al* case number BS171171; entry of appearance for Brian Chu, principal deputy counsel, in *Perroni v. County of Los Angeles, et al* case number BS171171; depositions of assistants Susan Osuna and Veronica Suquett 4/25/2018 in

Perroni v. County of Los Angeles, et al case number BS171171; declaration of Bruce Crouchet signed 4/20/2018 in *Perroni v. County of Los Angeles, et al* case number BS171171

In *Perroni v. Fajardo*, 2017 WL6350527 (12/13/2017), under California law, the prevailing party "shall" receive attorney fees in CPRA cases. But in my case, because I represented myself, the courts crafted a judicial exception to the mandatory language of the statute.

Investigatory records: Coroner 1981 file; LASD 1981 file

Newspapers/1981 death: Los Angeles Times, *Natalie Wood's Death Accidental Drowning: Coroner Says Actress Apparently Slipped While Leaving Yacht as Her Husband, Co-Star Argued,* Jones and Belcher (12/1/1981); Los Angeles Herald Examiner, *Some Drinks, a Fight, a Death. Natalie Wood Left Yacht While Husband and Co-Star Argued, Coroner Says,* Schorr and Furillo (12/1/1981); Daily Mirror (London) *Natalie's Last Hours,* Barry Wigmore (12/1/1981); Los Angeles Times, *Dispute Before Wood's Death Now in Doubt,* Jones and Harris (12/2/1981)

Newspapers/Sinatra: The New York Times, *3 Guilty of Racketeering in Westchester Theater Case,* Walter Waggoner (5/23/1979); Daily Mail (London) *The President, The Lady and The Godfather: A Story of Intrigue and Corruption at the Centre of Political Power* (9/20/1976); Brooklyn Eagle (Brooklyn, N.Y.) *Called Dago, Says Sinatra, The K. O. Kid* (4/9/1947); Daily News (New York, N.Y.) *Frankie & Carlo star in pic at theater trial* (12/7/1978); The Journal-News (Nyack, N.Y.) *Sinatra-Gambino photo evidence at trial,* M.J. Zuckerman (12/7/1978); The Bulletin (Bend, Ore.) *Sinatra wants Noguchi fired: 'Coroner of the stars' suspended,* Roger Bennett (3/12/1982); Los Angeles Times, *Saying Farewell to 'The Voice'* (5/21/1998)

Newspapers/Pitchess: Los Angeles Times, *Peter Pitchess, Sheriff Who Modernized Agency, Dies,* Myrna Oliver (4/5/1999); Los Angeles Times, *Former Sheriff Biscailuz Dies; Held County Posts 50 Years,* Henry Sutherland (5/17/1969); Los Angeles Times, *Deputies' Past Used to Win Attack Case,* Charles Maher (8/19/1979); Los Angeles Times, *Pitchess Is Remembered for Both Toughness and Charm,* Carla Rivera (4/9/1999)

Newspapers/other: Daily Mail (London) *"I Blamed Myself for Natalie's Death: Robert Wagner on the Night His Wife Disappeared"* (2/19/2009); Los Angeles Times, *Last of Old-Time Hollywood Press Agents: Ex-Studio Publicist Harry Brand Dies,* Burt A. Folkart (2/23/1989)

Online sources: Michael D. Antonovich biography, web.archive.org/web/2007120142916/http://antonovich.co.la.ca.us/bio/MDAbiography.pdf; LASD website, https://lasd.org/; Rick Porrello's American Mafia.com, *I Ain't No Band Leader!* John William Tuohy (6/2002) http://www.americanmafia.com/Feature_Articles_212.html; The Washington Post magazine, *AKA Frank Sinatra,* Jeff Leen (3/7/1999) https://www.washingtonpost.com/wp-srv/national/daily/march99/sinatra7_full.htm; FBI Records: The Vault re: Frank Sinatra, https://vault.fbi.gov/; Italian proverb, "The person who offends writes as if it was written on sand, and the person who is offended reads it as if it were written on marble." https://www.inspirationalstories.com/proverbs/t/about-offended/; The American Mercury magazine, *Frank Sinatra Confidential: Gangsters in the Night Club,* Lee Mortimer (8/1951) http://www.unz.com/print/AmMercury-1951aug-00029/; Joseph Kennedy quote, http://www.shoppbs.pbs.org/wgbh/amex/presidents/35_kennedy/filmmore/filmscript.html

Transcripts: 1/25/2018 hearing proceedings in *Perroni v. County of Los Angeles County,* *et al* case number BS171171; testimony of Sheriff Peter Pitchess in Nevada State Gaming Control Board transcript of recessed meeting for Frank Sinatra, consultant, entertainment and public relations, gaming license application, case number 80-51 (2/11/1981)

Witnesses: Kevin Brechner and Paul Wintler to SP

Chapter 17: Marching Orders

Books: *Natasha* (Finstad) p. 430 (Rasure/Pitchess "pulled his power"), 402-403 (Friday p.m./Saturday a.m.), 421-422 (Rasure's accident bias), 431 (Rasure "totally satisfied"), 432 (Rasure attacks Wayne), 438 (violated rules), 441-443 (Walken interviews); *Goodbye* (Rulli with Davern) p. 200 (no furniture moved), 281-283 ("shook up"); *Handbook* (Eliopulos) p. 24 (interior photography), 45 (fingernail scrapings), 101 (factors that solve crimes), 125 (witness appraisal), 127-151 (homicide investigations, altercation homicides), 195-196 (motive and opportunity), 231 (ethanol concentrations), 275-278 (drowning deaths); *Techniques* (Fisher) preface (written for crime scene and police investigators), p. 15 ("duty to the truth"), 35-38 (recording times, entering and protecting crime scene), 55 (objectives of crime scene investigations), 56 (don't draw premature conclusions), 58 (healthy skepticism), 93-99 (crime scene sketch, collecting evidence), 379 (homicide investigations require attention to detail), 380 ("suspect the worst"), 383-385 (signs of struggle), 386-390 (examination of body), 389 (hands in paper bags, fingernail clippings and scrapings), 397 (outdoor crime scenes), 412-413 (estimating time of death), 418-428 (abrasions, contusions or bruises), 426-427 (defensive injuries), 439-440 (drowning death), 448 (treat "accidental" investigation as homicide); *Pieces* (Wagner) p. 266 (Noguchi enrages Sinatra)

In 2001's *Natasha*, Finstad describes Rasure as an experienced "good-natured, self-described cowboy." In the numerous passages in which she mentions the detective, she never questions his capabilities. Yet on Pages 457-458 in the updated version of the book, she changes her tune, writing that she was "stunned by Rasure's incompetence" during her 1999 interview with him. Why it took her 22 years to do so could actually call into question her competence as a writer.

California law: California Penal Code § 187; *People v. Cole* (1903) 141 Cal. 88, 90 (false exculpatory statement); California Jury Instructions-Criminal 2.06 and 2.52 (consciousness of guilt)

Court documents and records: Hernandez deposition, p. 35 (Hamilton deceased)

Investigatory records: LASD 1981 file; Kroll report; Coroner 1981 file; Eaker report

Magazines: Vanity Fair (Kashner) pp. 214-233; Star, *Natalie Mystery Solved: Yacht skipper breaks his silence…at last* (7/23/1985)

Newspapers: The New York Times, *Natalie Wood Is Found Drowned On Yacht Visit to Santa Catalina* (11/30/1981); Daily Mirror (London) *Natalie's Last Hours*, Barry Wigmore (12/1/1981); Los Angeles Times, *Drowning Called Accidental: Natalie Wood Fell From Yacht, Coroner Believes*, Jones and Belcher (12/1/1981); Los Angeles Times, *Pitchess Is Remembered for Both Toughness and Charm*, Carla Rivera (4/9/1999)

Online sources: Duane Paul Rasure obituary (3/17/2014) https://www.findagrave.

com/memorial/126825038?search-true; CBS *48 Hours* interview of Duane Rasure (2011) https://www.youtube.com/watch?v=9KWpFDLHb3w

Transcripts: 12/1/1981 press release by Paul Ziffren for Robert Wagner as reported by Catherine Mann, *Entertainment Tonight*

Witnesses: Dr. Christina Stanley to SP; Det. Ralph Hernandez to SP

Chapter 18: Decades of Denial

Books: *Natasha* (Finstad) pp. 422, 442-443 (Davern's LASD statements); *Natalie Wood* (Lambert) pp. 528-539 (Wagner's narrative about weekend); *Goodbye* (Rulli with Davern) p. 180 ($150,000 to say "murder"), 186-187 (*Star* battle, $26,000 from *Star*), 197-199 (*A Current Affair*), 220, 223-225 ("billions" was hyperbole), 163, 282-284 (Davern's LASD statements), 206 ("I still grieve for Natalie"), 219 (*Now It Can Be Told*), dustjacket; *Pieces* (Wagner) pp. 260-262 (Wagner's theory on what happened, "hold no grudge"); *Heart to Heart* (Maychick) front cover flap

Investigatory records: LASD 1981 file

Magazines: Star, *The Untold Secrets of Natalie Wood's Life With Robert Wagner* (1/17/1984); People, *Natalie Wood: At last, the startling story of her life, loves and mysterious death–by her sister, Lana,* David Wallace (10/10/1983); Star, *Natalie Wood, Wagner and me–Christopher Walken tells own story of drowning* (6/18/1985); Star, *Natalie Mystery Solved: Yacht skipper breaks his silence…at last* (7/23/1985); Star, *Robert Wagner: How Natalie's Death Haunts Me* (8/27/1985); Playboy, *Playboy Interview: Christopher Walken* (9/1997); The Face, *Walken Talks,* Neal Norman (2/1985); Star, *Robert Wagner's 10 Years of Torment* (11/12/1991); National Enquirer, *Wagner Protected by 'Conspiracy of Silence'* (1/4/2016); National Enquirer, *Natalie Wood Probe Stalls as Cops Refuse to Talk* (5/23/2016); National Enquirer, *Natalie Autopsy Cover-up Exposed!* (8/29/2016); People, *From Any Distance, at Close Range Star Christopher Walken Comes Off as Edgy, Electric and Elusive* (5/26/1986) ("a —ing bore")

Newspapers: Los Angeles Herald Examiner, *Some Drinks, a Fight, a Death. Natalie Wood Left Yacht While Husband and Co-Star Argued, Coroner Says,* Schorr and Furillo (12/1/1981) (Walken quote); The Sun (San Bernardino County, Calif.) *Sheriff winding up Wood drowning case* (12/2/1981) (Walken quote on Noguchi); The Washington Post, *Behind the 'Heaven's Gate' Disaster,* Peter Brown (11/30/1980); Daily News (New York, N.Y.) *How Natalie Wood died: Her husband, bitter over stories, gives his views,* Bob Lardine (12/26/1981); Houston Chronicle, *Taped discussion clouds Natalie Wood's death,* Mike Daniel (2/19/1992); Atlanta Constitution, TV Watch: *You're On Candid Camera* (2/19/1992)

Online sources: Rulli blog; Inflation Calculator; CBS *48 Hours, Natalie Wood: Death in Dark Water* (2/3/2018) https://www.cbsnews.com/video/natalie-wood-death-in-dark-water-1/#x; Los Angeles Times, *Natalie Wood likely slipped and fell to her death: Christopher Walken* (11/18/2011) https://latimesblogs.latimes.com/lanow/2011/11/natalie-wood-death-christopher-walken.html; Christopher Walken biography, https://www.biography.com/actor/christopher-walken; 1979 Oscar awards for Christopher Walken and Michael Cimino, http://timelines.latimes.com/academy-awards/; Rotten Tomatoes rating of *Last Embrace,* https://www.rottentomatoes.com/m/last_embrace

Television: HBO documentary 1.13 (Delphine Mann, Natalie's secretary at the time of her death, and Josh Donen, son of Marion Marshall, who lived with the Wagners for a period of time, both stated they were invited to go on the Thanksgiving cruise but had to decline. While implying they believed Natalie accidentally slipped and fell in the ocean while attempting to retie the dinghy, both felt there would have been a different "dynamic" had they been there. The inconsistency establishes they both have doubts about what really happened Saturday night. Otherwise, what "dynamic" would they have altered?), 1.15 (Wagner's 2020 rendition of the weekend cruise), 1.22 (Crowley states Natalie's mother told him at the funeral, "If you had been on the boat my daughter would be alive.")

Transcripts: 12/1/1981 press release by Paul Ziffren for Robert Wagner as reported by Catherine Mann, *Entertainment Tonight*

Witnesses: Lana Wood, Marti Rulli and Stuart Miller to SP

Chapter 19: Politics as Usual

California's Public Records Act has its foundation in the California constitution and the effort to achieve public transparency. But the average citizen has been effectively denied access to its privileges by nightmarish procedures for enforcement of the act's mandate created by the California judicial system. Currently, as a practical matter, only the privileged and wealthy can take advantage of its provisions when an agency refuses to comply. This has emboldened state agencies to flaunt the act's legal mandates with impunity by delaying requests for records and employing private lawyers to frustrate access and drive up litigation costs. That needs to change.

When Finstad republished her book under a new title in 2020, it was billed as containing new evidence, including a passage on Page 458 about her alleged viewing of an LASD "murder book" containing the 1981 file that has now supposedly disappeared.

I spent 18 months litigating with the LASD, including taking the depositions of Hernandez, Corina and Smith and dealing with sworn representations to the Superior Court by Hernandez concerning what Finstad allegedly saw in 1999. And at no time did anyone mention the existence of a "murder book" in Natalie's case.

So, in 2021, we contacted former LASD Detective Louis Danoff, the man who Finstad says gave her the "murder book" in 1999, and we asked him if it, in fact, existed. In a sworn deposition, Danoff, who worked homicide—including its library of files—for nearly 30 years, adamantly denies giving Natalie's file to Finstad. So, as it stands, it looks like Finstad's imagination got the best of her. Danoff also said the term "murder book" was used to denote how all homicide bureau files in 1981 were stored in unexplained death cases. In other words, the term carries no implication that the LASD believed a murder occurred.

If you would like to watch the deposition testimony of Finstad and Danoff, please go to **www.nataliewoodbrainstorm.com**.

On June 23, 2021, more than six years after asking the LASD for "all records" on Natalie's death and eight months after filing my last CPRA case (*Perroni v. Villanueva*) for "any records showing who removed, checked out, or otherwise received access to" the sheriff's department file on Natalie Wood's death, there was a new development. Unexpectedly, the lawyer for Sheriff Villanueva sent copies of computerized records relating to LASD Library file #10108 for case file #1981-00898-1873 (Natalie Wood Wagner's file).

The documents reflect that the file was "ARCHIVED" on December 6, 2002, by Lynn Reeder. Thereafter, the records reveal the file was "CHECKED OUT" on November 15, 2007, by "Investigator" Albert Grotefend and returned four months later on April 2, 2008. I know of nothing that was happening in the world of Natalie Wood's death to prompt such access. Then, the file was "CHECKED OUT" on March 11, 2010, by "Investigator" Scott Lusk and returned on March 23, 2010, 12 days later.

Natalie's death investigation was officially "reopened" on November 17, 2011, 20 months after Lusk returned the file. So, why Grotefend and Lusk accessed the file remains a mystery. I have seen no evidence of their involvement in Natalie's case. Significantly, there are no entries after March 23, 2010. For all of Lt. Corina's and Detective Hernandez's boasting about conducting an exhaustive investigation, there is nothing to show that either of them looked at Natalie's file prior to the reopening of the case in 2011.

Apparently, my painstaking examination of the file for homicide evidence and a subsequent cover-up is unprecedented.

As of the date this book was published, I am still litigating with the LASD over the 1981 file in Natalie Wood's death investigation.

Books: *Goodbye* (Rulli with Davern) p. 38 (Wagner in wheelhouse), 126-140 (Friday night, Natalie impatiently waiting)

Court citations: Federal conspiracy indictment filed 11/20/2013 in *United States v. Gregory Thompson, et al* (U.S. District Court for the Central District of California No. CR 13-819); federal conspiracy indictment filed 8/8/2015 in *United States v. Lee Baca* (U.S. District Court for the Central District of California case number 15-0066 (A) – PA)

Court documents and records: Corina and Hernandez depositions, Captain David Smith deposition dated 6/1/2016 and tentative rulings by Superior Court Judge James C. Chalfant in *Perroni v. Fajardo* dated 9/27/2016 and 10/20/2016, pp. 9-10, 12; stipulation by the LASD dated 5/3/2016 in *Perroni v. Fajardo* regarding former Chief of Detectives William McSweeney's interview with the Los Angeles Times on 1/10/2012

Investigatory records: LASD 1981 file; Coroner 1981 file; Eaker report; Dr. L supplemental report

Magazines: Star, *Natalie Mystery Solved: Yacht skipper breaks his silence…at last* (7/23/1985); National Enquirer, *Natalie Wood's sister demands justice: 'Arrest Wagner'* (11/24/2014); Los Angeles, *The Downfall of Sheriff Baca*, Celeste Fremon (5/14/2015); National Enquirer, *Hollywood's Most Shocking Murder Mystery Blown Wide Open By Sensational New Claims* (6/29/2015) (LASD Hawaii trips)

Newspapers/1981 death: The Sun (San Bernardino County, Calif.) *Witness says she heard screams from direction of Wood's yacht* (12/4/1981)

Newspapers/2011 reopening: Los Angeles Times, *Natalie Wood case is reopened* (11/18/2011) (Baca quotes); Los Angeles Times, *Mystery of the reopened case*, Allen, Winton and Goffard (11/19/2011); The Californian (Salinas, Calif.) *Official says Wagner not a suspect*

in Wood death (11/19/2011)

Newspapers/Baca: Los Angeles Times, *Sheriff Offering a Badge and Gun to Celebrities*, Tina Daunt (6/18/1999); Los Angeles Times, *'Operation Pandora's Box' at heart of L.A. County's Sheriff Dept. scandal* (5/14/2015); Los Angeles Times, *Pandora's Box blew up in faces of sheriff's team*, Winton and Grad (2/11/2016); Los Angeles Times, *Baca to face feds in probe of jails* (4/12/2013); Los Angeles Times, *Tanaka subject of U.S. inquiry*, Chang and Kim (5/20/2014); LA Weekly, *Baca's Debacle*, Anson and Cogan (9/22/1999); Los Angeles Times, *L.A. Politicians Urged Pardon of Cocaine Dealer* (2/12/2001); LA Weekly, *Movin' On Up*, Sam Gideon Anson (12/1/1999); Los Angeles Times, *Sheriff Lee Baca was consumed by crises* (1/29/2014); Los Angeles Times, *Paris is freed; now it's Baca's turn* (6/27/2007); The Wall Street Journal, *ACLU Sues Los Angeles Sheriff Over Inmates' Treatment* (1/19/2012); Los Angeles Times, *Ex-L.A. Sheriff Lee Baca must pay $100,000 in jail beating verdict or face debtors court action* (2/10/2017); Los Angeles Times, *From the Archives: Secret clique in L.A. County sheriff's gang unit probed* (4/20/2012); Los Angeles Times, *L.A. County sheriff's deputies allege bosses hid FBI informant* (4/26/2013); Daily Bruin (UCLA, Los Angeles, Calif.) *Long-ill L.A. county sheriff Sherman Block dies at 74* (10/30/98)

Newspapers/Pitchess: Los Angeles Times, *Peter Pitchess, Sheriff Who Modernized Agency, Dies*, Myrna Oliver (4/5/1999); Independent (Long Beach, Calif.) *Sheriff confirms assistant* (1/15/1974)

Online sources: Rulli blog; 089.3 KPCC news and wires, *Natalie Wood's case reopened; skipper says he lied about her death*, https://www.scpr.org/news/2011/11/18/29942/natalie-woods-case-reopened-skipper-says-he-lied-a/; CBS *48 Hours*, *Natalie Wood: Death in Dark Water* (2/3/2018) https://www.cbsnews.com/video/natalie-wood-death-in-dark-water-1/#x; CBS News, *Natalie Wood's Fatal Voyage: "48 Hours" reveals new details in the investigation into the actress's 1981 death* (9/15/2012) https://www.cbsnews.com/news/natalie-woods-fatal-voyage/; The Oakland Press (Pontiac, Mich.) *Robert Wagner declines police interview in Natalie Wood death*, Anthony McCartney (1/18/2013) https://www.theoaklandpress.com/news/robert-wagner-declines-police-interview-in-natalie-wood-death/article_a7901f2b-774a-581b-9eae-8f89c2abe059.html; Huffpost Crime, *Natalie Wood Death Reopened: Robert Wagner Refuses Interview In New Inquiry* (1/18/13) (Walken interview and no suspects) https://www.huffpost.com/entry/robert-wagner-suspect-natalie-wood_n_2506306; Los Angeles Times, *Natalie Wood death: Detectives talked to owner of yacht* (11/19/2011); https://latimesblogs.latimes.com/lanow/2011/11/natalie-wood-death-detectives-talked-to-owner-of-yacht-.html; Los Angeles Times opinion, *The Natalie Wood mysteries* (11/22/2011) (Antelope Valley) https://www.latimes.com/opinion/la-xpm-2011-nov-22-la-ed-natalie-20111122-story.html

Press releases: LASD–Los Angeles County Sheriff's Department Information Bureau (SIB) Media Advisory: Natalie Wood Wagner Death Investigation Case Reopened (11/17/2011)

Television: CBS *48 Hours* TV special segment with *Vanity Fair* magazine concerning Natalie Wood's death (11/26/2011); ABC 7 News Los Angeles, ABC7.com staff (interview of Lt. Corina concerning "person of interest")

Transcripts: 1/27/2017 hearing proceedings in *Perroni v. Fajardo*

Witnesses: Correspondence from SP to Mathew Rosengart dated 10/27/2017 concerning Christopher Walken; Marti Rulli to SP (regarding Walken); correspondence from SP to Blair Berk dated 1/4/2018; Tommy Hudson, former homicide detective, to SP

Additional material: SP's inspection of Isthmus Cove and Blue Cavern Point, Santa Catalina Island, California

Chapter 20: Follow the Money

Books: *Pieces* (Wagner) pp. 29-30 (father against acting), 172-173 (small ranch, "the beautiful Marion"), 174 ("trial transcripts five feet high," financially strapped/on edge), 174-175 (father refused loan, Donen custody battle), 198 (Marion divorce), 202-204 (cleaned out, income tax matter, financial disparity), 298-299 (value of syndication, "partners" in *Hart to Hart*); *Goodbye* (Rulli with Davern) p. 134 (Wagner "ruined it" Friday night), 137 (October trip to NC, see a lawyer), 262 (*Splendour* given away); *My Life as a Mankiewicz: An Insider's Journey Through Hollywood*, Tom Mankiewicz and Robert Crane (University Press of Kentucky 2012) pp. 233-235 (50% of *Hart to Hart*)

Court citations: *Donen v. Donen*, Superior Court of Los Angeles County case number SM D-18714; file excerpts from *In the Matter of Peter and Joshua Donen* in the High Court of Justice, Chancery Division, case number 5/D. 1300; *Robert Wagner v. Marion Marshall Wagner*, Superior Court of Los Angeles County case number D 786834; *Wagner v. Columbia Pictures Industries, Inc.* (2007) 146 Cal. App. 4th 586; *Wagner v. Columbia Pictures Industries, Inc.* (2003) Superior Court of Los Angeles County case number BC298740, 2003 WL25774416; agreement, including Exhibit A, between Spelling-Goldberg Productions and Natalie Wood and Robert Wagner [*Love Song* contract] dated July 28, 1973; agreement, including Exhibit I, between Spelling-Goldberg Productions and Natalie Wood and Robert Wagner [*Charlie's Angels* agreement] dated 12/1/1977

Court documents and records: Probate file

Magazines: People, *Superdad Robert Wagner talks about the joys and heartaches of raising three daughters without Natalie*, Jeff Jarvis (7/4/1983)

Newspapers: Los Angeles Times, *Natalie Wood Wills Most of Estate to Mate, 2 Daughters*, Myrna Oliver (12/3/1981); Los Angeles Times, *Natalie Wood Leaves Estate to Family*, Myrna Oliver (12/4/1981); The New York Times, *TALKING MONEY WITH: STEFANIE POWERS; Lights! Camera! Caution*, Geraldine Fabrikant (7/12/1998)

Online sources: Inflation Calculator

Witnesses: Lana Wood to SP; Barry J. Jewell, probate, tax, estate planning and retirement plan expert, to SP

Additional material: grant deed title search for lot 25 in block 58 of Beverly Hills (603 N. Cañon Drive, Beverly Hills, California); *Globe* magazine FOIA request for FBI files on Spelling-Goldberg (11/2015)

Chapter 21: Person of Interest

Books: *Natalie Wood* (Lambert) pp. 236-237, 240-242 (engagement, wedding ceremony); 477-478 ("swishing her tail," Devane blowup), 508-509 (trip to N.C.), 509-510, 518

(suspected affair, location shooting in Hawaii), 515 (*Brainstorm* to LA), 517-518 (dinner at McDowall's), 521-522 ("demons came out," leaving LA), 527-543 (Wagner's version of weekend), 545 (Wagner call to Crowley); *Pieces* (Wagner) pp. 38-39 (fixer Harry Brand), 107-108 (Scott Marlowe, Nicky Hilton), 115 (N.Y. method actors), 135-137 (*Splendor in the Grass*, Warren Beatty), 139-142 (Wagner split from Natalie, "prepared to kill" Beatty), 137 (Elia Kazan: acting was Natalie's whole life), 249-250 (trip to N.C., location shooting in Hawaii), 254-258 (Wagner's rendition of weekend, Davern called at 1:30 a.m.); *Goodbye* (Rulli with Davern) p. 20 (no cruiser), 122 (tension to begin with), 122 (Wagner assaulted Natalie admirer); *Hairdresser to the Stars: A Hollywood Memoir*, Ginger "Sugar" Blymyer (www. InfinityPublishing.com 2000) p. 154 (visit at Cañon Drive, Natalie's children her priority), 221-223 (Wagner's drinking); *His Way* (Kelley) pp. 241-243 (Sinatra helped Joe DiMaggio with divorce); *Heart to Heart* (Maychick) pp. 121-122 (Wagner's version of weekend), 132-133 (Wagner's statement through friend), 140-143 (St. John); *One* (Powers) pp. 188-189 (Wagner's whereabouts November 20-22, 1981); *The Psychology of Jealousy and Envy*, Peter Salovey (The Guilford Press 1991) p. 79 (envy, discontent, hostility, superiority)

California law: California Jury Instructions–Criminal 8.47 (involuntary manslaughter, killing while unconscious due to voluntary intoxication) Spring 2011 Revision and Crim. 570 (voluntary manslaughter, heat of passion)

Court citations: *People v. Eric Christopher Bechler*, 2003 WL 2268395 (11/14/2003); *People v. Kerley* (2018) 23 Cal. App. 5th 513; *Donen v. Donen*, Superior Court of Los Angeles County case number SM D-18714, including defendant's exhibit 5, letter from Stanley Donen to Marion Marshall Donen dated 1/29/1962 and plaintiff's questionnaire on order to show cause dated 11/12/1964 signed by Marion Wagner; *Wagner v. Columbia Pictures Industries, Inc.* (2007) 146 Cal. App. 4th 586

Court documents and records: Corina deposition

Investigatory records: LASD 1981 file; Coroner 1981 file; Eaker report

Magazines: People, *Superdad Robert Wagner talks about joys and heartaches of raising three daughters without Natalie*, Jeff Jarvis (7/4/1983); Star, *Robert Wagner: How Natalie's Death Haunts Me* (8/27/1985); Vanity Fair (Kashner) pp. 214-233; Variety, *Just for Variety*, Army Archerd (12/1/1981)

Newspapers: Los Angeles Times, TV MOVIE REVIEW: *Natalie Wood Plays Heroine in 'Affair,'* Kevin Thomas (11/20/1973); Durham Morning Herald (Durham, N.C.) *Natalie Wood In Raleigh* (9/16/1981); The Honolulu Advertiser, *Hawaii Report*, Don Chapman (11/4/1981); The News and Observer (Raleigh, N.C.) *'Brainstorm' back on West Coast* (10/29/1981); Greensboro Daily News (Greensboro, N.C.) Tar Heel Living, *'Brainstorm' Top Hollywood Stars Filming Major Movie In North Carolina*, Jim Jenkins (9/24/1981); The Chronicle (Duke University, Durham, N.C.) *Guess Who's Reading The Chronicle?* (10/15/1981); The Chronicle (Duke University, Durham, N.C.) *Tinseltown in Durham? MGM to film at Duke* (9/3/1981); The Asheville Citizen (Asheville, N.C.) *'Brainstorm' Filming Ends* (10/29/1981); The Asheville Citizen (Asheville, N.C.) *Stars Highlight Hunt News Conference* (9/24/1981); Durham Morning Herald (Durham, N.C.) *Natalie Wood A Busy Lady* (9/22/1981); The Salemite (Salem, N.C.) *Actors Are People Too; Salem Student Observes Film Take* (11/6/1981); The Greensboro Record (Greensboro, N.C.) *WUNC radio fund-raiser pass-*

es goal (10/14/1981); Durham Morning Herald (Durham, N.C.) *Wood Was Angry, Slightly Intoxicated, Coroner Says* (12/1/1981); Los Angeles Herald Examiner, *Some Drinks, a Fight, a Death. Natalie Wood Left Yacht While Husband and Co-Star Argued, Coroner Says,* Schorr and Furillo (12/1/1981); The Greensboro Record (Greensboro, N.C.) *Detective says actor's argument an exaggeration* (12/2/1981); The Asheville Citizen (Asheville, N.C.) *Questions Raised In Wood Death* (12/4/1981); Durham Morning Herald (Durham, N.C.) *Natalie Wood Found Dead In Ocean* (11/30/1981); Durham Morning Herald (Durham, N.C.) *Husband, Friends Bid a Final Adieu to Natalie Wood* (12/3/1981); Daily News (New York, N.Y.*) How Natalie Wood died: Her husband, bitter over stories, gives his views,* Bob Lardine (12/26/1981)

In reading the North Carolina newspaper articles, I could sense the thrill and love the community had for Natalie during the filming of *Brainstorm*. And her presence there also had its lighter and more human moments. A maid innocently let a reporter into Natalie's suite in the Governor's Inn, and when asked about the experience of cleaning that suite, the maid said, "She's got the most beautiful clothes. But she's sort of messy." The report caused quite a stir in the hotel, but after a profuse apology by the management, Natalie just laughed it off. Another incident involved Natalie admiring a spectator's off-white cardigan and purchasing the sweater on the spot for $200 (about $565 today) to wear while filming *Brainstorm*. And when a local radio station had its annual on-the-air marathon, Natalie called in a donation. But the deepest feeling I got from the written material was how wounded the community was upon her death.

Online sources: Deputy Charles G. Guenther obituary (8/8/2014) https://www. legacy.com/obituaries/latimes/obituary.aspx?pid=172023453; Nicholas Gurdin obituary (11/7/1980) https://www.findagrave.com/memorial/7151157/nicholas-gurdin; Natalie Wood's Academy Awards nominations for *Rebel Without a Cause; Splendor in the Grass* and *Love with the Proper Stranger,* https://www.imdb.com/name/nm0000081/awards; Ron Wood reverse discrimination lawsuit, https://www.cbsnews.com/news/victory-in-reverse-discrimination-suit/

Press releases: LASD–Los Angeles County Sheriff's Department Information Bureau (SIB) Media Advisory: Natalie Wood Wagner Death Investigation Case Reopened (11/17/2011)

Professional journals: *Male sexual jealousy*, Daly, Wilson and Weghorst, *Ethology and Sociobiology*, 1982, 3(1):11-27; *Viewing the Bible Belt*, Tweedie, *Journal of Popular Culture*, 1978, 11(4):865-76

Television: HBO documentary 1.12 (Crowley declined cruise, Wagner and Walken argued "all the time")

Transcripts: Shorthand notes *In The Matter of Peter and Joshua Donen*, in the High Court of Justice, Chancery Division (London) case number 1962. D. No. 1840; 12/1/1981 press release by Paul Ziffren for Robert Wagner as reported by Catherine Mann, *Entertainment Tonight*

Witnesses: Karl Lack, Ron Hunter and Ginger "Sugar" Blymyer to Jan Morris; Karl Lack, Ron Hunter, Marian Cheshire and Mary Ann Clark to SP; Jan Morris, Linda Hudson, Tommy Hudson and Yvonne Cobourn to SP regarding Carolyn O'Brien, Danny Toler and Ron Wood; communications with Jan Morris regarding the Governor's Inn Hotel and the Triangle Research Institute; Sandra Sailer to Jan Morris; Lana Wood to SP; FOI communications with Hawa A. Wehelie, U.S. Coast Guard, Office of Information Management (EFOIA@uscg.mil) concerning transcripts of radio communications from the Isthmus, Catalina Island, from 10 p.m. November 28, 1981, to 10 a.m. November 29, 1981

Additional material: criminal record background check of Danny Lee Toler

Chapter 22: Summation

Since this chapter sums up details from previous chapters, mainly citations for new material are listed here.

Books: *Holy Bible: New Testament*, Revised Standard Version (Harper & Row, 1956) pp. 200, 219; *Natalie Wood* (Lambert) pp. 477-478 ("swishing her tail," drunken rage), 522 (leaving LA), 531 ("swishing her tail" at Walken); *Pieces* (Wagner) pp. 20-22 (excelled in swimming), 29 (scholarship for diving)

California law: California Penal Code § 188 (malice, express malice and implied malice, defined); California Jury Instructions-Criminal 2.00 (direct and circumstantial evidence, inferences), 2.01 (sufficiency of circumstantial evidence), 2.02 (sufficiency of circumstantial evidence to prove specific intent or mental state), 2.03 (consciousness of guilt, falsehood), 2.90, (reasonable doubt), 3.40 (cause "but for" test, generally), 8.10 (murder, defined), 8.11(malice aforethought, defined), 8.55 (homicide and caused, defined), 8.20 (deliberate and premeditated murder), 8.30 (unpremeditated murder of the second degree), 8.31 (second degree murder, killing resulted from unlawful act dangerous to life), 8.74 (unanimous agreement), 8.70 (degree of murder) and 370 (cause "but for" test, implied malice); California Evidence Code § 1250 (statement of declarant's then existing mental or physical state)

Court citations: *People v. Watson* (1981) 30 Cal. 3d 290, 300 (high probability of death); *People v. Boyer* (2006) 38 Cal. 4th 412, 467-472 (voluntary intoxication and second-degree murder); *People v. Whisenhunt* (2008) 44 Cal. 4th 174, 215-218 (failure to act *by itself* does not constitute an "intentional act" for implied malice murder); *People v. Kerley* (2018) 23 Cal. App. 5th 513; *People v. Beyah* (2009) 170 Cal. App. 4th 1241; *People v. Oliver* (1989) 210 Cal. App. 3d 138